Clara Ramirez Tr

D1284727

Conflict and Commerce in Maritime E

"Middle Kingdom"
"Han" "Ming"

New name of Taiwan

The Zheng family of merchants and militarists emerged from the tumultuous seventeenth century amid a severe economic depression, a harrowing dynastic transition from the ethnic Chinese Ming to the Manchu Qing, and the first wave of European expansion into East Asia. Under four generations of leaders over six decades, the Zheng had come to dominate trade across the China Seas. Their average annual earnings matched, and at times exceeded, those of their fiercest rivals: the Dutch East India Company. Although nominally loyal to the Ming in its doomed struggle against the Manchus, the Zheng eventually forged an autonomous territorial state located on Taiwan with the potential to encompass the family's entire economic sphere of influence. Through the story of the Zheng, Xing Hang provides a fresh perspective on the economic divergence of early modern China from Western Europe, its twenty-first-century resurgence, and the meaning of a Chinese identity outside China.

Xing Hang is Assistant Professor of History at Brandeis University. He is the author of the *Encyclopedia of National Anthems* (2011) and co-editor (with Tonio Andrade) of *Sea Rovers, Silver, and Samurai: Maritime East Asia in Global History, 1550–1700*.

Studies of the Weatherhead East Asian Institute,
Columbia University

The Studies of the Weatherhead East Asian Institute of Columbia University were inaugurated in 1962 to bring to a wider public the results of significant new research on modern and contemporary East Asia.

Conflict and Commerce in Maritime East Asia

The Zheng Family and the Shaping of the Modern World, c. 1620–1720

Xing Hang

Brandeis University

CAMBRIDGE
UNIVERSITY PRESS

CAMBRIDGE
UNIVERSITY PRESS

University Printing House, Cambridge CB2 8BS, United Kingdom

One Liberty Plaza, 20th Floor, New York, NY 10006, USA

477 Williamstown Road, Port Melbourne, VIC 3207, Australia

4843/24, 2nd Floor, Ansari Road, Daryaganj, Delhi - 110002, India

79 Anson Road, #06-04/06, Singapore 079906

Cambridge University Press is part of the University of Cambridge.

It furthers the University's mission by disseminating knowledge in the pursuit of education, learning and research at the highest international levels of excellence.

www.cambridge.org
Information on this title: www.cambridge.org/9781107558458

© Xing Hang 2015

First published 2015
First paperback edition 2017

A catalogue record for this publication is available from the British Library

Library of Congress Cataloging in Publication data
Hang, Xing, 1982–
Conflict and commerce in maritime East Asia : the Zheng family and the shaping of the modern world, c. 1620–1720 / Xing Hang (Brandeis University).
   pages   cm – (Studies of the Weatherhead East Asian Institute, Columbia University)
Includes bibliographical references and index.
ISBN 978-1-107-12184-3 (hardback : alkaline paper)
1. Zheng family.   2. Merchants – China – Biography.
3. Merchants – Taiwan – Biography.   4. China – Commerce – History – 17th century.   5. China – Foreign economic relations – Europe, Western.
6. Europe, Western – Foreign economic relations – China.
7. East China Sea – Commerce – History – 17th century.
8. South China Sea – Commerce – History – 17th century.
9. East Asia – Commerce – History – 17th century.
10. Social conflict – East Asia – History – 17th century.   I. Title.
HF3835.H365   2015
382.092′251–dc23

                                                           2015024719

ISBN 978-1-107-12184-3 Hardback
ISBN 978-1-107-55845-8 Paperback

Contents

Figures and maps

Figures

Maps

Tables in Appendix 3

Acknowledgments

The successful publication of this work owes, in large part, to the warm-hearted and generous assistance that I have received from numerous individuals along the way. My appreciation goes out to my fellow historians in late imperial Chinese, maritime East Asian, and global history. Among them, I must single out John E. "Jack" Wills, Jr., one of the towering pioneers of these fields. When reviewing my manuscript, he made his identity known and shared with me his unpublished work in progress, which was instrumental in shaping some of this project's themes. On top of that, Jack continued to offer advice and support afterward, giving meticulous, handwritten comments to my drafts, suggesting additional sources to use, and even correcting grammar and usage. The other reviewers remain anonymous, but I am equally grateful for the time that they have spent and their valuable feedback. Tonio Andrade read several renditions of my proposal and offered candid critiques both in writing and during extended phone and Skype conversations. Nie Dening of Xiamen University used all of his available resources and contacts to help me locate and scan a rare image from a book already out of print. I also give special thanks to the libraries and archives in mainland China, Taiwan, and the United States for opening their doors and making available their collections for me to peruse and analyze.

My graduate advisors at Berkeley, Yeh Wen-hsin, Kenneth Pomeranz, Jan de Vries, and the late Frederic Wakeman, helped shape and develop my project at its initial stages, and continue to inspire me as role models with their enlightening scholarship and sharp insight. I am deeply thankful to my colleagues at Brandeis, my new home after Berkeley, for providing such a warm and accommodating environment where my work could continue to mature. In particular, my former chair, Jane Kamensky, was always available as a resource, answering my questions at lightning speed over email, reading over my chapters, and giving me encouraging pep talks in her office. The students at Brandeis never cease to amaze me with their enthusiasm, broad interests, and thirst for knowledge. In discussion sections and seminars, many of them offered highly original perspectives pertinent to my project, and often from a unique angle outside of the history discipline. I probably learned much more from teaching them than they will ever learn from me.

I want to express my gratitude to my editor, Lucy Rhymer, and Cambridge University Press for their enthusiastic support for my project and for working with me to bring the manuscript to fruition. Last, but not least, I am deeply indebted to my family. My parents pushed me hard and encouraged me to challenge all boundaries. My in-laws read over my work and offered critiques from the perspective of educated outsiders with no prior knowledge of my topic. My wife, Kwun Suen, provided all kinds of support, and shared with me the emotional ups and downs of the manuscript process. Finally, Baby Sheng is my shining little beacon who gives me hope during times of frustration, when he does not add to it!

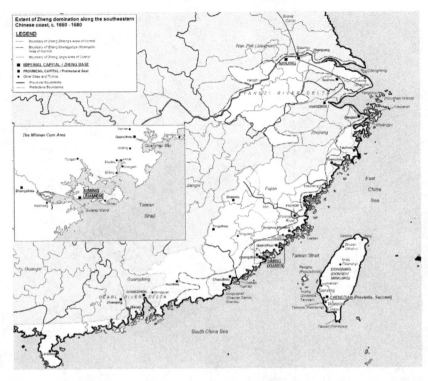

Map 0.1 Extent of Zheng domination along the southeastern Chinese coast, c. 1645–1680

Map 0.2 Maritime East Asia and the Indian Ocean zone, c. 1670–1680

Introduction

[handwritten: Zheng family dominated China's foreign trade]

During the seventeenth century, a single mercantile dynasty from Fujian, a province on the southeastern littoral of China, dominated the country's foreign commerce. The Zheng family's multinational and transnational enterprise traded extensively with ports across maritime East Asia. Its broad reach extended from the shores of Japan to the Strait of Melaka, thousands of kilometers away, and its powerful naval fleets roamed the East and South China Seas. The family competed fiercely and often successfully for control over this space with the Dutch East India Company (VOC), whose joint-stock model was considered a harbinger of the modern capitalist corporation.[1] In fact, sufficient quantitative evidence exists to show that the Zheng's revenues, on average, exceeded seventy million in 2014 US dollars during their over six decades in power, from 1622 to 1683.[2] *[handwritten margin: competition w/ VOC]*

The Zheng's impressive commercial activities formed part of a broader effort to secure their political survival and legitimacy. Under four generations of patriarchs they flexibly redefined their role in accordance with changing geopolitical circumstances. They began as one of many pirate bands that infested the China Seas during the final decades of the Ming dynasty (1368–1662). After the Manchu Qing (1636–1911) entered China in 1644, they morphed into a resistance force fighting on behalf of the beleaguered Han Chinese dynasty. When the Ming cause appeared all but doomed, the illustrious second-generation patriarch, Zheng Chenggong (1624–1662), seized the island of Taiwan from the Dutch East India Company in 1662, where he and his descendants forged a mercantile state with a sophisticated territorial administration. They undoubtedly aimed to eventually assert control over their entire economic sphere of influence in maritime East Asia, as demonstrated in their *[handwritten margin: stayed in power]*

---

[1] VOC is the Dutch abbreviation for Verenigde Oost-Indische Compagnie (United East India Company).

[2] Refer to Appendix 3 for the specific methodology and calculations behind the Zheng organization's revenues and profitability.

[handwritten:
① Pirates
② Pro Ming resistance
③ Rulers of Taiwan]

1

repeated plans to invade the Spanish Philippines and a renewed, ill-fated campaign on the mainland coast of China from 1674 to 1680.

The Zheng organization shaped and was, in turn, caught up in a unique confluence of regional and global history: a traumatic dynastic transition in China, the first wave of European expansion and colonization in East Asia, and its ever-tighter integration into a worldwide economic system. The prosperity of all four clan patriarchs depended upon their ability to manipulate and profit from the contradictions set into motion by these trends. Not surprisingly, they were among the most cosmopolitan, colorful, and conflicted individuals of their time. Indeed, the family left a far-reaching yet understudied imprint upon historical narratives from vastly different cultural contexts – from China, Japan, and Korea to the Netherlands, England, Portugal, and Spain. These historiographical traditions uniformly found it difficult to refrain from embellishing the Zheng's fantastic exploits and forging legends that grew out of, but eventually became inseparable from, the realities of their lives and times.

Zheng Zhilong (d. 1661), the founder of the family enterprise, was also known as Nicolas Gaspard and Iquan, plus countless orthographic variations of these aliases between and among the different languages whose speakers he interacted with throughout his eventful life. In his youth, he learned Portuguese and converted to Catholicism in Macao, married a Japanese woman, served as an interpreter for the Dutch East India Company in Taiwan, and plundered the Chinese coast as a pirate. In 1628, he submitted to the Ming and became an official and trade mogul whose wealth exceeded entire kingdoms. Yet his career ended abruptly when the Manchus took him captive to Beijing and later executed him.

His eldest son, the half-Japanese Zheng Chenggong, better known as Koxinga, transformed this enterprise into an anti-Manchu resistance with hundreds of warships and hundreds of thousands of troops, including entire special regiments of Japanese samurai warriors and African musketeers. He outmaneuvered the formidable Dutch East India Company to forge an economic and, increasingly, political hegemony over maritime East Asia. However, his crowning achievement, the seizure of Taiwan in 1662, took place amid a larger backdrop of defeat and demoralization by the Manchus on the mainland. Soon after this momentous victory, Koxinga perished amid the tropical island heat.

His eldest son and successor, Zheng Jing (1642–1681), started life as a wayward youth with a weak and emotional temperament, leading to an obsession with alcohol and sexual flings with older women. Surprisingly, these negative traits translated into benevolent, sensitive, and capable leadership, which came to define the majority of the organization's twenty final years on Taiwan. He became a visionary who transformed the militarily focused resistance movement of his father into a territorial state with a sophisticated bureaucracy founded upon filial piety to Koxinga's legacy and loyalty to an authentic "China" unblemished by the "barbarian" Manchus. In 1674, Jing took advantage of a domestic Qing uprising – the Rebellion of the Three Feudatories – to regain his family's lost mainland possessions. Although he suffered defeat in the end, he initially managed to seize control over more territory in southeastern China and came closer to his organization's avowed ideal of Ming restoration than any of his illustrious predecessors.

Zheng Jing's death in 1681, soon after the failure of his mainland adventure, and an ensuing succession struggle unexpectedly brought to power his twelve-year-old son, Zheng Keshuang (1671–1717), an immature and inexperienced youth who became the mere puppet of an oligarchy of high officials. After the Zheng fleets suffered a crushing defeat in an epic battle with the Qing navy in the Taiwan Strait, the organization surrendered in 1683. Yet the preceding two years, while brief, nonetheless witnessed momentous reforms which, had they continued, could have formalized a turn away from the Ming and toward the creation of a fully legitimate maritime Chinese kingdom. This orientation, already apparent under Koxinga, never fully had a chance to mature and became permanently stillborn with the surrender of the family to the Qing.

These four generations of leaders, who dominated the East Asian sea lanes for almost six decades, deserve a comprehensive narrative simply because their larger-than-life lives, filled with high-pitched drama and sordid tales of incest and intrigue, make for an incredible story that needs to be told. Beyond that, a multifaceted study of these individuals and their organization provides insight into the heated debates surrounding the question of how China, as well as the rest of East Asia and the world, came to be what they are today. During the seventeenth century, China's high-quality manufactures and voracious demand for silver weaved together a global network of trade. What role did the Zheng play in this integration, and how did their downfall contribute to the transformation of the Chinese economic core into an impoverished periphery two hundred years later? What does their story reveal about the character and contradictions of Chinese political and cultural identity, played out in the fierce conflicts between continental and maritime China, Ming and Qing, and in relation to neighboring East Asian states and Europe? Finally, this narrative provides some context for issues of importance in the early twenty-first century, such as the resurgence of mainland China and its new maritime orientation, disputes over islands in the China Seas, and the liminal political status of Hong Kong and Taiwan.

Myths made and unmade

The availability and credibility of sources have posed a tremendous barrier toward a comprehensive understanding of the Zheng and their historical significance. The original Zheng archival records suffered heavy destruction as a result of chaos and warfare, as well as purposeful Qing efforts to eradicate them after its occupation of Taiwan in 1683. The empire-wide literary purges of the eighteenth century, aimed at works deemed subversive to the court or anti-Manchu in character, further decimated what remained. Even so, a sizable quantity of materials has survived, remarkably against all odds. Most emerged out of hidden private collections or were discovered overseas, primarily in Japan – a major market for Chinese books – at the turn of the twentieth century. *Congzheng shilu* (*Veritable record of accompanying the expeditions*), purchased by researchers from a private collector in Fujian during the 1930s, is the most complete primary record to date. This meticulous year-by-year chronicle of the organization from 1649 to 1662 has been credibly attributed to Yang Ying (d. 1681), an official in charge of finances under Koxinga and Zheng Jing.[3] Other works include fragmentary collections of poems, edicts, memorials, and letters written by Zheng leaders and officials. Most of these materials only became widely available for scholarly use over the twentieth century.

The loss of much of the Zheng's own narrative meant that later historians increasingly had to rely upon the interpretations of others, along with the accompanying baggage of their agendas and biases. As Ralph Croizier's classic study has shown, vastly different understandings emerged over time between and within East Asian and Western historiographies. In China, contemporary Qing proclamations, memorials, and edicts primarily portrayed the Zheng as rebels and pirates acting against central authority. After their surrender in 1683, historical assessments of the family appeared whose primary focus involved meting out praise and blame to individuals according to Confucian moral standards. Officially sponsored histories perpetuated the negative narrative until well into the nineteenth century. Commoners in the Zheng home bases of southern Fujian and Taiwan, on the other hand, were the most unanimous in their praise for the family, and circulated legends and constructed shrines dedicated to their memory and exploits. In addition, former Zheng

[3] See the introduction to Yang Ying, *Congzheng shilu*, TWWXCK, 32 (1958), pp. 1–3.

"*historical memory*"

followers and private gentry scholars authored unofficial accounts, or wild histories (*yeshi*), which rely upon Qing records, access to family documents and archives, and oral testimonies from eyewitnesses, most of them unavailable today. Initially, they contained both positive and negative assessments of the Zheng's character.

The narratives of the family converged over the Qing. Zheng Zhilong came to be seen as a profit-seeking opportunist who did not hesitate to switch sides in pursuit of his interests, while Keshuang, the last ruler, was a weakling puppet of wicked advisors. Koxinga and Zheng Jing, on the other hand, received praise for their steadfast loyalty, even to a doomed dynasty. Koxinga was especially celebrated for sacrificing his filial obligations to his own father, Zhilong, for the Ming cause. The *Taiwan waiji* (*Unofficial record of Taiwan*), written in 1707 by Jiang Risheng, a southern Fujian gentry and son of a former Zheng commander, combined analytical narrative, moral judgment, and embellished dialogues and legends drawn from local folklore to solidify this tacit consensus. The work further transformed Koxinga into a hero of supernatural stature. During the middle of the nineteenth century, faced with French and Japanese designs on Taiwan and Fujian, the Qing court appropriated this discourse too. It deified Koxinga with an official shrine in Tainan, southern Taiwan, according him official sanction as a moral paragon to rally residents against foreign aggression.[4] This 180-degree turnabout in historical memory toward one of the Qing's bitterest former enemies had few parallels in China and elsewhere.

The Zheng inspired and continues to articulate modern nationalisms across East Asia. Books that came to reflect the Qing-era consensus on the Zheng were exported in large numbers to Japan over the Tokugawa (1600–1868) and early Meiji (1868–1912) periods, primarily via the port of Nagasaki. During the eighteenth century, narratives of the family patterned after their Chinese counterparts appeared in print. The Zheng also featured prominently in foreign affairs compilations and local gazetteers of Nagasaki, which drew largely upon Tokugawa official documents on international relations and interviews of incoming Chinese vessels at the Kyushu port. Many of these accounts, together with dramas and other fictional narratives, capitalized upon Koxinga's birth in Japan to a Japanese mother to nativize him as a Japanese cultural hero. Chikamatsu Monzaemon's (1673–1725) eighteenth-century masterpiece play *Kokusenya kassen* (*Battles of Coxinga*) portrayed Koxinga as a samurai

---

[4] For a detailed analysis of the evolution of the Zheng family's historical image, see Ralph C. Croizier, *Koxinga and Chinese nationalism: myth, history, and the hero* (Cambridge, MA: East Asian Research Center, Harvard University, 1977), pp. 12–37.

imbued with the "Japanese spirit" ("*Yamato damashii*"), whose bravery and prowess saved the Ming house from destruction. It became an instant hit and left a deep imprint upon the popular consciousness.

During Japan's fifty-year rule over Taiwan from 1895 to 1945, the authorities on the island promoted precisely this martial image of an adventurer and conqueror to inspire loyalty among their skeptical colonial subjects. The family's pan-Asian connections and business network also became useful in justifying imperial expansion and attempts to forge a Greater East Asian Co-prosperity Sphere in the Second World War. Japan's defeat and subsequent incorporation into an order dominated by the United States put a stop to its quest for political leadership. Accordingly, postwar Japanese popular and scholarly accounts portray Koxinga and the rest of the clan as generic, pan-Asian heroes devoid of a specific national belonging. Nonetheless, they continue to emphasize the family's trading network as harbingers of East Asian integration, reflecting the important position occupied by Japanese capital in the region.[5]

Likewise, the historical experience of the Zheng has undergone multiple reimaginations in a divided China that mirror its contested politics since 1949. At the height of the Cold War, from the 1950s to late 1970s, the Republic of China, defeated on the mainland and forced to withdraw to Taiwan, upheld Koxinga and Zheng Jing as moral paragons. Their anti-Qing resistance became an inspiration for the Guomindang's own agenda of recovering the mainland from the Communists, who, like the Manchus, were seen as destroying authentic Chinese culture.[6] Starting from the 1980s, amid closer cross-strait interaction and the loss of Taiwan's ability to represent "China" abroad in the face of the mainland's rise, advocates of a separate Taiwanese consciousness have gradually gained ground in both political and historical discourse. The new historiography engendered in this climate celebrates the Zheng as founders of an independent maritime kingdom and downplays their Ming loyalism because of the uncomfortable association of this ideology with China.[7]

On the mainland, representations of all four generations of the Zheng in scholarly articles, books, and other media have changed dramatically from the founding of the People's Republic of China (PRC) in 1949 to the second decade of the twenty-first century. Before the 1990s, the family

---

[5] Croizier, *Chinese nationalism*, p. 32; Jiang Renjie, *Jiegou Zheng Chenggong: Yingxiong, shenhua yu xingxiang de lishi* (Taipei: Sanmin Bookstore, 2006), pp. 43–88.

[6] Croizier, *Chinese nationalism*, pp. 63–70; Jiang Renjie, *Jiegou Zheng Chenggong*, pp. 118–123.

[7] Jiang Renjie, *Jiegou Zheng Chenggong*, pp. 127–130. See also Peter Kang, "Koxinga and his maritime regime in the popular historical writings of post-Cold War Taiwan and China," in Tonio Andrade and Xing Hang (eds.), *Sea rovers, silver, and samurai: maritime East Asia in global history, 1550–1700* (Honolulu: University of Hawaii Press, forthcoming).

was seen as an enlightened class of nascent capitalists who stood up successfully to European imperialism. Koxinga, in particular, acquired, and still enjoys, a reputation as a national hero (*minzu yingxiong*) for his momentous victory over the Dutch. However, during the 1990s, mounting cross-strait tensions called the family's official legacy into question. Koxinga's historical position was downplayed, while some scholars went as far as to accuse his son, Zheng Jing, of plotting Taiwanese independence. On the other hand, their enemies, the Kangxi emperor (b. 1654, r. 1662–1722) and Shi Lang (1621–1696), the Zheng defector who inflicted the final defeat upon the family, became celebrated as the main facilitators of Taiwan's reincorporation into the motherland. As China's interests become global in the early twenty-first century, the Zheng are acquiring renewed significance as harbingers of the country's naval power and maritime sovereignty. This shift reflects the transformation of official priorities, from the focus on national liberation and world communism to a more confident vision of a resurgent China.[8]

Surprisingly, historical interpretations of the Zheng in the West began earlier than in East Asia: soon after the Dutch loss of their Taiwan colony in 1662. Western sources draw upon the massive documentation left behind by administrators and employees of the Dutch and English East India Companies, and the Spanish colonial authorities and Roman Catholic missionaries of the Philippines. These materials, many of which are preserved in manuscript form at archives across Europe, provide information unavailable in any surviving Chinese materials. Because the Zheng presented a serious challenge to the very economic and political survival of these fragile European overseas outposts, the records naturally focus upon diplomatic exchanges with the organization, the number of its junks sailing to a given port, and the quantities and profitability of goods traded. They also vividly describe the appearance and demeanor of Zheng leaders and officials, and present them as complex, multidimensional personalities. The Chinese accounts, with their adherence to Confucian moral categories, typically leave out such details.[9]

Two early autobiographical narratives left a deep imprint upon Western historiography. In 1674, an account of Koxinga's attack on Taiwan and its subsequent surrender appeared in print in Amsterdam under the

---

[8] For more on the evolving historical image of the Zheng family on mainland China, see Xing Hang, "The contradictions of legacy: reimagining the Zheng family in the People's Republic of China," *Late Imperial China* 34.2 (2013).

[9] Leonard Blussé, "The VOC as sorcerer's apprentice: stereotypes and social engineering on the China coast," in W. L. Idema (ed.), *Leyden studies in Sinology: papers presented at the conference held in celebration of the fiftieth anniversary of the Sinological Institute of Leyden University, December 8–12, 1980* (Leiden: Brill, 1980) provides an insightful overview of how Dutch and Chinese sources view a similar set of events in vastly different ways.

pseudonym of C. E. S. Historians commonly attribute authorship to Frederik Coyett (1615–1687), the last governor of the island.[10] Around the same time, Vittorio Riccio (1621–1685), an Italian Dominican missionary, published a massive tome detailing his personal experiences on the southeastern coast during the 1650s and 1660s, as well as the work of the church across China. Since Koxinga permitted the Dominicans to establish a church and proselytize in Zheng-held areas, Riccio regularly interacted with Koxinga and his officials.[11] Both works contain highly negative portrayals of the Zheng, depicting them as amoral pirates who did not hesitate to renege upon their promises, and were responsible for the torture, maiming, and killing of hundreds of thousands of innocents. This appraisal came to define Western popular and scholarly works on the family until well into the twentieth century, although their tone acquired a greater degree of nuance over time.[12] Behind the shrill accusations lies a lingering sense of bitterness at the defeat of Europeans at the hands of what they considered to be a group of treacherous, heathen natives.

After the Second World War, the horizons of Western historiography broadened considerably amid intensified academic exchanges, first with Taiwanese scholars, archives, and academic institutions, and later, with their mainland counterparts in the waning years of the Cold War. From the 1950s to 1970s, scholars in Taiwan painstakingly compiled and annotated, under government sponsorship, a vast body of Chinese-language documents pertaining to the island's history and published them in a 354-volume series: the *Taiwan wenxian congkan* (*Taiwan historical documents collectanea*). Historians on the island further supplied exhaustive studies of these materials in academic journals such as *Taiwan wenxian* (*Taiwan historica*) and *Taiwan fengwu* (*Taiwan folkways*). Ming and Qing accounts related to the Zheng family feature prominently in these endeavors, which greatly facilitated access to Chinese-language sources on the subject in the West. The general influx of literature from the mainland starting in the late 1970s added to the body of available resources.[13]

---

[10] C. E. S. can be interpreted as the abbreviation for Coyett et Socii, Latin for Coyett and associates.

[11] Anna Busquets has undertaken an exhaustive analysis of Riccio's complete manuscript. See her "Dreams in the Chinese periphery: Victorio Riccio and Zheng Chenggong's regime," in Tonio Andrade and Xing Hang, *Sea rovers, silver, and samurai*. Although still unpublished in its entirety, parts of Riccio's narrative have appeared in José Eugenio Borao-Mateo, Pol Heyns, Carlos Gómez, and Anna Maria Zandueta Nisce (eds.), *Spaniards in Taiwan: documents*, 2 vols. (Taipei: SMC Publishing, 2002).

[12] Croizier, *Chinese nationalism*, pp. 29–31.

[13] A detailed introduction to the primary documents and historical accounts of the Ming-Qing transition from both Taiwan and mainland China, with significant sections on the Zheng family, can be found in Lynn Struve, *The Ming-Qing conflict, 1619–1683: a historiography and source guide* (Ann Arbor, MI: Association for Asian Studies, 1998).

Collectively, the large-scale influx of Chinese-language sources has ameliorated the previous Western negativity toward the Zheng. At the same time, because their narration style, character portrayals, and political agendas differ drastically from the traditional European historiography, they have presented new problems of interpretation for historians trained in the West. Research on the Zheng has largely become the provenance of two dynamic subfields. Late imperial Chinese historians, such as Lynn Struve and Wong Young-tsu, build upon the Qing historiographical tradition as later modified on both sides of the strait. They emphasize Zheng resistance against the Manchus and relations with the Ming loyalist courts. As Struve insightfully points out, the rise of the Zheng reflected the widespread militarization of Chinese society during the late Ming amid the systemic breakdown of civil institutions in the face of mounting internal and external crises. Wong correctly argues that the war-plagued southeastern coast reacquired political order by rallying around the family's banner of anti-Qing resistance.[14] However, neither scholar sufficiently accounts for aspects of the Zheng's behavior that may contradict their avowed Ming loyalism and the potential for shifts over time in response to altered circumstances.

The family constitutes an important subject of study for another group of historians: those whose expertise lies in maritime China, defined as a chain of ports, islands, and coastal territory stretching from the Liaodong peninsula in the north to Hainan in the south. For them, this littoral zone had a distinct past and identity characterized by profit-driven acquisitiveness and openness to the outside world, in contrast to the inward-looking continent and its rigid imperial autocracy and Confucian value system.[15] Experts of this dynamic field, whose focus is on the early modern period, or roughly the sixteenth to nineteenth centuries, are increasingly expanding beyond their disciplinary confines and seeking to understand China's

[14] Lynn Struve, *Southern Ming: 1644–1662* (New Haven CT: Yale University Press, 1984), pp. 6–7; Wong Young-tsu, "Security and warfare on the China coast: the Taiwan question in the seventeenth century," *Monumenta Serica: Journal of Oriental Studies* 35 (1981–1983), p. 133.

[15] The dichotomy of a maritime and continental China was first articulated in John King Fairbank, "Maritime and continental in China's history," in Fairbank and Denis Crispin Twitchett (eds.), *The Cambridge history of China* (Cambridge, UK: Cambridge University Press, 1983), vol. XII.1: Republican China, 1912–1949. The vast-ranging and pathbreaking research of John E. Wills, Jr. has built upon this analytical foundation to develop maritime Chinese history into an exciting and vibrant new field in its own right. One of his definitive works is "Maritime China from Wang Chih to Shih Lang: themes in peripheral history," in Jonathan D. Spence and Wills (eds.), *From Ming to Ch'ing: conquest, region, and continuity in seventeenth-century China* (New Haven, CT: Yale University Press, 1979). Deng Gang, *Maritime sector, institutions, and sea power of premodern China* (Westport, CT: Greenwood Press, 1999) offers a comprehensive, book-length treatment of maritime Chinese economic history.

position within a broader world that they see as interconnected and interdependent. Many cooperate closely with global historians or have come to define themselves as such. Others are joining forces with specialists in various geographic and disciplinary fields to articulate an East Asian maritime zone comparable to the Atlantic, Indian Ocean, and Mediterranean worlds. They conceive of this space, comprising the China Seas but with increasing inroads into the Indian and Pacific Oceans, as an integrated unit characterized by economic, diplomatic, and cultural exchanges whose internal dynamics exceed connections outside the region.[16]

Maritime historians build upon the rich Western historiography on the Zheng but dispense with the past negativity and emphasize the more neutral focus of these sources upon the family's trading network and multilateral ties with East Asia ex-China. Their works reveal a profit-driven, realpolitik side of the Zheng that Ming and Qing specialists have only lightly treated before and calls into question the family's commitment to the loyalist cause. The Zheng organization, they argue, should be treated as an entity separate from the dynastic transition on the mainland. Patrizia Carioti claims that the family established an "informal state," while Cheng Wei-chung goes farther, characterizing it as a fully independent sea-based kingdom.[17]

Many maritime scholars are merging their findings with the perspectives and arguments of late imperial Chinese historians. The pioneering works of John E. Wills, Jr., Leonard Blussé, and Tonio Andrade show that the Zheng inherited the legacy of a long line of merchant-mediators in the China Seas, who used their skills, connections, and military acumen to dominate the littoral and the seas. The success of these middlemen depended upon an ability to bridge their fluid maritime environment of

---

[16] Leonard Blussé has played a major role in the articulation of an integrated maritime East Asian regional history. See his "No boats to China: the Dutch East India Company and the changing pattern of the China Sea trade, 1635–1690," *Modern Asian studies* 30.1 (1996). It is important to note that the maritime East Asian and global perspectives are by no means mutually exclusive. Recent works that position the region within a global context include the collection of chapters in Angela Schottenhammer (ed.), *The East Asian Mediterranean: crossroads of knowledge, commerce, and human migration* (Wiesbaden, Germany: Otto Harrassowitz, 2008); François Gipouloux, and Jonathan Hall and Dianna Martin (trans.), *The Asian Mediterranean: port cities and trading networks in China, Japan and Southeast Asia, 13th–21st century* (Cheltenham, UK: Edward Elgar, 2011); and Blussé, *Visible cities: Canton, Nagasaki, and Batavia and the coming of the Americans* (Cambridge, MA: Harvard University Press, 2008).

[17] Patrizia Carioti, "The Zhengs' maritime power in the context of the 17th century far eastern seas: the rise of a 'centralised piratical organisation' and its gradual development into an informal 'state,'" *Ming-Qing yanjiu (Ming-Qing studies)* 5 (1996); Cheng Wei-chung (Zheng Weizhong), *War, trade and piracy in the China Seas, 1622–1683* (Leiden: Brill, 2013).

transnational markets, informal kinship networks, and cultural hybridity with the symbols of state orthodoxy on the Chinese continent.[18]

The new, transnational perspectives offered by maritime historians in the West have benefited scholarship in the Chinese world. In Taiwan, the massive editorial projects of Ts'ao Yung-ho, Chiang Shu-sheng, and others, often working closely with Blussé and Wills, has made available a growing number of European-language sources in published form, with some translated entirely into Chinese.[19] Through a careful reading and analysis of these resources alongside the Ming and Qing materials, the Taiwan historians have also authored sophisticated studies that often exceed their Western counterparts in the originality of their insights.[20] Most valuable are their meticulous identification of the plethora of spellings of Chinese person and place names mentioned in the European sources, which they link with the Chinese-language texts based upon their pronunciation in the southern Fujian, or Minnanese, dialect. Less ambitious translations of excerpts of core Dutch and Spanish texts have also appeared in mainland publications. Several mainland studies of the Zheng draw from these and the interpretation of Western maritime historians to question both the traditional Confucian and PRC orthodox interpretations of the organization's leaders.[21]

Despite great strides made in forging a balanced narrative, the maritime-centered approach toward the Zheng in the West remains largely that of an apolitical, sometimes even bordering on the stateless, family of self-interested armed traders. Like the Ming loyalist view

---

[18] See, e.g., Wills, "Maritime China from Wang Chih to Shih Lang: themes in peripheral history," in Spence and Wills (eds.), *From Ming to Ch'ing*; Leonard Blussé, "Minnan-jen or cosmopolitan? The rise of Cheng Chih-lung alias Nicolas Iquan," in E. B. Vermeer (ed.), *Development and decline of Fukien province in the 17th and 18th centuries* (Leiden: E. J. Brill, 1990), and Tonio Andrade, *How Taiwan became Chinese: Dutch, Spanish, and Han colonization in the seventeenth century*, Gutenberg E-book www.gutenberg-e.org/andrade, 2008.

[19] For instance, Blussé and Ts'ao collaborated for over a decade to arrange, annotate, and publish the official journal kept by the Dutch colonial authorities on Taiwan in Leonard Blussé, M. E. van Opstall, and Ts'ao Yung-ho (Cao Yonghe) (eds.), *De dagregisters van het Kasteel Zeelandia, Taiwan* (henceforth *Zeelandia dagregisters*), 4 vols. (The Hague: Institute for the History of the Netherlands, 1986–2000). Chiang Shu-sheng arranged to have all four volumes translated into Chinese.

[20] Cheng Wei-chung's Chinese monograph is quite representative of this trend of scholarship on Taiwan, which has, in the past few decades, emerged from obscurity to occupy a prominent place in mainstream historiography. See Zheng Weizhong (Cheng Wei-chung), *Helan shidai de Taiwan shehui: Ziranfa de nanti yu wenminghua de licheng* (Taipei: Qianwei, 2004).

[21] Nuanced and critical works of this nature include Chen Bisheng, *Zheng Chenggong lishi yanjiu* (Beijing: Jiuzhou, 2000); Deng Kongzhao, *Zheng Chenggong yu Ming-Zheng Taiwan shi yanjiu* (Beijing: Taihai, 2000).

espoused by late imperial historians, it does not adequately explain apparent contradictions in their words and actions.[22] In fact, it has comparatively done less to examine the nature of their organization on the home front, including core institutions and ideologies, attitudes toward the Ming and Qing, and the social composition of their subjects. Moreover, because of the nature of the primary records used, relations between the Zheng and Europeans are covered much more extensively than with other native players in the region. In East Asia, too, the maritime approach often serves to bolster existing agendas or legitimize new ones. Zheng interactions with the Europeans, for instance, reinforce the already-established mainland claim that they stood up to imperialism while presenting them in a fresh light as pioneers of Chinese maritime expansion.[23] Many Taiwan-based historians use the same evidence to prove the separateness of the island's historical experience from China.[24]

Toward a new historical narrative

On one level, this book aims to bridge the "split personality" of the Zheng, as reflected in the historiographical divide among East Asian narratives, between East Asia and the West, and between Western late imperial Chinese and maritime historians. It owes tremendous debts to the previous scholarship. In particular, it builds upon the view of John Wills and Lynn Struve that a politically autonomous, sea-based Chinese state with a developed civil bureaucracy posed a viable contingency during the seventeenth century.[25] Dahpon Ho views the Zheng as the prime drivers behind this Great Enterprise, parallel to Manchu ambitions

---

[22] Often, the contradictory portrayals appear in the same works without any attempt to reconcile them. Although Tonio Andrade, *Lost colony: the untold story of China's first great victory over the west* (Princeton, NJ: Princeton University Press, 2011), pp. 63–64, is convinced that Koxinga was a genuine Ming loyalist at heart, the core of his superb, fast-paced narrative on Zheng interactions with the Dutch reveals the man to be more of a self-aggrandizing lord of the seas.

[23] See Zheng Guangnan and Shanghai China Maritime Museum, *Xinbian Zhongguo haidao shi* (Beijing: Encyclopedia of China Press, 2014), pp. 308–312 and Ni Lexiong, "Zheng Chenggong shidai de haiquan shijian dui dangdai Zhongguo de yiyi," *Huadong shifan daxue xuebao zhexue shehui ban* 44.2 (2012).

[24] Examples include the numerous works of Ts'ao Yung-ho and Chiang Shu-sheng. Saying that there is an underlying agenda behind them does not in any way diminish the value of their scholarship, the product of years of dedicated research and labor that have single-handedly brought about a more comprehensive understanding of maritime East Asian history.

[25] John E. Wills, Jr., "The South China Sea is not a Mediterranean," in Tang Xiyong (ed.), *Zhongguo haiyang fazhan shi lunwenji* (Taipei: Research Center for Humanities and Social Sciences, Academia Sinica, 2008), vol. X, pp. 21–22; Struve, *Southern Ming: 1644–1662* (New Haven CT: Yale University Press, 1984), p. 7.

on land.[26] Cheng Wei-chung is another source of inspiration in his focus upon multilateral interactions between the organization and state and non-state actors across maritime East Asia, and not just the European colonial powers.[27] This book connects their perspectives to the work of Patrizia Carioti, who attributes the ultimate downfall of the Zheng organization to its inability to balance its advantages in maritime trade and overseas expansion with the dogmatic Ming loyalism of Koxinga and Zheng Jing.[28] It is hoped that their insights, merged together, allow for a comprehensive, post-ideological narrative of the family situated at the intersection of intellectual, political, economic, and cultural histories.

On another level, this book engages with Chinese, Dutch, English, Japanese, Korean, and Spanish historical records, reading them against one another in an effort to tell the story of the Zheng on their own terms – how they themselves viewed the world around them and how they devised strategies suited to their capabilities and limitations. Some of these archives, histories, and documents have been rarely utilized before.[29] In particular, this book pays special attention to newly available sources from mainland China. They include Zheng documents from private collections and Qing archives, especially those written in Manchu, used to keep government secrets and that promise to afford a more candid view of the family than records in Chinese. Many of them have been arranged and compiled into the *Taiwan wenxian huikan* (*Compendium of Taiwan historical documents*), published in 2004. This massive collection, comprising 100 volumes in seven parts, brings together most of the available primary materials related to Taiwan on the mainland. Other findings come from inscriptions and oral testimonies collected by the author during his fieldwork in Fujian.

Korean records provide another important, yet neglected, resource for better understanding the Zheng family and organization. Although the preeminent Qing tributary state, the Chosŏn Dynasty (1392–1910), especially its elite class, harbored strong pro-Ming sentiments. The Veritable Records of the Korean kings and accounts of tributary envoys

---

[26] Dahpon David Ho, "Sealords live in vain: Fujian and the making of a maritime frontier in seventeenth-century China," unpublished PhD dissertation, University of California-San Diego (2011), pp. 1–3.

[27] See Cheng (Zheng), *War, trade and piracy*.

[28] Carioti, "Zhengs' maritime power," pp. 52–53.

[29] For instance, Historiographical Institute, Tokyo University (ed.), *Tō tsūji kaisho nichiroku, Dai Nihon kinsei shiryō*, bk. 3, 7 vols. (Tokyo: Tokyo University Press, 1955), vol. I contains surviving fragments from the daily records of the Chinese Interpreters' Office at Nagasaki. Jin Ji (ed.), *Yongli Ningyang xianzhi, Riben cang Zhongguo hanjian difangzhi congkan xubian*, 10 (Beijing: Chinese Library Press, 2003) is a copy of a 1675 Fujian gazetteer compiled by a Zheng official that has survived in Japan.

to Beijing exhibited particular interest in irredentist resistance movements to Manchu rule.[30] Moreover, heavy storms frequently washed
Zheng junks onto the shores of Cheju Island, situated as it was in the
middle of the China-Japan route, one of the busiest lanes for sea traffic in
seventeenth-century East Asia. Especially valuable are interviews of the
shipwrecked Zheng merchants, conducted via interpreters or written
exchange in Chinese characters with local officials, which provide rare
insight into the opinions and self-identification of individuals in the
organization beneath the elite stratum.[31] The Korean records thus reveal
a pro-Ming viewpoint from a third party able to counterbalance the cold,
often negative, appraisals in the Qing and European sources.

Based upon new and existing primary evidence and a synthesis of the
academic consensus, this study advances three key arguments. For one, it
contends that the Zheng organization successfully applied and adapted
the bureaucratic structure and Confucian orthodoxy of the Chinese continent to govern a constituency of primarily merchants and military men
in a hybrid, transnational maritime zone. Chinese merchants were officially relegated to the bottom of the social and moral hierarchy during the
Ming and Qing. In practice, as recent scholarship has shown, they played
key roles in the smooth functioning of a highly complex, commercialized
economy. However, the court supported their activities only to the extent
that they supplemented its primary aim of perpetuating a stable agrarian
order.[32] Likewise, the late imperial hierarchy degraded and excluded
military men from elite status.[33] The Zheng, on the other hand, created
civil institutions to harness and tie mercantile and martial interests to
state power. They granted merchants and military commanders positions
of authority equivalent or superior to Confucian scholar-officials and
landed gentry, the traditional elites of late imperial China.

The Zheng made similar modifications in the realm of foreign relations.
The Ming court had idealized a hierarchical world order centered upon

[30] For a detailed study of pro-Ming sentiments in Korea, refer to Sun Weiguo, *Da Ming
qihao yu xiao Zhonghua yishi: Chaoxian wangchao zun Zhou si Ming wenti yanjiu* (Beijing:
Commercial Press, 2007).
[31] One representative record of these conversations frequently cited in this book is Sŏng Haeun,
Chŏngmi chŏnshinrok, in Hanguk gochŏn bŏnyŏkwon, www.itkc.or.kr/MAN/index.jsp
(2007).
[32] Important works on the subject of merchant relations with the state in China include Ho
Pingti, *Ladder of success in imperial China* (New York: Columbia University Press, 1962);
Ray Huang, *1587: a year of no significance, the Ming dynasty in decline* (New Haven, CT:
Yale University Press, 1981); R. Bin Wong, *China transformed: historical change and the
limits of European experience* (Ithaca, NY: Cornell University Press, 1997); and Craig
Clunas, *Superfluous things: material culture and social status in early modern China*
(Honolulu: University of Hawaii Press, 2004).
[33] Struve, *Southern Ming*, pp. 5–6.

China as the Middle Kingdom (Zhongguo) – the superior realm and bastion of civilization. Lesser, "barbarian" lands around it were expected to pay regular homage before the Ming emperor – the universal Son of Heaven – and present a tribute of their native products. The envoys received, in return, gifts of much-coveted goods, such as silk and porcelain, worth many times the value of their tribute as a demonstration of his generosity and the prosperity of his realm. A more extensive private trade was also permitted at the capital in Beijing and the mission's designated port of entry. Within this framework, foreign trade functioned as a political instrument to reward subservient tributary states. As such, the court tried to confine outside contacts and exchange to the missions, and permitted them to come to China only according to fixed intervals. It concurrently restricted and, at times, banned its own subjects from private trade and travel abroad.[34]

The Zheng organization did not need to carry this diplomatic baggage, for it was, in theory, subordinate to the Ming, and to a pretender desperately fleeing the Qing onslaught in southwestern China, far away from its main bases. The Zheng thus had the freedom to ally, trade, and compete with foreigners on equal terms, which, in fact, allowed them to control overseas commerce and advance Chinese interests abroad more effectively than the original tributary system. In contrast to the negligence, suspicion, or outright hostility that continental dynasties exhibited toward subjects beyond China's borders, the organization protected their interests before Asian rulers and European colonial authorities. The Zheng, in turn, enjoyed strong support from overseas Chinese merchants and immigrants, who served the organization as agents and spies, and paid it duties and taxes. As a result, the family came to exercise an informal economic hegemony over much of maritime East Asia.

Secondly, the Zheng converted this massive clout into a sustained program of state building and overseas expansion. The organization transformed from an ad hoc military authority based in tenuous, resource-deficient southeastern Chinese coastal outposts into a Taiwan-centered territorial government after Koxinga seized the island from the Dutch in 1662. His successors, Zheng Jing and Keshuang, cemented his legacy by forging a centralized administration able to mobilize resources and enforce laws at a level of grassroots penetration that the thinly

---

[34] John King Fairbank provides a classic, but still highly relevant, introduction to the theoretical role of trade within the Chinese tributary system, especially as applied to maritime East Asia, in *Trade and diplomacy on the China coast: the opening of the treaty ports, 1842–1854* (Stanford, CA: Stanford University Press, 1964), pp. 23–37. A much-needed and enlightening update comes from David C. Kang, *East Asia before the West: five centuries of trade and tribute* (New York: Columbia University Press, 2011).

stretched Ming and Qing bureaucracies could only dream of doing. Moreover, in contrast to the arbitrary personal leadership style of their predecessors, the two men made decisions through consultation with an oligarchy of advisors. Taiwan, however, only served as the initial step in a broader vision of a maritime realm encompassing the family's entire sphere of influence in maritime East Asia.

Finally, the Zheng tried, throughout their existence, to justify their maritime orientation according to continental modes of legitimacy. To this effect, the organization alternated, according to the geopolitical situation, between the political models of an autonomous feudatory of a restored Ming, a Korean-style Qing vassal, and an independent maritime kingdom. Moreover, the Zheng held talks with their Qing enemies on at least twenty occasions to end hostilities and normalize their relationship. The two sides often came close to a political settlement, which could have resulted in two Chinese states or a unified Chinese empire with a dynamic, expansive dependency. A realistic contingency existed for both entities to maintain an active diplomatic and commercial engagement with the emerging globalized economic system as core regions rather than being passively drawn in later as peripheries.

The Zheng family in a global comparative framework

Although a narrative primarily set in the seventeenth century, the story of the Zheng organization offers fresh insights into China's agonizing transition to a global periphery in the nineteenth century. According to R. Bin Wong, Eric Jones, and others, the Ming and Qing political economy, aimed at upholding the status quo of a prosperous agrarian empire, constituted the main factor behind this drastic reversal of fortunes. Unlike the revenue-starved states of Western Europe, in constant conflict with one another and their domestic elites, Chinese rulers saw little need to raise funds by affording legal protection for merchants and opening new markets through overseas expansion. These measures would have provided a supportive climate for the generation of capital to engage in scientific innovation and industrial development.[35]

Kenneth Pomeranz builds upon this scholarly consensus, but emphasizes that Western Europe, in particular, England, could not have succeeded without the windfall of natural resources from its New World

---

[35] See R. Bin Wong, *China transformed*; Jean-Laurent Rosenthal and R. Bin Wong, *Before and beyond divergence: the politics of economic change in China and Europe* (Cambridge, MA: Harvard University Press, 2011); Eric Jones, *The European miracle: environments, economies, and geopolitics in the history of Europe and Asia*, third edition (Cambridge, UK: Cambridge University Press, 2003); and Gipouloux, *Asian Mediterranean*, pp. 142–143.

colonies. Overseas expansion, a product of the multistate system, allowed Europe to break free of dependence upon domestic agricultural surpluses and generate massive quantities of capital for industrialization. While the Zheng organization proved similarly capable of armed penetration into the resource-rich Southeast Asian periphery, it lacked the legitimacy and active support from the mother country to sustain its operations.[36] As a result, China remained caught in a labor-intensive agrarian regime.

These conclusions are solid, but it should be noted that their treatment of the political economies of China and Western Europe reflects the late eighteenth-century outcome of a highly contingent process. In fact, the preceding century was a time of state building and competitive boundary setting across Eurasia.[37] In Europe, Hapsburg Spain had an opportunity and, indeed, tried to unify the entire continent. Only with its defeat at the hands of the Dutch in the Eighty Years' War did the Treaty of Westphalia, signed in 1648, institutionalize the cutthroat competition of European states through balance-of-power politics. Likewise, the assumption of a unified Chinese empire does not take into account of the fact that East Asia during this period was a region characterized by intense rivalries. The Zheng, along with the Ming loyalist courts, Zungar Mongols, and insular Southeast Asian sultanates, should be treated equally with the Manchus, Russians, and other "winners" of the contest: as entities with similar potential to create durable state structures. Viewed from this perspective, the Qing victory in China was neither inevitable nor guaranteed to be complete.

Faced with a similar geopolitical climate, the Zheng organization naturally shared many parallels with contemporary European joint-stock corporations, especially the Dutch East India Company. Both the Zheng and the VOC monopolized a significant portion of their mother countries' foreign commerce, and combined trade with plunder in a quest to dominate the same Asian sea lanes. Both subscribed to their mother countries'

---

[36] According to Kenneth Pomeranz, *The great divergence: China, Europe, and the making of the modern world economy* (Princeton, NJ: Princeton University Press, 2001), p. 204, the fortuitous discovery of local coal mines also helped Western Europe break through the ecological barrier.

[37] Seventeenth-century state building is the common subject of a vast body of literature that spans traditional historical fields. Representative works include Frederic Wakeman, *The great enterprise: the Manchu reconstruction of imperial order in seventeenth-century China*, 2 vols. (Berkeley, CA: University of California Press, 1985) for the Manchus; Victor Lieberman, *Strange parallels: Southeast Asia in a global context, c. 800–1830*, 2 vols. (Cambridge, UK: Cambridge University Press, 2003) and Anthony Reid, *Southeast Asia in the age of commerce: 1450–1680*, 2 vols. (New Haven, CT: Yale University Press, 1988–1993) for mainland and insular Southeast Asia; Peter Perdue, *China marches west: the Qing conquest of central Eurasia* (Cambridge, MA: Harvard University Press, 2005) for Inner Asia; and Jones, *European miracle* for Western Europe.

ideal of resistance against foreign invasion; the Dutch company vowed to end Spanish commercial and military hegemony, while the Zheng desired the expulsion of the Manchus from China. Both also enjoyed significant and growing autonomy over time, transforming from armed commercial enterprises into expansive territorial states.[38] For this reason, the VOC is often utilized as a point of reference and comparison in this study of the Zheng organization.

Certainly, one must bear in mind the tremendous differences, whether in terms of internal structure or external environment, between the two quasi-official entities. The Dutch East India Company is commonly believed to be the prototype of a modern capitalist enterprise, with its separation of ownership and management, limited liability, and tens of thousands of contract employees.[39] The States General, the governing body of the Dutch Republic, chartered and actively supported the VOC as a means to expand the mother country's trade with Asia and assist in the struggle for independence from Spain by attacking Iberian interests overseas. The Zheng organization, on the other hand, maintained little distinction between bureaucracy and commerce, and official and private interests. Moreover, it flourished amid the growing inability of the Ming court to control the maritime frontier. While the China Seas constituted the family's main sphere of influence, the Dutch operated on a greater scale, encompassing, in addition, Western Europe and the Indian Ocean. Also, unlike the Zheng, the Dutch were originally outsiders to maritime East Asia, and stood at an initial disadvantage in accessing product sources and the culturally specific personal ties and knowledge base of Chinese and other diaspora networks.[40]

Still, enough mitigating factors exist to balance out these differences. By the 1630s, when the Zheng organization was only beginning to take shape, the Dutch had already been involved in maritime East Asia for over a quarter of a century. They had formed alliances and partnerships with native rulers, primarily in Southeast Asia but also with Japan, and built a formidable network of colonies and bases throughout the region.[41] They further maintained cooperative ties with the Chinese diaspora; they founded cities on the sites of existing Chinese trading communities and actively recruited Chinese immigrants to their main colonies in Java and Taiwan. As a result of these endeavors, the company reaped handsome

---

[38] Although Gipouloux, *Asian Mediterranean*, p. 131 believes that the objective of the Dutch East India Company was primarily commercial and "never territorial," even he admits that the ultimate effect of its actions led to creation of a colonial system.
[39] Gipouloux, *Asian Mediterranean*, p. 127.   [40] Ibid., pp. 126–132, 323.
[41] Jonathan I. Israel, *Dutch primacy in world trade, 1585–1740* (Oxford, UK: Oxford University Press, 1989), p. 86.

profits throughout the 1630s, when its fortunes in East Asia neared the peak.[42] It would be a stretch to call the Dutch "outsiders" during this period, even if they were not fully integrated into the regional network.

In fact, a certain degree of detachment does not necessarily constitute a disadvantage compared to those completely inside the system. Where the Dutch East India Company either could not or refused to adapt to local norms, it could force its will upon others to a certain extent by means of its powerful ships, deadly guns, and sturdy fortresses.[43] This advantage in military technology, along with their apparent freedom from local entanglements, made the Dutch highly sought after, at least initially, as a potential ally. Oftentimes, they could acquire significant privileges, such as exclusive access to product sources and trading concessions, in exchange for their assistance.[44] In contrast, the "insider" Zheng constantly faced the looming specter of extermination at the hands of a Manchu court determined to eradicate this threat to its absolute control over China. They further experienced frequent interruption to their product sources due to warfare and purposeful blockade. Not surprisingly, the Qing often requested, and, at one point, even received, Dutch assistance to eradicate them.[45]

Because of the delayed head start and lack of support from the mother country, the Zheng organization was, in its earlier years, admittedly characterized by more arbitrary, and hence less institutionalized elements than the VOC. It also operated on a smaller scale. Nonetheless, the overall trajectory of the two converged over time. The Zheng organization achieved growing sophistication in its institutions, especially in its final two decades. It successfully adapted the Ming imperial system to formalize the once informal, lineage-based patron-client connections based on reciprocal debt obligations commonly practiced in southeastern China and among overseas Chinese. This rationalization differed from a conventional European model, but it effectively responded to the Zheng's unique mix of challenges and opportunities.[46] Unlike the Dutch East India Company, which needed to coordinate operations

---

[42] Blussé, "No boats," pp. 63–66.   [43] Andrade, *Lost colony*, pp. 35–37.

[44] A good example is the alliance forged between the Dutch and the northern half of Vietnam, or Tonkin, against Quảng Nam, its rival in the south. See Hoáng Anh Tuấn, *Silk for silver: Dutch-Vietnamese relations, 1637–1700* (Leiden: Brill, 2007).

[45] The most comprehensive monograph on the Qing-Dutch alliance to date is John E. Wills, *Pepper, guns, and parleys: the Dutch East India Company and China, 1662–1681* (Cambridge, MA: Harvard University Press, 1974).

[46] Even the VOC fell short of a perfectly rationalized model in the modern sense. Julia Adams argues that patrimonialism frequently caused severe agency problems that ultimately led to the company's demise. See her "Trading states, trading places: the role of patrimonialism in early modern Dutch development," *Comparative Studies in Society and History* 36.2 (1994).

over vast distances, they aimed to stabilize volatile production sources and markets, often located in hostile territories.

Moreover, just as their European counterparts expanded eastward into East Asia, the Zheng gravitated toward the opposite direction: the Indian Ocean. This movement, beginning in the late 1650s, was driven by the onset of fundamental shifts within the global economic structure that continued well into the late eighteenth century. These included India's replacement of China as the world's preeminent production center, voracious Chinese demand for natural resources, and Japan's turn toward import substitution.[47] The net effect was a decline in trade within East Asia and the tighter integration of parts of the region into a fledging global economy. To better access the Indian Ocean network, the Zheng formed partnerships with crucial intermediaries, such as Indian merchants, Southeast Asian kingdoms, and the English. They further worked to assert direct control over the new product sources by conquering Taiwan, making plans to seize the Philippines, and engaging in import substitution to organize the production of their own textiles.

In sum, the differences between the Zheng and the VOC largely cancel each other out, enabling a rough framework of comparison between the two entities to be established. As this study shows, the Zheng institutions proved as equally capable as the joint-stock corporations in stimulating investment, accumulating capital, and maximizing profits. For the years when sufficient quantitative data are available to make a comprehensive estimate, the organization is demonstrated to have matched or exceeded the VOC in revenues and profitability. It also adapted effectively to the profound economic shifts already under way during the late 1660s.

On a broader level, a comparative approach juxtaposing the Zheng organization and the Dutch East India Company can shed light upon the political economies of their respective mother countries: China and the Netherlands, and, by extension, the Western European state system. Although both were autonomous entities, they still embodied the institutions and values of their native lands in compact form. While far from perfect, this framework provides a promising alternative to direct comparisons between an integrated but diverse Chinese empire and compact but more homogenous European states, which often pose problems because of vast differences in scale, natural

---

[47] John L. Cranmer-Byng and John E. Wills, Jr., "Trade and diplomacy with maritime Europe, 1644–c. 1800," in Wills (ed.), *China and maritime Europe, 1500–1800: trade, settlement, diplomacy, and missions* (Cambridge, UK: Cambridge University Press, 2011), pp. 207–222.

endowments, and diplomatic traditions.[48] It can also take into account the dynamic and contested process of state building across Eurasia.

It is a key contention of this book that the late imperial Chinese system, when faced with serious alternatives to its legitimacy, proved capable of allying with mercantile interests and sponsoring the search for new markets and resources abroad as a means of enhancing state power. At the same time, however, the ideal of a unified Confucian hierarchy under Heaven worked powerfully against attempts to institutionalize the competitive climate. The Zheng ultimately lost in this battlefield of ideas, paving the way for a unified agrarian empire under the Qing. Nonetheless, elements of the family's legacy remained influential for centuries after in shaping maritime Chinese business and community organizations and the articulation of a Chinese identity outside China. It is also significant in light of the PRC's ambitious initiative to territorialize maritime East Asia and integrate it as one core of a global Silk Road economic belt.

---

[48] Pomeranz, *Great divergence*, 7 offers a credible alternative framework by focusing upon the main economic centers: England in Europe and for China, the Yangzi River Delta, which includes an area around present-day Shanghai. The main shortcoming of this otherwise solid approach is that the Chinese core lacked a central authority akin to the English crown.

1 Setting the stage

The province of Fujian is short on arable land and densely populated. Very few of the five grains are produced. For this reason, residents along the coast all view the junk as their home, the seas as their fields, and trade with the barbarians as their livelihoods.

Memorial of the Fujian Censorate to the Ming court, 1593.[1]

The province of Fujian is traditionally known as a "seaside Lu and Zou [respective hometowns of the ancient sages, Confucius and Mencius]." In recent years, however, the people do not cherish the values of old. Their customs have become vulgar, and they are prone to violence.

From the *Fujian sheng li* (*Regulations of Fujian Province*).[2]

The Zheng organization emerged out of Fujian, a province roughly the size of Portugal (about 121,000 sq. km) situated along the jagged, meandering southeastern Chinese littoral. Surrounded from three sides by mountains, afflicted by an acute shortage of arable land, but endowed with fine harbors and inlets, Fujian's livelihood depended upon its maritime zone. The destitute found employment in fishing and salt gathering, while gentry and merchants invested their capital in seafaring ventures. More importantly, the littoral of the province served as a conduit for the flow of goods, information, and culture between China and the world beyond.[3]

Three levels of integration

Starting at least from the time of Christ, China had been a key participant in long-distance trade. Silk, porcelain, and other exports prized for their refined and sophisticated craftsmanship traveled as far as the shores of the Mediterranean. In exchange, China received spices, precious metals, and luxury goods, either carried on the backs of camel caravans traversing the Middle East and Central and Inner Asia, or onboard seagoing vessels

[1] Ming shilu *Minhai guanxi shiliao*, *TWWXCK*, 296 (1971), p. 87.
[2] *Fujian sheng li*, *TWWXCK*, 199 (1964), p. 1032.
[3] Wong Young-tsu, "Security," pp. 115–116.

22

sailing from port to port along the Persian Gulf, Indian Ocean, and South China Sea. Some scholars view this vibrant Eurasian network of land and maritime Silk Roads as an early stage or variety of transregional economic integration. The resulting interdependent unit, known as a world system, would eventually expand to encompass all continents.[4] According to these scholars, the Fujian coast played an important role in this initial period of globalization. From the seventh to fourteenth centuries, the port of Quanzhou had served as the eastern terminus of the maritime Silk Road. With a population of a million during its heyday and frequented by Chinese, Arab, Indian, and Persian traders, it was one of the biggest and most cosmopolitan cities in the world.[5]

Historians of Ming and Qing China, in contrast to specialists of earlier periods in Chinese history, depict a more fragmented landscape. The classic model proposed by G. William Skinner continues to serve as an indispensable framework of reference. Instead of a unified market, Skinner divides the late imperial Chinese realm into nine loosely linked, but largely distinct, macroregions. Each of them maintained an organic coherence based upon economic ties, environmental conditions, and socialization patterns.[6] Dahpon Ho has modified this model, originally applied to continental China, toward an examination of its maritime zone. The result was a similar fragmentation into four overlapping maritime spaces from north to south, each "defined in shape and scope by the networks of primary and secondary ports that allowed intra-region and inter-region trade." Ho lists a domestic coastal trading circuit hugging the Chinese coast; a zone linking the highly commercialized Yangzi River Delta with Korea and Japan; Greater Fujian, consisting of shorelines on both sides of the Taiwan Strait and Okinawa; and the Cantonese-speaking South China water world. These spaces connected loosely to the separate networks of North and Southeast Asia.[7]

Indeed, certain patterns in late imperial coastal Fujian conform closely to Ho's model. In fact, Greater Fujian can be further split according to dialect: Mindong and Minbei in the north, spoken in and around the provincial capital of Fuzhou, and Minnan in the two southeastern

---

[4] Two of the most representative works from the world-system school are Janet L. Abu-Lughod, *Before European hegemony: the world-system, AD 1250–1350* (Oxford, UK: Oxford University Press, 1991) and André Gunder Frank, *ReOrient: global economy in the Asian age* (Berkeley, CA: University of California Press, 1998).

[5] Abu-Lughod, *Before European hegemony*, pp. 335–337.

[6] See Skinner's introduction to the macroregion in his "Regional urbanization in nineteenth-century China," in Skinner (ed.), *The city in late imperial China* (Stanford, CA: Stanford University Press, 1977).

[7] Ho's dissertation, "Sealords," pp. 41–44, speaks of six spaces, but two of them – maritime Southeast Asia and North Asia – are not directly related to maritime China.

prefectures of Zhangzhou and Quanzhou, as well as settlements in Okinawa and Taiwan. Xinghua, or Putian, lying between Fuzhou and Quanzhou, constitutes a buffer zone whose speech contains elements of both. Together, these dialects differed markedly from the Hakka spoken in the mountainous interior of the province and Jiangxi farther to the west, Wu to the north in Zhejiang, and Cantonese. Diverse tongues and physical barriers encouraged particularistic ties of family and community – often perceived as insularity and suspicion of outsiders – that came to revolve around strong lineage organizations, another means of subdivision.[8] Since population growth had placed severe strains on the limited supply of arable land by the fourteenth century, parts of Fujian also participated in the coastal trading circuit, importing grain from neighboring provinces even in good years.[9]

Yet other patterns do not appear to fit so neatly into these maritime spaces. Besides Taiwan and Okinawa, Minnanese traders journeyed and settled throughout China, while Minnanese seafarers colonized parts of Zhejiang, eastern Guangdong, the Leizhou Peninsula of western Guangdong, and Hainan Island. Others went to Japan and Southeast Asia, where they established mercantile outposts and some of the first Chinese communities overseas.[10] Such vast-ranging activities have prompted some scholars to stake a middle ground between the Skinnerian macroregion and the long-term globalization models proposed by world-systems theorists. Hamashita Takeshi and Giovanni Arrighi suggest the concept of an East Asian world-region extending from Central to Southeast Asia. Others, such as François Gipouloux and Angela Schottenhammer, argue for a more circumscribed "Asian Mediterranean" consisting of major urban centers and ports along the waterways from Manchuria to the Strait of Melaka.

However, the two schools agree that, despite significant internal diversity, the overall density and frequency of economic, political, and cultural linkages within these zones of interaction exceeded those with the outside.[11] Moreover, they share the belief that the centrality of China and its

---

[8] For an in-depth look at how these lineage groups formed and evolved into stable and durable local units of power and authority, refer to Michael Szonyi, *Practicing kinship: lineage and descent in late imperial China* (Stanford, CA: Stanford University Press, 2002).

[9] Evelyn Sakakida Rawski, *Agricultural change and the peasant economy of south China* (Cambridge, MA: Harvard University Press, 1972), pp. 59, 178–180.

[10] Wang Gungwu, "Merchants without empire: the Hokkien sojourning communities," in James D. Tracy (ed.), *The rise of merchant empires: long-distance trade in the early modern world, 1350–1750* (Cambridge, UK: Cambridge University Press, 1990), pp. 406–407.

[11] The concept of a world-region is defined in Giovanni Arrighi, Hamashita Takeshi, and Mark Selden, "Introduction," in Arrighi, Hamashita, and Selden (eds.), *The resurgence of East Asia: 500, 150, and 50 year perspectives* (London: Routledge, 2003), pp. 4–10. For

tributary system constituted the single most important characteristic of their respective regional models. Where the perspectives of the world-region and Mediterranean proponents diverge lies in their assessment of China's contribution to East Asian integration. For advocates of an East Asian world-region, this centrality facilitated regional coherence. Supporters of an Asian Mediterranean believe that the maritime zone formed an organic entity characterized by robust, multilateral circuits of private exchange precisely because of the absence of an effective, sustained Chinese state presence.[12]

Both arguments contain much merit. Trade among East Asian ports certainly exceeded their continental connections. Yet world-region scholars are also correct to point out that maritime and continent remained closely tied in a cultural and political sense, if not economically, during the early modern period. Coastal Fujian is a good case in point. Although access to the rest of China proved difficult, it enjoyed a tradition of fielding successful civil-service examination candidates and bureaucrats to serve the imperial court. It was also a birthplace of neo-Confucianism, which became the orthodoxy of China, Korea, Japan, and Vietnam after the fourteenth century.[13] The world-region model thus appears to be more applicable for the period covered by this study. Still, because of the intensity of commercial exchange on the sea lanes, it considers maritime East Asia to constitute a special subset of the broader world-region.

The three different perspectives presented above – on the extent of translocal and transnational integration through history – do not, in fact, contradict each other. It might be more instructive to view the macroregional, world-regional, and global areas as separate but overlapping layers able to simultaneously coexist and develop in planned and decentralized ways.[14] Yet the relative importance and degree of internal cohesion of any one layer changes over time. These shifts create profound stress and contradictions within the balance of interests that had profited from the previous arrangement, while introducing new parties from outside the system. The resulting process of negotiation and conflict holds the possibility of multiple outcomes. Coastal Fujian's geography, its participation in these multiple layers of integration, and the layers' complex and uneasy interplay provided the stage for the Zheng organization to act out its historical role.

more on the Asian Mediterranean, see Schottenhammer, *East Asian Mediterranean* and Gipouloux, *Asian Mediterranean.*
[12] See, for instance, Gipouloux et al., *Asian Mediterranean*, p. 322.
[13] Wang Gungwu, "Merchants without empire," p. 403.
[14] Gipouloux, et al., *Asian Mediterranean*, p. 23.

The prelude

The story begins in the fourteenth century, when Zhu Yuanzhang (b. 1328, r. Hongwu, 1368–1398) established the Ming dynasty after driving out the Mongols. In his desire to stabilize the realm from decades of warfare, he sought to realize his Daoist-inspired vision of a society of self-sufficient peasants overseen by a small corps of scholar-officials and gentry.[15] He further imposed a strict interpretation of Confucian orthodoxy that placed merchants, artisans, and other itinerant groups at the bottom of the social hierarchy and discouraged commerce and luxuries. As an extension of this principle to foreign relations, he issued the Maritime Prohibitions (*haijin*), which banned private trade and travel abroad. All interactions and commerce with other countries could only take place within the official tributary system. Strict regulations stipulated the size of embassies, types of goods exchanged, intervals for visits, and a designated port of entry. In effect, the Ming tried to monopolize access to Chinese goods and use them to entice foreign rulers to recognize its centrality and legitimacy. The focus upon ritual, hierarchy, and trade limitations had appeared in various forms in previous dynasties, but the Ming combined them into a bureaucratized framework as never before. These measures were fundamentally defensive, meant to neutralize the threats of internal rebellion and external invasion at the lowest cost.[16]

Zhu Di (1360–1424, r. Yongle, 1402–1424), the third Ming emperor, adopted a more vigorous approach aimed at expanding and enforcing the Confucian order. He built a fabulous new capital at Beijing, briefly occupied Vietnam, secured Japan's submission as a vassal state, and recognized the newly established Ryukyu kingdom in present-day Okinawa. Most famously, he and his successors outfitted seven maritime voyages under his eunuch, Zheng He (1371–1433), whose massive fleets sailed as far as India, the Middle East, and East Africa. One aim of these ambitious expeditions was to coopt the vigorous private commercial networks that had thrived in competition with official trade in the China Seas and Indian Ocean. This effort encountered much success, as countries far and wide came to pay tribute to and recognize the centrality of the Chinese Son of Heaven. However, influential Confucian officials at

[15] For a succinct overview of Zhu Yuanzhang's vision, see Timothy Brook, *The confusions of pleasure: commerce and culture in Ming China* (Berkeley, CA: University of California Press, 1999), pp. 17–19.

[16] John E. Wills, Jr., "Introduction," in Wills (ed.), *China and maritime Europe*, p. 7; Wills, "Relations with maritime Europeans, 1514–1662," in Denis Twitchett and Frederick W. Mote (eds.), *The Cambridge history of China* (Cambridge, UK: Cambridge University Press, 1998) vol. VIII.2: The Ming dynasty, 1368–1644, p. 333; Deng Gang, *Maritime sector*, pp. 124–125.

court complained bitterly about the exorbitant costs associated with a proactive foreign policy, leading to its permanent abandonment shortly after the Yongle emperor passed away.[17]

Nonetheless, the Ming-centered world order forged under Zhu Yuanzhang and Zhu Di had solidified in East Asia. On the one hand, it contributed to the disruption and decline of the maritime Silk Road that had forged a Eurasian-wide exchange of luxury goods. No longer would Arab, Persian, and Indian traders sail to the shores of China.[18] On the other hand, the tributary system fused East Asia into an integrated world-region. Besides close political and cultural exchange, the localized patterns of trade in the maritime zone became subsumed into a larger economic system. During the fifteenth century, the Ryukyu kingdom became the key intermediary of this integration on account of its unique geographic position at the confluence of the East and South China Seas and its privileged status as a trusted tributary vassal. Its ships procured Chinese silk, porcelain, and copper, and exchanged them for spices, marine products, and aromatic woods from Southeast Asia, which they then sold to China, Korea, and Japan. The Sultanate of Melaka, another Ming tributary state overlooking the narrow strait bearing its namesake, served as the terminus of the maritime East Asian network and the main gateway for commerce with the Indian Ocean world.[19]

In coastal Fujian, Ming policies brought about the decline of Quanzhou as an international port. In contrast, Fuzhou rose to prominence because of its role as the designated port of entry for Ryukyu missions after 1465. Nonetheless, southern Fujian continued to contribute actively to the maritime East Asian economy. Minnanese often served as interpreters, crewmembers, and even tribute envoys onboard Ryukyu ships. They also participated in the domestic coastal trade.[20]

In the sixteenth century, the carefully managed, official framework of tribute trade began to show visible strain. The Ming was experiencing population growth, regional specialization and proto-industrial

---

[17] For more on the Yongle emperor's exploits, with a particular focus upon the Zheng He voyages, see Louise Levathes, *When China ruled the seas: the treasure fleet of the dragon throne, 1405–1433* (New York: Oxford University Press, 1996).

[18] Abu-Lughod, *Before European hegemony*, pp. 359–361.

[19] Anthony Reid, "Chinese on the mining frontier of Southeast Asia" and Hamashita Takeshi, "The *Lidai baoan* and the Ryukyu maritime tributary trade network with China and Southeast Asia, the fourteenth to seventeenth centuries," p. 27, both in Eric Tagliacozzo and Chang Wen-chin (eds.), *Chinese circulations: capital, commodities, and networks in Southeast Asia* (Durham, NC: Duke University Press, 2011).

[20] Chang Pin-ts'un, "Maritime trade and local economy in late Ming Fukien," in E. B. Vermeer (ed.), *Development and decline of Fukien province in the 17th and 18th centuries* (Leiden: E. J. Brill, 1990), pp. 66–67; Wang Gungwu, "Merchants without empire," p. 407.

development, the rise of a vibrant merchant class and urban culture, and increased mobility at all levels. Greater wealth, albeit unevenly distributed, stimulated demand for exotic luxury imports beyond those supplied by tributary missions.[21] Many residents along the resource-scarce Chinese littoral, eyeing the vast potential of the domestic market, sailed abroad in defiance of the maritime ban. At this point, the Ming had registered a drastic decline in its naval capabilities since the Zheng He voyages. Its growing inability to project power beyond the immediate shoreline left open a vast, stateless space encompassing the China Seas. Not surprisingly, coastal Fujian proved well positioned to fill in the vacuum. Local gentry covertly provided capital and protection through lineage networks to support the illicit overseas ventures of merchants and sailors, often their kinsmen and neighbors. Xiamen, close to Quanzhou, and Yuegang (Moon Harbor), near Zhangzhou, emerged as major smuggling depots, enabling merchants to bypass the official tributary entry points of Fuzhou and Guangzhou in neighboring Guangdong Province.[22]

Southeast Asia was the prime destination for the smugglers. Soon large Chinese trading communities sprang up in Melaka, Ayutthaya in Siam, and other major ports. It was in these ports that the Chinese first encountered a strange-looking group of newcomers from the far western end of Eurasia. Beginning in the late fifteenth century, the Portuguese had circled the Cape of Good Hope and reached India. In their quest to dominate the flow of spices to Europe, a key ingredient in the flavoring and preservation of food, they went on to conquer Melaka in 1511, acquiring a foothold in Southeast Asia for the first time. There they initiated contact with Chinese merchants, who directed them to the smuggling depots off Fujian and other parts of the China coast. In the following years, as they participated in this illicit trade, the Portuguese repeatedly tried to secure permission from the Ming court for direct, legitimate commercial relations, but these efforts ended in abject failure.[23]

In the meantime, China developed a voracious appetite for silver currency, which proved crucial in greasing the engines of its commercialization.

---

[21] Brook, *Confusions*, pp. 86–252.

[22] Ho, "Sealords," pp. 57–63; Blussé, "Minnan-jen," p. 247; Zheng Guangnan and Maritime Museum, *Xinbian haidao shi*, pp. 329–334; Wills, "South China Sea," p. 21; and Wills, "Yiguan's origins: clues from Chinese, Japanese, Dutch, Spanish, Portuguese, and Latin sources," in Tonio Andrade and Xing Hang (eds.), *Sea rovers, silver, and samurai.*

[23] Jurgis Elisonas, "The inseparable trinity: Japan's relations with China and Korea," in John Whitney Hall (ed.), *The Cambridge history of Japan* (Cambridge, UK: Cambridge University Press, 1991), vol. IV: Early Modern Japan. pp. 250–252; John E. Wills, Jr., "Maritime Europe and the Ming," in Wills (ed.), *China and maritime Europe*, pp. 25, 32.

With domestic mines failing to keep up, silver fetched a far greater value in terms of gold than anywhere else. In Japan, some of the enterprising Kyushu-based warlords (daimyo) came up with a solution; they opened mines within their domains to alleviate the shortage across the sea. By the end of the sixteenth century, the country was producing up to a third of the world's silver, most of it ending up in China. Exports of the metal, in turn, stimulated the rise of an elite class of Japanese consumers hungry for Chinese silk and other luxuries, which they were willing to purchase at up to ten times the original price.[24] The China-Japan exchange quickly became the backbone of the maritime East Asian economic system.

Despite its newfound economic prosperity, Japan was torn apart at the time by warfare and lack of a powerful central authority. Chinese merchants and their gentry sponsors took advantage of the chaos to hire Japanese soldiers of fortune to protect their illicit operations from Ming harassment. Bands of armed smugglers soon terrorized the seas and raided settlements all along the mainland coast. Although collectively labeled "Japanese pirates" (wokou), Chinese formed the majority of their ranks and occupied key leadership positions. Many operated from ports in southwestern Japan, where they received the protection of the warring daimyo. Hirado, a small domain in northwestern Kyushu controlled by the Matsuura clan, grew into a major base. The scale and frequency of the predation reached their height during the 1540s. The freebooters forged an illicit emporium on the island of Shuangyu, off Zhejiang. It was located near Ningbo, the official gateway for Japanese tributary missions, and the Yangzi River Delta, site of the main commercial and production centers for silk and other goods. The Portuguese and many Southeast Asians joined the ranks of these smugglers and pirates.[25]

Ming attempts to crack down on piracy became the key catalyst that set into motion the historical events culminating in the rise of the Zheng mercantile dynasty. In 1548, Ming forces destroyed the multinational smuggling den of Shuangyu. Shortly thereafter, the court terminated the official tribute trade with Japan, which by then was already in decline. The Ming crackdown demonstrated that, when mobilized for large, targeted campaigns and put under effective commanders, its forces could still pull off major successes. However, the engagement also revealed severe

---

[24] Naohiro Asao and Bernard Susser (trans.), "The sixteenth-century unification," in Johon Whitney Hall (ed.), *The Cambridge history of Japan*, Cambridge, UK: Cambridge University Press, 1991, vol. IV: Early modern Japan, pp. 60–61; Sakuma Shigeo, *Nichi-Min kankeishi no kenkyū* (Tokyo: Yoshikawa kōbunkan, 1992), pp. 251–252; Richard von Glahn, *Fountain of fortune: money and monetary policy in China, 1000–1700* (Berkeley, CA: University of California Press, 1996), pp. 113–114.

[25] Wills, "Maritime Europe," pp. 32–33; Elisonas, "Inseparable trinity," pp. 251–252.

structural problems with the entire military system, built upon an official network of garrisons (*wei-suo*) and manned by hereditary military house-holds according to the vision of the dynastic founder two hundred years ago. Increased opportunities for social and spatial mobility generated by commercial expansion over the sixteenth century caused many qualified soldiers to desert their posts for other professions. This outflow was reinforced by a neo-Confucian orthodoxy and civil bureaucracy that looked down upon soldiers and did everything possible to discourage the military as a channel for legitimate social advancement. Poor leader-ship and the low caliber and morale of those who remained behind made most coastal garrisons ill-suited for defense against lower intensity but more consistent predation.[26]

Faced with continued threats to maritime security, the court author-ized individual military commanders to directly recruit mercenary volun-teers to supplement or replace the garrison troops. The famed general Qi Jiguang (1527–1588) successfully trained a ragtag band of peasants and miners to score major victories against *wokou* marauders in the Yangzi River Delta. The campaigns forced the pirate bands to gravitate farther south. Coastal Fujian became the new focal point for their activities. Located at a safer distance from the main centers of political power, its rich seafaring heritage further gave its ports intermediacy, the ability to concentrate and control a large share of the flow of traffic and goods between the Chinese core area and overseas destinations. From 1556, Yuegang, already an illicit depot for trade with Southeast Asia, replaced Shuangyu as the main hub for the Sino-Japanese exchange.[27]

However, Yuegang soon came under attack from the Ming navy under the command of Yu Dayou (1503–1579). He employed a similar practice as Qi, recruiting mercenaries from among merchants and fishermen through the intermediation of local gentry. Yu also secured the surrender of smugglers and converted them and their vessels for government use. His fleets had successfully vanquished or neutralized most of the smug-gling confederations in the Yuegang area by 1569.[28]

Nonetheless, the Ming authorities came to realize that military campaigns, while devastating for individual piratical groups, could not stem maritime predation at its root. They had to admit that the vibrant commercial integration of the East Asian world-region, and especially its maritime component, had long outgrown the bureaucratic straitjacket of

[26] Ray Huang, *1587*, pp. 160–162; Struve, *Southern Ming*, pp. 5–6.
[27] Ho, "Sealords," pp. 50–51; Elisonas, "Inseparable trinity," pp. 251–252; Ray Huang, *1587*, p. 162.
[28] Chang Pin-ts'un, "Chinese maritime trade: the case of sixteenth-century Fu-ch'ien," unpublished PhD dissertation, Princeton University (1993), pp. 247–248.

the tributary system. In fact, some local officials were already making practical adjustments at their own initiative. After the Portuguese backed out of their collusion with Chinese pirates and turned their fleets around to suppress piratical activities, the Guangdong authorities granted them permission to establish an enclave at Macao, a small peninsula in Xiangshan County, during the 1550s. Their presence would gradually receive acceptance from higher levels of Ming officialdom in the following decades. Macao provided a valuable loophole within the tributary system that both the Portuguese and enterprising Chinese merchants readily sought to exploit. A flourishing traffic soon emerged involving trade with Southeast Asia, particularly the Portuguese stronghold of Melaka.[29]

In 1567, more breaches appeared in the dike when the Ming court authorized private licensed trade with Southeast Asia at Yuegang, which it renamed Haicheng county. Although carefully regulated and heavily taxed, the measure brought a substantial part of the smuggling back into legal channels. Chinese merchants flooded ports across maritime East Asia. The immigrant population also grew rapidly, from 10,000 in the mid-Ming period to over a million by 1650. The maritime ban remained in place for Japan, the most important destination for Chinese junks, but clandestine contacts continued. In addition, semi-legal alternatives emerged in place of formal ties. After 1567, significant numbers of Japanese merchants and soldiers of fortune sailed for Southeast Asian ports, where they conducted a lively trade with the Chinese. Many settled down permanently.[30] In 1571, Portuguese missionaries acquired the port of Nagasaki from a minor daimyo in Kyushu and developed it into a formidable competitor to Hirado. Along with Macao, this new settlement made possible direct and legitimate private trade between China and Japan. Needless to say, the Portuguese prospered tremendously from this enviable intermediary role, as many Chinese ships chose to fly their flag and purchase their trading passes.[31]

Enticed by the prosperity of the maritime East Asian sea lanes, Portugal's Iberian neighbor and rival, Spain, also entered the game. The Spanish seized most of the Philippine Islands over the 1560s and, in 1571, founded Manila on the basis of an existing Chinese settlement. The city rapidly became a prime destination for junks sailing from the

---

[29] For a concise narrative of how the Portuguese secured Macao and their relations with the Ming in general, refer to Wills, "Maritime Europe," pp. 25–40.

[30] Chao Zhongchen, *Ming dai haijin yu haiwai maoyi* (Beijing: People's Publishing House, 2005), pp. 289–290. The classic treatment of Japanese settlements in Southeast Asia is Iwao Seiichi, *Nanyō Nihonmachi no kenkyū* (Tokyo: Iwanami Bookstore, 1966).

[31] Roderich Ptak, "Sino-Japanese maritime trade, circa 1550: merchants, ports and networks," in Ptak (ed.), *China and the Asian seas: trade, travel, and visions of the other (1400–1750)* (Brookfield, VT: Ashgate Variorum, 1998), pp. 295–300.

China coast, which exchanged their cargoes for products from the New World: tobacco, food crops, and, especially, silver and gold. Extracted from the mines of Potosí, in present-day Bolivia, through the ruthless exploitation of Native American labor, these metals were transported by pack mules on a tortuous mountain route through the Andes to the port of Acapulco, Mexico. They were then shipped across the Pacific to Manila almost annually on board the famous galleons.[32] Until the 1630s, the New World supplied the largest quantity of bullion to China, greatly exceeding imports from Japan.[33] The transpacific route, along with Portuguese spice shipments to Europe via the Cape of Good Hope, linked the entire world, for the first time, into an integrated world system. However, the connections that they forged still remained tenuous and subject to significant volatility, in contrast to the far denser and more predictable intra-East Asian trade.[34]

Meanwhile, the warfare and disunity that had colored Japan through-out the late fifteenth to sixteenth centuries drew to a close. In 1587, Toyotomi Hideyoshi (c. 1536–1598) finalized his hegemony over the daimyo. Flush with victory, he set out to construct a Japan-centered version of the Chinese tributary system that, like the Ming, monopolized foreign trade. He outlawed *wokou* piracy, placed the Portuguese enclave of Nagasaki under central control, and permitted only select merchants, foreigners, and daimyo bearing licenses stamped with his vermillion seal (*shuin*) to send ships to Southeast Asia. He further demanded vassalage from authorities across the region, from Siam to Manila, and, in 1592, even tried to subjugate China by invading Korea, the premier Ming tributary kingdom. Yet, successful resistance from Ming and Korean forces, and his own death six years later, put an end to his universalistic vision.[35]

The Tokugawa shogun who dominated Japan after Hideyoshi took a more pragmatic stance toward foreign relations. Like him, they refused to subject the country to the Chinese tributary system, but decided not to

---

[32] Timothy Brook, *Vermeer's hat: the seventeenth century and the dawn of the global world* (New York: Bloomsbury Press, 2008), pp. 64, 133, 152–184.

[33] One scholar has estimated that a whopping 50,000–90,000 kg of silver entered China from Manila in a good year. See William Atwell, "Ming China and the emerging world economy, c. 1470–1650," in Denis Twitchett and Frederick W. Mote (eds.), *The Cambridge history of China* (Cambridge, UK: Cambridge University Press, 1998), vol. VIII.2: The Ming dynasty, 1368–1644, pp. 389–392.

[34] Jan de Vries, "Connecting Europe and Asia: a quantitative analysis of the Cape route trade, 1497–1795," in Dennis Flynn, Arturo Giráldez, and Richard von Glahn (eds.), *Global connections and monetary history, 1470–1800* (London: Ashgate, 2003).

[35] Kenneth Swope offers a comprehensive account of the Japanese invasion of Korea within an East Asian-wide context in *A dragon's head and a serpent's tail: Ming China and the first Great East Asian War, 1592–1598* (Norman, OK: University of Oklahoma Press, 2009).

pursue his wild imperial dreams. Instead, they tried to benefit as much as possible from the existing East Asian economic order. To this effect, the Tokugawa inherited Hideyoshi's practice of issuing *shuin* permits for vessels to Southeast Asia. After attempts to establish commercial ties with China on the basis of status parity fell flat, they turned to Korea and Ryukyu, both close Ming vassals, using them as additional intermediaries for Chinese goods. In 1609, the Tokugawa normalized diplomatic relations with the Chosŏn court. That year, the Shimazu, daimyo of the Kyushu domain of Satsuma, attacked Ryukyu and forced its king to submit to their hegemony, although it was encouraged to continue its tributary relationship with the Ming. As a result, Ryukyu's once flourishing trade with Southeast Asia, already in decline because of strong competition from Portuguese and Chinese merchants, came to an end.[36]

Iberian and Japanese expansion into maritime East Asia, combined with the anti-piracy campaigns on the southeastern Chinese littoral, greatly narrowed the space for the non-state *wokou* bands. The prominent exception was the mountainous, sparsely populated island of Taiwan. Portuguese mariners sailing past its eastern shore, enthralled at the stunning landscape, gave it an alternate name: Formosa, or beautiful. It was primarily inhabited at the time by mutually hostile Malayo-Polynesian tribal confederations. Ming observers derisively labeled these aborigines "Eastern Savages" (*dongfan*), who do not observe proper Confucian distinctions of superior and inferior, "do not count the days or keep records, and run around naked."[37] Although just 180 kilometers east of the narrow Taiwan Strait from the crowded Fujian coast, Taiwan surprisingly lacked any large-scale Chinese settlement before the seventeenth century other than some makeshift Minnanese fishing villages off the western shore. Fantastic descriptions of the hostile waters around the island intensified perceptions of its "foreignness" from China.[38]

Taiwan naturally became a haven for pirate bands fleeing the Ming naval onslaught. After withdrawing from the Guangdong coast in the 1570s, Lin Daoqian and Lin Feng, partners and competitors in predation, continued their raids from bases at Wankan, an aboriginal settlement near present-day Jiayi, and the narrow sandbar of Tayouan farther south, outside of Tainan. Ming naval fleets eventually dislodged them

---

[36] Ronald Toby, *State and diplomacy in early modern Japan: Asia in the development of the Tokugawa bakufu* (Stanford, CA: Stanford University Press, 1991), pp. 23–52.

[37] Shen Yourong, *Minhai zengyan, TWWXCK*, 56 (1959), p. 25.

[38] Emma Jinhua Teng, *Taiwan's imagined geography: Chinese colonial travel writing and pictures, 1683–1895* (Cambridge, MA: Harvard University Asia Center, 2004), p. 38.

and destroyed their bases.[39] Smaller-scale smugglers continued to operate on Taiwan, using it as a covert meeting ground with *shuin* ships from Japan.

In the early seventeenth century, the Japanese merchants attempted, with the blessing of the Tokugawa shogun, to occupy the island as a base to pursue direct commercial relations with the Ming. In 1609, a reconnaissance expedition was dispatched to Taiwan under the Christian samurai Arima Harunobu (1567–1612), but he soon withdrew after encountering ferocious opposition from warlike aboriginal tribes. Unfazed, some *shuin* traders decided to press ahead with a full-scale invasion. In 1616, a massive force led by another Christian, Murayama Tōan (d. 1619), and consisting of thirteen ships and 4,000 warriors, sailed for Taiwan. Again, the attempt ended in disaster. A typhoon blew nearly all of the ships onto the mainland Chinese coast, where their crews went on an orgy of pillaging, killing, and kidnapping before returning. The one ship that actually made it to Taiwan encountered a deadly ambush from aborigines on a small creek. Short of men and weapons to effectively resist, all of the men onboard committed suicide.[40]

Suspicions over Tokugawa designs on Taiwan, combined with intelligence on the invasion of Ryukyu, prompted the Ming court to reissue the maritime ban for the Yangzi River Delta region in 1613, and order the expulsion of the Japanese community at Macao. To ensure more consistent coastal defenses and regular patrols in the Taiwan Strait, the Fujian authorities created a permanent mercenary force out of the fishermen, merchants, and surrendered pirates previously mobilized only on an ad hoc basis for major campaigns. Although charged with enforcing the ban on trade with Japan, the provincial gentry at the helm of the new force sought to use their position as gatekeepers to take a cut of the lucrative profits from smuggling. In 1618, they allied with the largest pirate on Taiwan at the time, Lin Jinwu (d. 1621), and charged him with regulating the activities of Chinese and Japanese merchants who sailed to the island and collecting fees from them. The Fujian authorities turned a blind eye to the shady dealings of the mercenary network, since they saw Taiwan as a useful stateless buffer zone that could keep hostile foreign forces from attacking the mainland shore.[41]

---

[39] Igawa Kenji, "At the crossroads: Limahon and *wakō* in sixteenth-century Philippines," in Robert J. Antony (ed.), *Elusive pirates, pervasive smugglers: violence and clandestine trade in the greater China Seas* (Hong Kong: Hong Kong University Press, 2010), pp. 80–81. For an original record of this campaign, see Shen, *Minhai zengyan*.

[40] Wills, "Maritime China," pp. 214–215; Charles Ralph Boxer, *The Christian century in Japan: 1549–1650* (Berkeley, CA: University of California Press, 1951), pp. 274–275, 298.

[41] Cheng (Zheng), *War, trade and piracy*, p. 23.

After Lin's death in 1621, the island's operations underwent further consolidation at the hands of Li Dan (d. 1625), a prominent Chinese merchant based out of Hirado. An informal leader of the Chinese communities in Hirado and Nagasaki, he went by the respectful nickname of "Captain China." Li maintained close contact with well-placed clan members and gentry in his native Quanzhou prefecture, and, through them, the mercenaries and Fujian authorities. Meanwhile, his warm relationship with the Matsuura daimyo of Hirado allowed him to acquire the Tokugawa shogun's *shuin* passes. Li's associate, Yan Siqi (d. 1625) looked after his business on Taiwan. Yan also had the support of lineages in his native Zhangzhou, which ensured access to the sole legal port of Haicheng.[42] By making himself indispensable to both ends, Li and his network of smugglers dominated the Taiwan Strait area of the China-Japan route, overshadowing his Fujianese mercenary allies and keeping out Japanese merchants and adventurers. By the early 1620s, the maritime East Asian exchange had stabilized and its spoils divided among four different players: the Spanish, Portuguese, Japanese *shuin*, and Ming mercenary networks.

However, the appearance of menacing newcomers in regional waters was already upsetting the fragile balance. The English East India Company (EIC), chartered in 1600, a fierce competitor of Portugal for the India market, acquired a foothold in the spice trade in 1603, when it established a permanent trading post, or factory, at Banten, in western Java. England's neighbor across the North Sea, the Dutch Republic, had been locked in a life-and-death struggle for independence against the Hapsburg throne of Spain since 1568. The union of the Spanish and Portuguese crowns in 1580, which led to blockades of spice shipments and New World silver to the Netherlands from the port of Lisbon, forced the young state's mercantile elites to form their own companies to trade with Asia. To avoid internal competition and present a unified front against the Iberian enemies abroad, they were, in turn, consolidated into a single joint-stock corporation – the United East India Company (VOC) – in 1602.

---

[42] Charles Ralph Boxer, "The rise and fall of Nicholas Iquan (Cheng Chih-lung)," *T'ien Hsia monthly* 11.5 (1941): 402–404. Andrade, *Taiwan became Chinese*, ch. 2 and Chiang Shu-sheng (Jiang Shusheng), *De missiven van de VOC-gouverneur in Taiwan aan de Gouverneur-generaal te Batavia* (*Letters from the VOC governor in Taiwan to the governor-general at Batavia*), 1 vol. (Taipei: SMC Publishing, 2007–), vol. I, pp. 133, 174, 216 convincingly refute the claims of Boxer and Iwao Seiichi, "Ming mo qiaoyu Riben Zhinaren Jiabidan Li Dan kao," in Xu Xianyao (ed. and trans.), *Helan shidai Taiwan shi lunwen ji* (Yilan, Taiwan: Foguang renwenshe, 2001), p. 71, that Yan Siqi and Li Dan were the same person.

The VOC followed the English into India and Banten, but rapidly outstripped them in the scale and success of its operations. The Dutch fully utilized European advantages in military technology, including advanced weaponry, impregnable fortresses, and sturdy and fast ships, to establish a political hegemony over the main spice production centers on the Indonesian archipelago. They intervened, often violently, into the internal affairs and diplomacy of its petty principalities. By 1623, the VOC had also expelled the Portuguese, while brutally quashing attempts by the English to ally with the native kingdoms against it. Four years earlier, in 1619, the VOC board of directors in Amsterdam had established the Council of the Indies, a territorial authority headed by a governor-general, to better supervise its burgeoning Asian operations. The Dutch further seized Jakarta, a dependency of Banten lying to its northeast, and renamed the settlement Batavia, an archaic Latin name for their home country. In 1621, the city became the VOC's Asian headquarters. From there, the company administered a growing network of factories and colonies across the region.[43]

As they fought bitterly over control of the spice flow to Europe, the Dutch and the English, like the Iberians before them, developed an interest in the lucrative trade of maritime East Asia. Yet early efforts to establish a foothold outside of Macao and Manila proved unsuccessful. A 1596 English mission bound for the China coast was shipwrecked before reaching its intended destination.[44] The Dutch fared somewhat better; in 1604, an expeditionary fleet under Wijbrand van Waerwijck (c.1566–1615) set anchor at Penghu, a chain of volcanic islets lying midway in the strait between Taiwan and Fujian. Home to a small community of Minnanese anglers, the islands also went by the name of Pescadores ("fishermen"), given by the Portuguese, the first Europeans to sight them. From there, van Waerwijck sent envoys to Fujian with lavish bribes to influential officials in the hopes of securing free trade from the Ming court. What the Dutch got instead was a Ming fleet of fifty junks whose commander ordered them to withdraw. Since the Song dynasty (960–1279), Penghu was administered off and on under Quanzhou prefecture, and thus remained, however tenuously, integral to the empire. The commander did promise a workable trading arrangement if Van Waerwijck relocated farther to Taiwan, outside of effective Chinese

---

[43] A succinct overview of Dutch policies in insular Southeast Asia is found in George Masselman, "Dutch colonial policy in the seventeenth century," *Journal of economic history* 21.4 (1961).

[44] Marguerite Eyer Wilbur, *The East India Company: and the British empire in the Far East* (Stanford, CA: Stanford University Press, 1945), p. 318.

control. The Dutch decided not take up the offer and sailed back to Southeast Asia.[45]

In 1609, the two companies finally got their big break, not in China as they had desired, but in Japan, where the Matsuura daimyo welcomed the VOC to open a factory at Hirado, and allowed the English to follow suit two years later. At first, both of them made profits by plundering the cargoes of the larger but weaker Chinese junks on the Manila and Macao routes, and selling the booty in Japan. In 1619, the Dutch and English even put aside their differences and briefly formed a joint Fleet of Defense to coordinate their seizures at sea.[46] Although they reaped sizable fortunes at the expense of the Iberians and Fujian mercenaries, they also realized that merely skimming off the intra-East Asian trade could only go so far. Because of the importance of the China–Japan exchange, they needed, in addition to the Japanese market, a permanent foothold on the Chinese end with easy and regularized access to product sources.

As a result, both companies renewed their attempts to establish a sustained presence along the China coast. However, they differed in their approach. The kind but gullible head of the English factory at Hirado, Richard Cocks (1566–1624), cultivated a friendship with Li Dan, hoping to use his connections to the Fujian authorities to persuade them to open up trade. These efforts ultimately came to naught, with the money and gifts that Cocks entrusted as bribes for the officials most likely ending up in the pockets of the wily Captain China.[47]

The Dutch, on the other hand, opted to seize either Manila or Macao by force. However, several attempts to invade the two cities in the first two decades of the seventeenth century floundered in the face of typhoons and firm resistance from their defenders.[48] In 1622, after suffering one such defeat outside Macao, a Dutch fleet once again ended up in Penghu. This time, the commander, Cornelis Reijersen (d. 1625), took on a more assertive stance than his predecessor. He ordered fortifications built, and from their new base, the Dutch attacked ports and plundered shipping all along the Fujian coast in attempts to force open the Chinese market.[49]

A series of complicated negotiations ensued, with the Fujian authorities ordering the VOC to withdraw to nearby Taiwan, which they confirmed was not Chinese territory, unlike Penghu. In exchange, they would allow the mercenaries to organize smugglers to sail to the island and meet the

[45] Wills, "Maritime Europe," pp. 67–68.
[46] Cheng (Zheng), *War, trade and piracy*, pp. 27–31.
[47] Iwao, "Li Dan kao," pp. 77–82.
[48] Cheng (Zheng), *War, trade and piracy*, pp. 27–31.
[49] Wills, "Maritime Europe," pp. 68–69.

Dutch. It was essentially the same arrangement offered to them more than a decade earlier. The Dutch tried to have their cake and eat it too by agreeing to move to Taiwan but stalling on their promise to evacuate Penghu. This hazy arrangement worked until February 1624, when the Fujian military forces came under the command of Yu Zigao (d. 1628). The son of the famed *wokou*-fighter, Yu Dayou, he adopted a tough line, amassing ships and soldiers and sailing directly into Penghu to confront the tiny VOC garrison. Under heavy pressure, the outnumbered Dutch dismantled their fortress and relocated to Taiwan in August 1624.[50]

Reijersen and his men established a permanent settlement along the southwestern coast of the island, at Tayouan, the lively Sino-Japanese smuggling outpost outside present-day Tainan. It was located on top of a sandbar cut off on three sides from the main island by a small body of inland sea, the Tai Bay. At the head of Tayouan, a formidable fortress, Casteel Zeelandia, was built to defend the settlement. A shallow channel, named Lu'ermen (Lakjemeuse or Deer's Ear), led into the inland sea through a narrow opening to the north of the sandbar, and provided a convenient entryway to the rest of Taiwan. On the main shore opposite the bay, the VOC annexed the aboriginal settlement of Saccam (Chikan) from a nearby tribe and built a new town on its grounds, named Provintia. A governor assisted by a council and who answered directly to Batavia oversaw the affairs of the new colony.[51] It did not take long for the VOC to realize the strategic value of Taiwan. From their new foothold on the island, the Dutch could completely shut down the trade of Macao and Manila, since vessels plying the sea routes between these Iberian colonies and China and Japan had to pass through nearby waters. However, the company still lacked the power to dislodge two other deeply entrenched interest groups in the area: Li Dan and the Fujian mercenaries. Some framework for cooperation had to be worked out with them.

Li Dan, too, proved willing to accommodate the Dutch. The predation in the waters around China brought severe disruption to his business. Faced with skyrocketing debt, Li sailed personally to Taiwan, where he took on the role of mediator to prevent further conflict. He cultivated friendly ties with Yu Zigao, gathering intelligence on the Dutch for him, and incorporated the head of the Fujian mercenaries, Xu Xinsu (d. 1627), into his illicit network. At the same time, Li helped the VOC open up a smuggling route from Fujian, while he and Yan Siqi partici-pated in the plunder of Chinese junks on the Macao and Manila routes.

[50] Chiang (Jiang), *Missiven*, vol. 1, pp. xx–xxiii, 46.
[51] Ts'ao Yung-ho (Cao Yonghe), "Taiwan as an entrepôt in East Asia in the seventeenth century," in John E. Wills, Jr. (ed.), *Eclipsed entrepôts of the Western Pacific: Taiwan and central Vietnam, 1500–1800* (Burlington, VT: Ashgate, 2002), p. 6.

By ensuring his indispensability to all the major players in the Taiwan Strait area – the Fujian authorities, mercenaries, and the Dutch – Li hoped to maintain control over the mainland China-Taiwan-Japan route and recover access to its once lucrative profits.[52] One associate who participated fully in these dealings was a young man named Zheng Zhilong. He and his descendants would soon occupy the center of this vast and intricate maritime stage.

Coastal Fujian was caught in several tumultuous transitions over the fourteenth to seventeenth centuries. With the decline of the Eurasian luxury trade, it gradually lost its importance as a terminus of the maritime Silk Road. However, it preserved its accumulated skills in seafaring, long-distance travel, and entrepreneurship to stake out a new role as a nexus within the Greater Fujian and domestic coastal maritime zones, as well as the East Asian world-region. During the sixteenth century, the loosening of the Ming tributary order opened up a vast, stateless zone in maritime East Asia centered upon the exchange of Chinese luxuries for Japanese silver. At the same time, the entry of European powers into the China Seas drew some of its ports into a dynamic new global economic system. Bolstered by government policies on overseas trade, coastal Fujian acquired the intermediacy to emerge once again as a central player within these platforms. Yet, despite the maritime economic orientation, the littoral remained politically and culturally tied to the continent through the imperial system and Confucian orthodoxy.

Coastal Fujian's shifting emphasis upon, and participation in, different levels of local, regional, and global integration opened up multilayered outcomes for its subsequent trajectory. John Wills depicts two realistic contingencies for the Fujian coast throughout the seventeenth century: the center of a politically autonomous maritime China or a reintegrated part of a mainland province.[53] Zheng Zhilong and his descendants embodied and developed this dichotomy in new directions. They would benefit tremendously from, and be severely constrained by, coastal Fujian's overarching structures.

---

[52] Iwao, "Li Dan kao," pp. 102–104; Cheng (Zheng), *War, trade and piracy*, pp. 33–37.
[53] John E. Wills, "Contingent connections: Fujian, the empire, and the early modern world," in Lynn Struve (ed.), *The Qing formation in world-historical time* (Cambridge, MA: Harvard University Asia Center, 2004), pp. 197–198 and "South China Sea," pp. 21–22.

Now, within and without, we are one family. The Emperor is the father and the people are like his sons. The father and sons are of the same body; how can they be different from one another? If they are not as one then it will be as if they had two hearts and would they then not be like the people of different countries? ... All residents ... will fulfill the order to shave their heads ... Those who follow this order belong to this country; those who hesitate will be considered treasonous bandits and will be heavily penalized ... As for other apparel, unhurried change is permitted, but it cannot differ from the system of our dynasty.

Qing Haircutting Edict, 1645.[1]

What today is called 'aiding the ruler' is really a means by which a restoration can start from a very small beginning. Over the whole vast area, we can rely only on the scattered troops of each province, each issuing its own commands, all hoping to have good luck in contributing to the restoration.

Zheng Zhilong in *Jingguo xionglue* (*Grand strategy for ordering the country*).[2]

In the first half of the seventeenth century, two groups of people from opposite frontiers of the East Asian landmass organized and unified under capable leaders. The meteoric rise to power of Nurhaci (1596–1616) and his Jurchen confederation in the Northeast Asian forests owed to his adaptation of the political systems, worldviews, and commercial practices of the neighboring Mongol and Tungusic tribes, Koreans, and Ming.[3] Likewise, Zheng Zhilong and his band of southern Fujianese armed merchants represent the culmination of the hybridity characteristic of the sixteenth-century China Seas. Zhilong himself spoke Portuguese,

---

[1] Janet Chen, Cheng Pei-kai, and Michael Lestz with Jonathan Spence (eds.), *The search for modern China: a documentary collection*, third edition (New York: W. W. Norton, 2014), p. 27.

[2] Zheng Dayu and Zheng Zhilong, *Jingguo xionglue*, quoted in Wills, "Contingent connections," pp. 181–182.

[3] The rise of the Manchus has been well studied. See, for instance, Frederic Wakeman, *Great enterprise* and Pamela Kyle Crossley, *The Manchus* (Oxford, UK: Blackwell, 2002). Dahpon Ho is the first to point out the intriguing connection between Zheng Zhilong and Nurhaci.

converted to Catholicism, married a Japanese woman, whom he soon left behind for the life of a pirate, and later became a Ming official. Both enterprises came of age in a time of global crisis. Nurhaci's descendants, who redefined themselves by the new ethnic label of Manchu, conquered China and became its new rulers. Zheng Zhilong, on the other hand, transformed his organization from one of many illicit bands roaming the seas into a multinational commercial network able to share maritime dominance with his partner and bitter rival: the Dutch East India Company. The Qing and Zheng enterprises would meet, negotiate, and clash along the southeastern Chinese littoral.

The making of Zheng Zhilong

As *wokou* piracy subsided and new avenues of legitimate trade opened up in maritime East Asia in the seventeenth century, many Chinese joined the European and Japanese business networks, purchasing their passes, flying their flags, and settling down at ports under their protection. In large part, the Portuguese, Spanish, and Dutch solidified their shaky hold over their East Asian colonies through a framework of interdependency with Chinese immigrants that Tonio Andrade calls "co-colonization." The diaspora, through close ties to their homes and relatives in coastal China and collusion with local gentry, provided access to lucrative product sources otherwise unavailable to the outsider Europeans. The Chinese further supplied much-needed taxes and labor that the native populations of these possessions could not, at least at the same level of efficiency and cost-effectiveness. In return, European laws and infrastructure protected and promoted the livelihoods of these overseas communities.[4]

The spectacular emergence of Zheng Zhilong from humble obscurity to one of the richest moguls in the early modern world precisely occurred within this framework of cross-cultural cooperation. And his origins were obscure, indeed. Even his date of birth remains a subject of dispute, with the primary records giving a range of years from 1590 to 1610. The most accurate estimation should fall between 1592 and 1595, since this window positions him at the most appropriate life stage during each of the major events in his subsequent career.[5] It is established that he was

[4] Andrade, *Taiwan became Chinese*, Conclusion.
[5] Liao Hanchen provides a useful list of the conflicting versions of Zheng Zhilong's birth-date in Liao Hanchen, "Zheng Zhilong kao: shang, *Taiwan wenxian* 10.4 (1959): 63–70. John Wills plays around with the sexagenary stems and roots used to record the dates on the traditional Chinese lunar calendar to convincingly arrive at 1592 or 1594 as possible years of birth. Refer to Wills, "Yiguan's origins: clues from Chinese, Japanese, Dutch, Spanish, Portuguese, and Latin sources," in Tonio Andrade and Xing Hang (eds.), *Sea*

born in Shijing, a seaside town in Nan'an county, Quanzhou prefecture. Most accounts claim that he was the eldest son of Zheng Shaozu, a grain storage clerk at the prefectural government office. Wills has identified yet another name for his father: Xiangyu.[6] The more authoritative Zheng genealogy lists the name as Shibiao, but does not provide any additional details about his occupation. Nonetheless, judging from the modest character of the family's ancestral home, he probably came from a lower-class background with some means and access to a rudimentary education, the typical profile of a low-level Ming functionary.[7]

It is incredibly hard to separate fact from legend in Zheng Zhilong's early life, but the often contradictory sources, chock full of tantalizing apocryphal tales, are consistent and credible about several basic events, upon which a narrative will be attempted. As a child, Zhilong had probably already acquired the nickname of Yiguan, commonly used to denote the eldest brother or son in the Minnanese dialect. Later on, Europeans and many Japanese would exclusively use the term, spelled Iquan or a dizzying variety of other orthographic variations, to refer to him. His father, like others with high hopes for their sons, wanted him to study and memorize the Confucian Classics so that he could someday pass the civil service examinations and become an official, the main avenue of legitimate success in imperial China. However, the young boy felt bored at the prospect of pushing papers in a government office for the rest of his life. Instead, he roamed the streets, vandalizing property and picking fights. During his mischievous escapades, he must have stopped occasionally to glance at the trading junks entering and leaving the nearby port of Anhai (also known as Anping), and imagined a thrilling future of adventure on the seas.

For reasons not entirely clear, Zhilong had a nasty falling-out with his father as a teenager. Some accounts mention that Shibiao had grown disgusted with the out-of-control behavior of his son and drove him out of the house, while others mention Zhilong running away of his own accord. More sensational but implausible versions portray him as a lust-filled lad who was forced to flee when caught feeling up one of his father's concubines. At any rate, he left his home for Macao, most likely in 1610, while in his late teens. There, he became an apprentice for his maternal

rovers, silver, and samurai: maritime East Asia in global history, 1550–1700 (Honolulu: University of Hawaii Press, forthcoming). The Taiwanese scholar Tang Jintai comes up with the equally credible estimate of 1595 through exhaustive analysis of fragmentary Chinese and Japanese records in Kaiqi Taiwan di yi ren: Zheng Zhilong (Taipei: Guoshi, 2002), pp. 38–39.

6 Wills, "Yiguan's origins."
7 Zheng Guangnan and Maritime Museum, Xinbian haidao shi, p. 201; Wills, "Yiguan's origins"; personal visit to the Zheng ancestral home, Shijing, Fujian, August 2009.

uncle, a merchant named Huang Cheng, helping him sail ships on the routes to Japan and Southeast Asia.[8]

The powerful lineage networks of Minnan provided a transnational platform for the restless young man to realize his pent-up ambitions. During his residence in Macao, Zhilong embraced Catholicism, receiving the baptismal name of Nicolas Jaspar. The sincerity of his conversion is questionable. Years later, after he had become more established, European visitors to his mansion viewed with shock the layout of his private chapel, which had a crucifix placed together with idols of native gods, while the Mass took place alongside traditional ceremonies. Regardless of his real intentions, the new religion proved highly beneficial for him. He befriended several well-placed priests and learned from them the Portuguese language, an important *lingua franca* in the maritime East Asian sea lanes. Through their intermediation, he made several visits and even resided for some time at Manila, that other great trading emporium and religious center.[9]

Important connections from a different direction followed suit. While on his layovers in Japan, he appeared to have caught the fancy of the powerful Captain China, Li Dan, who adopted him as a son. This arrangement, common to southern Fujian, amounted to an apprenticeship whereby young men of relatively poorer backgrounds entered the service of wealthy households. The patron would raise and support the "son," and, when he grew older, provide him ships and capital to trade on behalf of his "father," who stayed behind. Often, as in the case of Zheng Zhilong, the relationship took on a homoerotic dimension. One early Chinese account mentions Li taking a fancy to his youthful appearance, and becoming his male lover.[10]

While a form of servitude, Zhilong's status as an adopted son nonetheless provided decent opportunities for mobility. Through the introduction of his patron, he became acquainted with the highest echelons of power in Japan. In 1612, he and Zuguan, presumably another associate of Li Dan, visited the Tokugawa patriarch, Ieyasu (1543–1616), at his castle in Sunpu (present-day Shizuoka). Since they were considered "men of the Great Ming, from across the azure sea," the two likely still resided at

[8] Jiang Risheng, *Taiwan waiji*, TWWXCK, 60 (1960), pp. 2–3; Zheng Yiju, "Zheng Chenggong zhuan," in *Zheng Chenggong zhuan*, TWWXCK, 67 (1960), p. 1; Ji Liuqi, *Ming ji beilue*, TWWXCK, 275 (1969), p. 174. Estimates of the year of arrival in Macao and Zhilong's age come from Wills, "Yiguan's origins."
[9] Boxer, "Rise and fall," pp. 411–412, 427–428; Anna Busquets, "Dreams."
[10] Andrade, *Lost colony*, p. 25. For more on the system of adopted sons, see Han Zhenhua, "Zheng Chenggong shidai de haiwai maoyi he haiwai maoyi shang de xingzhi: 1650–1662," in Xiamen University History Department (ed.), *Zheng Chenggong yanjiu lunwen xuan* (Fuzhou: Fujian People's Publishing House, 1982), pp. 170–172.

the time in Macao. In fact, during the audience, they informed Ieyasu about the latest news from China and presented a gift of Chinese medicine.[11]

Zhilong additionally handed to the patriarch a manual on military strategy that he had been putting together, entitled the *Jingguo xionglue* (*Grand strategy for ordering the country*).[12] By then, he had developed a keen interest and expertise in military affairs, a surprising but appropriate combination of his earlier Confucian education, street passion for martial arts, and lust for adventure. Perhaps the boredom occasioned by the long intervals spent at sea on his patron's junks gave Zhilong plenty of time to read, reflect, arrange his sources, and put his own thoughts in writing. The *Grand strategy* contains quotes and passages from a diverse selection of Ming sources pertaining to military matters, with special attention to maritime East Asia. It covers themes such as the use of stars for navigation and astrological signs to determine auspicious times for warfare, as well as detailed descriptions of Chinese provinces and foreign countries, complete with maps and the state of their defenses, weapons, and battlefield formations and tactics. The manual remained a work-in-progress for Zhilong throughout his life. The version that he presented to Ieyasu in 1612 contained twenty chapters (*juan*). When it reached its final form in 1645, it had expanded to eighty chapters. By then, he had possessed sufficient resources to hire ghostwriters from among his lineage kin.[13]

One might suggest that Ieyasu agreed to the audience precisely because of this manual, with its wealth of strategic information on China and other foreign lands, and Zhilong's own expertise. Zhilong also did not forget to flatter the Tokugawa patriarch by including a detailed description and maps of Japan in his book, the most comprehensive out of all the countries covered.[14] Suitably impressed by the interview, Ieyasu bequeathed upon the young man a long-term residence in Nagasaki. Accordingly, Zhilong moved his base of operations from Macao and Manila to the port city, where, for several years, he served as Li Dan's agent. Zhilong quickly became a local sensation. The two magistrates, appointed by the

[11] Japanese records are consistent about Zhilong's visit to Sunpu. See, for instance, Hayashi Akira, *Tsūkō ichiran*, 8 vols. (Tokyo: Kokusho kankōkai, 1912–1913), vol. V, p. 238, and Kawaguchi Chōju, *Taiwan Tei shi kiji*, *TWWXCK*, 5 (1958), 2. A comprehensive list of the sources recording the audience with Ieyasu, and meticulous philological research upon them, can be found in Ishihara Michihiro, *Min matsu Shin sho Nippon kisshi no kenkyū* (Tokyo: Fuzanbō, 1944), pp. 262–263.

[12] Hayashi Akira, *Tsūkō ichiran*, vol. V, p. 238.

[13] Zheng Dayu and Zheng Zhilong (eds.), *Jingguo xionglue*, Harvard University Yenching Library (ed.), *Meiguo Hafo daxue Yanjing tushuguan cang Zhongwen shanben huikan* (Beijing: Commercial Press, 2003), vol. XX, pp. 256–265.

[14] Refer to the table of contents in Zheng Dayu and Zheng Zhilong, *Jingguo xionglue*, vol. 19, pp. 13–20.

Tokugawa shogunate (*bakufu*) in Edo to administer the port city, "really loved him."[15] He also became fast friends with the wealthiest and most powerful man in town: Suetsugu Heizō Masanao (1546–1630), a *shuin* merchant with extensive interests in Southeast Asia, and, like him, a nominal Catholic.[16] These connections would serve the Zheng family's commercial enterprise well in the years to come.

Zhilong must have performed his tasks capably, since he would relocate to Hirado, Li's home turf, signaling a major promotion. In that equally famed and cosmopolitan port, he rubbed shoulders with the local daimyo, Japanese samurai and merchants, and the English and Dutch. Jacques Specx (1585–1652), the first director (*opperhoofd*) of the VOC factory, became a business partner and close friend.[17] It was also there that he met the daughter of a low-ranking samurai foot soldier (*ashigaru*), Tagawa Matsu. Sparks of passion flew, and they soon tied the knot.[18] In 1624, his new wife gave birth to their son, the famed Koxinga, on top of a rock washed by the salty waters of the East China Sea while taking a stroll on the beach, as local lore would later have it. By then, she may have already given birth to a daughter. Soon afterward, within the space of a few months, Zhilong left Hirado for good, and did not see her again for two decades. During this period, she conceived another son named Shichizaemon (b. 1628). Since he could only have resulted from an illicit affair, the infant took her surname.[19]

What could draw the young Zhilong away from a life of conjugal bliss in the comfortable, multicultural setting of Hirado? As it turned out, Li afforded him the opportunity for more adventure by sending him to Taiwan. His patron needed his assistance in restoring the smooth operation of illicit trade on the island, which had come under threat from the VOC's occupation of Penghu and raids on the China coast. Because of Zhilong's knowledge of Portuguese, Li assigned him to serve as an interpreter on behalf of the Dutch during their difficult negotiations with the Fujian officials that resulted in the VOC's agreement to remove its trading outpost to Taiwan. Undoubtedly pleased with the outcome, the company

---

[15] Wu Weiye, *Luqiao jiwen*, *TWWXCK*, 127 (1961), p. 59. One magistrate resided at Nagasaki, while the other stayed at Edo, with the two switching places at intervals.

[16] Kawaguchi Chōju, *Taiwan kakkyoji*, *TWXXCK*, 1 (1958), p. 56 and Inagaki Kigai, *Tei Seikō* (Taipei: Taiwan keisei shinpōsha, 1929), pp. 224–227.

[17] Yuan Bingling and Bao Leshi (Leonard Blussé) (trans.), "Guanyu Zheng Zhilong gei Helan Badaweiya cheng zongdu Sibeikesi de liang feng xin," *Fujian shizhi* (July 1994): 28.

[18] Boxer, "Rise and fall," p. 416.

[19] Lian Heng, *Taiwan shihui zawen chao*, *TWWXCK*, 224 (1966), p. 27. Before Tagawa Matsu, perhaps in his childhood, Zhilong had been betrothed to a girl of the Chen family, but apparently the union never materialized, since he fled from home. See *Tei shi kankei bunsho*, *TWWXCK*, 69 (1960), p. 36.

kept Zhilong on its payroll as an employee. The young man remained an important liaison for all parties, especially since Li Dan arrived in Taiwan shortly afterward, and took his cooperation with the Dutch to a new level. Besides collaborating in the smuggling on the mainland coast, Li and his local affiliate, Yan Siqi, made a deal with the company whereby they would help it intercept and plunder junks in the Taiwan Strait caught sailing to or from Manila and Macao.[20] The Dutch could achieve their aim of diverting all Chinese vessels away from ports belonging to the Spanish and Portuguese; the two men could get a handsome share of the spoils.

Zheng Zhilong also turned pirate and smuggler, leading a squadron of junks under Yan's command. He was the youngest and most junior member, but rapidly acquired prominence within the ranks. He earned the respect of his leader and associates through demonstrations of bravery and audaciousness in the seizure of junks and booty. He further tapped into his lineage network back home in coastal Fujian. Since his father, Shibiao, passed away during this time, his three brothers and scores of clan relatives came to join his squadron on Taiwan.[21]

The good times did not last long. In July 1625, Li Dan, struck by illness contracted in the tropical heat on Taiwan, returned to Hirado and soon passed away. Three months later, Yan Siqi, too, came down with a severe case of pneumonia after a hunt in the mountains and died on his sickbed. Chinese accounts are full of colorful anecdotes of what happened next. According to one variation, Yan's nine squadron commanders immediately met to cast lots to determine the successor; Zhilong won and inherited the deceased's ships and assets.[22] Another version has the nine pirates kneeling before a sword stuck deeply into a sack of rice to ascertain the will of Heaven. When it came to Zhilong's turn, the sword fell out of the sack, prompting the others to uphold him as their new leader.[23]

However, this storybook narrative of a charismatic leader elected by popular consensus and favored by destiny sanitizes the messy, bloody, and contested nature of the succession. After the concurrent demise of Li and Yan, no individual possessed the clout or stature to tie together their sprawling network. Some of Yan Siqi's associates preferred to rally behind Zhilong, but others formed competing groups. One line of division may have run through geography and clan networks. Leonard Blussé and Ang Ka-in speak at length about a Quanzhou alliance under Zheng

---

[20] Chiang (Jiang), *Missiven*, vol. I, pp. 152, 234.
[21] Jiang Risheng, *Taiwan waiji*, pp. 13, 16.   [22] Ibid., pp. 14–15.
[23] Kawaguchi, *Tei shi kiji*, pp. 3–4.

Zhilong pitted against a clique of Zhangzhou pirates.[24] However, brilliant new studies by John Wills and Lu Zhengheng have shown that, while hometown solidarity mattered, a great degree of overlap occurred in practice. Zhilong had many Zhangzhou followers, while Quanzhou men joined the Zhangzhou-led groups.[25] Perhaps it would be more accurate to describe the conflict as one between the gentry and mercantile interests of each prefecture that provided funding and protection for the pirates. The alliances between Li, a Quanzhou man, and Yan, from Zhangzhou, had temporarily shelved these differences. Now, with them gone, the two elite groups fought by proxy to determine which Minnan port would acquire preeminent intermediacy: officially sanctioned Haicheng or the rising Quanzhou smuggling centers of Anhai and Xiamen.

Other players also took a keen interest in the contest. Both the VOC and the Fujian authorities cultivated allies among the pirate leaders and played them off against each other. The Dutch saw a golden opportunity to present themselves and their powerful ships and weapons as the solution to the predation before the Ming authorities in exchange for direct access to Chinese product sources, cutting out the troublesome middlemen. Yu Zigao and Xu Xinsu, on the other hand, could continue to justify their usefulness to the court and reap fortunes as gatekeepers of the illicit trade.[26] To further complicate the picture, remnants of Li's Hirado-based network, now under the leadership of his son, Augustin Li Guozhu, sailed to Taiwan to reclaim the family patrimony.[27] With so many different interests overlapping and colliding with one another, rampant piracy and vicious infighting engulfed the Taiwan Strait area for the next few years. Because of this waterway's strategic location in the middle of the China and Japan routes, ships across maritime East Asia found it all but impossible to conduct normal trading activities.[28]

Zheng Zhilong was initially one of the pirates supported by the VOC. The governor of Taiwan, Gerrit Fredericksen de Witt, outfitted him and his followers with ships and weaponry. The company also allowed him to inherit and maintain the Wankan base north of Tayouan, and fly the

---

[24] Weng Jiayin (Ang Ka-in), *Helan shidai Taiwan shi de lianxuxing wenti* (Taipei: Daoxiang, 2008), pp. 147–180; Blussé, "Minnan-jen," pp. 256–257.

[25] Wills, "Yiguan's origins." See also Lu Zhengheng, "Guan yu zei zhijian: Zheng Zhilong baquan ji 'Zheng bu,'" unpublished MA thesis, National Tsinghua University (2013), pp. 83–90.

[26] Yang Yanjie, *Heju shidai Taiwan shi* (Taipei: Linking, 2000), pp. 52–53.

[27] Iwao Seiichi, "Ming mo qiaoyu Riben Zhina maoyishang Yiguan Augustin Li Guozhu zhi huodong," in Xu Xianyao (ed. and trans.), *Helan shidai Taiwan shi lunwen ji* (Yilan, Taiwan: Foguang renwenshe, 2001), pp. 141–142.

[28] Yang Yanjie, *Heju shidai*, pp. 52–53.

Dutch flag in his raids.[29] Through a combination of persuasion and superiority in violent firepower, Zheng Zhilong won over a sizable share of the resources and manpower left behind by Li and Yan. He then took steps to consolidate and expand his organization. He appears to have introduced hierarchical ranks among his new followers in place of the more informal fraternal cooperation of regular smuggling and pirate bands.[30] He also gradually substituted the outright plunder of ships for a more elaborate protection racket. He set up floating markets on his junks off the Penghu Islands to trade and levy duties, known informally as water payments (*baoshui*), upon passing vessels.[31] He even took advantage of a devastating famine in Fujian at the time to acquire more followers by encouraging refugees to migrate and settle at his Wankan base.[32]

Moreover, Zhilong found a lucrative outlet for most of his spoils in his old friend, Suetsugu Heizō Masanao. Ever the calculating businessman, Masanao had seized upon a series of anti-Christian campaigns in Japan to renounce his faith, convert to Buddhism, and sell out a former co-religionist, Murayama Tōan, leader of the second failed expedition to Taiwan. After Tōan and his entire clan were beheaded by the *bakufu*, Masanao replaced him as the shogunal deputy (*daikan*) of Nagasaki.[33] This position, of equal importance as the magistrates, put him in charge of supervising the entire foreign trade of the city. Both the Chinese entering port and Japanese merchants buying and selling from them had to go through Masanao. He also exercised influence over the consortium of big wholesalers from Osaka, Kyoto, and Sakai who formed the silk allotment guild (*itowappu*). Established in 1605, the guild was given the exclusive legal privilege of importing raw silk at fixed prices and reselling them domestically.[34] Masanao, along with another merchant, also acquired *shuin* passes from the *bakufu* for Taiwan, where Zhilong offered him a rich selection of high-quality products from the Yangzi River Delta.[35]

Although Zhilong's organization was but one of many pirate bands in the Taiwan Strait at the time, and by no means the largest, it certainly

---

[29] Cheng (Zheng), *War, trade and piracy*, p. 40; Chiang (Jiang), *Missiven*, vol. I, pp. 216, 234.

[30] Wong Young-tsu, "Security," p. 123.

[31] Zha Jizuo, *Zuiwei lu xuanji, TWWXCK*, 136 (1962), p. 255.

[32] Jiang Risheng, *Taiwan waiji*, pp. 16–17; Ni Zaitian (ed.), *Xu Ming jishi benmo, TWWXCK*, 133 (1962), p. 175.

[33] Inagaki, *Tei Seikō*, p. 225.

[34] Nakamura Tadashi, *Kinsei Nagasaki bōekishi no kenkyū* (Tokyo: Yoshikawa kōbunkan, 1988), pp. 267–268.

[35] Kawaguchi, *Taiwan kakkyoji*, p. 56 and Adam Clulow, *The company and the shogun: the Dutch encounter with Tokugawa Japan* (New York: Columbia University Press, 2014), pp. 210–211.

ranked among the most cohesive, well-armed, and prosperous. By 1627, the VOC had decided that he had grown too big for comfort, and watched with trepidation his increasingly intimate collaboration with the Japanese. An aggressive, headstrong new governor of Taiwan, Pieter Nuyts (1598–1655), sought talks with the Ming, offering to liquidate Zhilong in exchange for an agreement from the court to obtain unfettered access to Chinese goods.[36] At the same time, the company started to collect tolls from incoming Chinese and Japanese ships at Tayouan in an attempt to limit direct contact between them.

These actions harmed the interests of the powerful Suetsugu Heizō Masanao, who had reaped huge fortunes in this formerly free-for-all smuggling zone. In response, he ordered his vessels to defy the new Dutch regulations and continued doing business directly with Zheng Zhilong. When the VOC insisted upon enforcement, Masanao angrily protested and even tried, unsuccessfully, to get his Tokugawa overlords to launch an invasion of Taiwan. Tensions reached a climax on June 29, 1628, when the captain of one of his ships, Hamada Yahyōe, and 150 of his crew attacked Nuyt's residence at Tayouan by surprise and held the governor at knifepoint. The standoff ended within hours; the governor was released after he paid compensation to the crew and sent his son as a hostage to Japan. However, the Nuyts incident, as it later became known, triggered a systemic crisis in the relationship between the Dutch East India Company and Japan. Although Masanao did not get his invasion, he persuaded the *bakufu* to reject two subsequent VOC embassies and shut down its Hirado factory, effectively suspending all bilateral trade.[37]

In the meantime, Nuyts had to deal with another existential threat to the young colony at Tayouan. Upset at the chronic disruption of the trade between the China coast and Manila, and recognizing Taiwan's strategic value, the Spanish authorities decided to establish their own settlement on the island to directly compete with the VOC. In 1626, the Spanish landed on a small island facing present-day Jilong, on the northern tip of Taiwan, where they built a fortress. A year later, they constructed another fortification at Danshui, on the western shore, overlooking the vast and fertile Taipei plain.[38]

---

[36] Cheng (Zheng), *War, trade and piracy*, p. 45.
[37] Andrade, *Taiwan became Chinese*, ch. 2; Inagaki, *Tei Seikō*, pp. 204–223; Clulow, *Company and Shogun*, pp. 225–228.
[38] For more on the Spanish colonization of northern Taiwan, which they called Isla Hermosa, see Andrade, *Taiwan became Chinese*, ch. 4 and José Eugenio Borao-Mateo, *The Spanish experience in Taiwan, 1626–1642: the Baroque ending of a Renaissance endeavour* (Hong Kong: Hong Kong University Press, 2009).

The failed attempts by the VOC to secure free trade from the Ming, along with the Spanish and Japanese pushback, revealed before Zheng Zhilong the vulnerability of the Dutch; freedom from the company's manipulation to become a naval power in his own right no longer seemed like a distant goal. More importantly, he learned to appreciate the value of a stable base with regularized access to product sources, as well as the importance of symbolic capital, especially legitimacy and legality, in achieving this aim. For Zhilong, submission to the Ming could offer all of these and more. It possessed a powerful political infrastructure and the wealth and cultural eminence for him to maximize the potential of his organization and grant him tremendous leverage over rival pirate leaders. Moreover, he felt confident that he held a sufficient advantage over the empire on the seas to allow him to dictate the terms of his submission and maintain the greatest possible independence of action afterward. This option acquired added urgency and attraction amid Dutch efforts to form their own alliance with the imperial court at his expense.

In 1627 and 1628, Zhilong launched devastating raids upon the mainland coast that took the form of full-scale military invasions. He captured and looted several county seats in Quanzhou and Zhangzhou prefectures, killing one garrison commander and sinking hundreds of the best Ming ships. During his raids, Zhilong won over more adherents to his organization by restricting his plunder to the wealthy and distributing some of the spoils to the poor. In 1628, he occupied Xiamen, headquarters of the Ming anti-piracy squadron, and forced Yu Zigao to flee. Before withdrawing voluntarily, Zhilong captured Xu Xinsu and chopped off his head, and detained several of Yu's subordinates.[39] Zhilong then initiated contact with the gentry of Quanzhou, especially those of his hometown and Anhai with ties to his clan. Through them and the captured Ming officers whom he subsequently set free, he forwarded a request to the Fujian authorities to submit to their authority and fight piracy on their behalf to demonstrate his sincerity.[40]

Zhilong's estimation of his comparative advantage vis-à-vis the Ming proved right on the mark. Other than imposing the maritime ban on Fujian again in 1628, the court could do little to counter his onslaught. It was confronted with too many challenges elsewhere, from the emerging Manchu threat on the northeastern Asian frontier to peasant uprisings in the northwest, fueled by natural disasters and government mismanagement.[41] Moreover, Yu Zigao did not enjoy the full support and trust of the court, since he belonged to the eunuch faction of Wei Zhongxian

---

[39] Wong Young-tsu, "Security," pp. 123–126; Chao, Ming dai haijin, p. 256.
[40] Lu, "Guan yu zei," pp. 83–90.   [41] Chao, *Ming dai haijin*, p. 254.

(1568–1627), whose followers the emperor was purging from the ranks of government. The commander's incompetence in handling piracy suppression and the loss of his own base provided additional fuel for his political enemies.[42]

In July 1628, Xiong Wencan (d. 1640) assumed the post of Fujian governor. With the support of the Minnanese gentry and the newly enthroned Emperor Sizong (b. 1611, r. Chongzhen, 1627–1644), he ordered that Yu Zigao be removed from his post, imprisoned, and executed. However, a deep split occurred toward Zheng Zhilong's request for submission. The gentry of Zhangzhou, where the brunt of his attacks occurred, additionally feared the loss of Haicheng's influence and supported continued military action against him; those from Quanzhou took his side. In the end, Xiong recommended him for an official position in exchange for his surrender. Shortly afterward, the court approved the decision. And remarkably, perhaps awed by his show of strength, impressed by his moral compassion to the destitute, moved by the advice of gentry with prior contacts with him, or a combination of the above, it appointed Zhilong to replace the disgraced Yu. Of course, the reformed pirate started out at the most basic rank of patrolling admiral (youji), and was given three years to test his reliability and loyalty to the dynasty.[43]

Toward the pinnacle

Zheng Zhilong's transformation from outlaw to Ming official caused even greater worries for the Dutch East India Company authorities in Taiwan. Having just suffered a severe reversal in relations with Japan, they feared that he would soon possess the clout to corner the supply of Chinese products and deny the company access to the Fujian coast. If completely shut out of the China-Japan exchange, the colony of Taiwan would no longer have any reason to exist. Indeed, Suetsugu Heizō Masanao had already put enormous pressure upon the VOC to vacate the island and threatened to take military action if it did not. Some officials at the company headquarters of Batavia also felt that Taiwan was no longer worth keeping.[44]

Notwithstanding the disaster of the Hamada affair, Governor Nuyts decided to take yet another risk: lead a Dutch expedition to the China coast to ensure the stable flow of goods. Although similar forays had been made before over similar issues, the Fujian authorities viewed the

---

[42] Lu, "Guan yu zei," pp. 85–86.
[43] Lu, "Guan yu zei," p. 87; Kawaguchi, *Tei shi kiji*, p. 5.
[44] Andrade, *Taiwan became Chinese*, ch. 2.

presence of their ships as unnecessary provocations and a breach of the tacit agreement whereby only Chinese merchants would sail to Taiwan. The officials further feared a crackdown from the court. This time, the expedition outdid previous ones in its audacity. Nuyts's fleet sailed straight into Xiamen harbor and anchored near the headquarters of Zheng Zhilong, the new head of piracy suppression for the Ming. He invited Zhilong onboard his ship, the *Texel,* and held him hostage for a month until he agreed to unfettered commercial privileges for the VOC.[45]

Nuyts evidently believed that the new position of this former company interpreter gave him a decisive role in determining Ming policy toward foreigners. Yet, Zhilong was actually more vulnerable than he seemed on the surface. As a condition for surrender, he had to disperse his private piratical force and entrust his followers to several commands in the regular Ming army. Rather than submit to this fate, many of his subordinates fled to sea again, taking with them the majority of his men and junks. They joined forces with his competitors into new outlaw bands that again ravaged the Taiwan Strait. In a repeat of Zhilong's earlier performance against Yu Zigao, the pirates twice captured his military base of Xiamen, briefly driving him away from the city. Zhilong's inability to control his followers raised suspicions among some Ming officials and gentry of the sincerity of his commitment to the dynasty. To put a check on him, Fujian authorities decided to secure the surrender of other pirates and grant them official posts. The former enemies were then forced to work together against those still refusing to submit.[46]

Zhilong remained unfazed in the face of these severe challenges. He retained a core following of 600 troops, whom he split under the command of him and his brothers. He further recruited peasants into his ranks on land and outfitted a fleet of fishing vessels at sea. From these humble foundations, he rebuilt a mercenary force from scratch with a clearly developed sense of hierarchy and no longer subject to the presence of his former headstrong, free-willed allies. After several major engagements throughout 1630, Zhilong crushed most of the pirate bands and foiled attempts by the Fujian authorities to enlist individual pirates to threaten his unique position. With the coastal areas in relative peace again, the maritime ban was lifted the following year.[47]

During these campaigns, Zhilong surprisingly received the timely assistance of the Dutch, whose ships sailed to the China coast again, this time as welcome allies of the Ming. The dramatic turnabout probably had something to do with the assumption of his friend and business partner

---

[45] Cheng (Zheng), *War, trade and piracy,* pp. 54–55.   [46] Lu, "Guan yu zei," pp. 91–92.
[47] Cheng (Zheng), *War, trade and piracy,* pp. 55, 63; Lu, "Guan yu zei," pp. 95–101.

from Hirado, Jacques Specx, to the post of governor-general at Batavia in 1629. Zhilong specially wrote a letter addressed to him for the occasion, congratulating him and reminiscing about their time together in Japan. He also promised Specx that the Fujian coast would remain open for business with the Dutch. Zhilong basically reiterated voluntarily what he had promised Nuyts earlier on under pressure. Without doubt, the governor-general reciprocated in kind. Besides the personal amity, the company now depended upon him as the only reliable source for Chinese goods at a time when it faced highly limited options in maritime East Asia.[48]

With his position stabilized for the time being, Zhilong turned toward the consolidation and growth of his commercial enterprise. He moved his base from Xiamen to nearby Anhai, to the north, and built up the seaside town as a commercial port, capitalizing upon the town's rich mercantile tradition.[49] He organized a private fleet to participate in the intra-East Asian trade and forced other merchants in his sphere of influence to purchase his passes and fly his flag. These ships followed a traditional triangular route that brought Chinese silk to Japan for silver, which, in turn, went to purchase spices, aromatic woods, exotic foodstuffs, and ingredients for Chinese medicine in the ports of Southeast Asia. The bullion surplus repatriated back home in this manner allowed him to rapidly acquire a fortune. As the most immediate consequence, he reneged upon his earlier promise to grant the VOC free and unfettered access to the China coast. He left the Taiwan route in the exclusive care of two old smuggling associates: Hong Xu (d. 1665), a native of Jinmen, an island just ten kilometers away from Xiamen, and Zheng Tai (d. 1663), a destitute young man whom he adopted into the clan.[50]

Developments in his personal life proceeded in tandem with his career. He married again, this time taking the hand of Yan Siqi's daughter. By appropriating this crucial aspect of Yan's legacy, Zhilong could solidify his reputation as the rightful heir of all the smuggling networks in the Taiwan Strait, and win over the fragile loyalty of his former comrades-in-arms. In a maritime twist to the Confucian obligation of the wife toward

---

[48] Tonio Andrade, "The company's Chinese pirates: how the Dutch East India Company tried to lead a coalition of pirates to war against China, 1621–1662," *Journal of World History* 15.4 (2004): 433–435; Yuan and Bao (Blussé), "Zhilong gei Sibeikesi."

[49] Cheng (Zheng), *War, trade and piracy*, p. 70.

[50] Hong Xu is almost certainly the subordinate of Zheng Zhilong known in Dutch sources as Gampea. For a detailed study on this identification, see Yang Yanjie, "Zheng Chenggong bujiang Gampea kao," in Fang Youyi (ed.), *Zheng Chenggong yanjiu* (Xiamen: Xiamen University Press, 1994). For more on Zheng Tai's background, see Hayashi Shunsai and Ura Ren'ichi (ed.), *Ka'i hentai*, 2 vols. (Tokyo: Tōyō bunko, 1958–1959), vol. I, p. 46.

her mother-in-law, his new wife would assist Zhilong's mother or step-mother, Lady Huang, in managing his business and keeping accounts at Anhai and other ports in coastal Fujian. Lady Huang enjoyed a position of great influence within the family in her own right; even Zhilong deferred to her on some major matters. In fact, VOC officials often found themselves dealing directly with her when he was away performing official duties on behalf of the Ming.[51]

Zhilong's new marriage by no means conflicted with his previous union to Tagawa Matsu. Chinese merchants commonly maintained wives at multiple ports in maritime East Asia because of the lengthy layovers and the need to coordinate trading activities over long distances.[52] It is not inconceivable that Tagawa was looking after her Chinese husband's interests at Hirado and Nagasaki, major destinations for most of the exports onboard his ships. Her second son, Shichizaemon, who eventually assumed the position of Zheng agent in Japan, may have very well acquired his mercantile training through an apprenticeship with his mother. Of course, as the shadowy circumstances of Shichizaemon's birth demonstrate, Tagawa, too, could freely take on other lovers when Zhilong was away.

Besides cultivating trade routes and marriage connections, Zheng Zhilong did not neglect to groom an heir to carry on his legacy. Just like in any traditional Chinese family, the responsibility fell squarely upon his firstborn, Koxinga. Zhilong wrote to his Japanese wife several times ordering her to accompany their son to China. However, Tagawa Matsu consistently refused on the grounds that Koxinga's brother, the two-year-old Shichizaemon, was too young for her to leave him. Finally, husband and wife agreed to let Koxinga make the journey on his own. In 1630, the six-year-old boy arrived in Fujian. Koxinga's mother and toddler brother would relocate to Nagasaki, which, during this time, enjoyed a more regularized circuit of communication with the Chinese coast.[53]

Zheng Zhilong's meteoric ascent proved uncomfortable for the Ming. To separate him from his burgeoning power base, the authorities assigned him to battle bandits in mountainous western Fujian, close to the border of Guangdong and Jiangxi. His preoccupation with the outlaws left him unable to tend to matters on the coast, leaving it wide open for a renewed onslaught of maritime predation. Pirates hostile to Zhilong's monopoly

[51] Wills, "Yiguan's origins"; Ho, "Sealords," pp. 23, 106–107.
[52] Wills, "Yiguan's origins"; Lynn Pan, Sons of the Yellow Emperor: a history of the Chinese diaspora (New York: Kodansha International, 1994), p. 157. In addition to his two main wives, Zhilong also had two concubines. See Tei shi kankei, p. 36.
[53] Kawaguchi, Tei shi kiji, pp. 8, 10.

rallied under the leadership of Liu Xiang (d. 1634), a Zhangzhou native, and consolidated into a competing syndicate. Allied to them was a large Quanzhou contingent under Li Dan's son, Augustin Li Guozhu.[54] Their ships ravaged the Taiwan Strait, making navigation and trade all but impossible.

In 1631, the court appointed Zou Weilian (d. 1635) as governor of Fujian to replace Xiong Wencan. Faced with this formidable maritime menace, Zou believed that only Zhilong possessed the knowledge, skills, and connections to pacify the seas. Accordingly, the governor recalled him to Xiamen in the spring of 1632, after he successfully exterminated the mountain bandits, and placed him in charge of spearheading the campaign against Liu Xiang. Zhilong also received a promotion to Fujian vice-commander (*fu zongbing*), a sign that the Ming authorities had decided to end his trial period and welcome him into the formal hierarchy as a trusted official.[55]

Meanwhile, the Dutch East India Company dropped its friendly attitude toward Zheng Zhilong and initiated its own raids on shipping along the China coast. Several factors brought about this sudden turnaround. Hans Putmans (d. 1656), who succeeded Nuyts as governor of Taiwan in 1629, prioritized violence as a means to shape reality on the ground. Disappointed in the growing concentration of Taiwan's trade into the hands of Hong Xu and Zheng Tai, he hoped to foment enough disorder to discredit Zheng Zhilong in the eyes of the Ming officials and force them to negotiate on VOC terms. Jacques Specx had provided an effective check on Putmans, but no more obstacles existed after the governor-general stepped down in 1632.[56]

By then, the Dutch position in maritime East Asia had witnessed a marked improvement. In 1630, Suetsugu Heizō Masanao, the biggest obstacle to VOC trade in Japan, had passed away. Although the position of deputy was hereditary, his son and successor adopted a friendlier attitude toward the Dutch. The company took advantage of this fortuitous turn of events to mend relations with the *bakufu*. In 1632, in a rare act of contrition, it handed Pieter Nuyts over to the Tokugawa authorities, who clamped him into a Japanese prison for four years. The *bakufu*, which had considered the headstrong Nuyts as the main culprit for the downturn in bilateral relations, happily restored the suspended diplomatic and commercial ties with the VOC.[57]

---

[54] Cheng (Zheng), *War, trade and piracy*, pp. 72–73; Iwao, "Augustin Li Guozhu," pp. 144–145.

[55] Cheng (Zheng), *War, trade and piracy*, p. 75.   [56] Andrade, "Chinese pirates," p. 436.

[57] Andrade, *Taiwan became Chinese*, ch. 2; Inagaki, *Tei Seikō*, pp. 224–225, 240–241; Clulow, *Company and Shogun*, pp. 229–254.

For these reasons, Putmans now had a freer hand from Batavia to pursue his agenda of opening up China by force. In June 1633, he personally led a fleet of ten ships that sailed directly into Xiamen harbor and launched a surprise attack on Zheng Zhilong's shipyard. At the time, Zhilong was constructing thirty vessels modeled according to the latest European designs and outfitted with state-of-the-art cannons. Now, he could only watch in shock and helplessness as all but four of the ships were sunk and destroyed. Despite the devastating loss, he firmly refused Putmans's demand to establish a trading post on Gulang Island, in Xiamen harbor.[58]

Putmans decided to step up his attacks and also make overtures to Liu Xiang and Augustin. The VOC and the pirate coalition soon participated in each other's raids and split the profit between them.[59] To add insult to injury, pirate ships attacked the Zheng bastion of Anhai, looting the town and killing several of Zhilong's relatives.[60] Zhilong was determined to exact revenge for his devastating losses and, more importantly, break the cooperation of his rivals, which could potentially destroy his maritime enterprise and end his blossoming political career.

He first took aim at the Dutch. In October 1633, after waiting several weeks for a severe typhoon to weaken Putmans's fleet, he lured the main part of it into Xiamen harbor and cut off all avenues of retreat by blockading the entrance. As he completed his encirclement, pirate ships sailing with the company fled in panic. Then, Zhilong's 150 junks swarmed in from all sides. Some of the ships were deliberately set on fire and hurled toward the enemy, destroying and sinking two major Dutch vessels. Putmans beat a hasty retreat back to Taiwan. A year later, in a classic case of blowback, Liu Xiang's piratical fleets turned upon their former comrades. They raided the coastline of southern Taiwan and, at one point, surrounded Fort Zeelandia, before the Dutch finally repulsed their attack.[61]

The fiasco forced Putmans back into a cooperative mode with Zheng Zhilong. In subsequent peace negotiations, the governor agreed to the licensed, restricted trade that prevailed before the piratical upsurge. Zhilong proved surprisingly reasonable in his terms. In exchange for Dutch recognition of his supremacy in the Taiwan Strait, he promised to prevent his own ships and those affiliated with him from sailing directly to Japan in accordance with Ming regulations. This decision effectively removed organized Chinese competition for the VOC from the Japanese

[58] Andrade, "Chinese pirates," p. 437.   [59] Ibid., p. 436.
[60] Lu, "Guan yu zei," p. 111.
[61] Andrade, "Chinese pirates," pp. 439–440; Cheng (Zheng), *War, trade and piracy*, pp. 87–88.

market. Its Taiwan colony could finally actualize its potential to become a thriving entrepôt able to exceed Macao, Manila, and the Japanese *shuin* traders in the lucrative intra-East Asian exchange. The island prospered greatly for the rest of the decade.[62]

With the Dutch placated, Zheng Zhilong could devote his entire attention to his archenemy, Liu Xiang. His core private force, along with assistance from the official Ming military, defeated the pirate's massive fleets in seven brilliant naval campaigns over the next three years. His successes allowed him to secure the surrender of Liu's ally, Augustin Li Guozhu, who assisted the Ming in several of the later engagements. During the climactic final battle off the coast of Guangdong at the end of 1635, Liu Xiang, under fierce fire, blew himself up onboard his flagship.[63] Augustin then defected again, but Zhilong tracked down his ships and eliminated him during a short skirmish.[64] After the demise of the pirate bands, Zhilong initiated a purge of peaceful business rivals. Although the Zhangzhou merchants Hambuan and Jocksim purchased his passes, their enterprises had reached a similar scale to his and offered credible alternatives for the Dutch in the Taiwan trade. He used his official position to obstruct their business whenever possible and extort from them tremendous sums of money. In 1640, Hambuan perished when his ship sank in a typhoon near Penghu, while Jocksim disappeared from the records.[65] With the Zhangzhou-supported pirates and traders out of the way, Zhilong's supremacy was complete.

Consolidation amid crisis

The seventeenth century, in contrast to the economic growth and expansion of the previous century, was a time of severe depression for many parts of the world, including the East Asian world-region. Some historians perceive of this downturn as a common global phenomenon known as the seventeenth-century crisis, although much about it remains a subject of controversy, including its causes, timeframe, severity, and universal applicability. Nonetheless, these scholars agree that average temperatures dropped, whether because of natural climate change or dust from meteors and volcanic eruptions. The resulting droughts, floods, and other abnormal weather patterns severely affected the food supply. In a world where growth still heavily depended upon agrarian

---

[62] Blussé, "No boats," pp. 64–66.   [63] Wong Young-tsu, "Security," p. 129.
[64] Iwao Seiichi, "Augustin Li Guozhu," pp. 148–149.
[65] For more on Hambuan and Jocksim, see Nagazumi Yōko, "Helan de Taiwan maoyi," in Xu Xianyao (trans.), *Helan shidai Taiwan shi lunwen ji* (Yilan, Taiwan: Foguang renwenshe, 2001), pp. 273–307.

surpluses, a marked contraction in handicraft production and consumption followed suit, in the worst cases leading to massive deaths amid famine and pestilence. Since the amount of available resources could not support as many state entities or elites, economic woes often triggered political crises in the form of rebellions, coups, and military invasions. The malaise presented opportunities for ambitious state-builders and monopolists to overturn the existing order, eliminate their competitors, and build more uniform, consolidated enterprises.[66]

In maritime East Asia, the seventeenth-century crisis peaked during the 1630s. Silver production from New World mines declined, causing only a trickle to flow into Manila and Macao during some years. More bad news for the Spanish and Portuguese came in 1639, when two galleons from Acapulco laden with the metal sank into the Pacific. Combined with poor harvests, the dismal trading conditions contributed to a massacre of Manila's Chinese population between 1639 and 1640 by the Spanish that claimed a total of 20,000 lives. The worldwide decline of Spain as a political power exacerbated the situation. The Dutch successfully built a narrowing arc of containment around the Iberian colonies. Dutch predation frequently rendered the Manila and Macao routes unusable. The VOC also continued to make steady advances into Southeast Asia, seizing the prized Portuguese possession of Melaka in 1641 and controlling the narrow strait that tied the Indian Ocean to the China Seas.[67]

Meanwhile, Japan was beset by a famine of epic proportions; popular discontent boiled over into a major rebellion in 1637 on the Shimabara peninsula, east of Nagasaki. Under these circumstances, the *bakufu* viewed with trepidation the power wielded by the Suetsugu household and Kyushu daimyo, whose influence derived from foreign trade and contacts, particularly converts to Catholicism. It feared their potential to mobilize angry commoners to subvert Tokugawa rule in collusion with Spanish and Portuguese traders and missionaries and overseas Japanese Christians. The *bakufu* was determined to root out the Kyushu elites' access to alternative channels of authority. In five edicts promulgated between 1633 and 1639, known collectively as Maritime Prohibitions (*kaikin*), it proscribed Christianity, permanently expelled the Iberians, discontinued the *shuin* system, and forbade subjects from leaving or returning to Japan on pain of death. It further sought to monopolize access to overseas trade by institutionalizing ties with the neighboring

---

[66] For an introductory overview of the seventeenth-century crisis, refer to Geoffrey Parker and Lesley M. Smith, "Introduction," in Parker and Smith (eds.), *The general crisis of the seventeenth century*, second edition (London: Routledge, 1997), pp. 7–17, 19–22.

[67] William S. Atwell, "A seventeenth-century 'general crisis' in East Asia?" *Modern Asian Studies* 24.4 (1990), pp. 669–670 and "Emerging world economy," pp. 408–409.

states of Ryukyu and Korea. The *bakufu* also restricted all private trade in the hands of Chinese merchants and the VOC, and, in 1640, confined their presence solely to the port of Nagasaki to better supervise their activities.[68]

As a result of the maritime ban, total silver exports from Japan declined from an average annual high of four to five million taels (150,000 to 187,500 kg) in the early seventeenth century to fewer than 1,500,000 taels (56,250 kg) in 1642.[69] The edicts struck further blows to Manila and, especially, Macao, which had thrived as an intermediary for Japanese silver. For at least the next two decades, the Iberian colonies were plunged into a severe economic depression. Conversely, the new laws proved to be a windfall for the Dutch by automatically removing or marginalizing all other organized competition in the China-Japan exchange. Of course, the more numerous Chinese merchants at the port collectively constituted a bigger commercial presence, but they lacked the scale of the company and the backing of a strong state. The company could hope to harness their activities by issuing passes and encouraging them to fly the Dutch flag, while stepping up the confiscation and plunder of those caught without them.[70]

However, the VOC's favorable position contained one key weakness; it depended, in large part, upon continued access to the Chinese product sources provided by Zheng Zhilong. And Zhilong was not about to let the Dutch enjoy all the profits for themselves. In 1641, he violated his previous agreement with the company as well as the existing Ming prohibition on trade with Japan by sailing his junks from Anhai directly to Nagasaki. In the following years, his personal ships accounted for a quarter of all Chinese vessels, and some 80 percent of their cargoes. According to incomplete estimates, he realized revenues, on average, worth 402,400 taels (15,090 kg) of silver between 1640 and 1646.[71] Many other traders, of course, purchased his passes. His brilliant move provided greater coherence and organization to the Chinese merchants.

Naturally, Zhilong's actions cut into the profits of the Dutch and affected the viability of their entrepôt of Taiwan. The company representatives at Nagasaki repeatedly requested the magistrates to authorize the plunder of his junks at sea in revenge for the perceived betrayal at his hands. Despite their bitter complaints, the authorities adamantly ordered

---

[68] Toby, *State and Diplomacy*, pp. 11–13.
[69] Atwell, "Emerging world economy," p. 411. For a guide to measurement and currency conversions, refer to Appendix 2.
[70] Clulow, *Company and Shogun*, p. 175.
[71] For a quantitative analysis, see Table 1.1 in Appendix 3.1 and Ishihara, *Nippon kisshi*, pp. 272–278.

them, in the name of the shogun, to desist from harming Zhilong's vessels and those of other Chinese or face the death sentence.[72] The *bakufu*, too, benefited from the counterweight presented by him to VOC designs to monopolize the market share at Nagasaki. The *bakufu*'s firm stance on his behalf marked the beginning of an alliance with his family that would last for over half a century.

In addition to Japan, Zhilong maintained a close commercial relationship with the native kingdoms and European colonies in Southeast Asia, although the quantity and value of the goods exchanged remain unclear. After the onset of the Tokugawa maritime restrictions, he became a crucial intermediary who carried cargoes on behalf of the Spanish and Portuguese between Macao and Manila and Nagasaki. The shipments into Japan included bibles, Christian texts, and religious iconography, in direct violation of Tokugawa laws. Zhilong also purchased African slaves from the Portuguese. Because of their skillful use of muskets and deadly marksmanship, he used them as his personal bodyguards, and later put together an entire elite infantry division consisting of some 300 of these "black boys."[73]

Zhilong's ties with Macao and Manila contained a genuine personal element, for he recalled his earlier days there with great fondness and remained grateful to the Catholic priests whom he had encountered even if his own conversion was less than sincere. His junks transported Spanish and Portuguese missionaries traveling to and from the China coast at his own cost, while his port of Anhai provided food and refuge for shipwrecked Iberian sailors. He also had family from Macao. After the promulgation of the maritime restrictions, non-Japanese Christians were expelled from Japan. According to Portuguese accounts, Zheng Zhilong's daughter was part of this exodus. She settled down in Macao and married a Portuguese or mestizo Macanese man. When Zhilong learned of her whereabouts, his ships brought her, her husband, and her father-in-law, a man named Manuel Bello, to reside with him in Anhai.[74]

Zheng Zhilong invested his massive capital from overseas trade into other economic sectors. After Macao's direct trade to Japan was shut down because of the Tokugawa maritime restrictions, Zhilong recruited 150 skilled weaving families from Guangzhou and set them up in Anhai. He supplied them raw silk and looms purchased from merchants from the Yangzi River Delta. He also purchased landholdings in Fujian and Guangdong and supervised, with great success, the production and

---

[72] Ibid., p. 290.
[73] Andrade, *Lost colony*, p. 326; Boxer, "Rise and fall," p. 437; Wills, "Iquan's origins."
[74] Boxer, "Rise and fall of Nicolas Iquan," pp. 426–432; Wills, "Iquan's origins."

processing of porcelain and sugar.[75] Under him, Anhai subverted officially sanctioned Haicheng to become China's preeminent international
port despite the theoretical illegality of its existence. Zhilong, too, became
an incredibly wealthy man valued at tens of millions of silver taels in
annual income, and had assets that rivaled entire kingdoms.[76]

In 1640, Zheng Zhilong received a promotion to the rank of Fujian
military commander (zongbing). His new post, which gave him responsibility over the soldiers and military installations of the entire province,
became a legitimate pretext for him to privatize a substantial number of
government forces and tie them to him through a personal chain of
command. He managed to have his brother Hongkui (d. 1653) succeed
him as vice-commander. Other relatives and allies assumed crucial positions, especially at strategic coastal defense installations. The proceeds
from his commercial network funded purchases of arms and equipment
for the troops. The emergence of this privatized "Zheng clique" in the
Ming Fujian military command, in turn, bolstered his ability to regulate
foreign trade; his system of passes expanded from Anhai and Xiamen to
incorporate the entire Fujian littoral. His subordinates further assumed
leadership positions beyond Zhilong's home province: in Chaozhou prefecture, right across the border in eastern Guangdong, and Wenzhou and
Taizhou in southern Zhejiang.[77]

Like other upwardly mobile merchants during the late Ming period,
Zhilong sought to transform his economic power into legitimate political
and cultural capital.[78] He compiled a genealogy to sanitize his shady past and
reinterpret his life and career along Confucian lines. He ensured that his son,
Koxinga, received a strict, traditional education, expecting him to one day
pass the civil service examinations and become a high-ranking official
(Figure 2.1).[79] He aped the practice of model local elites in supervising the
repair of a Song-era sea bridge connecting Anhai with the town of Shuitou,
across a narrow bay. A consortium of Quanzhou gentry and Zhilong's
merchant associates, primarily from the Huang, Zeng, Ke, and Chen clans,
donated 200 taels of silver to the effort. Men from these lineages later served
the Zheng organization loyally as key officials and commercial agents.

Finally, to drive home his exalted status, Zhilong built a splendid
mansion overlooking Anhai's busy harbor to serve as his headquarters.

---

[75] Chen Bisheng, Zheng Chenggong yanjiu, pp. 131–132 and Tang, Zheng Zhilong,
pp. 188–190.
[76] Wong Young-tsu, "Security," p. 129.
[77] Lu, "Guan yu zei," pp. 130–140. Note that Lu translates the Zheng clique as the "Zheng
Ministry."
[78] Clunas, Superfluous things, p. 162.
[79] Huang Zongxi, Cixing shimo, TWWXCK, 25 (1958), p. 1.

Figure 2.1 The Pavilion in the Heart of the Water. This tablet, erected in 1637 at the orders of Zheng Zhilong, lies in the middle of the Anping Bridge, which runs between Anhai and Shuitou. He had supervised and collected funds for its renovation and reconstruction. Note the list of gentry donors to the project on the left-hand side of the tablet. Photograph by author, July 2009.

The Chinese accounts, perhaps with a healthy dose of hyperbolic exaggeration, noted that the compound came fully equipped with a canal connected to the sea that allowed ships to sail directly into his bedroom.[80]

However, Zhilong's newfound success largely came at the expense of the other part of his patrimony: his bases in Taiwan. With him gone, the Dutch could advance unhindered beyond their outposts of Tayouan and Provintia. As they moved northward, they seized land from the aborigines by playing off one tribe against another. In 1642, VOC forces compelled the Spanish to abandon Danshui and Jilong, bringing the entire northern and western coastal area under its control.[81] Meanwhile, because of Zhilong's domination of the China-Japan exchange, Taiwan gradually lost its role as a regional entrepôt. Instead, over the 1640s, the island came to resemble a colonial economy characterized by a sugar monoculture and the extraction of deer, hunted by aborigines in the forests and mountains. Some of these products enjoyed significant demand in Japan; sugar went to flavor food in Japanese candies and sweetmeats, while deerskins were prized as part of decorative covering for sword cases and ceremonial armor in samurai outfits.[82] Deer meat, on the other hand, found a receptive market in China. Large numbers of Chinese immigrants soon poured into Taiwan to till the land and trade with the aborigines, bringing the total population of the once sparsely settled island to over ten thousand in the 1640s.[83]

Nonetheless, Zhilong's residual influence over Taiwan remained sizable. Besides controlling all mainland shipping to the island, he retained special privileges from his pirate days, including the levying of taxes over Chinese fishermen and customs duties for merchants. He also operated gold mines in eastern Taiwan, largely beyond the reach of the Dutch authorities.[84] Some of his former associates, including a trader and interpreter named He Tingbin, remained behind to assist the VOC in regulating the affairs of the burgeoning Chinese community. However, they never completely cut off their ties to the Zheng and often continued to obey the family's directives.[85]

---

[80] Wong Young-tsu, "Security," p. 129.

[81] Andrade, *Taiwan became Chinese*, ch. 5, ch. 9. Due to high, forbidding mountains, running in five ranges from north to south, the eastern two-thirds of the island remained largely off-limits, inhabited by ferocious head-hunting tribes.

[82] Ts'ao(Cao), "Taiwan as entrepôt," p. 7; Nara Shuichi, "Zeelandia, the factory in the Far Eastern trading network of the VOC," in Leonard Blussé (ed.), *Around and about Formosa: essays in honor of Professor Ts'ao Yung-ho* (Taipei: Ts'ao Yung-ho Foundation for Culture and Education, 2003), pp. 172–173.

[83] Chen Guodong, *Taiwan de shanhai jingyan* (Taipei: Yuanliu, 2006), pp. 408–409; Shi Lang, *Jinghai jishi*, TWWXCK, 13 (1958), p. 60.

[84] Tang, *Zheng Zhilong*, pp. 188–190.

[85] Jiang Risheng, *Taiwan waiji*, pp. 36, 47–48; Tonio Andrade, "Chinese under European Rule: the case of Sino-Dutch mediator He Bin," *Late Imperial China* 28.1 (2007), p. 8.

These primarily unilateral rights later led to tense disputes with the Dutch under Koxinga.

By the early 1640s, Zheng Zhilong had unified Li Dan's piracy network and Xu Xinsu's mercenaries, acquired the support of the Quanzhou gentry, asserted economic supremacy over Zhangzhou, and foiled Ming and VOC attempts to use him for their own ends. Moreover, he institutionalized and legitimated his positions according to the official ranks and titles of the Chinese imperial system. The Ming court, for good reason, made continued attempts to dilute his influence. The governor often dispatched him to the mountains to combat bandits and transferred his command several times from Anhai to Nan'ao, an island straddling the Guangdong border, ostensibly to fight pirates but actually a form of disguised exile. Memorials to the court in the 1640s even suggested that Zhilong lead his entire naval squadron to Liaodong against the Manchus. Through stalling tactics and bribes paid to well-placed gentry and officials with access to the central bureaucracy, he never strayed too far from his power base. More importantly, the Ming court saw no better option than Zhilong in maintaining order along the troublesome littoral at a time when it was confronted with an existential crisis of an unprecedented nature, one that eventually brought about its downfall.[86]

Between Ming and Manchus

The seventeenth-century crisis, while hugely beneficial for Zheng Zhilong and his clique, ironically threatened the very survival of the Ming, his protector and source of legitimacy. A steep drop in the agrarian surplus of grain-producing areas led to widespread famine from the desolate northwestern backwater and the resource-deficient southeastern coast to even the most prosperous urban centers of the Yangzi River Delta. The Tokugawa prohibitions, Iberian decline, and Anglo-Dutch predation exacerbated the problem by limiting the supply of currency to an economy and court heavily dependent for their revenues upon imported silver. Moreover, much of the bullion that flowed into China entered and remained within Zhilong's sphere of influence.[87] As a result, deflation worsened, and the severe fiscal shortfalls in the government treasury

---

[86] Chen Bisheng, *Zheng Chenggong yanjiu*, p. 91; Lin Renchuan, "Shi lun zhuming haishang Zheng shi de xingshuai," in Academic Division of the Zheng Chenggong Scholarly Discussion Group (ed.), *Zheng Chenggong yanjiu lunwen xuan xuji* (Fuzhou: Fujian People's Publishing House, 1984), p. 202.

[87] Professor Zheng Yongchang of National Chenggong University in Tainan gives this highly original but sound conjecture of Zheng Zhilong's contribution to the Ming fiscal crisis (personal correspondence, 2008).

prevented effective famine relief and grain transfers in the places most needed.[88] Peasant rebellions soon broke out and spread across the entire empire.

The Ming imploded under the weight of these domestic and external pressures. In the summer of 1644, Beijing fell to peasant rebels led by Li Zicheng (1606–c. 1645), and the Chongzhen emperor committed suicide. By that time, the Manchu descendants of Nurhaci had established the institutions for a powerful, centralized Qing state with the help of Han collaborators in northeast Asia. Dorgon (1612–1650), the Manchu prince regent for the five-year-old Emperor Shizu (1638–1661, r. Shunzhi, 1644–1661), allied with the Ming general Wu Sangui (1612–1678) to occupy Beijing in the name of crushing the rebellion. Qing forces secured most of North China by the end of the year.[89]

Meanwhile, Ming officials and military commanders scrambled to reconstitute the imperial court south of the Yangzi River at the subsidiary capital of Nanjing. They rallied around an imperial descendant, Zhu Yousong (1607–1646), who assumed the throne as the Hongguang emperor (r. 1644–1645). Zheng Zhilong assigned a fleet of ships led by his brother, Hongkui, to patrol the Yangzi River on behalf of the pretender, forming the frontline of defense against an imminent southward Manchu advance. However, the Zheng brothers were far more concerned about the preservation of their home base in Fujian. When the Manchus began crossing the Yangzi in early 1645, Hongkui abandoned his positions without a fight. Qing forces entered Nanjing with minimal resistance and captured the pretender, ending the short-lived Hongguang court.[90]

Hongkui withdrew to Hangzhou, the Zhejiang provincial seat, where he encountered another imperial prince, Zhu Yujian (1598–1646), who was also fleeing the Manchu onslaught. Hongkui escorted the prince to Fuzhou, where he took refuge under the military protection of Zheng Zhilong. Meanwhile, many prominent Ming officials, along with local gentry, congregated in the city, a bastion of stability amid the chaos enveloping the tottering empire. They made an effort to regroup and reorganize in the face of the Manchu onslaught. Their enthusiastic support, along with the backing of Hongkui, persuaded Zhilong to uphold Zhu Yujian as the new Ming ruler. The prince's enthronement as the Longwu emperor (r. 1645–1646) took place in August 1645. To demonstrate his gratitude, and to maintain the loyalty of his new benefactors, Zhu showered high ranks and honors upon Zhilong and the rest of the

---

[88] Atwell, "General crisis," p. 666.
[89] For more on the Qing conquest and consolidation, refer to Wakeman, *Great enterprise*, vol. I, pp. 818–821.
[90] Struve, *Southern Ming*, pp. 57–58, 77.

Zheng family, and placed them and members of their clique in charge of all military affairs in the province.[91]

Despite a genuine initial effort at cooperation, the two men soon fell out with one another. Their worldviews and the interests of themselves and their adherents diverged in fundamental ways. Zheng Zhilong hoped to utilize the emperor as a figurehead to legitimize and bolster the autonomy of his Fujian satrapy and commercial network in maritime East Asia. Yet the Longwu pretender proved to be a highly competent and vigorous ruler, a mature man with an independent will not easily susceptible to manipulation from others. With the support of the civil officials at his court, he constantly made plans for a campaign of dynastic restoration to expel the Manchus and unify China under his rule.[92] He and his retinue refused to be confined within the boundaries of a province like Fujian, which he considered "a puny place."[93] The traditional disregard held by civil officials for military men and merchants fueled personality differences and conflicts at the individual level and dampened enthusiasm for a much-needed united front.[94] From the perspective of the refined and arrogant central bureaucrats, Zhilong and his clique, many of them former smugglers and pirates, came across as coarse and violent.

A deadlock ensued. On the one hand, the Longwu emperor lacked substantial forces of his own to undertake his cherished campaign of restoration. The military commanders, answering primarily to Zheng Zhilong and stationed at the strategic mountain passes leading into Fujian, refused to budge, citing war preparations that never seemed to end and food shortages that never got resolved.[95] On the other hand, Zhilong did not have an independent source of symbolic capital and political legitimacy. He could not justify the prioritization of his military clique and commercial enterprise above the Confucian obligation of a loyal minister to aid the Son of Heaven in regaining his rightful place at the center of the cosmos. Without the ranks and titles from the Longwu emperor, he could only depend upon his personal charisma, potentially leaving him with undependable allies rather than subordinates, a regression back to his days as an outlaw.

Scholars have commonly represented the imperial pretender's ideal of restoration as an unrealistic fantasy, in contrast to Zhilong's more pragmatic approach based upon a rational assessment of the limits of his

---

[91] Chen Bisheng, *Zheng Chenggong yanjiu*, p. 92; Struve, *Southern Ming*, pp. 77, 87
[92] Struve, *Southern Ming*, pp. 4, 80–82.   [93] Wills, "Contingent connections," p. 182.
[94] Chen Bisheng, *Zheng Chenggong yanjiu*, pp. 92–94 lists several of these personality conflicts.
[95] Struve, *Southern Ming*, pp. 88–89.

military protection.[96] Despite putting a positive spin on the latter's character, this perspective tends to be too trusting of the traditional, Confucian-inspired view of him as an amoral opportunist. As John Wills has pointed out, Zhilong shared the Longwu emperor's vision, and made great efforts to reconcile them with his personal interests. Shortly before he welcomed the ruler to Fuzhou, he had undertaken a significant expansion and revision of his book, *Grand strategy for ordering the country*, to serve as an advisory manual on policy and military strategy for the Ming court. The new edition outlined his version of how to achieve a restoration. Only through regional autonomy, he believed, could support be rapidly built up across the empire from the grassroots level for a task as massive as the expulsion of the Manchu invaders. This decentralized effort would involve the initiative of individual provinces, each utilizing its own resources and manpower.[97] Thus, the positions espoused by Zhilong and the Longwu pretender both contained elements of idealism, which precisely made their disagreement all the more bitter.

Their uncompromising attitudes also masked a deeper panic at an increasingly desperate situation on the ground. The 1640s were extremely bad years for the southeastern coast; crop failures and droughts caused food prices to skyrocket. The destitute, having eaten everything within reach and in sight, resorted to cannibalism. Others joined roving bands of displaced peasants, fishermen, and lower gentry that waged class warfare across towns and villages in a Robin Hood-like manner, killing officials and plundering wealthy families, and robbing public granaries.[98] Meanwhile, the chaos and warfare caused by the Qing invasion of the Yangzi River Delta drastically decreased the supply of raw silk to Zheng Zhilong's ports in Fujian.[99]

Seen in this light, the Longwu emperor's platform of restoration was not as unrealistic as it seems. His solution would broaden the resource base by incorporating more agriculturally fertile provinces, such as rice-producing Jiangxi and Huguang, into his domain to support the anti-Qing resistance. Zhilong, on the other hand, feared that any departure from Fujian would dilute his power base and influence over the pretender, who could readily avail himself of the support of other Ming loyalist commanders. Zhilong thus opted to squeeze as much as possible from Fujian

---

[96] See, for instance, Wills, "Contingent connections," p. 180; Ho, "Sealords," p. 124.

[97] Zheng Dayu and Zheng Zhilong, *Jingguo xionglue*, quoted in Wills, "Contingent connections," pp. 180–182; Ho, "Sealords," p. 123.

[98] Robert J. Antony, *Like froth floating on the sea: the world of pirates and seafarers in late imperial China* (Berkeley, CA: University of California Institute for East Asian Studies, 2003), pp. 30–31.

[99] Cheng (Zheng), *War, trade and piracy*, pp. 137–138.

regardless of its impoverished state. He raised taxes and extorted huge sums of money and grain from gentry and wealthy commoners, and, increasingly, impoverished peasants, to pay and feed his troops in the hopes of riding out the crisis.[100]

When these measures proved untenable, Zheng Zhilong looked for relief overseas, rather than the interior. In late 1645 and early 1646, he sent two missions to Nagasaki with the aim of securing armaments and samurai warriors from the Tokugawa shogun. Japan was an ideal choice in this regard. It had been a leading exporter of mercenaries before the ban on overseas travel. Both the European colonial authorities and native rulers in Southeast Asia valued them for their bravery and ferocity.[101] Zhilong himself already maintained an entire division of 1,000 Japanese mercenaries commanded by his brother and fully armed with muskets.[102]

Moreover, Zhilong recently scored a triumph regarding a more personal matter: his Japanese wife, Tagawa Matsu. Now that Shichizaemon had matured into a fifteen-year-old teenager, she felt ready to join her husband and elder son in China. However, the attitude of the *bakufu* remained unclear. When the Tokugawa maritime ban first came into effect, all Japanese wives of Chinese merchants were strongly encouraged to depart.[103] However, over five years had passed since then, and it was by no means certain that the *bakufu* would allow Japanese subjects to leave the country once the rules had been set in stone. Therefore, he must have felt greatly pleased when he received permission for Tagawa Matsu to set sail, after numerous petitions from him and Koxinga.[104] Zhilong probably felt confident that he possessed sufficient clout to make the Japanese authorities bend the rules for him once more on the issue of military assistance.

The first mission carried a letter from his subordinate, Zhou Hezhi, who, like him, had once resided in Japan and cultivated close ties to *bakufu* officials and daimyo. The second one represented Zhilong himself, and forwarded his personal gifts and requests targeted at all levels of the Japanese establishment, from the shogun in Edo and emperor at

---

[100] Struve, *Southern Ming*, pp. 84–85.

[101] For a fascinating case study of the role of Japanese mercenaries in the Indonesian archipelago, see Adam Clulow, "Unjust, cruel and barbarous proceedings: Japanese mercenaries and the Amboyna incident of 1623," *Itinerario* 31.1 (2007).

[102] Sekisai Ugai, *Min Shin tōki* (Rare books collection, National Taiwan University Library), n.p.

[103] Like Tagawa, many other women chose to stay behind. The policy toward Japanese spouses of the Chinese proved highly lenient compared to the wives and mistresses of the Europeans, along with their interracial children, who faced forcible expulsion. See Michael S. Laver, *The sakoku edicts and the politics of Tokugawa hegemony* (Amherst, NY: Cambria Press, 2011), p. 148.

[104] Kawaguchi, *Tei shi kiji*, pp. 7, 20–21.

Kyoto to the magistrates at Nagasaki. In addition to military aid, the letter to the shogun pressed the ruler to authorize Koxinga's younger brother, Shichizaemon, to leave Japan and join him in China, along with "ten ladies-in-waiting and slaves" to serve his homesick wife. Zhilong further used the opportunity to update the *bakufu* on the status of his eldest son, boasting of the ranks and honors Koxinga had received as a military commander in the service of the Ming pretender.

The *bakufu* officially turned down the first request, citing the lack of formal diplomatic ties between China and Japan since the sixteenth century. In response to the second mission, it returned Zhilong's gifts and questioned the envoy about the inappropriate use of language when referring to the emperor and shogun in the letters.[105] In private, however, many within the ruling circles at Edo staunchly favored intervention. Serious deliberations ensued, and detailed plans were even drawn up for an invasion of the Chinese coastline and mobilization of daimyo and samurai across western Japan. Further action was prevented only when news arrived at Nagasaki in December 1646 of the fall of Fuzhou to the Manchus three months earlier.[106]

By early 1646, Zheng Zhilong, faced with crippling shortages, could no longer feed or pay his men to defend the entire province. Compounded by his feeling of alienation at the hands of the Longwu emperor and his civil officials, Zhilong decided to abandon the court. He withdrew his men from the strategic mountain passes separating Fujian from Zhejiang in the north and Jiangxi to the west, and relocated them to guard his maritime enterprise along the littoral. Meanwhile, he entered into talks with the Qing via the mediation of several trusted Quanzhou gentry now collaborating with the Manchus. He presently received an imperial rescript from the Shunzhi emperor granting him the title of King of Three Provinces (*Sansheng wang*), with full authority over Zhejiang, Fujian, and Guangdong. The offer sounded attractive, since it gave him the regional autonomy that he had always sought after but could no longer maintain under the Longwu court. However, as a condition, he had to travel to Beijing for an imperial audience, where the Qing ruler could "hear more of his extraordinary merit and accomplishments."[107] The wily Zhilong

---

[105] Transcripts of these missions and the ensuing deliberations can be found in Hayashi Shunsai, *Ka'i hentai*, vol. I, pp. 11–25.

[106] The most authoritative studies on the requests for Japanese aid from Ming loyalists, including the Zheng family, which occurred in the half century or so between 1645 and 1692, are Ishihara, *Nippon kisshi* and Huang Yuzhai, "Ming Zheng Chenggong deng de kang Qing yu Riben," *Taiwan wenxian* 9.4 (1958). See also the groundbreaking new study by Patrizia Carioti, "The Zheng regime and the Tokugawa *bakufu*: asking for intervention," in Tonio Andrade and Xing Hang (eds.), *Sea rovers, silver, and samurai*.

[107] Sekisai, *Min Shin tōki*.

probably sensed a trap, an attempt to separate him from his power base. As a result, the negotiations dragged on, with Zhilong likely holding out to secure a waiver of the audience.

In the fall of 1646, Manchu troops entered Fujian with minimal resistance and soon captured Fuzhou. The Longwu emperor, who was attempting to create a loyalist resistance force of his own separate from Zhilong, fled for Jiangxi, to the power base of another Ming commander. However, he was chased down in the mountains close to the provincial border and executed on the spot.[108] Zheng Zhilong had ordered members of his clique not to resist the Manchus to demonstrate his sincerity. However, the Qing had grown impatient with the slow progress of the negotiations and decided to turn up the pressure on him. Manchu forces continued their rampage even when they reached his core territories along the coast. They torched his fabulous mansion at Anhai, and humiliated, to the point of suicide, his wife, Tagawa Matsu.[109]

When Zhilong angrily protested at what he saw as a breach of mutual understanding, the Manchu commander immediately called off the attacks and invited him to a banquet to discuss the details of his new position. At this point, the majority of the Zheng clique, led by his brother Hongkui and eldest son Koxinga, came out strongly against the idea of submission. The suspicious character of the Shunzhi emperor's edict, the unruly behavior of the Manchus in Fujian, and the sudden turnaround in the Qing commander's attitude gave cause for grave suspicion as to the sincerity and trustworthiness of the new dynasty. Hongkui and Koxinga got down on their knees and cried bitterly, begging the stubborn patriarch not to attend the banquet. After all, they reasoned, he still possessed formidable military power and a naval fleet of 500 war junks, more than enough to protect his territory and interests.[110]

The members of the clique must have also learned, by then, of the Qing edict of July 1645, drafted by the regent Dorgon, ordering all subjects, on pain of decapitation, to shave their heads and adopt the queue of the Manchu conquerors, as well as their tight-collared riding jackets. Yet, the majority of Han Chinese – elite and commoner alike – prized their loose-flowing robes and, especially, their long hair, which they normally coiled into a bun on the top of their heads. For them, cutting it not only violated Confucian injunctions against harming the bodies given to them by their parents, but also insulted their very manhood, being tantamount to

---

[108] Jiang Risheng, *Taiwan waiji*, p. 94. Some sources say that the Longwu emperor fled the approaching Qing troops on his horse, and was never seen again. See *Minhai jillue, TWWXCK*, 23 (1958), p. 2.

[109] Huang Zongxi, *Cixing shimo*, p. 2.

[110] Zheng Yiju, "Zheng Chenggong zhuan," pp. 4–5.

spiritual castration. More so than the dynastic change itself, Dorgon's draconian order triggered the emergence of a proto-racial ethnic conscious-ness among many Han subjects. Irrespective of class, they took up arms to combat what they perceived to be the desecration of their "civilized" way of life.[111] Zhilong's subordinates, aside from the desire to preserve their political and commercial interests, undoubtedly felt genuine disdain for these "barbarian" invaders, and cringed even more at the thought of undergoing the ultimate humiliation of becoming just like them.

Zhilong fully understood their sentiments, but he also emphasized that with the Qing in control of over two-thirds of China, resistance from only his forces stationed in several resource-deficient coastal bases could never turn the tide in favor of the Ming. Why not take a risk for the chance to become "a hero who understands the times" and obtain a prominent position in the new dynasty? This arrangement even promised to expand the clique's sphere of influence to include all three southeastern coastal provinces. Unmoved, the majority of Zhilong's commanders refused to go along with him.[112]

Equally unfazed, Zhilong kept his appointment and entered the camp of the Manchu commander in Fuzhou. Three days and nights of wild feasting and drinking followed. The Manchus initially showed signs of willingness to accept Zhilong's submission on his own terms and hash out the details of his new official post. However, the Qing general grew suspicious of the sincerity of Zhilong's submission. He had only brought along part of his family and a corps of several hundred African guards; none of the core subordinates in his clique showed up. After much discussion with the civil officials in his camp, the commander decided to capture Zhilong, bring him to Beijing for an imperial audience, and keep him as a hostage in the capital. Without an effective leader, the Manchu general surmised, the Zheng clique would quickly disintegrate into disunited components that the Qing could finish off one at a time. Accordingly, in the middle of the night after the third day of the banquet, the commander suddenly ordered the camp dismantled, and had his men capture Zhilong and disarm his guards. He and his relatives were taken north and placed under effective house arrest.[113]

As Dahpon Ho points out, Zheng Zhilong was the unique product of a frontier zone. Like his counterpart from that other borderland, Nurhaci, Zhilong transcended the manipulation of state actors to forge

---

[111] Wakeman, *Great enterprise*, vol. I, pp. 648–674.
[112] Huang Zongxi, *Cixing shimo*, p. 2; Zheng Yiju, "Zheng Chenggong zhuan," pp. 4–5; Andrade, *Lost colony*, p. 66.
[113] Wong Young-tsu, "Security," pp. 131–132; and Struve, *Southern Ming*, pp. 97–98.

a consolidated enterprise of his own that rationalized his liminal set-tings.[114] He achieved military supremacy along the Fujian and a large part of the southeastern coasts, established maritime East Asian com-mercial dominance, and acquired recognition from the Ming. His des-cendants would combine all the elements of this triple legacy to forge a powerful, expansive quasi-state that increasingly asserted political con-trol over its sphere of economic influence, starting with the realization of their patriarch's unfulfilled designs over Dutch Taiwan.

Yet unlike the Zheng, Nurhaci and his descendants successfully grafted their tribal customs and militarized hierarchy onto the Confucian ortho-doxy espoused by the Ming ruling class to govern a massive, sedentary Chinese empire for almost three centuries. Here, the Qing rulers could refer to a rich history of conquests from both Chinese and Inner Asian unifiers. Zhilong's organization, on the other hand, lacked any vocabulary or successful historical precedent to describe its effort to dominate mar-itime East Asia, which did not involve toppling an established dynastic order in China but somehow coexisting as a distinct entity. Its unclear legal status and inability to free itself from a legitimacy bequeathed by outsiders made it inherently fragile, a fact made all too apparent when it confronted the Qing enterprise in Fujian. For the rest of the organiza-tion's existence, Zhilong's successors would engage in a slow and difficult translation and nativization of the imperial orthodoxy of Chinese dynas-ties to order their maritime realm.

[114] Ho, "Sealords," p. 3.

3 Between trade and legitimacy

> I most pity how difficult it is to fulfill the two obligations of loyalty [to the ruler] and filial piety. Whenever I think of my father's residence, tears flow in the four directions.   Poem by Koxinga, undated.[1]

> This coastal area is what I firmly possess. The profits from the Eastern and Western Oceans are those I create and cultivate … how can I agree, on the contrary, for others to restrict what I sit upon and enjoy?   Letter from Koxinga to Zheng Zhilong, 1653.[2]

The Manchus, whose traditional strength lay in the rapid advancement of their cavalry, lacked the mobility or naval power to control the mountainous and meandering coastline, bays and harbors, and islands along the littoral. As a result, resistance continued within the maritime zone of southeastern China. Nonetheless, the Qing felt confident that it would only be a matter of time before this marginal frontier submitted. After all, the Manchu commander's prediction appeared to have come true; with Zheng Zhilong gone, his followers scattered all over the place. Some members of his clique fled north to the Zhoushan Islands off Zhejiang, where they joined a gentry militia led by Zhang Mingzhen (d. 1656) and Zhang Huangyan (1620–1664). The two men had upheld Zhu Yihai (1618–1662), the imperial prince of Lu, as their ruler. This regime had coexisted uneasily with the Longwu court farther south in a relationship fraught with mutual suspicion and jealousy.[3] Others surrendered to the Qing. However, the majority of the Zheng clique's following remained along the Fujian coast, where they formed resistance groups largely independent of one another. Two of the biggest contingents came under Zhilong's clan relatives Zheng Cai and Zheng Lian (b. 1650). Based on the islands of Xiamen and Jinmen, they nominally recognized the prince of Lu and eventually took him under their protection.[4]

---

[1] "Yanping er wang yiji," in *Zheng Chenggong zhuan*, *TWWXCK*, 67 (1960), p. 129.
[2] Yang Ying, *Congzheng shilu*, p. 43.
[3] For more on the prince of Lu, his role in the anti-Qing resistance, and relations with the Longwu court, see Struve, *Southern Ming*, pp. 108–117.
[4] Struve, *Southern Ming*, p. 110.

During this time, Koxinga, Zhilong's eldest son, was a minor player, only controlling his family's shattered inheritance at Anhai with 300 followers and a handful of ships.[5] Yet the young man emerged, in the course of a few years, to dominate the entire maritime resistance, driven by a schizophrenic combination of intense idealism, thirst for revenge, and ruthless pragmatism that reflected the inherent contradictions of coastal Fujian. Throughout his life, he also faced a subtle but wrenching conflict within his bicultural Sino-Japanese background, especially the prioritization of loyalty to the ruler in Japan as opposed to the equal or greater emphasis on filial obedience in China. The pressure to submit to the Manchus to release his father from captivity, anger at the violent deaths of his mother and the Longwu pretender at the hands of these "barbarians," and the powerful appeal of Ming loyalism all stretched him to the mental breaking point. At the same time, his inner conflict gave him the flexibility to objectify these values and manipulate both the Ming and Qing to provide the best legitimate justification for his goals. He proved to be the right person to transform an enterprise similarly riveted with political, social, and economic contradictions from the "centralized piratical organization" of his father's days into a rational "informal state" that encouraged trade and maritime economic expansion.[6]

Early years

Koxinga was, in his words, "born where the sun rises" at the port of Hirado, Japan, in 1624.[7] With Zhilong absent from the home since he was of a very young age, the boy received a largely Japanese upbringing from his mother, Tagawa Matsu. Originally named Sen, the character for "Forest," he went by the nickname of Fukumatsu, or "Auspicious Pine," as a child. His favorite pastimes included archery and swordplay, typical of boys from samurai families.[8] He also internalized the warrior ethic of *bushidō*, which emphasized the bond of a vassal to his lord above all other ties.[9] Young Fukumatsu's early years in Japan, along with the deep attachment he developed toward his mother, profoundly shaped his personality and behavior. The Italian Dominican Vittorio Riccio, who spent many years in his retinue, saw traits in him that stood out from the "pure Chinese." These included his fairer skin and indirect expression of displeasure or anger through a "feigned and hearty laughter" rather than

---

[5] Chen Bisheng, *Zheng Chenggong yanjiu*, p. 120.
[6] Carioti, "Zhengs' maritime power," p. 29.   [7] Hayashi, *Ka'i hentai*, vol. I, p. 45.
[8] Jiang Risheng, *Taiwan waiji*, p. 39; Ishihara, *Nippon kisshi*, p. 121.
[9] For more on the ideal lord-vassal bond, see Robert Bellah, *Tokugawa religion: the cultural roots of modern Japan* (New York: Free Press, 1985), pp. 70, 93.

straightforward rebukes or threats.[10] He also handled a variety of weapons, including the harquebus and cannon, with great expertise, and had almost perfect aim. Like a model samurai, he valued personal valor and courage, and frequently led the charge into battle, ranking among the first to suffer injury.[11]

In 1630, at the age of six, his life changed dramatically when, at Zhilong's request, he left his sheltered surroundings and sailed for Fujian, an ancestral home to which he felt little attachment, to join a father of whom he had no recollection. In a strange new land among unfamiliar relatives, who often taunted and shunned him for being "different," Zheng Sen badly missed his mother, and frequently gazed eastward at night.[12] He soon learned to respect and fear his father. Zhilong placed high hopes in his eldest son and imposed strict discipline over him. Sen spent his childhood and teenage years at a school in Anhai. In 1643, at nineteen, his father sent him to the prestigious Imperial Academy in Nanjing, the subsidiary capital. Under the tutelage of Qian Qianyi (1582–1664), the most renowned neo-Confucian scholar of the day, Sen internalized the classics of the Chinese tradition and learned to compose eloquent poetry. The commentaries to the *Spring and Autumn Annals*, which emphasized loyalty to the ruler and the clear delineation of boundaries between China and "barbarians," became a favorite text, along with *The Art of War*, a famous handbook of military strategy by Sunzi (c. 544–496 BCE).[13]

In 1645, after the fall of Beijing and Nanjing, he left for Fuzhou, where he had his first imperial audience with the Longwu pretender. Expressing amazement at the young man's remarkable features and lamenting his own lack of an heir, the ruler bestowed upon him the royal surname of Zhu and the formal name of Chenggong, or "Achieving Merit." This act effectively made him crown prince. From then on, Chenggong became widely known as Guoxingye, or its Minnanese pronunciation, Koxinga: Lord of the Imperial Surname. He also received the title of Generalissimo Who Summons and Quells (Zhaotao dajiangjun) and was given command of the elite imperial bodyguard.[14] While there was probably genuine admiration for the young man, the pretender's honors formed part of a broader strategy aimed at courting Zhilong and motivating his clique to support the court. For Koxinga, however, the audience, and the many subsequent opportunities for close interactions with the Longwu emperor

---

[10] Borao-Mateo et al., *Spaniards in Taiwan*, vol. II, pp. 589–590.
[11] Examples of his valor abound in the textual sources. See, for instance, Yang Ying, *Congzheng shilu*, p. 37 and Jiang Risheng, *Taiwan waiji*, pp. 129–130.
[12] Jiang Risheng, *Taiwan waiji*, p. 39.   [13] Huang Zongxi, *Cixing shimo*, p. 1.
[14] Xia Lin, *Haiji jiyao*, *TWWXCK*, 22 (1958), pp. 1–2.

as part of his assigned duties, deeply impressed him and instilled within him genuine loyalty and affection for his ruler.[15]

Historians commonly assume that such feelings exceeded those for Zhilong, to the point that he substituted political loyalty for filial piety.[16] The Longwu emperor, according to one scholar, effectively became Koxinga's surrogate father.[17] Indeed, when it became apparent that Zhilong would abandon the court and defect to the Qing, his son knelt before the pretender and promised, in tears, to "remain steadfast to Your Majesty and return your favor with death!"[18] Later on, in a final attempt to dissuade Zhilong from surrendering, Koxinga reminded him that it was he who taught his son "never to serve a second master."[19]

However, this perspective overlooks Koxinga's often contradictory effort to remain filial to his father's will. While head of the imperial bodyguard, he used his proximity to the Longwu emperor to help Zhilong spy on the ruler, covertly reporting to his father everything the pretender said and did.[20] Koxinga's final conversation with Zhilong also contained a more cynical component. Most of the Ming princes, except for Zhu Yujian, he recognized, were incompetent and "not worth upholding." Koxinga advised Zhilong to sit on the fence in terms of his political loyalties, relying upon his familiarity with the coastal geography and powerful ships for self-preservation. If "Heaven has not yet tired of the Ming," he suggested, "then we can and should uphold it. If not, you can live out your days along the coast in happiness," an obvious euphemism for autonomy or independence.[21] Zhilong, of course, did not listen and ended up a hostage in Beijing. The subsequent need to ensure his safety and secure his release, if fortune permitted one day, meant that Koxinga had to remain engaged with the Qing, and even appease it.

It was not an easy thing to do, especially since the misfortune of his ruler and father was compounded by the rape and suicide of his beloved mother. According to one bizarre Chinese account, after the young Koxinga recovered her body, he cut open her belly and cleansed her intestines "according to barbarian custom."[22] The author of the narrative must have given a confused description of Japanese ritual suicide

---

[15] Chen Bisheng, *Zheng Chenggong yanjiu*, p. 145.

[16] See, for instance, Wills, "Maritime China," pp. 227–228 and Struve, *Southern Ming*, p. 163. Nonetheless, these historians recognize that significant ambiguity existed in Koxinga's preference for ruler over father, since he continued to have strong feelings for Zhilong and grieved at his misfortune.

[17] Croizier, *Chinese nationalism*, pp. 46–47.   [18] Xia Lin, *Haiji jiyao*, p. 2.

[19] Zheng Yiju, "Zheng Chenggong zhuan," p. 5.

[20] Ji Liuqi, *Mingji nanlue*, TWWXCK, 148 (1963), p. 317.

[21] Shen Yun, *Taiwan Zheng shi shimo*, TWWXCK, 15 (1958), p. 11.

[22] Huang Zongxi, *Cixing shimo*, p. 2.

(*seppuku*), which Tagawa could have only inflicted upon herself. Nonetheless, the story highlights the extreme extent of Koxinga's grief and desire for revenge, which became inseparable from more abstract Confucian injunctions against serving another ruler and opposition to the draconian haircutting order. In his words, "no person, wise or stupid, is willing to become a slave with a head that looks like a fly," a reference to the Manchu shaven pate.[23] He thus developed strong personal and ideological deterrents against accommodation with the Qing.

The need to stake out two moral positions – loyalty and filial piety – increasingly at odds with each other plagued Koxinga's conscience for the rest of his life. On the flip side, the conflict proved immensely liberating, since it allowed him to selectively choose the stance most suitable for his interests. Koxinga jealously guarded this freedom and flexibility of action, and refused to bend to any higher authority. He desired only to utilize others, but never agreed to be utilized.[24]

Rise to power

In the wake of the Zheng clique's collapse, Koxinga fled to his family's coastal Anhai base, where he raised the banner of resistance against the Qing. His slogan called for "exterminating my father to repay the country." Yet, ironically, it was Zhilong's lucrative commercial network, which he inherited almost intact, that provided him with ample funds to recruit manpower and construct ships for military and commercial purposes. He also received timely support from two powerful figures in the former Zheng clique: his uncles, Hongkui and Zhiwan. They offered their services as Koxinga's advisors and allies out of sincere respect for Zhilong, and because they saw in the son the capability and potential to carry on their elder brother's legacy. From a modest beginning of 300 followers, Koxinga's movement quickly expanded to several thousand men.[25]

Unlike most of the other warlords along the southeastern coast, he steadfastly held onto the Longwu reign title, and refused to pledge allegiance to the prince of Lu, ostensibly because of the hostility between the two rulers and his continued remembrance of the pretender. More likely, however, he hoped to avoid his father's mistake of having a potent symbol of authority too close by and thus constantly able to interfere with his decisions. In fact, when another imperial prince, Zhu Youlang (1623–1662, r. Yongli, 1646–1662), emerged as a new rallying point for

---

[23] Shen Yun, *Taiwan Zheng shi*, p. 11.   [24] Yang Yang, *Congzheng shilu*, pp. 62–63.
[25] Chen Bisheng, *Zheng Chenggong yanjiu*, p. 120; Xia, *Haiji jiyao*, p. 4; Jiang Risheng, *Taiwan waiji*, p. 115.

Ming loyalists in western Guangdong, far away from Koxinga's main power base, he immediately submitted to the new pretender. Nonetheless, he maintained a loose cooperation with the more numerous adherents of the prince of Lu against the greater enemy: the Manchus.[26]

In 1648, Koxinga and his uncles initiated campaigns against the Qing to recapture Quanzhou and its counties. After gaining some territory and then losing it again, they advanced into Guangdong and attacked Chaozhou, with similar results. At this point, Koxinga realized the need for a more stable base of operations to fight a protracted war against the Manchus. He set his sights upon Xiamen and Jinmen, once Zhilong's headquarters and now under the control of Zheng Lian and Zheng Cai, his clan uncles. Separated from the mainland by a narrow body of water, the islands resembled a massive fortress able to repel any invasion from land.[27]

Hongkui advised Koxinga to act during the fall of 1650, on the occasion of the Mid-Autumn Festival, which celebrated the full moon and signified the reunion of loved ones. As in previous years, they and their soldiers joined those of his relatives at Xiamen to drink wine and enjoy the delicacy of mooncakes. On this festive occasion, however, Koxinga led an inebriated Zheng Lian to a cave amid some rocky hills in the southwestern part of the island. There, his troops secretly lay in wait. They pounced upon Lian and decapitated him on the spot, and quickly disarmed his uncle's men without any struggle. He and Hongkui proceeded to target Cai, forcing him first to flee and then surrender his own troops. Cai, out of shock or despair, fell ill and died shortly afterward. With his greatest clan rivals eliminated or marginalized, Koxinga became recognized as the new Zheng patriarch and Zhilong's rightful successor. In the meantime, his following had grown to some 40,000 soldiers, and he possessed several hundred powerful war junks.[28]

The character of Koxinga's Ming loyalism

Most historians in East Asia and the West characterize Koxinga as a "Ming loyalist." Wong Young-tsu, for instance, believes that his devotion to the cause of dynastic restoration was "fanatical" and free of any selfish motivation, a position that Tonio Andrade largely endorses.[29] Prominent

---

[26] Shen Yun, *Taiwan Zheng shi*, pp. 12–14.

[27] Zheng Yiju, "Zheng Chenggong zhuan," pp. 5–7.

[28] Zheng Yiju, "Zheng Chenggong zhuan," p. 8. The cave where Zheng Lian met his unfortunate end is located today in the Xiamen Botanical Gardens. It is marked by a sign that reads "Spot where Zheng Chenggong slaughtered Zheng Lian."

[29] Wong Young-tsu, "Security," p. 133; Andrade, *Lost colony*, p. 80.

exceptions include Ralph Croizier and Chen Bisheng, who point to convincing evidence of opportunistic behavior contradicting this avowedly determined stance.[30] Lynn Struve and John Wills, on the other hand, take the middle ground, showing how Koxinga managed to "conflate his own interests with those of the Ming, and perform his best for the loyalist cause."[31] This last explanation appears to be the most plausible, but one must take into account what exactly constituted Koxinga's program of restoration, as well as changes over time and in the relative power balance between the loyalist courts and the Qing.

Without doubt, Koxinga idealized a reconstituted Ming, but he wanted, like his father, to enjoy the greatest possible autonomy within it. Thus, while his official title of Generalissimo Who Summons and Quells only entitled him to lead troops on behalf of the dynasty, he and his subordinates referred to himself in private as "feudatory" (fan), a term reserved for imperial vassals who possessed personal armies and fiefdoms. This position would be more autonomous than those of his Qing counterparts, Shang Kexi (1604–1676) and Geng Jimao (d. 1671), who were awarded bases in Guangdong for helping the Manchus pacify southern China. Although these men had a private military staff, they enjoyed only limited privileges in civil affairs.[32] Another inspiration was the Tokugawa bakufu of Japan, where Koxinga spent his childhood. Theoretically a subordinate authority representing the samurai class, it evolved into a parallel central government that eclipsed the largely ceremonial imperial court in Kyoto.[33] However, China, unlike Japan, was too vast for Koxinga alone to completely dominate. His ideal lay between the two poles: an autonomous regional lord with absolute de facto control over the southeastern coastal provinces of Fujian, Zhejiang, and Guangdong in exchange for expelling the Manchus.

Yet, before 1651, Koxinga appeared to have placed genuine sentiments for Ming restoration above his personal interests, even if he fell short of

---

[30] See Chen Bisheng, Zheng Chenggong yanjiu, pp. 235–241; Croizier, Chinese nationalism, pp. 17–27.

[31] Quote from Struve, Southern Ming, p. 156. See also Wills, "Maritime China," p. 226.

[32] Zha Jizuo, Lu chunqiu, TWWXCK, 118 (1961), p. 136. For more on the establishment of the Qing feudatories and their privileges and limitations, see Liu Fengyun, Qing dai Sanfan yanjiu (Beijing: Renmin University Press, 1994), pp. 111–114.

[33] The institution of the bakufu itself draws upon the Chinese historical precedent of a tent government (mufu), which functioned like a large, highly centralized regional authority with control over several provinces, according to Hung Chien-chao, "Taiwan under the Cheng family 1662–1683: sinicization after Dutch rule," unpublished PhD dissertation, Georgetown University (1981), p. 125. Andrade, Lost colony, p. 64 points out, presciently, that Koxinga may have found resonance in his official title, since it sounded similar to that of the Japanese shogun, the barbarian-quelling generalissimo (seii taishōgun).

the Confucian archetype of a selfless minister. He was, after all, a hot-headed youth in his twenties, ready to change the world according to his vision. And the external climate gave much hope to young idealists. The Yongli court received a major boost in 1649 and 1650 when two major Qing commanders defected to its ranks. The pretender further secured the surrender of the bulk of the peasant rebels who had brought down the Ming in 1644, led now by Li Dingguo (1621–1662) and Sun Kewang (d. 1660). This invigorated movement quickly captured almost half of the country and inflicted heavy losses upon the Qing, including the lives of several senior commanders.[34] In 1651, Li Dingguo made it as far as the gates of Guangzhou. From there, he wrote a letter to Koxinga, calling upon him to join forces in a northern expedition to recapture Nanjing and Beijing from the Manchus.[35]

With restoration appearing imminent, Koxinga did not hesitate to mobilize the majority of his forces and lead them into Guangdong to initiate the rendezvous. He left behind a small garrison under Zheng Zhiwan to defend Xiamen. Even before the campaign began, however, he ran into the determined opposition of his left vanguard, Shi Lang, who undoubtedly spoke for a majority of his other subordinates. Xiamen, Shi stressed, was the organization's main base of operations. There, Koxinga, his relatives, and top commanders stored several years' worth of reserves in warehouses in the form of bullion, trading goods, and grain. Many of his officers and men had families, houses, and graves maintained for generations in and around the island. By drawing large numbers of troops away from Xiamen, he left it vulnerable to an enemy attack that could shatter morale and threaten the very survival of his organization. Despite Shi's reasonable objections, Koxinga overruled him and stubbornly continued to push ahead.[36]

True to the worst fears of Shi and other subordinates, Qing soldiers under Ma Degong (d. 1664) took advantage of the absence of his main forces to strike Xiamen. Zheng Zhiwan, assigned to garrison the island, fled without a fight, fearing for the safety of his elder brother, Zhilong, if he resisted. For days, Qing soldiers killed and raped residents, set fire to houses, and plundered the city of nearly all its wealth. Koxinga's wife, Madame Dong (d. 1681), barely escaped with the spirit tablets used to worship his ancestors, which she protected with her bare hands. In the end, Zheng Hongkui came to the rescue, inflicting severe losses upon Ma Degong and surrounding the Qing forces. However, Ma forced Hongkui

---

[34] For a detailed narrative and analysis of these events, see Struve, *Southern Ming*, pp. 148–150.
[35] See Li's letter to Koxinga in Yang Ying, *Congzheng shilu*, pp. 39–41.
[36] Yang Ying, *Congzheng shilu*, p. 14.

to release them after threatening adverse consequences for the Zheng family members who had surrendered to the Qing.[37] Both uncles chose to succumb to enemy blackmail over Koxinga's orders because of their seniority within the lineage and because they possessed independent chains of command.

When news of what transpired reached Koxinga's ranks, his followers wailed loudly and refused to advance any further. With his men on the verge of mutiny, he reluctantly turned them around and sped back to Xiamen, where he convened a meeting of his subordinates. He promptly ordered the execution of Zhiwan and some of his uncle's subordinates for their cowardice, and displayed their severed heads prominently on the city gate. He also took the opportunity to destroy their hierarchy and scatter their soldiers among his own divisions. This public display of mechanic ruthlessness, sparing not even kin, scared Hongkui out of his wits. However, the young leader decided to spare his life, since he had always been kind to Koxinga and taken his side on major issues. Hongkui saw where the wind was blowing and promptly surrendered his men and retired to a stockade on a nearby island, where he lived in seclusion until his death in 1654. Koxinga now had complete, unchallenged control over his clan.[38]

On the flip side, the Xiamen debacle worsened his relationship with Shi Lang, a commander highly valued for his wise leadership and bravery. Because of his accurate prediction of Xiamen's vulnerability, Shi grew increasingly arrogant and often took unilateral action contrary to Koxinga's orders in battles against the Qing. In late 1651, unable to bear his insubordination any longer, Koxinga imprisoned him on a boat with his father and younger brother. Shi, a popular commander, escaped to Qing-held territory with the help of sympathetic subordinates. Upon hearing of his defection, a furious Koxinga responded by putting his accomplices and captive family members to death. This act would earn him the lasting hatred of Shi Lang and ensured that bringing down the Zheng organization became a lifetime goal.[39]

The severe setback of 1651 rapidly drew Koxinga out of the naivety of youth, and made him realize that before launching any restoration campaign on behalf of others, he needed to make sure he had a strong, cohesive organization of his own. He thus withdrew from active involvement in the loyalist cause, and instead worked hard to cultivate a "loyalist mystique" among his followers. In public, he displayed utmost deference to the Yongli pretender, memorializing every action and decision,

---

[37] Zheng Yiju, "Zheng Chenggong zhuan," p. 8; Jiang Risheng, *Taiwan waiji*, pp. 116–117.

[38] Yang Ying, *Congzheng shilu*, p. 18; Zheng Yiju, "Zheng Chenggong zhuan," p. 8; Jiang Risheng, *Taiwan waiji*, pp. 118–119.

[39] Chen Jiexian, *Bu titou yu Liangguo lun* (Taipei: Yuanliu, 2001), p. 149.

kowtowing in front of imperial edicts, and even rejecting "undeserved" ranks and titles.[40] He needed the symbolism to effectively tie together a movement riveted by sharp socioeconomic divisions among classes, elite groups, and dialects.

The core of the organization's talent and leadership consisted of Koxinga's relatives and his father's former subordinates in the Zheng clique. These men of military and mercantile background grew up in Minnan, knew the coastal harbors and inlets, and acquired naval expertise through years at sea and distant lands. Many, like Hong Xu, were Zhilong's pirate associates before joining the Ming.[41] Even though they could possess a high degree of ethnic sentiment and dynastic loyalty, they were amenable to pragmatic compromises with the enemy as long as such a deal could advance their interests. Shi Lang's case best exemplifies this ambiguity.

Among others who joined Koxinga's ranks were prominent former central bureaucrats such as Xu Fuyuan (1599–1665), a prime figure in late Ming intellectual societies. Minnanese gentry, including Li Maochun and Wang Zhongxiao (1593–1666), also sought protection from him. As Koxinga's power grew, he incorporated the Zhejiang resistance movement of Zhang Mingzhen and Zhang Huangyan, who took refuge in Xiamen in 1652 after the entire province fell to the Qing. They brought along their ruler, the prince of Lu, and other illustrious Ming imperial descendants, such as Zhu Shugui (1617–1683), the prince of Ningjing.[42]

On an official level, Koxinga treated these men as honored guests and consulted them on all matters of state. However, significant tensions characterized their relationship. As in the days of Zhilong, these refined elites disdained the merchants and military men who constituted the backbone of the organization. Zhang Mingzhen and Zhang Huangyan, in particular, viewed themselves as Koxinga's equals under a common Ming cause, and jealously maintained an independent chain of command. Regional prejudices compounded the difficulty of cooperation. Koxinga was known to have "detested Zhejiang people" in general. Not surprisingly, frequent disputes erupted between him and the two Zhang, and scuffles occasionally broke out among their men. Some narratives even make the unsubstantiated claim that Zhang Mingzhen's death in 1654 resulted from poisoning by Koxinga.[43]

---

[40] For examples, see Yang Ying, *Congzheng shilu*, pp. 39–40; Jiang Risheng, *Taiwan waiji*, p. 119.

[41] Chen Bisheng, *Zheng Chenggong yanjiu*, pp. 162–164; Xia, *Haiji jiyao*, p. 13.

[42] Zha, *Lu chunqiu*, pp. 65–66.

[43] Shao Tingcai, *Dongnan jishi*, TWWXCK, 96 (1961), pp. 33–34, 128; Yang Ying, *Congzheng shilu*, p. 94.

More ominously for Koxinga, while the two gentry leaders upheld the distant Yongli court in public, they treated the Xiamen-based prince of Lu as their true ruler. Because of his proximity, they saw in him a more potent figurehead to lead the maritime-based resistance. Koxinga, however, feared a repeat of Zheng Zhilong's disastrous relationship with the Longwu court, and did everything possible to ensure that the prince and his Zhejiang allies could never assert their collective will upon the organization. No doubt under heavy pressure, the prince "voluntarily" renounced all his titles in 1652. When an edict from the Yongli emperor reinstated them in 1659, the only time the pretender ever issued a command of substance, Koxinga openly refused to recognize it. Instead, he exiled the prince of Lu to Penghu.[44]

Significant numbers of Qing defectors also acquired prominence in the organization. The most prominent of these include Ma Xin (d. 1662), the Qing military commander of Taizhou, in southern Zhejiang, and the vice-commander of the Zhangzhou Garrison, Liu Guoxuan (1628–1693).[45] Since they came from outside coastal Fujian and did not speak its dialects, the defectors lacked the connections to form strong local power bases and thereby remained entirely dependent upon Koxinga for their positions. They often became some of the organization's most trusted men, even above the Minnanese, and acted as a check on their activities. Both Ma, who hailed from north China, and Liu, a Hakka from Tingzhou, deep in mountainous western Fujian, would rise to the enviable position of second-in-command, the first under Koxinga and the second, Zheng Jing. As if trying to atone for their past affiliation with the Qing, the defectors also tended to be the most idealistic of Zheng commanders, and the most aggressive advocates of Ming restoration. They further brought to the organization valuable strategies and techniques in land-based infantry warfare, which would serve it well in campaigns against the Manchus.

Residents of coastal Fujian formed the grassroots base of Koxinga's organization. They supplied the majority of infantry and sailors for his navy, paid him taxes and surcharges, and rendered labor service. The burdens were numerous and often onerous, forcing many into bankruptcy; some had to sell their wives and children to make ends meet. Destruction to their livelihoods also occurred because of warfare and marauding troops, whether his own men, local rebels, or the Manchus. Some places at the periphery of his control changed hands frequently, causing them to experience repeated rounds of raping, killing, burning, and looting at the hands of transient occupiers. Nonetheless, in many crucial respects, Koxinga's leadership proved far superior to both the

[44] Zha, *Lu chunqiu*, p. 73.   [45] Yang Ying, *Congzheng shilu*, p. 92.

Ming and Qing courts. He promoted the livelihood of coastal Fujianese commoners, based upon fishing, salt production, and, especially, maritime trade. These, in turn, stimulated other opportunities, from cash cropping and artisan crafts to shipbuilding and services. The continental dynasties, on the other hand, severely hampered these activities.[46]

Despite significant tensions and mutual distrust, Koxinga successfully bridged these diverse socioeconomic interests and put them firmly under his leadership. He could now set his sights beyond his twin bases of Xiamen and Jinmen. In a series of brilliant campaigns beginning in 1652, he captured most of the counties in Zhangzhou and Quanzhou, and laid siege, albeit unsuccessfully, to their prefectural cities. He further blockaded Quanzhou harbor, and caused the death of Chen Jin, the governor-general of Fujian and Zhejiang.[47] Meanwhile, Koxinga's navy extended his maritime jurisdiction along a 13,000-kilometer-long coastline, from southern Zhejiang to eastern Guangdong. This zone, consisting of offshore islands and a narrow strip of hinterlands, functioned as key nodes in the shipment of products between the commercial centers of China and overseas ports.

The Qing earlier paid little attention to the southeastern coast because of the more pressing threat posed by the Yongli court. However, Koxinga's remarkable offensive demonstrated to the Qing that the maritime resistance, once believed to have been safely marginalized, had regrouped around an effective leader able to seriously challenge its rule. However, the construction of a navy, the most effective way to combat him, required a heavy commitment of time and money that the resource-poor coastal provinces proved ill-equipped to provide at the time. Moreover, the Shunzhi emperor assumed personal rule in 1651, after Dorgon's death. The young ruler reversed many of the regent's draconian policies toward Han Chinese, and proved more willing to entrust them with positions of responsibility.[48] With the Shunzhi emperor's approval, the Qing authorities decided to invite Koxinga for talks. Even if the two sides could not reach any settlement, the court figured, the negotiations would keep him from fully joining with the main Yongli forces to form a united front across southern China.[49]

In 1653, the Shunzhi emperor unilaterally proclaimed a ceasefire on the southeastern coast. In several edicts addressed to Koxinga, he

[46] Chen Bisheng, *Zheng Chenggong yanjiu*, pp. 161–162.
[47] Struve, *Southern Ming*, pp. 158–159; Xia, *Haiji jiyao*, pp. 9–11.
[48] *Qing Shizu shilu xuanji* (henceforth *Shunzhi shilu*), *TWWXCK*, 158 (1963), p. 105; Wakeman, *Great enterprise*, vol. II, pp. 896–904.
[49] Chen Jiexian, *Bu titou*, pp. 142–143; Wu Zhenglong, *Zheng Chenggong yu Qing zhengfu jian de tanpan* (Taipei: Wenjin, 2000), p. 49, n. 68–69, 62.

acknowledged the policy errors of his uncle Dorgon, and sacked Ma Degong and other officials in Fujian responsible for the surprise attack on Xiamen. He also brought Zheng Zhilong out of captivity, and showered him and his relatives with ranks and titles rarely accorded to subjects of their status. The emperor then placed Zhilong and the Fujian officials in charge of the negotiations, hoping to utilize the lure of the new dynasty's leniency and familial ties to coax this troublesome adversary into submission.[50] Although Koxinga initially complained of being dragged into the talks against his will, he soon agreed to cease hostilities to "display trustworthiness to the Qing Dynasty."[51] Both formal Qing envoys and Zheng Zhilong's bondservants and sons shuttled back and forth between the capital and the Fujian coast several times in each of the subsequent four years to transmit messages from both sides and hold meetings with the organization's representatives.

Many historians in East Asia and the West believe that Koxinga did not treat the negotiations seriously and primarily utilized it as a stalling tactic to build up his resistance movement.[52] There is much truth to this perspective, but as mainland scholar Chen Bisheng and his Taiwanese counterpart, Wu Zhenglong, have shown, Koxinga could very well have thrown in his lot with the Qing given sufficiently attractive terms.[53] A settlement conducted in a manner able to win over his trust would institutionalize his sphere of influence on the southeastern coast without undertaking risky campaigns of restoration on behalf of the Ming. On a personal level, he could ensure the safety – or even the release from hostage – of his father and relatives in Beijing.

From the beginning, however, vastly different understandings of what each side wanted to get out of the negotiations hampered the progress of the talks. The Qing hoped to grant attractive concessions to make Koxinga "feel good about surrendering," while he wanted to discuss the offer on an equal footing and arrive at a mutually acceptable compromise, a subtle yet important difference.[54] In letters and highly charged meetings, the Qing officials and envoys presented their terms as ultimatums, pressuring him to accept or face adverse consequences, with no room to bargain for more favorable terms. Their conduct only deepened his hatred for the Manchus and strengthened his mistrust of their intentions.

---

[50] Yang Ying, *Congzheng shilu*, p. 73.   [51] Chen Jiexian, *Bu titou*, pp. 32–45, 83–84.

[52] See, for instance, Zhuang Jinde, "Zheng-Qing heyi shimo," *Taiwan wenxian* 12.4 (1961): 1, and Wills, "Contingent connections," p. 187. As Struve puts it in *Southern Ming*, p. 160, Koxinga "put on the most cunningly deceptive performance of his career."

[53] Chen Bisheng, *Zheng Chenggong yanjiu*, pp. 142–143 and Wu Zhenglong, *Tanpan*, pp. 180–181.

[54] Quote from Struve, *Southern Ming*, p. 146. See also Yang Ying, *Congzheng shilu*, p. 62.

Not without a sense of vindication, he wrote to Zhilong, asking "since my father has erred in front, how can I follow your footsteps?"[55]

Moreover, Koxinga found the Qing concessions, which acquired full form around 1654, highly unattractive. The court essentially planned to treat him in the same manner as its feudatories in Guangdong, Shang Kexi and Geng Jimao. Koxinga was given jurisdiction over the prefectures of Zhangzhou and Quanzhou in southern Fujian, and Chaozhou and Huizhou in eastern Guangdong. Although he could exercise full control over his troops, all civil officials within his four prefectures required central approval. He could continue to operate his overseas trading network, but had to forward customs duties to Beijing.[56] More unappealing was the Qing order for him and his men to shave their heads as an absolute precondition for these limited concessions. Even if he could overcome his personal hatred of the Manchus and rationalize his submission morally, he still faced potential mutiny from his commanders and soldiers, especially if the command came too suddenly.[57] The benefits that Koxinga could receive from the Qing not only did nothing to enhance his authority, but also cut into his existing privileges.

Nonetheless, Koxinga tried hard to drive home a bargain. He tacitly accepted the offer of the four prefectures and agreed to "adopt the Qing calendar ... if not for the sake of the land and its mortals, then to bend on behalf of my father."[58] However, he refused to alter his hair and clothing or accept limits to his authority. He told the Qing envoys that if they desired peace, then "there are precedents in the Koryŏ (918–1392) and Chosŏn" dynasties of Korea.[59] He hoped to formalize his coastal sphere of influence within the framework of an autonomous vassal kingdom like Korea, which was permitted to maintain their Ming-style robes and long hair after becoming a Qing vassal. At the same time, Koxinga remained open to the idea of adopting Manchu coiffure, but only if he could receive much more attractive concessions than the ones already offered him. For him and his men to "put down their hearts and shave their hair," he demanded complete jurisdiction over the three coastal provinces of Fujian, Zhejiang, and Guangdong, the same offer that the Manchus had once dangled before Zhilong.[60] The Qing court refused to consider any of his demands. The Shunzhi emperor officially cut off the talks at the end

---

[55] Yang Ying, *Congzheng shilu*, p. 59.
[56] Su Junwei, "Qing chao yu Ming-Zheng hezhan hudong celue jianlun qi dui liang'an guanxi de qishi," unpublished MA thesis, National Taiwan University (2008), pp. 172–176.
[57] Yang Ying, *Congzheng shilu*, p. 67.
[58] Yang Ying, *Congzheng shilu*, p. 108; Jiang Risheng, *Taiwan waiji*, p. 163.
[59] Yang Ying, *Congzheng shilu*, p. 48.   [60] Ibid., p. 54.

of 1654, although sporadic exchanges of letters and envoys continued into 1657.

Lynn Struve correctly argues that Koxinga emerged out of the negotiations in a much stronger position than at the beginning; the Qing, on the contrary, "expended a good deal of time and energy only to lose actual ground."[61] Yet, as Chen Bisheng shows with equal insight, Koxinga actually benefited less at the expense of the Qing than the Ming loyalist cause. During the negotiations, he received renewed calls from Li Dingguo to join forces for another northern expedition. In response, Koxinga either engaged in never-ending preparations or sent token troops into eastern Guangdong that lingered for a long time to raid for supplies, only to conveniently "miss" the appointment, citing adverse winds and bad weather. By keeping his best forces unmoved and unused, he allowed the Qing to focus its undivided attention upon the Yongli court.[62] Once the pretender was marginalized and eliminated, the Qing would come back to finish off Koxinga. This strategy of divide and conquer proved quite effective in the long term.

A comfortable ambiguity

Nonetheless, for most of the 1650s, Koxinga found himself in an enviable position. As he told his younger brother, whom Zhilong had dispatched from Beijing in a desperate final attempt to sway him, he "can become a man of Qing if it trusts my words. If not, then I will stay a minister of the Ming."[63] Like a shrewd businessman, Koxinga carefully avoided antagonizing either side so that, in the event one party won, he could receive the greatest possible concessions as "rewards" for his "assistance." He thus devoted the bare minimum of military support possible for Ming restoration to convince the Yongli emperor of his loyalty. Meanwhile, he kept talking with the Qing, ready to accept any arrangement that could overcome his mistrust and ethnic sensitivities, and ensure his father's survival.

While he kept both sides busy, he focused upon building the institutions to strengthen control over his organization. Koxinga divided his troops into seventy-two divisions (zhen), complete with infantry, cavalry, and navy. His commanders had wide latitude in selecting their own men or, if they surrendered from the Qing, could keep their original divisions intact. One of these units consisted of the elite African bodyguards inherited from his father. Fearsome in appearance and armed with Dutch muskets, they were

---

[61] Struve, Southern Ming, p. 161.
[62] Chen Bisheng, Zheng Chenggong yanjiu, pp. 154–156.
[63] Yang Ying, Congzheng shilu, p. 62.

placed under his trusted second-in-command, Ma Xin, who led them into battle dressed in European clothes.[64] When Koxinga's men did not participate in raids or campaigns, he kept them busy with drills; officers and soldiers from inland areas practiced naval skills, while those from the coast learned archery and horseback riding.[65]

Koxinga was quick to recognize accomplishments among his men and lavished them with gifts and honors. He established at Xiamen a Hall for Nourishing Descendants (Yuzhouguan) to provide generous financial support for relatives of deceased officers and a Confucian education for their sons.[66] On the other hand, he practiced a harsh and impersonal discipline that spared not even his closest relatives, as seen vividly in the execution of his own uncle, Zheng Zhiwan. Those found in violation of his commands were decapitated, forced to commit suicide, poisoned, or, for more minor offenses, severely beaten. If lucky, a prominent subordinate could receive a suspended capital sentence, to be abolished if he won a victory in the next battle.[67] Needless to say, Koxinga's discipline kept his men in constant fear and anxiety. It often failed to account for a reasonable degree of human error, and directly triggered quite a number of defections to the enemy. Still, the rules were generally fair and, balanced with the rewards, motivated Koxinga's units to excel in battle, and earned him the lasting gratitude and respect of most of his followers.

Shortages of food and basic provisions remained a perennial problem for him and his soldiers throughout their years on the mainland. It is estimated that, throughout the 1650s, the number of people under Koxinga not engaged in any form of productive activity stood at no less than 300,000. They included officers, soldiers, Ming princes and loyalist gentry, and their families. Only taking into account the military personnel, one town in southern Fujian had to support, on average, 1,500 men.[68] To meet the needs of this massive retinue, Koxinga and his soldiers often resorted to outright plunder, known euphemistically as "taking grain" (quliang), primarily directed at Qing-held territories. From 1649 to 1660 they engaged in at least forty-four forays into prefectures in Fujian, Guangdong, and Zhejiang.[69] To his credit, Koxinga tried his best to temper these abuses,

---

[64] Andrade, *Lost colony*, p. 122.

[65] Huang Dianquan, *Zheng Chenggong shishi yanjiu* (Taipei: Taiwan Commercial Press, 1975), p. 21.

[66] Yang Ying, *Congzheng shilu*, pp. 71, 96–97, 109; Xia, *Haiji jiyao*, p. 14.

[67] Instances of punishments meted out to subordinates abound in Yang Ying's work. See, e.g., *Congzheng shilu*, pp. 38–39, 88–89, 98, 135.

[68] Chen Bisheng, *Zheng Chenggong yanjiu*, p. 165.

[69] Dahpon Ho provides a harrowing description of the atrocities committed by Zheng forces, as well as other contenders for the southeastern coastal region, and brings to life the massive scale of human suffering in "Sealords," pp. 177–197.

ordering his soldiers to target the wealthy first and avoid raping women.[70] However, looting and pillaging towns and villages provided only several months' worth of rations at any one time. He needed a longer term strategy for acquiring food and supplies.

In the areas under his direct control or influence, Koxinga imposed a regular tribute, known as a "primary tax" (*zhenggong*), of grain or bullion upon the residents. They also had to provide additional "donations" (*zhuxiang*) and "voluntary offers" (*leshu*) that were often anything but voluntary to fulfill special requisitions for his troops.[71] The port of Haicheng became a supply depot that concentrated these contributions and forwarded them across the narrow stretch of sea to Xiamen. In general, residents along the southeastern coast paid out staggering sums to the Zheng coffers. Yang Ying shows that for 1654 alone, Zhangzhou prefecture contributed an equivalent of 1,080,000 taels (40,500 kg) of silver, while neighboring Quanzhou coughed up more than 750,000 taels (28,125 kg). To alleviate the onerous exactions, Koxinga ordered some of his troops to open up new land and grow crops for themselves in eastern Guangdong. He further intensified the cultivation of his family fields in the Zhangzhou and Quanzhou area.[72]

After negotiations with the Qing began, Koxinga took advantage of the ensuing ceasefire to expand his territorial possessions and sphere of influence, citing the inability of his barren strongholds to adequately supply his large armies. Because the Qing feared that any strong action could place the promising talks in jeopardy, his men ran into little resistance. At the same time, Koxinga advanced into the mountains to attack and subjugate independent, "neither Qing nor Ming" (*bu Qing bu Ming*) militias that had fortified themselves in stockades to defend against harassment from outside soldiers irrespective of ideological persuasion.[73] Through a skillful combination of bloody military campaigns and deft diplomacy, Koxinga successfully secured a sizable land perimeter around his main bases of Xiamen and Jinmen.

Starting from 1654, he established formal bureaucratic offices to govern his expanding territory. Although he carefully represented them

---

[70] Zhuang Jinde, "Zheng shi junliang wenti de yantao," *Taiwan wenxian* 12.1 (1961): 55, 76; Wu Micha, "Zheng Chenggong zheng Tai zhi beijing: Zheng Shi zhengquan xingge zhi kaocha," *Shiyi* 15 (1978): 33.

[71] Wu Micha, "Zheng Tai beijing," 32; Wong Young-tsu, "Security," p. 132.

[72] Yang Ying, *Congzheng shilu*, pp. 43, 63; Liu Xianting, *Guangyang zaji xuan*, TWWXCK, 219 (1965), p. 32.

[73] *Bu Qing bu Ming* carries the double meaning of "neither clear nor bright," a pun on the unclear political stances of these militias. For a list and brief summary of Koxinga's campaigns upon their stockades and fortresses, see Chen Bisheng, *Zheng Chenggong yanjiu*, pp. 166–170.

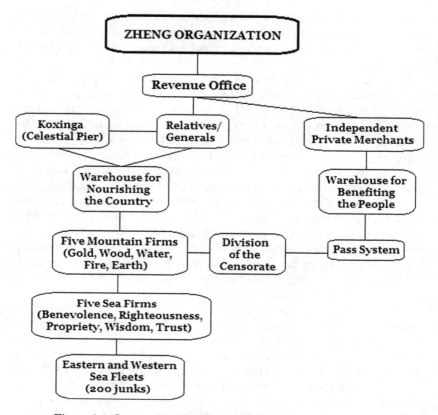

Figure 3.1 Structure of the Zheng commercial enterprise.

as local extensions of the Ming, in reality he redefined positions and created new ones to suit conditions on the southeastern coast. Xiamen, which he renamed Siming (Cherishing the Ming), became his administrative and military headquarters.[74] With the approval of the Yongli emperor, he created the Six Offices (Liuguan): namely, Works, Rites, Punishment, Revenue, Military, and Personnel. Officially a regional branch of the Ming imperial Six Boards (Liubu), it served as a central cabinet for the Zheng organization. He also established a Confucian academy at Xiamen and dispatched promising students to southwestern China to take the civil service examinations at the Yongli court.[75] However, a great part of Koxinga's territorial holdings changed hands

[74] Zheng Yiju, "Zheng Chenggong zhuan," pp. 5–8.   [75] Xia, *Haiji jiyao*, pp. 13–14, 21.

frequently and lacked the stability to move beyond crude military occupation aimed at extracting surpluses for campaigns and defense. As a result, most offices, staffed with exiled Ming gentry and officials, primarily fulfilled empty symbolic roles or offered menial clerical jobs. The few strategic posts, such as Military and Revenue, were led exclusively by relatives or his core following of armed mercantile elites.[76]

The institutions of overseas commerce

The Revenue Office was the most important of the Six Offices in the 1650s. As shown in Figure 3.1, it oversaw several institutions that collectively monopolized all major economic activity within Zheng-held areas. The Warehouse for Nourishing the Country (Yuguo ku) served as a central repository of capital for Koxinga and his subordinates.[77] Its interest-bearing silver deposits funded the operations of Koxinga's own company, known as Celestial Pier (Tianhuang), which bought and sold goods directly on his behalf through ten subsidiary firms (hang).[78] The Five Mountain Firms (Shan wushang), each of them named after one of the elements of gold, wood, water, fire, and earth, operated deep in Qing territory, procuring silk, porcelain, and other luxuries and ensuring their timely delivery to Xiamen.[79] They also served as marketing centers for foreign goods. Disguised as ordinary storefronts, the firms had its main headquarters in Hangzhou, where the chief manager, Zeng Dinglao, was stationed. Under him were four assistant managers, each in charge of a branch office. Three of them were located in Suzhou and Nanjing, major commercial centers in the heart of the Yangzi River Delta and strategically sited near rural production bases. Another operated in Beijing, right under the nose of the Qing court.[80]

The firms played an additional role as collection points for intelligence on Qing campaign plans and troop movements, and provided shelter for spies, often the same long-distance traders responsible for transporting goods to and from the Zheng camp. Buddhist monks also became crucial eyes and ears for the organization on account of their shaven pates and reputation as itinerant wanderers. The spies carried with them a flag and bronze tally plated with gold as tokens of connection to the Zheng.[81] Zeng

---

[76] Struve, *Southern Ming*, p. 180.   [77] Yang Ying, *Congzheng shilu*, p. 111.
[78] Historiographical Institute, *Tō tsūji*, vol. I, pp. 180–181.
[79] *Zheng shi shiliao xubian*, TWWXCK, 168 (1963), p. 911.
[80] Liu Xianting, *Guangyang zaji*, p. 32.
[81] Taiwan Research Institute of Xiamen University and China Number One Archives (eds.), *Zheng Chenggong dang'an shiliao xuanji* (Fuzhou: Fujian People's Publishing House, 1985), pp. 408–409.

Ruyun, the son of Zeng Dinglao, befriended lower Qing gentry degree holders, often through bribery, in the hopes of securing their collusion and protection for these covert activities.[82] Koxinga's Five Mountain Firms were connected to a broader, overlapping Ming loyalist espionage network centered upon the Yangzi River Delta. This circuit, maintained by Wei Geng (1614–1662), a Zhejiang-based poet and recluse, and his associate Qian Zuanzeng (d. 1662), kept the various anti-Qing resistance movements in contact with one another and with the Yongli court in southwestern China.[83] Another important point of contact was Zheng Zhilong in Beijing. Under the guise of formal negotiations, the father's envoys opened a private channel of communication that supplied Koxinga with everything from paternal advice on how to run the organization to the latest news direct from the capital.[84]

These covert passageways facilitated the exchange of information and goods with Xiamen, headquarters of the Five Sea Firms (Hai wushang) (see Figure 3.1). Named after the cardinal Confucian principles of benevolence, righteousness, propriety, wisdom, and trust, they handled the shipment of products to and from overseas destinations.[85] Other than Xiamen, the firms had branches along the entire southeastern littoral, most prominently the main overseas trading port of Anhai and the Zhoushan archipelago in Zhejiang. The Five Sea Firms also supervised the construction of new vessels for commercial and military use. The small port of Shacheng, lying on the border of Fujian and Zhejiang, provided convenient access to excellent shipbuilding timber in the mountainous forests of the interior.[86] A merchant named Lin Xingke specialized in floating logs downstream along the Min River to the coast, where he hired carpenters to process some of them into wooden planks bound for Xiamen, and hid the others at covert warehouses placed strategically in several villages. A typical vessel was a massive affair, measuring 8 *zhang* (30.7 m) in length and 2 *zhang* (7.7 m) in width, with a depth of around 2 *zhang*. It had twenty-five compartments for living space and the storage of cargo.[87]

[82] *Shiliao xubian*, p. 911.

[83] He Lingxiu, *Wukuzhai Qing shi conggao* (Beijing: Xueyuan, 2004), pp. 281–294.

[84] One Qing official complained that Koxinga's information gathering was so good that he "knew of Beijing's orders for troop movements before he did." Quoted in Wills, "Contingent connections," p. 190.

[85] Taiwan Research Institute of Xiamen University and China Number One Archives (eds.), *Kangxi tongyi Taiwan dang'an shiliao xuanji* (Fuzhou: Fujian People's Publishing House, 1983), p. 82.

[86] Chen Xiyu, *Zhongguo fanchuan yu haiwai maoyi* (Xiamen: Xiamen University Press, 1991), p. 92.

[87] *Zheng shi shiliao sanbian*, TWWXCK, 175 (1963), pp. 216–217.

Each firm operated twelve junks, adding up to a total of sixty vessels that were, in turn, subdivided into the Eastern Ocean Fleet and the Western Ocean Fleet. The fleets organized along a Ming-era geographic division of the world's oceans into the Eastern and Western Oceans, with the line between them running roughly through the island of Borneo.[88] They differed primarily in the focus of their trade and composition of their cargo. The junks of the Eastern Ocean Fleet specialized in trading with Japan, Dutch Taiwan, and the Philippines, while the Western Ocean Fleet focused on Siam, Batavia, Cambodia, and other Southeast Asian ports. Since most of the ships followed a triangular route, they often included stops in each other's jurisdictions on their return journeys. Due to dependence upon the prevailing monsoon and currents in a given season, it took about a year to complete a roundtrip journey, with significant layover in different ports. Although rarer, direct travel among ports in one ocean also occurred.[89] To defend against predation on the seas, junks were heavily armed with cannons and often traveled in groups of four or five.[90]

Koxinga's relatives and subordinates enjoyed privileged access to his firms. Chen Yonghua (1634–1680), a classmate and close advisor of his son Zheng Jing, earned several thousand taels of silver per year simply from engaging in occasional trade.[91] Others started subsidiary firms, complete with their private fleets of junks. Examples included the Xuyuan firm, owned by Hong Xu, who headed the Revenue Office until his transfer to the Military Office in 1657, and the Dongli firm of Zheng Tai, Koxinga's clan brother and Hong's successor.[92] Overseas trade provided for Zheng officials a stock option outside of regular stipends, giving them a strong material incentive to remain loyal to the organization.

A corps of agents known as official merchants (*guanshang*) worked under Koxinga and his subordinates in a labor arrangement that differed from the formal contractual employment found in the Dutch East India Company. Official merchants fall under two distinct categories. The first were recruited from the adopted sons of Zheng relatives and commanders, Zheng Tai being the most prominent and successful example. The other, and more common category, involved a relationship based upon

---

[88] See Zhang Xie, *Dongxiyang kao* (Beijing: Zhonghua Bookstore, 1981), pp. 170–171.
[89] Nie Dening, "Ming-Qing zhi ji Zheng shi jituan hai shang maoyi de zuzhi yu guanli," in Xiamen University History Department (ed.), *Zheng Chenggong yanjiu lunwen xuan* (Fuzhou: Fujian People's Publishing House, 1982), p. 336.
[90] Sŏng, *Chŏngmi chŏnshinrok*, pp. 277_003d-004b.
[91] Yu Yonghe, *Pihai jiyou, TWWXCK*, 44 (1959), p. 51.
[92] *Shiliao xubian*, p. 456; Xia, *Haiji jiyao*, p. 48; Historiographical Institute, *Tō tsūji*, vol. I, p. 181.

long-term debt obligations, whereby independent merchants borrowed capital or ships to trade on behalf of Zheng leaders. After paying back the accrued interest to Koxinga or his subordinates at a discount and splitting the profit, they acquired a new principal for investment.[93] Zeng Dinglao and Lin Xingke fit into this group. Agents were organized into an employment hierarchy based upon their expertise, experience, and amount of capital at hand to make investments. The reciprocal nature of relations allowed the Zheng to entrust official merchants of both categories with large sums of money across vast distances.

Indeed, this labor system functioned effectively far out at sea. The crew of a typical Zheng junk, to take the example of one vessel that washed onto the shores of Cheju in 1667, consisted of around a hundred official merchants, primarily men in their thirties, along with their wives and children. A head merchant acted as spokesman and liaison at foreign ports, while the manager supervised affairs onboard during the journey. The entourage also included a keeper of the accounts, an expert on the compass and ocean currents, and a religious specialist who burnt incense to the sea goddess for good luck. Others handled more technical matters, such as repairing the junk, cooking meals, and operating the sails.[94] The crewmembers observed strict distinctions. When Korean officials threw a feast in their honor, only the head merchant and managers occupied guest seats at the table. The rest had to sit outside the entrance to the building, or, in the case of the lowliest operators of the ship, on the steps and in the middle of the garden.[95]

The revenues from Koxinga's business provided capital for future investments and financed his campaigns against the Manchus. To prevent opportunities for embezzlement and abuse, the Division of the Censorate (Chayan si) conducted regular audits (Figure 3.1). The censors, whose traditional duty in Ming and Qing bureaucracies was to expose the wrongdoings of officials before the emperor, assumed a role here akin to corporate watchdogs. They checked the principal and interest of deposits in the Warehouse for Nourishing the Country against the income and expenditures of the Five Mountain and Sea Firms, and reported discrepancies.[96]

Besides his and his subordinates' agents, Koxinga welcomed unaffiliated private merchants to participate in his network. They ranged from

---

[93] The borrowing cost, equivalent to 1.3% per month or 15.6% per annum in 1655, appears to have been a great bargain, below the market norm of 1.5% per month charged by major pawn shops. See Han Zhenhua, "Zheng Chenggong maoyi, pp. 172–173.

[94] Sŏng, *Chŏngmi chŏnshinrok*, pp. 277_003d-004b. See also Zhang Xie, *Dongxiyang kao*, pp. 171–172.

[95] Sŏng, *Chŏngmi chŏnshinrok*, pp. 277_003d-004b.

[96] Yang Ying, *Congzheng shilu*, pp. 111–112.

small traders to gentry families employing their own adopted sons. As in Zhilong's days, anyone could travel and trade overseas as long as they purchased a permit (*paixiang*) issued in Koxinga's name, depending upon the size of the vessel and distance of the destination.[97] They further had access to capital from the Warehouse for Benefiting the People (*Limin ku*), a Xiamen-based bank that specialized in private lending. This was an adaptation from the system of Ming preparedness granaries that loaned out grain at interest to the destitute in times of need.[98]

The system also had enough flexibility to ensure that the lines of division among different categories of merchants participating in the Zheng organization's business network could overlap with minimal conflict of interest. Koxinga often consigned his Celestial Pier goods onboard the Dongli vessels of his clan brother Tai on voyages to Japan.[99] Likewise, private traders hired cargo space from the Zheng agents, traveled with them, or even rented entire ships directly from the Five Sea Firms.[100] Official merchants, too, could conduct their private business on the side, with many becoming fabulously wealthy in their own right.

The large Chinese – primarily Minnanese – diaspora in Japan and Southeast Asia epitomizes the multiplicity and interpenetration of these roles. Their numbers included not only merchants, but also Ming loyalist refugees, a strange mix of ideological purity and hard economic reality that mirrored the complex societal composition of coastal Fujian. Their sheer diversity meant that they differed from one another in their relationship to the organization. Some participated as independent traders, while others served as agents for him and his subordinates. A select number of overseas Chinese, on account of their wealth, influence in their communities, or close personal relationship with local rulers, became Koxinga's official representatives in the area, with responsibility for purchasing goods, selling permits, and supervising his trade.[101] These men occupied a Janus-faced role, maintaining an often precarious co-allegiance to both Koxinga and local rulers or European authorities, while serving as conduits of communication between them.

The Zheng organization's commercial institutions employed Chinese bureaucratic practices to rationalize the customary networks of patronage and kinship native to the southeastern coast into a formal hierarchy that reported directly to the Revenue Office. This skillful adaptation allowed

[97] Ōta Nanpo, *Ichiwa ichigen*, 2 vols. (Tokyo: Yoshikawa kōbunkan, 1928), vol. II, p. 733.
[98] Brook, *Confusions*, pp. 70–71.   [99] Historiographical Institute, *Tō tsūji*, vol. I, p. 179.
[100] *Shiliao xubian*, pp. 589–590.
[101] Jian Huiying, "Ming-Zheng shiqi Taiwan zhi haiwai maoyi ji qi zhuanyun diwei zhi yanjiu," unpublished MA thesis, National Taipei University (2000), p. 57.

Koxinga to achieve a greater level of official control over foreign trade than any of the Ming maritime restrictions in the past. His system fused a large segment of Chinese, whether living deep within Qing territory or in Japan and Southeast Asia, into a unified economic bloc. This immense influence inevitably became politicized over time. At the most basic level, Koxinga's permit entitled the bearer and crew to armed escorts from his powerful navy, dispatched by the Five Sea Firms. Those without one risked having their junks plundered at sea by hostile powers like the Dutch. Something similar would happen if Koxinga's ships caught them, in addition to severe fines and punishments for themselves and their family members in China.[102] Moreover, the use of an agent to issue licenses and collect fees at overseas ports automatically entailed responsibility for a mobile group of traders across a theoretically unlimited area. The Zheng trading network thus increasingly acquired the characteristics of a maritime state. All it needed was the resolve and ability to actualize its potential.

Despite Koxinga's maritime dominance, a sizable number of ships continued to sail without its permits, primarily to ports in Southeast Asia. The semi-autonomous Qing feudatories, Shang Kexi and Geng Jimao, exploited their geographical advantage to outfit their own mercantile fleets from their base in Guangzhou. Merchants from Macao, whether Portuguese, Macanese, or Chinese, also competed with the organization, especially in the Malay Peninsula and Indonesian archipelago, Portugal's former sphere of influence.[103] The remainder consisted of small, independent merchants, mostly from ports in northern China, far away from the Zheng sphere of influence.[104]

Tracing the intra-East Asian triangle

During the 1650s and early 1660s the Zheng organization engaged in a fierce economic and geopolitical competition with the Dutch East India Company over control of the lucrative intra-East Asian trade. As with the VOC, Japan constituted the mainstay of Koxinga's business. The Japanese market became even more attractive after 1655, when the *bakufu* abolished the five-decade-old silk allotment guild and introduced direct procurement for all Japanese merchants able to pay. This system, known as *aitai shōbai*, gave both the Dutch and Zheng a free hand to set

---

[102] Zheng Ruiming, "Taiwan Ming-Zheng yu Dongnanya zhi maoyi guanxi chutan: Fazhan Dongnanya maoyi zhi dongji, shiwu ji waishang zhi qianlai," *Guoli Taiwan shifan daxue lishixue bao* 14 (1986), 24.
[103] Cheng (Zheng), *War, trade and piracy*, pp. 169, 172.   [104] *Shiliao xubian*, p. 647.

much higher sale prices, since they had practically no rivals but each other, in contrast to the large number of Japanese buyers.[105]

An average of fifty Chinese ships visited Nagasaki each year from 1650 to 1662. Nearly all of them either directly belonged to Koxinga and his subordinates or purchased his passes. Besides the main cargo of raw silk, Zheng junks carried gold and processed textiles, porcelain, medicine, and books from the mainland coast. Tonkin, in northern Vietnam, and its rival in the center and south of the country, Quảng Nam, became alternate sources of silk and gold. These cheaper varieties appealed to a segment of lower elites and wealthy commoners in Japan.[106] Other products from Southeast Asia, especially animal hides, found a ready market at Nagasaki.

The total value of Koxinga's exports to Japan amounted to an annual average of 1,563,259 taels (58,622.2 kg) worth of silver. Silver constituted some 70 percent of the return shipment. Others included knives and swords, armor, muskets, and cannons for use in campaigns against the Qing on the mainland coast. Tar and resin formed essential ingredients in the construction of naval junks. Copper went to forge Koxinga's weapons and "cast Yongli-era coins" that circulated in the areas under his control.[107] The same selection of items found their way on a smaller scale into Tonkin and Quảng Nam to fund their longstanding civil war. Since Japanese exports were mostly consumed as currency or in warfare during this period, they held less intrinsic commercial value. In sum, the Japan trade generated for Koxinga at least 2,350,386 taels (88,139.4 kg) in revenues in a given year, netting a profit of 1,513,093 taels (56,740.9 kg) for a rate of return of 181.1 percent.[108]

In contrast, the Dutch East India Company lacked reliable sources of Chinese silk, which generated the highest premiums on account of their superior quality. The Zheng family strictly controlled access to the luxury, only agreeing to sell at more expensive rates via Taiwan. The Dutch tried all they could to get around the monopoly. They made persistent but failed attempts to acquire another base off the Chinese coast. They also experimented in exports from Tonkin. In return, they formed an alliance with its ruler, Trịnh Tráng (1577–1654, r. 1623–1654), and provided weapons to assist his campaigns against Quảng Nam. However, the quality of Tonkin silk proved too variable to generate a high value-added demand in Japan. When all seemed hopeless, the Dutch

[105] Nakamura, *Nagasaki bōekishi*, pp. 267–268.
[106] Hoáng, *Silk for silver*, pp. 98–99; Li Tana, *Nguyễn Cochinchina: southern Vietnam in the seventeenth and eighteenth centuries* (Ithaca, NY: SEAP Publications, 1998), pp. 80–81.
[107] Jiang Risheng, *Taiwan waiji*, pp. 105, 190; *Shiliao xubian*, p. 325.
[108] See Appendix 3.2 for the methodology behind the revenues and profit margins.

discovered, to their great fortune and delight, white silk from their Bengal factory.[109] After 1655, Bengali silk sold well at Nagasaki, although it could never outpace the Chinese variety so long as sufficient supplies of the latter could be obtained.[110] Despite this success, the mean of 7.2 Dutch ships calling at port per year exported 708,564 taels (26,571.2 kg) worth of goods during this period, less than half of their rivals.[111]

Dutch Taiwan and Manila were the two other main destinations in the Eastern Ocean. Through their relations with the Indian Ocean and New World, these European colonies connected parts of the western Pacific to a broader global world system. Zheng junks carried massive cargoes of gold from the mainland coast to Taiwan. The VOC relied upon the metal to procure Indian silk and cloth bound for Nagasaki.[112] Manila offered a subsidiary market for Chinese goods free of Dutch competition. Luxuries such as silk and porcelain found ready demand among Spanish elites in the Philippines and across the Pacific, in the New World. Shiploads of American silver traveled the other way.[113] Compared to the previous decade, however, bilateral trade took a hit because of depression in Spain's worldwide possessions and the dynastic transition in China.[114] In sum, the global linkages afforded by Taiwan and Manila remained overshadowed by the denser intra-East Asian framework during the 1650s.

If not repatriated back to China, most of the silver surplus generated from the Japan trade, and, secondarily, Taiwan and Manila, bought into markets across the Western and Eastern Oceans. Ports in Siam, Cambodia, Vietnam, insular Southeast Asia, the Philippines, and Taiwan offered a largely similar mix of consumer goods. Zheng and Dutch merchants fought to secure big-ticket items, such as sugar, pepper and other spices, and deerskins. More exotic luxuries, including sappan-wood, ivory, and rhinoceros horns, either served as ingredients in medicine or fulfilled the conspicuous consumption of Chinese and Japanese elites. Zheng vessels also loaded abundant primary resources, including rice and timber for shipbuilding, on their return journeys to alleviate shortages and feed and supply Koxinga's soldiers back home.[115] The Zheng dispatched sixteen to twenty vessels to the Western Ocean alone

---

[109] Wills, *Pepper, guns, and parleys*, pp. 24–25.
[110] Nara, "Zeelandia, the factory in the Far Eastern trading network of the VOC," pp. 172–173.
[111] See Appendix 3.2.   [112] Cheng (Zheng), *War, trade and piracy*, pp. 179–180.
[113] Borao-Mateo et al., *Spaniards in Taiwan*, vol. II, p. 582.
[114] Atwell, "General crisis," pp. 669–670. See also Table 2.5 in Appendix 3.2.
[115] Jian, "Ming-Zheng haiwai maoyi," p. 44; J. de Hullu (ed.), *Dagh-register gehouden int Casteel Batavia vant passerende daer ter plaetse als over geheel Nederlandts-India* (henceforth *Batavia dagregisters*), 31 vols. (The Hague: Martinus Nijhoff, 1904), 1656–1657, pp. 37–38.

in a typical year. Revenues, consisting of imports into the Western Ocean and exports to the China coast, equaled 1,724,960 taels (64,686 kg). According to an incomplete estimate, profits stood at 356,960 taels (13,386 kg) worth of silver.[116]

Adding just the comparatively better-documented Western Ocean and Japanese figures, and ignoring the substantial trade that Koxinga maintained with the Eastern Ocean destinations of Taiwan and Manila, yields 4,075,346 taels (152,825.4 kg). This sum serves as a rough estimate of the total commercial revenues realized by the Zheng organization from 1650 to 1662. To put it in today's terms, the Zheng took in some 91 million in 2014 US dollars every year. Gross profits, or the raw difference between sale and purchase prices, were at least 1,870,053 taels (70,126.9 kg).

In comparison, the more meticulously documented revenues of the Dutch East India Company, based upon all products exchanged within the China Seas and Indian Ocean, and sent from the Cape of Good Hope to the Netherlands, equaled 8,546,867 guilders (112,458.8 kg), less than three-fourths of the Zheng figures. Gross profits amount to 6,014,955 guilders (79,144 kg), barely ahead of its Chinese competitors. The lead achieved here primarily emanates from incomplete information on the part of the Zheng. In fact, if one looks solely at average annual income generated from VOC trade and colonial revenues in Asia, a more direct comparison, the total of 4,114,123 guilders (54,133 kg) trails Koxinga and his adherents.[117] Undoubtedly, the Zheng organization reigned supreme in the intra-East Asian exchange during this period.

Maritime horizons

What the Dutch could not achieve through fair competition, they tried to obtain through coercion. The company put enormous pressure upon its trading partners to exclude the Zheng, or at least deprive them of any privileges it itself held in local markets. On a few occasions, it resorted to outright seizures of Zheng vessels and the confiscation of their cargoes. The imposing and technologically sophisticated Dutch broadside ships proved to be formidable adversaries on the high seas.[118] Like his father, Zhilong, Koxinga could still defeat the Dutch through unusual methods, but this option best suited a war involving the full-scale mobilization of military resources. Moreover, from the standpoint of Sunzi's *Art of War*, Koxinga's favorite reading material, he should only choose armed conflict

---

[116] See Appendix 3.2.   [117] See Table 2.6 in Appendix 3.2.
[118] Andrade, *Lost colony*, pp. 13–15.

as a measure of last resort.[119] Another source of inspiration was certainly Tokugawa Japan, whose complex web of laws successfully curbed the VOC's tendency to get its own way in the country through violent means.[120] Examples, both past and present, thus taught him the value of diplomacy and alliances as effective alternatives to violence in advancing his interests while neutralizing Dutch attempts at sabotage.

Soon after Koxinga achieved dominance in the family, he introduced a framework for international relations adapted from the China-centered tributary system. He positioned his organization at the center of a smaller, more intricate hierarchy of partners that incorporated maritime states and elites – particularly those of Japan – that were denied participation in the original Ming order. This arrangement allowed Koxinga to forge ties based upon status parity, characterized by the mutual "dispatch of embassies according to a calendar of diplomatic ritual, cordial encounters, and equivalent treatment of these foreign rulers through regulation and practice."[121] The Ming, as the Celestial Dynasty above all other kingdoms, could never lower itself to accept such an arrangement. However, the Zheng could view a relationship based upon rough equality as completely legitimate, since all remained subordinate, in theory, to the Yongli pretender. Within Koxinga's framework, vassalage represented an insult meant to humiliate hostile states, often as an initial step toward actual territorial conquest and direct administration.

Japan. In 1651, as soon as he achieved supremacy on the southeastern Chinese coast, Koxinga dispatched an envoy to Nagasaki with a letter congratulating the new shogun, Ietsuna (b. 1637, r. 1651–1680). Greatly pleased, the ruler agreed to forge an alliance with the Zheng organization. For the *bakufu*, close ties with Koxinga, who led the biggest segment of Chinese merchants in maritime East Asia, ensured that it could interact with them as a unified bloc under a reliable partner knowledgeable of Japanese practices. He could ensure their compliance with its regulations and serve as an effective counterweight to the Dutch. Support of Koxinga also accorded well with genuine pro-Ming sentiments prevalent among most Japanese at the time. After the Manchu entry into China, the *bakufu* still favored "only those Chinese merchants under anti-[Qing] auspices" to trade at Nagasaki, and provided a haven for Ming refugees.[122]

However, the exact nature of the relationship between Koxinga and the *bakufu* remained ambiguous, and perhaps purposefully so. Chinese narratives claim that Ietsuna agreed to a fictive uncle-nephew protocol

---

[119] Ibid., p. 175.   [120] Clulow, *Company and Shogun*, pp. 201–202.
[121] Kenneth R. Robinson, "Centering the king of Chosŏn: aspects of Korean maritime diplomacy, 1392–1592," *Journal of Asian Studies* 59.1 (2000): 110.
[122] Toby, *State and diplomacy*, pp. 138–139.

(*shengli*) based upon status parity, with Koxinga as the more junior member.[123] However, this interpretation appeared to be only that of Koxinga. In subsequent years, he sent regular embassies bearing letters and gifts alongside his trading vessels. However, they never visited Edo, nor, according to available sources, did the *bakufu* ever dispatch envoys to his bases along the Chinese coast.

While Japanese accounts are silent on the *bakufu*'s view, its actions toward him and his half-brother Shichizaemon appeared to treat them more as its own vassals charged with supervision over a stateless foreign community. Indeed, the brothers were Japanese subjects by default because of their birth to a samurai mother. Yet their lowly position in the domestic hierarchy as foot soldiers (*ashigaru*) meant that they could only deal with the *bakufu* as subordinates of the Nagasaki magistrates, usually of the standard-bearer (*hatamoto*) rank.[124] Thus, the relationship that took shape between the Zheng organization and Japan was neither entirely foreign nor domestic but had the qualities of both. As one Zheng official later put it, "the ties between us are like those of one family" and "the subjects of Japan are like our subjects."[125] This ambiguity gave Koxinga a free hand on the China-Japan trade route, to the great benefit of himself and his network, other Chinese merchants, and the authorities at Edo and Nagasaki.

Koxinga formed a highly collegial relationship with all levels of the Nagasaki hierarchy through two of the most important figures in his organization. Shichizaemon, based in Nagasaki, served as head agent and ambassador at the port. His residence in the Motohakatachō district hosted visiting Zheng traders and doubled as a guildhall and silk exchange, where Chinese and Japanese merchants socialized and made deals.[126] It also became a community center that regulated the affairs of the large population of long-term Chinese residents.

Through Shichizaemon, Koxinga continued his father's cordial relations with the two *bakufu*-appointed magistrates and shogunal deputy at Nagasaki. The organization, in fact, stored its trading passes at their offices. Private merchants could pick up the permits upon entering port by paying Shichizaemon and his subsidiary agents and securing a written proof of purchase. These permits had to be renewed annually, and

[123] Jiang Risheng, *Taiwan waiji*, p. 123. However, this fictive kinship by no means constituted a fixed hierarchy, since death and succession on either side could change the ritual order of the relationship.

[124] W. G. Beasley, *The Japanese experience: a short history of Japan* (Berkeley, CA: University of California Press, 2000), p. 155.

[125] Hayashi Shunsai, *Ka'i hentai*, vol. I, p. 73.

[126] Ehara Uji, *Nagasaki mushimegane*, NBS, 1.5 (1973), p. 44.

their proceeds forwarded to Xiamen. Koxinga made only ten new ones available each year to ensure a dominant cut of the business for himself and his subordinates.[127] The magistrates assisted in enforcing payment. In 1653, when the ship owner Wang Yunsheng arrived at Nagasaki with an expired permit from ten years ago, they ordered the coastal garrison forces to detain him, confiscated the goods on his vessel, and handed him over to Zheng agents. Only through Shichizaemon's entreaties did Koxinga forgive this transgression.[128] Others without Wang's luck faced bankruptcy and the organization's harsh punishments after returning to China.

With Shichizaemon's assistance, Koxinga also brought all cases of predation on his vessels, primarily undertaken by his VOC competitors, before the Nagasaki magistrates for adjudication. In one landmark case in June 1657, Dutch ships plundered the Japan-bound junk of a Zheng agent named Chen Zhenguan near Johor, on the tip of the Malay Peninsula. The Dutch took the crew captive and placed the men on several ships that sailed for Taiwan. However, a severe storm blew one of the vessels, the *Urk*, off course, causing it to run aground in the shallow waters off Kyushu. The Chinese made a daring, successful escape to shore. On August 23, they arrived at Nagasaki and went straight to the magistrates' office to file a petition to Edo. Two months later, the *bakufu* ruled in their favor, ordering the VOC to compensate their losses and warning it to desist from future predation on junks headed to Japan or face permanent expulsion. In a subsequent 1661 ruling, the *bakufu* further ordered the Dutch to compensate Chen by paying him more than 20,000 taels of silver in damages.[129] This and other decisions effectively brought Koxinga under the protection of Japanese domestic law, which he could brandish to neutralize Dutch violence anywhere in maritime East Asia. The *bakufu* could also use its protection of his interests to extend its own influence thousands of kilometers beyond Japan's own shores.[130]

The other official in charge of the Japan trade was Koxinga's elder clan brother, Zheng Tai, who, after 1657, controlled the finances of the organization at Xiamen as Revenue Officer. A frequent visitor to Nagasaki as a young man, he utilized his acumen and charming

---

[127] Ōta, *Ichiwa ichigen*, vol. II, p. 732.

[128] This incident exposes an agency problem between the brothers. Shichizaemon may have been taking bribes from individual merchants in exchange for turning a blind eye to their trading pass requirement. See Ōta, *Ichiwa ichigen*, vol. II, p. 733.

[129] Ehara, *Nagasaki mushimegane*, pp. 45–46; Tanabe Mokei, *Nagasaki jitsuroku taisei*, *NBS*, 1.2 (1973), p. 217.

[130] For a detailed analysis of the *Urk* incident and its broader ramifications, see Cheng (Zheng), *War, trade and piracy*, p. 186 and Clulow, *Company and Shogun*, pp. 171–202.

personality to expand Zhilong's established web of mercantile connections.[131] Tai's main point of contact was the semi-autonomous municipal corporation, headed by a group of hereditary city elders (*toshiyori*). Although nominally ranked under the centrally appointed authorities, they often enjoyed more local influence than the *bakufu* officials.[132]

These relationships formed the basis for a joint Zheng-Japanese administration over Chinese merchants and residents at Nagasaki. One way Koxinga asserted his will was through the Chinese Interpreters' Office (*Tō tsūji kaisho*). A semiofficial organ overseen by the city elders, it communicated *bakufu* policies and pronouncements to the Chinese community, and gathered news and intelligence on China and other foreign countries. Its interpreters were drawn from long-term residents in the community, and adopted Japanese names when they entered its service.[133] Many of them became close friends with Zheng Tai. He complemented this popularity with rich bribes and gifts, making them powerful lobbyists for the Zheng family in front of the city elders and magistrates.[134] The interpreters further allowed him to store silver on behalf of Koxinga and himself, which they marked under separate accounts, to serve as emergency funds and working capital. By 1662, he had deposited 300,000 taels at the office.[135]

Koxinga and his representatives also cultivated ties with prominent exiled Ming loyalists, viewing them as surrogate gentry able to keep the other Chinese residents in line and forge valuable contacts with Japanese elites and officials outside of the Zheng's immediate circle. Among them were the renowned Confucian scholar Zhu Shunshui (1600–1682), Li Feng, a former military governor, and Lin Huanguan, leader of a loyalist militia. Koxinga and, later, Zheng Jing, issued them complimentary permits at the beginning of each year for participation in the lucrative maritime trade.[136] In addition, the organization maintained cordial ties with Yinyuan (Ingen, 1592–1673), the highly esteemed head abbot of Huangbo Temple in northeastern Fujian and transmitter of the Huangbo (Ōbaku) sect of Chan (Zen) Buddhism to Japan. In 1654, when the monk

---

[131] Yang Ying, *Congzheng shilu*, pp. 88, 111; Hayashi Shunsai, *Ka'i hentai*, vol. I, p. 46; and Borao-Mateo et al., *Spaniards in Taiwan*, vol. II, p. 618.

[132] For a detailed breakdown and analysis of the structure of local government at Nagasaki, see Charles Ralph Boxer, *Dutch merchants and mariners in Asia, 1602–1795* (London: Variorum Reprints, 1988), pp. 146–149.

[133] Patrizia Carioti provides an excellent description of the Chinese Interpreters' Office and its main functions in "Asking for intervention."

[134] For one instance of such gift-giving, see Hayashi Shunsai, *Ka'i hentai*, vol. I, p. 253.

[135] Hayashi Shunsai, *Ka'i hentai*, vol. I, p. 49; Historiographical Institute, *Tō tsūji*, vol. I, pp. 92, 180.

[136] Sŏng, *Chŏngmi chŏnshinrok*, pp. 277_011b–012a.

and twenty disciples set sail from China at the invitation of the Kōfukuji temple in Nagasaki, Koxinga dispatched soldiers to travel alongside them on land and used his own ships to escort them to their destination.[137]

Because of the special relationship with Japan, the *bakufu*'s maritime prohibitions naturally did not apply to the Zheng. In fact, the majority of non-silver items on the return cargo of Zheng ships consisted of weapons and strategic materials whose export abroad was forbidden. Like his father, Koxinga additionally sought Japanese manpower to augment his forces. In 1647, before he had fully consolidated his position on the Chinese coast, he sent a mission to Nagasaki asking for "tens of thousands of warriors."[138] His appeal never received a reply. It marked the first of a total of three petitions made by Koxinga on the matter.[139] Yet requests made directly to Edo apparently only occurred when the organization encountered major crises or challenges requiring a massive mobilization of troops that only the *bakufu* could coordinate.

More commonly, during most of the 1650s, Koxinga attempted to recruit smaller numbers of Japanese soldiers at a time, but on a regular basis through less formal channels. For this task, he secured the assistance of the Nagasaki-based Zhu Shunshui, whose neo-Confucian scholarship and ardent Ming loyalism earned him significant respect and influence among elite circles within the country. One of Koxinga's surviving letters to Zhu specifically instructed him to request "troops of any size from the daimyo of Japan."[140] Main targets of persuasion included Mito, the domain northeast of Edo, and Satsuma. Their lords ranked among the most fervent proponents for intervention when Zheng Zhilong appealed for aid in 1646.[141] Zhu did not restrict his focus to Japan; he also embarked on an epic journey through Southeast Asia, home to a large population of Japanese diaspora unable to return home once the Tokugawa ban took effect.[142]

The effect of these efforts remains poorly understood. However, eye-witnesses from a 1649 Ryukyu mission and later authors of Nagasaki local

---

[137] Tanabe, *Nagasaki jitsuroku*, p. 255.   [138] Hayashi Shunsai, *Ka'i hentai*, vol. I, p. 29.

[139] Patrizia Carioti, "Asking for intervention" and Huang Yuzhai, "Zheng yu Riben" believe that although the *bakufu* seriously considered Koxinga's appeals, it ultimately rejected them, but avoided an official response in order to preserve flexibility of action. Nonetheless, a close examination of the primary sources yields fresh evidence that, while still not entirely conclusive, complicates the excellent work of Huang Yuzhai and Carioti and bolsters the claim of Ishihara, *Nippon kisshi*, pp. 57–60, that many samurai from Japan actually settled in China and joined Koxinga's ranks.

[140] The full text of the letter is found in Ishihara, *Nippon kisshi*, p. 54.

[141] Shao, *Dongnan jishi*, pp. 97, 125.

[142] For more on Zhu's requests for troops and journeys in Japan and Southeast Asia, see Zhu Zhiyu, *Zhu Shunshui ji* (*The Collections of Zhu Shunshui*) (Taipei: Hanjing, 2004) and Xu Xingqing (ed.), *Xinding Zhu Shunshui ji buyi* (*Newly Compiled Additions to the Collections of Zhu Shunshui*) (Taipei: Taiwan University Press Center, 2004).

gazetteers described entire expatriate Japanese communities on islands off the Fujian coast. They preserved the customs of their homeland, wearing kimonos and placing pine and bamboo decorations at their doorsteps to celebrate the New Year.[143] These communities could well have been present since before the enactment of the maritime prohibitions. Nonetheless, they probably saw an influx from Southeast Asia, thanks to Zhu Shunshui's recruitment drive. In Vietnam and Siam, Japanese diaspora are documented to have taken up service with the Dutch East India Company. It is not inconceivable that they would similarly provide their martial and mercantile expertise to the Zheng.[144]

Apparently, Japanese also went in large numbers to the Chinese coast directly from Japan. In fact, as one shipwrecked Zheng merchant recalled before Korean authorities in 1667, Koxinga "had been borrowing troops from Japan for a long time."[145] Zhu may have picked up individual warriors from domains across the country, most likely from among the large number of unemployed samurai (rōnin) made redundant with the coming of peace and maritime restrictions. Indeed, things went well enough for Koxinga to confidently boast of the imminent arrival of "troops from foreign countries like Japan and Cambodia to aid the cause of righteousness," as he remarked in a 1653 letter to his imprisoned father, Zhilong.[146]

Once in China, Japanese from both Japan and Southeast Asia formed the core of a special samurai division known as "iron men" (tieren), inherited from Zhilong's time. Chinese likely made up a majority of the 5,000–8,000 soldiers, but the Japanese possessed and disseminated crucial skills, from battlefield tactics to the handling of weapons. Heavy armor decorated with intricate motifs covered the bodies of the men, leaving only small holes for the eyes and mouth. During battle, each unit of the division, marked by a flag bearing a distinct animal, specialized in one weapon. They performed capably in campaigns against the Manchus, striking fear into the enemy's hearts with their terrifying and exotic appearance as much as their actual power.[147] In terms of both composition and division of labor, the iron men marked the final

---

[143] Hayashi Shunsai, Ka'i hentai, vol. I, p. 32; Nishikawa Joken, Nagasaki yawasō (Nagasaki: Nagasaki Municipal Government, 1926), pp. 42–43.

[144] For a study of the Japanese diaspora, especially after the bakufu's maritime prohibitions, refer to William D. Wray, "The seventeenth-century Japanese diaspora: questions of boundary and policy," in Ina Baghdiantz McCabe, Gelina Harlaftis, and Ioanna Pepelasis Minoglou (eds.), Diaspora entrepreneurial networks: four centuries of history (New York: Berg, 2005).

[145] Sŏng, Chŏngmi chŏnshinrok, pp. 277_022a-022b.

[146] Yang Ying, Congzheng shilu, p. 43.

[147] Ji Liuqi, Ming ji nanlue, pp. 331–332 and Jiang Risheng, Taiwan waiji, p. 170.

evolution and institutionalization of the *wokou* bands that once ravaged the Chinese coastline.

Many of these mercenaries concurrently participated in the China-Japan trade. For instance, a Zheng junk from Macao bound for Nagasaki that happened to run aground onto Cheju Island in 1670 contained a crew donning both Chinese and Japanese hairstyles and outfits.[148] This fact proves particularly surprising, because vessels arriving at Nagasaki were subject to rigorous searches for goods and people found in violation of the prohibitions.[149] It is thus hard to imagine that Japanese subjects could enter or leave the port without at least tacit approval from the *bakufu*. As Carioti correctly argues, the *bakufu* wished to avoid a nationwide mobilization required for a risky continental venture, especially one involving direct confrontation with the powerful Manchu cavalry. At the same time, leaving the initiative to individual daimyo could strengthen these regional lords at the expense of the Tokugawa hegemony.[150] For this reason, the *bakufu* left Koxinga's appeal unanswered in 1647. On the other hand, a China plagued by warfare and chaos provided a much-needed safety valve to direct unorganized and rootless elements of society away from their discontent toward the *bakufu*.[151]

Vietnam. Despite the foundational importance of Japan, smooth relations with other rulers ensured Koxinga access to crucial subsidiary linkages within the intra-East Asian structure. In 1654, he signed treaties with both of the rival contenders for the Lê dynasty of Vietnam. Trịnh Tráng, the lord of Tonkin and the real power behind the kings in Hanoi, granted Koxinga the privilege of sending four junks per year to procure locally produced silk. This agreement gave Koxinga the added benefit of undercutting the business of the already troubled Dutch factory.[152] Meanwhile, the powerful warlord Nguyễn Phúc Tần (1620–1687, r. 1648–1687) of Quảng Nam also welcomed Zheng traders to fund his war against the VOC-Tonkin alliance. As a result, Zheng junks became the dominant presence at the free port of Hội An.[153]

---

[148] Wu Han (ed.), *Chaoxian Li chao shilu zhong de Zhongguo shiliao* (*Historical Documents on China found within the Chosŏn Yi Dynasty Veritable Records*), 12 vols. (Beijing: Zhonghua Bookstore, 1980), vol. IX, p. 3968.

[149] Laver, *Sakoku edicts*, pp. 70–71.   [150] Carioti, "Asking for intervention."

[151] Conrad Totman, *Early modern Japan* (Berkeley, CA: University of California Press, 1995), pp. 126–128.

[152] Willem Phillippus Coolhaas (ed.), *Generale missiven van gouverneurs-generaal en raden aan Heren XVII der Verenigde Oostindische Compagnie*, 11 vols. (The Hague: Martinus Nijhoff, 1960), vol. II, p. 778; Hoáng, *Silk for silver*, pp. 98–99.

[153] Li Tana, *Nguyễn Cochinchina*, pp. 80–81.

Siam. Siam was the biggest and most important emporium in the Western Ocean. In 1644, King Prasat Tong (1600–1656, r. 1630–1656) had signed a treaty with the Dutch granting them exclusive purchasing rights in cowhides, pepper, and other strategic commodities. In 1652, he also became a Qing vassal and paid tribute at Guangzhou.[154] However, he grew incensed at the Dutch for not assisting him during a rebellion within his vassal states and became dissatisfied with the limited nature of official trade with the Qing. Accordingly, he dispatched an envoy to Xiamen in 1653 to initiate ties with Koxinga. Without doubt, the Zheng organization was primarily responsible for the subsequent increase in junks sailing from China to the port of Ayutthaya, from six in 1653 to a peak of twenty-one in 1659. Bilateral relations underwent a further boost in 1656, when, through the mediation of Koxinga's official merchants, the ruler reestablished trading links with Japan after numerous failed attempts on his own. Commercial ties with the Tokugawa *bakufu* had been severed since 1630, when Prasat Tong usurped the throne and torched the Japanese settlement in Ayutthaya in retaliation for supporting his rival.[155]

Koxinga's ties to the large diaspora community in Siam proved additionally beneficial for his business. The king employed Chinese merchants as agents of his royal monopoly on the kingdom's foreign commerce. Besides navigating Prasat Tong's ships and collecting customs duties, they became trusted advisors and assumed major positions at court.[156] Many highly placed traders purchased licenses from Koxinga and assumed double identities as official merchants of him and his subordinates.[157] Due to this interpenetration of roles, the Siamese king, like Japan, protected Zheng vessels with his laws and ordered the VOC to desist from preying on them. At the same time, he bent other laws, turning a blind eye when Zheng merchants purchased goods at any quantity they chose in blatant disregard of company privileges. Prasat Tong's successor, Narai (1633–1688, r. 1657–1688), continued the favorable policies in his early years.[158]

Spanish Philippines. Since the peace agreement at Westphalia between Spain and the Netherlands in 1648 had removed the legal basis for VOC predation on shipping to Manila, Koxinga could send junks to the Philippines without fear of retribution. He interacted with the Spanish

---

[154] Sarasin Viraphol, *Tribute and profit: Sino-Siamese trade, 1652–1853* (Cambridge, MA: Council on East Asian Studies, Harvard University, 1977), pp. 11–12.

[155] Cheng (Zheng), *War, trade and piracy*, pp. 162, 187.

[156] Zheng Ruiming, "Ming-Zheng yu Dongnanya," pp. 75–76; Viraphol, *Tribute and profit*, pp. 19–22.

[157] Jian, "Ming-Zheng haiwai maoyi," pp. 42–43.

[158] Cheng (Zheng), *War, trade and piracy*, p. 200.

authorities through the approximately 8,000 Chinese residents of Manila, known as Sangleyes, who lived in the Parián, a segregated district outside the city walls, and formed a majority of the urban population. However, ties remained tense, as bilateral trade hit rock bottom during the 1650s. Disputes flared when the New World galleons consistently failed to show up between 1651 and 1653, and again in 1655. Shortages of silver hit Manila, causing Koxinga's traders to suffer tremendous losses. He also complained bitterly about the abuse and extortion suffered by his merchants at the hands of unscrupulous and corrupt Spanish customs officials. The ill-feeling would pave the way for a full-scale embargo on the Manila trade in 1655.[159]

The VOC. Although the Zheng organization and the VOC were fierce competitors, the two sides worked hard during the earlier part of the 1650s to promote friendly ties and seek out areas of common interest on the basis of equality. Koxinga fully engaged the company, from Batavia to its dependencies and factories. His ships often visited the company headquarters to purchase pepper and other spices. He exchanged polite, routine letters and presents with Governor-General Carel Renierszoon (b. 1604, r. 1650–1653) and his successor, Joan Maetsuyker (1606, r. 1653–1678). Other important contacts included members of the Council of the Indies and the influential Pan Mingyan (Bingan, d. 1663), headman of the Chinese community.[160] On its part, the VOC authorized its factories to issue passes to select Zheng agents to guarantee their safe passage.[161] In 1654, in a further sign of goodwill, it dispatched a physician, Christiaen Beyer, to reside at Xiamen to personally attend to Koxinga's needs.[162]

When crises did occur, the two sides worked hard to minimize the damage. On August 23, 1653, two Dutch ships assisting the forces of Tonkin against its Quảng Nam enemies seized a junk from Hội An that carried Koxinga's permit. When the news reached him, Koxinga wrote an angry letter demanding a compensation of three times the value of the junk's cargo. On June 29, 1654, Governor-General Reniers responded with a partial repayment and additional presents to him of cloth and pepper, which appeared to have mollified him.[163]

---

[159] Ibid., p. 170.
[160] Cheng Shaogang (trans. and annot.), *Helan ren zai Fuermosha* (Taipei: Linking, 2000), p. 511.
[161] Cheng (Zheng), *War, trade and piracy*, p. 186.
[162] Johannes Huber, "Relations between Cheng Ch'eng-kung and the Netherlands East India Company in the 1650s," in Leonard Blussé (ed.), *Around and about Formosa: essays in honor of Professor Ts'ao Yung-ho* (Taipei: Ts'ao Yung-ho Foundation for Culture and Education, 2003), pp. 225–226.
[163] Ibid., pp. 220–221, 228–229.

The colony of Taiwan, on Koxinga's doorstep, became a focal point for cooperation. Koxinga maintained frequent correspondence with the governors, the Formosa Council, and ten Chinese headmen whom the Dutch had selected from among prominent merchants and ship owners to supervise the routine affairs of its majority Chinese immigrant population.[164] Many of them had handled the island's trade since the days of Zheng Zhilong, and continued to serve Koxinga as his agents in the lively commercial exchange with the mainland coast. The Dutch granted the headmen and select large merchants exclusive legal rights to purchase deerskins from aboriginal tribes and lucrative tax farms on an emerging sugar monoculture.[165] Through simultaneous allegiance to Koxinga and the company, they acquired spectacular wealth and gradually took on characteristics of a local bourgeoisie enjoying a high degree of self-rule.[166]

Koxinga continued to enforce his father's residual rights over Taiwan, including the taxation of fishermen and property. Most of these extraterritorial claims remained unknown and hence unrecognized by the VOC authorities, who imposed their own charges in a double taxation scenario. Nonetheless, some of his activities eventually came to light. In 1651, VOC authorities discovered one of his ships levying duties on fishing vessels off the coast of Wankan, his father's former base. When the Dutch requested him to desist in the future, he claimed that he had inherited the right to do so directly from Zhilong and threatened to seek compensation from the anglers' relatives in China if hindered in his collection efforts. This act would effectively kill the fishing industry, from which the VOC also drew handsome revenues. Because of Koxinga's angry outbursts, the company often kept quiet and let him have his way for the sake of maintaining cordial relations.[167] However, the company viewed his extraterritorial exactions as a severe affront to its own sovereignty over Taiwan. The colonial authorities feared, correctly as it turned out, that Koxinga could utilize these privileges as a foundation to expand his political control over the entire island at the expense of the VOC.

The Zheng organization, which flourished amid dynastic transition, diverged significantly from the Dutch East India Company, born out of the rise of the Netherlands as a world power. The company operated, no matter how loosely, according to an official charter outlining a wide range of responsibilities and privileges. On the other hand, while Koxinga's

---

[164] Andrade, *Taiwan became Chinese*, ch. 10.
[165] Yamawaki Teijirō, "The great trading merchants, Cocksinja and his son," *Acta Asiatica: Bulletin of the Institute of Eastern Culture* 30 (1976): 110.
[166] Zheng (Cheng), *Taiwan shehui*, pp. 306–308.
[167] Blussé et al., *Zeelandia dagregisters* (1996), Part III: 1648–1655, pp. 205, 219.

official title of Generalissimo Who Summons and Quells only granted him limited power to command troops on behalf of the Ming, he could overstep his prescribed bounds with impunity because of his distance from the Yongli court. As a result, the Zheng organization appears to lack the rational, clearly defined institutional structure of the Dutch East India Company. Cheng Wei-chung contrasts the sound legal protections granted by the Dutch to Chinese immigrants on Taiwan with the arbitrary exactions and corrupt nepotism of Zheng family members and officials.[168] Others argue that Koxinga's business relied primarily upon irregular "trade to a shifting set of constantly besieged mainland ports," while his widely fluctuating profits aimed solely at "obtaining sustenance for his military" to fight the Manchus at the expense of civil administration.[169]

These observations are true to a certain extent, but they only capture the initial snapshot of a longer process of consolidation. By the middle of the 1650s, Koxinga had established a rudimentary bureaucracy and framework of international relations adapted from the Ming. He further utilized the imperial system to formalize the complex patronage-based trading structure of southern Fujian into an official hierarchy that gave militarists and merchants a larger role in administration. These institutional innovations, primarily in the economic realm, allowed him to compete successfully with the VOC in the intra-East Asian luxury exchange. In fact, they often proved more effective than the Dutch in advancing mercantile interests and promoting capital generation. His organization thus contained traces of the international trading corporation, carrier, and credit institution – some of the hallmarks of "modernity" – combined into one.

---

[168] Zheng (Cheng), *Taiwan shehui*, pp. 190–272.
[169] Pomeranz, *Great divergence*, p. 204; Struve, *Southern Ming*, p. 180.

4 Brave new world

Even at this time, there are no wise ministers within to rectify their ruler ... outside, there are arrogant generals whose armies have no discipline ... they have become self-satisfied at their accomplishments and form factions, to the point of causing heroes to lose hope and the hearts of the people to crumble. How can we hope for a restoration in the future?   Koxinga to eunuch envoy from the Yongli court, 1655.[1]

Taiwan is close to Penghu, therefore this land must also be under the government of China. ... The residents of both shores [Tayouan and Provintia], being Chinese, have occupied and cultivated these lands for ages.   Koxinga's proclamation to the Dutch garrison of Fort Provintia, 1661.[2]

Koxinga's organization grew rapidly within the interstices of the conflict between the Ming loyalist movement and the Qing. However, the tide gradually turned in favor of the Manchus starting from the middle of 1655. That year, their troops drove Li Dingguo into the remote southwest province of Guizhou, joining the Yongli emperor who had preceded him in retreat. A nasty power struggle soon developed between Li and Sun Kewang that aggravated factional politics within the court and fueled open internecine warfare. At the end of 1657, the imperial pretender fled again, this time to Yunnan, and toward increasing marginalization. A bitter and revengeful Sun surrendered to the Qing. The Shunzhi emperor now stood ready to launch a massive final offensive into Guizhou from the central-southern provinces of Huguang and Guangxi.[3] The Yongli court's rapid descent into defeat meant that the Qing would soon redirect all its armies and resources against Koxinga on the southeastern coast.

Meanwhile, because of incessant disorder accompanying the dynastic transition and the onset of another economic depression at the end of the 1650s, China began to undergo a gradual transformation from a producer

---

[1] Jiang Risheng, *Taiwan waiji*, p. 145.
[2] Blussé et al., *Zeelandia dagregisters* (2000), Part IV: 1655–1662, p. 352.
[3] Struve, *Southern Ming*, pp. 149–154, 167–169.

of coveted luxury goods to an importer and processor of raw materials.[4] Chinese supply sources declined in relative importance, while the emergence of the Indian subcontinent as a global manufacturer underlay the successful Dutch efforts to find an alternative source of raw silk. On the other hand, Southeast Asia, especially Taiwan and the Philippines, became increasingly attractive on account of its natural resource wealth and ready accessibility to products from outside of maritime East Asia. Here, one can detect the haphazard beginnings of a loosening of economic exchange within the East Asian world-region and the tighter integration of its components into a global world system. Under these circumstances, Koxinga fought stubbornly to preserve his existing privileges on the mainland. Yet he had the foresight and flexibility to convert his economic influence in Taiwan and the Philippines into a creeping political authority that set them up for outright military seizures by his forces.

New crises, new horizons

As the Shunzhi emperor grew increasingly confident of victory over the Yongli pretender, he found it less necessary to keep the peace with Koxinga or negotiate an amicable settlement with him. In 1655, the ruler issued a final ultimatum to him and dispatched the princeling Jidu (1633–1660), along with 30,000 elite soldiers from the Manchu Eight Banners, to the Fujian coast to cower him into submission.[5] Koxinga, incensed at the Qing court's attempt to intimidate him, once again adamantly rejected its terms. Jidu's troops responded with an all-out offensive on Xiamen and Jinmen in April 1656. Despite inflicting a crushing defeat on the invaders, Koxinga had to abandon his defensive perimeter of Zhangzhou and Quanzhou after razing their main cities to the ground and applying a scorched-earth policy to the surrounding countryside to slow down their advance. The family's main port of Anhai was abandoned and destroyed, and commercial operations moved to Xiamen. Earlier in the year, Qing armies elsewhere had routed his men in eastern Guangdong and retook Zhoushan after all its defenders perished in battle.[6]

In this new climate of belligerence, Zheng Zhilong's value as a bargaining chip for the Qing to secure Koxinga's submission decreased, and he was placed in prison under the convenient pretext of collusion with the

---

[4] von Glahn, *Fountain of fortune*, p. 207.
[5] Su, "Qing yu Ming-Zheng," p. 155; Struve, *Southern Ming*, p. 166.
[6] Yang Ying, *Congzheng shilu*, p. 91; Su, "Qing yu Ming-Zheng," p. 157; Struve, *Southern Ming*, p. 181.

enemy. In public, Koxinga appeared entirely unmoved by this news and ignored the earnest, last-ditch written appeals of Zhilong and the tearful entreaties of his personal envoys and relatives to submit. His father, he proclaimed, had only himself to blame for "plunging into the tiger's den" of his own accord. Yet, away from the public eye, Koxinga's subordinates often saw him getting up in the middle of the night to cry bitterly as he faced north.[7]

On top of the military reversals and personal misfortune came devastating news in July that Huang Wu (d. 1674), a commander entrusted with defending the crucial supply depot of Haicheng, turned himself and the city over to the Qing. Huang soon regretted his decision and requested to rejoin Koxinga's ranks. He claimed that his new masters treated him with suspicion and deprived him of personal command over his soldiers. However, Koxinga, devastated at having lost years of reserves of grain, equipment, and trading goods stored at the town, rejected his request.[8] Driven by revenge, Huang, together with Shi Lang and other defectors, divulged to the Qing court every secret that they knew about the Zheng organization and called for stringent measures to cut its access to food and product sources, thereby starving it into disintegration. On August 6, the Shunzhi emperor acted upon their advice and issued a ban on all private maritime trade and travel. His edict vowed to prevent even a "single piece of wood from entering the sea."[9] The authorities also began to hunt down agents of Koxinga's Five Mountain Firms, break his covert spy rings, and seize merchants caught transporting goods to areas under his control.[10]

The ban itself proved ineffective, as merchants in Qing-held territories continued to openly smuggle goods to Koxinga's agents.[11] However, Lynn Struve and others correctly note that the measure signaled "the first steps in what became, over several years' time, an increasingly successful ... policy of cutting off contact between people on the [mainland] and [Zheng's] men."[12] Indeed, the disruption to his supply lines and Five Mountain Firms meant that silver entering the southeastern coast from abroad could no longer smoothly flow into the broader mainland economy, especially the highly commercialized Yangzi River Delta. Monetary deflation ensued, contributing to a depression that caused the production of silk and other luxuries in the region to dwindle.[13]

[7] Yang Ying, *Congzheng shilu*, p. 107; Xia, *Haiji jiyao*, p. 19.
[8] Yang Ying, *Congzheng shilu*, pp. 116–117.   [9] *Shiliao xubian*, p. 501.
[10] For one example, see *Shiliao xubian*, pp. 526–532.
[11] Wong Young-tsu, "Security," pp. 143–144; Ura Ren'ichi and Lai Yongxiang (trans.), "Qing chu Qianjieling kao," *Taiwan wenxian* 6.4 (1955): 113.
[12] Quote from Struve, *Southern Ming*, p. 181. See also Wong Young-tsu, "Security," p. 144.
[13] von Glahn, *Fountain of fortune*, p. 214.

The decreasing window of opportunity on the mainland struck the first blow to the intra-East Asian trade centered upon the exchange of Chinese silk for Japanese silver. In the short term, however, the higher risk of acquiring fewer goods with huge demand overseas allowed Koxinga to widen his profit margins.[14]

During this time, a trading circuit primarily involving the sale of Indian textiles and Southeast Asian primary resources to China and Japan for gold and copper began to take shape. Southeast Asia, located at the intersection of the Indian Ocean and China Seas, additionally acquired immense strategic value as a meeting ground and transit point for these products. Accordingly, Koxinga increased his involvement in its ports over the 1650s. His merchants formed new relationships with Muslim traders from Bengal and the Coromandel Coast at Ayutthaya, where they purchased Indian silk and cotton goods with Japanese silver and Chinese gold. These textiles were in high demand in Japan and most Southeast Asian destinations. On certain occasions, the Muslim merchants even traveled on board Zheng junks to Nagasaki.[15]

Koxinga and his affiliated merchants further sought cheaper substitutes for Indian textiles within the intra-East Asian trading structure. Demand from them and the VOC stimulated the transformation of China and Japan into secondary cotton producers within the emerging system. A coarse, processed cloth known as *cangan* sold well in Taiwan and the Philippines, fetching on average 300,000 taels (11,250 kg) in revenues per year. It met the demand of the impoverished native population of the islands themselves and also in Spain's American colonies.[16]

As the trading structure underwent a fundamental shift, the scope of cooperation between the Zheng organization and the VOC narrowed while competition intensified. The Dutch stranglehold over crucial sectors of the resource-rich Southeast Asian kingdoms and principalities, and their dominance over spices, made it difficult for Zheng ships to profitably conduct trade in the region, especially at Batavia. Tensions escalated when Koxinga formed private pacts with the native rulers of VOC dependencies on the Malay Peninsula and Indonesian archipelago to procure pepper at more favorable rates. The Dutch reacted rudely and violently to this incursion upon one of their most lucrative businesses. In 1655, company vessels seized 400 piculs (23,880 kg) of pepper from a

---

[14] Hayashi Akira, *Tsūkō ichiran*, vol. 4 (1912), 325–328 shows that the value of Koxinga's exports into Japan remained at a consistent level both before and after the Qing enacted the maritime ban.

[15] Cheng (Zheng), *War, trade and piracy*, p. 188.

[16] Cheng (Zheng), *War, trade and piracy*, pp. 188–189. For more on *cangan*, see Chen Guodong, *Taiwan shanhai*, pp. 451–478.

junk that formed part of Koxinga's fleet trading with Melaka and Palembang. In a letter dated June 17, Governor-General Maetsuycker explained to him that the sultans had prior agreements to sell exclusively to the company, and requested him to confine future procurement to Batavia.[17]

Meanwhile, Koxinga's new ties with Muslim merchants at Siam made possible direct linkages to the Indian Ocean and decreased the desirability of sending gold via Dutch Taiwan. Instead, he acquired a new appreciation for how natural resource exports had greatly enriched the island and its Chinese headmen. He Tingbin (Pinqua), his father's former connection, became the colony's most influential man, for he "handled the greatest volume of trade and possessed the most land."[18] A continued influx of Chinese immigrants transformed Provintia, on the main island facing Casteel Zeelandia across the Tai Bay, into a bustling commercial quarter filled with shops and residences. In fact, their numbers grew so large that, in 1653, an additional fort, named after the town, was built to deter rebellion.[19] Koxinga would cast an increasingly covetous glance at this prosperous colony next door in conjunction with developments on the mainland.

Koxinga's grand strategy

Sometime in 1655, when it became evident that talks with the Qing would go nowhere, and faced with an attack from Jidu, Koxinga decided to launch a campaign to seize the Yangzi River Delta. According to many Chinese historians, this northern expedition exemplifies beyond a doubt his unwavering loyalty to the Ming and willingness to stake everything he had for a doomed cause.[20] John Wills sees a similar desperation, but one emanating primarily out of increasingly aggressive Qing policies toward him, which "aggravated food shortages," and pushed him "further north in search of grain stores and trading opportunities" and to break the tightening noose.[21] There is much truth to their assertions, but it must be emphasized that Koxinga also possessed the confidence to confront the Qing directly after a decade of military and commercial expansion. In 1657, he possessed a powerful, battle-hardened force consisting of some

---

[17] Huber, "Cheng and the Company," p. 232; Blussé et al., *Zeelandia dagregisters*, Part III, p. 582.

[18] Cheng, *Helan Fuermosha*, p. 513. Pinqua appears to be the transcription of the Minnanese for Binge, or "Elder Brother Bin."

[19] Andrade, *Taiwan became Chinese*, ch. 9.

[20] See, for instance, Li Shunping, "Zheng Chenggong zusun sandai jingying Taiwan de qianhou," *Taibei wenxian* 38 (1976): 261.

[21] Wills, "Contingent connections," p. 190.

180,000 men and 3,000 war junks.[22] As Lynn Struve and Chen Bisheng have shown, rather than passively reacting to the Qing onslaught, Koxinga appeared to have carefully planned out the campaign well in advance.

In fact, the expedition formed but one part of a brilliant vision that represented nothing short of a wholesale redirection and redefinition of his priorities in the face of a changing geopolitical environment. His grand strategy took into account both his ideological convictions and material interests. On a tactical level, if he could occupy the Yangzi River Delta, the most prosperous region in the empire and the largest source of the Qing's revenues, he could permanently resolve his organization's pressing need for food and supplies. He could gain direct access to the primary production bases of silk and other luxuries and ship them directly overseas from its fine harbors, thereby lifting the economy out of depression. His Five Mountain Firms would be reestablished as legitimate companies protected by his soldiers, free of interference from Qing harassment and embargoes. He could also turn the tables on the Qing and cause it to experience resource shortages by cutting off the Grand Canal, the major artery for grain shipments to Beijing, and even use it to continue his advance northward to capture the capital itself.[23] Moreover, with the bulk of Manchu forces tied down in difficult battles with the Ming resistance in the southwest, the Yangzi River Delta was left thinly defended and vulnerable to attack by sea.[24]

On a strategic level, Koxinga hoped that the invasion would tip the power balance back toward the Ming loyalist movement, rallying the Yongli court and others sympathetic to its cause to rise up against the Manchus. In the best possible scenario, Koxinga would receive, for his prize, a huge chunk of the empire, including the Yangzi River Delta region and the entire southeastern coastal littoral, as an autonomous part of a restored Ming. To this effect, in 1657 he dispatched an envoy skilled in the art of persuasion to talk Li Dingguo and Sun Kewang into ending their infighting and coordinating their campaigns with his.[25] Should this effort come to naught, he calculated that the renewed empire-wide resistance would at least delay Manchu troops until he had conquered the Yangzi River Delta. He could then either watch from the sidelines, as before, or force a greatly weakened Qing to grant him the same recognition of his autonomy as the Yongli pretender.[26]

---

[22] Su, "Qing yu Ming-Zheng," p. 154.   [23] Liu Xianting, *Guangyang zaji*, p. 32.
[24] For more on the weak state of Qing defenses, refer to *Shiliao xubian*, pp. 979–981.
[25] Jiang Risheng, *Taiwan waiji*, pp. 164–165.
[26] Xia, *Haiji jiyao*, p. 24; Yang Ying, *Congzheng shilu*, p. 156.

Finally, if everything else failed, Koxinga made preparations for exile abroad in Southeast Asia. He could take advantage of its bountiful natural resources to support himself and his soldiers and export these goods to China, while intensifying his ties with product sources outside maritime East Asia. Dutch Taiwan and the Spanish Philippines became the most ideal targets. Both had huge Chinese immigrant populations, which comprised the overwhelming majorities in Zeelandia and Provintia as well as Manila. While the colonial authorities depended upon them for the goods and services that only they could provide, they constantly came under suspicion for plotting insurrections and subversion. In response to perceived or actual acts of rebellion, the Spanish systematically massacred the Chinese at Manila in 1603, killing more than 20,000, and again in 1639. The Spanish also conducted arbitrary confiscations of traders' goods and demanded from them heavy bribes on a frequent basis.[27] In Taiwan, widespread discontent and anger simmered among Chinese farmers over a heavy mandatory poll-tax imposed by the Dutch, as well as the extortion they had to suffer in its collection. These sentiments erupted into a full-scale revolt in 1653, led by the headman Guo Huaiyi (d. 1653). It was quickly and brutally crushed.[28]

Tonio Andrade has shown that, other than suppressing domestic dissent, both colonies lacked sufficient manpower or fortifications to repel an invasion, especially from an East Asian entity determined enough to seize them.[29] At the time, Manila was defended by only 600 Spanish soldiers, of whom 200 "were in condition to endure the hardships of a campaign or service on the walls."[30] Taiwan fared better, with 1,500 Dutch troops stationed at Casteel Zeelandia. However, the majority of them consisted of untrained young recruits or had become incapacitated because of illness.[31] The Spanish and Dutch had to rely upon mercenaries recruited from the aboriginal tribes and play them off against the Han Chinese to maintain order. Koxinga could thus readily exploit these internal weaknesses to take over either colony.

For Koxinga, Taiwan took precedence because of its proximity to his Xiamen base and the scale of his father's patrimony on the island. Moreover, he had to demonstrate filial piety toward Zhilong's will. The issue of Taiwan came up in written exchanges with Zhilong during

[27] Andrade, *Taiwan became Chinese*, Conclusion.
[28] Johannes Huber, "Chinese settlers against the Dutch East India Company: the rebellion led by Kuo Huai-i on Taiwan in 1652," in E. B. Vermeer (ed.), *Development and decline of Fukien province*, pp. 280–283.
[29] Andrade, *Taiwan became Chinese*, Conclusion.
[30] Coolhaas, *Generale missiven* (1974), vol. IV, p. 463.
[31] C. E. S., *Verwaerloosde Formosa*, p. 86; Yang Ying, *Congzheng shilu*, p. 185.

Koxinga's negotiations with the Qing, and probably became part of the incriminating evidence used to clamp the elder Zheng in jail. In one letter, he admonished his son, "should your enterprise come to naught, you can always find security on Taiwan similar to Qiuran." He referred to a famed seventh-century knight-errant whose name means "Bearded Warrior." Qiuran had abandoned the scramble for China to the Tang dynasty (618–907) and exiled himself to Manchuria, where he seized the throne of a local kingdom.[32] For Koxinga, the conquest of Taiwan served as a legitimate option of last resort in case his mainland adventures failed to yield any fruit.

Expansion on land and sea

Indeed, before he even initiated the northern expedition, Koxinga worked to ensure that Taiwan and the Philippines could serve as viable contingencies for him and his men. In August 1655, he fired the opening salvo by banning all ships from sailing to Manila on the pain of harsh punishments. He cited the years of insults endured by his traders and Chinese residents of the Parián at the hands of the Spanish, who possessed a "heart like that of a dog or pig."[33] At the same time, he ordered the governor of Taiwan to enact his embargo against Manila to prevent Chinese traders from using the island as an illicit transit point. While the Dutch harbored no good feelings for the Spanish, the authorities refused to cooperate, as they had no direct orders from Batavia. Incensed by the reaction, Koxinga extended his embargo to Taiwan on June 27, 1656.[34]

As soon as the bans came into effect, careful searches were undertaken on all incoming vessels at Xiamen. Those caught with products from Taiwan and Manila had their cargoes confiscated and their right hands chopped off. More serious offenders faced imprisonment or even execution.[35] Although some of Koxinga's personal vessels still went to trade, the sanctions had a devastating effect on both colonies, contributing to deflation and increased destitution among the common people. On one level, the harsh measures, as Cheng Wei-chung has shown, attempted to disguise the shortage of luxury goods from China resulting from the economic downturn and Jidu's invasion, and squeeze higher prices for

---

[32] Chen Lunjiong, *Haiguo wenjianlu*, *TWWXCK*, 26 (1958), p. 21. For more on Qiuran, see Du Guangting, "Qiuranke zhuan," in Zhang Youhe (ed.), *Tang-Song chuanqi zhuan* (Beijing: People's Literary Publishing House, 1962).

[33] Huber, "Cheng and the Company," p. 234; Blussé et al., *Zeelandia dagregisters*, Part III, p. 558.

[34] Yang Ying, *Congzheng shilu*, p. 113.

[35] Blussé et al., *Zeelandia dagregisters*, Part IV, pp. 94–95; C. E. S., *Verwaerloosde Formosa*, p. 86.

fewer future exports. Yet sanctions also became the initial step for him to convert his massive economic clout into more direct political control over Taiwan and the Philippines.[36] For instance, Koxinga took advantage of the embargo to dispatch Sausinja, a minor official, to Taiwan with instructions to "visit all junks and inspect their loaded manufactures and other goods, and ... make a report."[37] Acts like this clearly aimed at wresting the colonies away from their European masters by delegitimizing their laws and regulations while establishing a shadow government of his own.

The Spanish became the first to back down before his harsh measures. In late 1656, Governor-General Sabiniano Manrique de Lara (r. 1653–1662) sent an apology mission to Xiamen to restore ties. In return, Koxinga dispatched his representative, Singsic, who arrived at Manila the following year. He received the warm welcome of Lara and all the Manila elites, who entertained him with an extravagant procession and lodged him at the home of the mayor of the Parián, a significant honor. The purpose of the envoy's visit was to restore commercial ties, but he acted as if he had come to take possession of the land. Singsic rode on a sedan chair made out of tiger skin and borne by eight Chinese residents, while a retinue of armed guards walked alongside him with his official insignia. Besides bearing himself "with the same majesty and pomp as in his land," he hosted events attended by the entire expatriate community, including a grand ceremony of floating bamboo lanterns in celebration of Lunar New Year. He ordered local Chinese to contribute funds for his return journey and even attempted to administer Koxinga's harsh punishments on Sangley criminals; this last act the Spanish barely dissuaded him from doing.[38] Although the Zheng representative exhibited an almost unbearable arrogance, Lara's appeasement worked. Ties were reestablished, and Koxinga left Manila alone for the time being.

In March 1657, the Dutch, too, softened their position. Officials in Batavia admitted that the embargo, "if it should continue like this for much longer, would spell total ruin for the company."[39] Governor Frederick Coyett sent Taiwan's preeminent headman, He Tingbin, to negotiate with the Zheng authorities at Xiamen. Pinqua reported back to

[36] Cheng (Zheng), *War, trade and piracy*, pp. 168, 180.
[37] Blussé et al., *Zeelandia dagregisters*, Part IV, pp. 94–95; C. E. S., *Verwaerloosde Formosa*, p. 86.
[38] Casimiro Díaz, *Conquistas de las islas Filipinas: la temporal, por las armas del señor don Phelipe Segundo el Prudente; y la espiritual, por los religiosos del orden de nuestro padre San Augustin: fundacion, y progressos de su provincia del santissimo nombre de Jesus*, 2 vols. (Valladolid, Spain: L.N. de Gaviria, 1890), vol. II, pp. 553–555; Borao-Mateo et al., *Spaniards in Taiwan*, vol. II, pp. 582–584.
[39] Quoted in Andrade, *Taiwan became Chinese*, ch. 10.

Coyett that Koxinga's only condition for the resumption of trade was for the Dutch to stop plundering his junks and harassing his traders in the future. Finding the terms highly reasonable, the governor authorized the headman to agree to them, and, in a written reply to Koxinga, promised to treat his merchants at Taiwan better "than they would receive from any other nation anywhere else in the world."[40]

Yet, unknown to Coyett, Pinqua served as the Zheng organization's chief spy on Taiwan and regularly forwarded crucial and sensitive intelligence on the island's affairs to Koxinga. As early as 1654, Pinqua had run into trouble with the company for hiring divers to conduct unauthorized surveys of the depths of a bay near the northern port of Jilong under the guise of recovering treasure from a sunken Spanish vessel.[41] Unfazed, he conducted another survey in 1657; he ordered one of his associates to map out the sea route toward the main Dutch settlements in southern Taiwan while disguised as a fisherman.[42] These covert endeavors no doubt constituted only a small part of many other operations that escaped any documentation.

Now, during the negotiations with Koxinga to end the embargo, Pinqua privately agreed to an additional demand, which he carefully concealed from Coyett. Taiwan would render Koxinga an annual tribute of 5,000 taels of silver, 100,000 arrow shafts, and 1,000 *dan* (59,700 kg) of sulfur for his war effort against the Manchus. To come up with the payment for the tribute, Pinqua leased from the Revenue Officer, Zheng Tai, the right to levy duties on all junks traveling between Taiwan and the mainland coast. For those unable to promptly fulfill their obligations, the headman advanced funds to them at interest after they handed over a written promise to return the money at a specified future date. Anyone who refused to pay had their names, ships, and cargoes written down and reported to Koxinga.[43] Needless to say, this position of unchecked privilege generated opportunities for great personal profit from extortion and bribery. Koxinga's move essentially bypassed the Dutch and directly dealt with Pinqua as the representative of his interests in Taiwan. It represented a humiliation that neither Coyett nor the company could accept if they learned the full scope of the terms, since it was just one step short of outright occupation.

Meanwhile, Koxinga had begun his northern expedition, which in reality was a series of northward thrusts that occurred in several stages from 1656 to 1659. Initially, progress was modest due to his

[40] Ibid., ch. 11.   [41] Blussé et al., *Zeelandia dagregisters*, Part III, p. 295.
[42] Jiang Risheng, *Taiwan waiji*, p. 165.
[43] C. E. S., *Verwaerloosde Formosa*, pp. 67, 193; Blussé et al., *Zeelandia dagregisters*, Part IV, pp. 222–223, 246–247.

preoccupation with sanctions against the Spanish and Dutch. Nonetheless, by the autumn of 1657, after a year of seesawing battles with Qing forces, Koxinga had secured the coastal area of northern Fujian and captured the strategic southern Zhejiang port of Taizhou. These gains, along with his growing confidence in Manila and Taiwan as viable bases for his men in case of failure, laid the groundwork for a larger-scale penetration into the Yangzi River Delta.[44] In late spring of 1658, Koxinga departed Xiamen with 100,000 soldiers and over a thousand junks. Yet things went unexpectedly awry when the expeditionary force neared the Yangshan Islands, at the mouth of the Yangzi. An especially violent typhoon struck, drowning 10,000 men, or one-tenth of his total troop strength, several of his sons and concubines and 231 other household members, and one hundred ships. Koxinga had no choice but to retreat to Taizhou to rest his forces.[45]

Unfazed, Koxinga carefully prepared for another offensive. Besides training his core forces, he dispatched the Zhejiang militia, under Zhang Huangyan's exclusive command following the death of Zhang Mingzhen in 1654, to the Yangzi River Delta. The mission would scout out the terrain based upon the militia's extensive knowledge of the region.[46] It would also cooperate with Wei Geng's gentry spies to contact and secure the allegiance of key Qing generals and elites, and help Koxinga determine the best route and timing for his strikes.[47]

In July 1658, Koxinga further dispatched a junk to Nagasaki with a crew of 147 people bearing a letter and lavish gifts to the Tokugawa shogun in an effort to secure armaments and manpower. Since he could previously obtain both through private channels, his dispatch of a formal mission, the first time in over a decade and unprecedented in its scale, appeared highly unusual. Indeed, what he asked for was nothing short of a massive influx of aid requiring a logistical effort that only the *bakufu* could coordinate or tacitly approve. Upon receiving the appeal, the shogunal advisory body (*rōjū*) in Edo carefully studied and debated over the request for two months. As before, it avoided a direct response and sent the presents and mission home in September.[48] Direct intervention remained off the cards, but, given the promising state of affairs in China, the *rōjū* took a middle approach. It arranged for daimyo and the Chinese community at Nagasaki to construct ships and recruit Ming loyalist exiles and *rōnin* on behalf of the Zheng organization. The ultimate goal was to attack Beijing by sea in coordination with the northward march of Zheng troops.

[44] Chen Bisheng, *Zheng Chenggong yanjiu*, pp. 178–179.
[45] Struve, *Southern Ming*, pp. 185–186.   [46] Yang Ying, *Congzheng shilu*, p. 142.
[47] *Haidong yishi*, TWWXCK, 90 (1961), p. 89.
[48] Ehara, *Nagasaki mushimegane*, p. 44; Hayashi Shunsai, *Ka'i hentai*, vol. I, p. 45.

Zhu Shunshui soon traveled to China to serve as a liaison between Koxinga and the planned expeditionary force.[49]

Bolstered by these developments, Koxinga renewed his offensive in the summer of 1659. His first target was the island of Chongming, right outside Shanghai, which he hoped to transform into a new base like Xiamen. Its maritime environment and strategic location would allow his men and their families, whom he had brought onboard his ships, to operate in familiar territory and gradually adapt to conditions in the interior. He could further use it as a port to receive the ships and soldiers expected to arrive from Japan.[50] However, after encountering a small but sturdy Qing garrison, Koxinga chose to avoid a fight and move farther into the Yangzi in spite of the strong protests of his commanders.[51] In the long run, his failure to secure the island as a forward base for his troops severely handicapped his consolidation over the region.

For the time being, however, he proved enormously successful. Koxinga seized Guazhou, on the northern bank of the Yangzi, and Zhenjiang, directly facing it on the southern shore, both strategic garrison towns with a chokehold over the Grand Canal. This move cut off the flow of grain and communications to Beijing for an entire month.[52] When word reached a shocked Shunzhi emperor, he ordered the mobilization of armies across the empire – from the southeastern coast to as far afield as remote Ningxia in the northwest – to aid the Yangzi River Delta. He also dispatched elite Manchu imperial guards under the command of the chamberlain Dasu (d. 1661). The emperor even contemplated leading soldiers in person.[53]

Meanwhile, across the Yangzi River Delta, Qing garrisons, including at major cities such as Hangzhou and Ningbo in Zhejiang, fled, remotely announced their submission, or sat on the fence.[54] Residents abandoned towns still under Qing control to "weaken the defenders, who forbade but could not stop them."[55] Popular uprisings flared north of the Yangzi and in neighboring Huguang and Jiangxi.[56] Gentry and commoner alike greeted the expeditionary troops with enthusiasm, often shedding tears at the sight of their flowing robes and long hair.[57] Ming fashion soon became the rage, driving up the price of raw silk and demand for tailors.[58] When a fleeing Qing officer stopped to eat at a village restaurant and

---

[49] Zhu Zhiyu, *Zhu Shunshui ji*, pp. 676–678.
[50] Cheng (Zheng), *War, trade and piracy*, pp. 192–193.
[51] Yang Ying, *Congzheng shilu*, p. 143.   [52] *Shiliao xubian*, pp. 1012–1013, 1067.
[53] *Shunzhi shilu*, pp. 159–160.
[54] Zha, *Lu chunqiu*, pp. 83–84; Zheng Yiju, "Zheng Chenggong zhuan," p. 16.
[55] Zha, *Lu chunqiu*, p. 71.   [56] *Shiliao xubian*, pp. 1143–1146.
[57] Shao, *Dongnan jishi*, p. 113.
[58] Peng Sunyi, *Jinghai zhi*, *TWWXCK*, 35 (1959), p. 48.

inquired about the latest news, the old storekeeper, not knowing his identity, clasped her hands together and thanked Heaven that the "northerners [Manchus] will soon be exterminated!"[59] The entire region lay on the brink of defection. Capitalizing upon this momentum, Koxinga's men pressed onward to the gates of Nanjing, which they surrounded and besieged on August 27, 1659.[60]

By this point, however, the fault lines within the organization, which Koxinga had integrated into a seamless whole in the southeastern coast, began to surface. The expedition had received an enthusiastic reception from Qing defectors, former Ming bureaucrats and gentry, and the Zhejiang militia. In fact, Koxinga relied upon Ma Xin, a Mandarin-speaking northerner, and the Wu-speaking Zhang Huangyan to persuade key Qing commanders to submit to the organization. However, at this critical moment, discord broke out between Koxinga and the Zhejiang militia. Whether out of jealousy or hatred, he sent Zhang Huangyan to pacify cities and towns upriver under the pretext of holding back Qing reinforcements, but in reality marginalizing him. Although Zhang could hardly undertake such a formidable task with less than a thousand men and a hundred ships under him, Koxinga refused to provide any reinforcements.[61]

On the other hand, Koxinga's core Minnanese followers, who comprised the majority of his divisions, remained reluctant to fight on unfamiliar terrain so far from home. A victory would benefit them in the long term by securing a large, fertile base. Yet they faced devastating immediate losses in delayed harvests, the conversion of junks into warships, and diversion away from fishing grounds and overseas markets. In fact, before the thrust into the Yangzi, many of his Minnanese generals had advocated a return to Xiamen, where they could adopt a wait-and-see approach, "advancing to fight and retreating to defend."[62]

Partly because of the regional rivalries, the discipline of Koxinga's troops grew laxer as the siege dragged on. Despite their huge numbers, they surrounded only a fourth of Nanjing's massive walls.[63] Even his elite vanguard soldiers gambled and drank, and left their camps unguarded to hunt and fish.[64] Instead of reinforcing the strict standards for his men that gained him fame and notoriety on the southeastern coast, Koxinga let the

---

[59] Huang Zongxi, *Cixing shimo*, p. 6.   [60] Yang Ying, *Congzheng shilu*, p. 152.
[61] Zha, *Lu chunqiu*, p. 83.   [62] Jiang Risheng, *Taiwan waiji*, p. 164.
[63] Chen Bisheng, *Zheng Chenggong yanjiu*, p. 205; John E. Wills, Jr., "The hazardous missions of a Dominican: Victorio Riccio, O. P., in Amoy, Taiwan, and Manila," in *Actes du IIe colloque international de sinologie: les rapports entre la Chine et l'Europe au temps des lumières* (Paris: Les belles lettres, 1980), vol. IV, p. 251.
[64] Zheng Yiju, "Zheng Chenggong zhuan," p. 17; Peng, *Jinghai zhi*, pp. 110–111; Yang Ying, *Congzheng shilu*, p. 158.

behavior continue. He himself had grown complacent from his streak of victories in the Yangzi River Delta. After he abandoned his effort to occupy Chongming, he disregarded his subordinates' advice to slow down his advance and establish an alternative base around the Grand Canal. Indeed, other than garrisoning some captured territory on an ad hoc basis, Koxinga did little to capitalize upon the wave of elite and popular support in the delta to establish a durable civil government. Without a credible alternative administration, Qing commanders saw little appeal in switching sides, despite the best efforts of Ma and Zhang. On a tactical level, since Koxinga idealized "a maximally large victory" at Nanjing, a city of momentous historic and symbolic significance, he refused to attack promptly but gave the beleaguered Qing garrison an ultimatum of two weeks to surrender. In the meantime, he put on grand spectacles for his men and allowed them to celebrate his birthday.[65]

The grace period allowed the Qing defenders to recover from their initial panic and regain their fighting resolve. They received a further boost in their numbers and morale from a contingent of Manchu soldiers, who, fresh from victory in Guizhou, happened to pass by the city and broke through the siege lines to reinforce the beleaguered garrison.[66] When it became apparent that the defenders did not plan to surrender Nanjing, Koxinga finally made preparations to storm the city. However, Qing forces acted before him; late on the night of September 8, they burst out of a side gate and launched a surprise offensive. Koxinga's soldiers fought back ferociously, with some divisions resisting to the last man. Ultimately, his main contingents broke ranks and fled. A total of fourteen division leaders and other high-ranking military and civil officials perished in the fiasco or were captured by Qing soldiers and later executed.[67] The two-week long siege of Nanjing had come to an end.

Dramatic turnarounds

Koxinga retreated with his navy back to Zhenjiang, gathering thousands of his scattered men along the way. Although he had suffered some ten thousand casualties in battle out of a total of 85,000 men, his naval forces remained unscathed, and managed to sink two Qing vessels that tried to cut off his retreat. He still controlled the coastline from Zhejiang to Fujian and possessed significant infantry capability, with five thousand fresh

---

[65] Struve, *Southern Ming*, pp. 185–186.   [66] Ibid., p. 188.
[67] Xia, *Haiji jiyao*, pp. 24–25; Yang Ying, *Congzheng shilu*, pp. 160–162; Jiang Risheng, *Taiwan waiji*, p. 182.

crack troops who had not yet seen any action.[68] For this reason, his allies Zhang Huangyan and Wei Geng encouraged him to hold onto Zhenjiang and use it as a base to prepare for a renewed offensive at a later time. However, Koxinga believed that his forces were too demoralized to operate again in unfamiliar territory. Even more distressing for him, his invasion had failed to rejuvenate the Ming loyalist forces in the southwest or even slow down the Manchu advance. In February 1659, Qing forces under Wu Sangui successfully pinned down Li Dingguo's remnants on the edge of Yunnan and forced the Yongli emperor to flee into neighboring Myanmar.[69] The Qing could soon concentrate all its energies upon his bases in southeastern China.

On September 14, acting against the earnest entreaties of his allies, Koxinga's men plundered Zhenjiang for provisions and sailed away into the Yangzi. This unilateral withdrawal amounted to a vicious betrayal of Zhang Huangyan, as it cut off his escape route via the sea. When cities and towns upriver from Nanjing learned of Koxinga's defeat, they defected back to the Qing. Stranded deep within hostile territory, Zhang and a handful of his Zhejiang militia disguised themselves as commoners and fled on foot. They traveled day and night through narrow, tortuous mountain roads, with Qing soldiers in hot pursuit. Despite several close calls, they returned to the southeastern coast alive at the end of 1659.[70]

Meanwhile, Koxinga decided to try his luck again at negotiations with the Qing court. On September 19, he brought his forces to the mouth of the Yangzi and anchored at Shanghai, headquarters of the Qing regional commander, Ma Fengzhi (d. 1661). Koxinga dispatched a trusted envoy, Rites Censor Cai Zheng (d. 1668), to his camp with a request for his assistance in restarting the talks. Ma had long enjoyed close relations with key figures in the Ming loyalist resistance even as he engaged them in battle. Not surprisingly, he was one of the commanders who sat on the fence during the siege of Nanjing. Koxinga thus trusted Ma as the only person on the Qing side whose attitude toward him was genuine and who would not sell out his interests.[71]

In preparation for the upcoming talks, Koxinga tried to seize Chongming again. The belligerent move, he calculated, would allow him to bargain for more favorable conditions from the Qing court, and,

---

[68] The casualty figure comes from Zha, *Zuiwei lu*, p. 135.

[69] Shao, *Dongnan jishi*, p. 120; Zha, *Lu chunqiu*, p. 84; Struve, *Southern Ming*, pp. 170–171, 188.

[70] For Zhang's account of his escape, which reads like an adventure novel, see Zha, *Lu chunqiu*, pp. 84–90.

[71] Yang Ying, *Congzheng shilu*, p. 164. Ma Fengzhi's biography is in *Qing shi liezhuan xuan*, *TWWXCK*, 274 (1968), pp. 83–85.

if not successful, at least frighten it enough to delay or prevent the imminent attack on the southeastern coast.[72] From Chongming, he could also plan for a renewed expedition into the Yangzi in the event the talks failed. However, Koxinga's offensive on the island, launched on September 23, stalled in the face of unexpectedly fierce resistance from the Qing garrison, whose defenders inflicted significant casualties upon his men. Loud calls came from his ranks to abandon the campaign altogether.[73] As Koxinga pondered his options, an envoy of Ma Fengzhi burst into his camp with a message from Ma calling upon him to return to his coastal bases and calmly await the results of the negotiations.[74] After boasting to the Qing envoy, and partly consoling himself, that his show of strength outside of Chongming had instilled sufficient fear into the court, Koxinga complied and sailed away with his ships back to Xiamen.[75]

Cai Zheng, in the meantime, traveled to Beijing, where he had an audience with the Shunzhi emperor. The ruler gave his blessing for the talks by showering the envoy with gifts and instructing him to return to Shanghai to confer with Ma Fengzhi.[76] However, the negotiations soon encountered strong opposition from other high-ranking Qing officials. In memorials to the court, they questioned why Koxinga attacked Chongming when he should "encamp in an empty and open terrain to await the results of the talks" if he truly intended to surrender.[77] They further questioned Ma Fengzhi's motives for encouraging the talks at a time when military action could readily eliminate Koxinga's newly defeated army. One official openly accused Ma of secret collusion with the enemy to "slow down our forces."[78]

On November 17, after a month of indecision, the emperor reversed his previous leniency. In a menacing ultimatum, he ordered Koxinga to signal his loyalty and sincerity to the dynasty by shaving his hair prior to any concrete discussions. At the same time, the ruler issued another edict promising amnesty and rewards for any of Koxinga's followers able to "capture him alive" or "cut off his head and come to surrender."[79] The ruler then instructed elite Manchu banner troops under Dasu to march to Fuzhou from Nanjing. They would join the regular Han Green Standard armies and hundreds of recently constructed ships from the three

[72] Struve, *Southern Ming*, p. 188; Wu Zhenglong, "Nanjing zhi yi hou Zheng-Qing heyi zai jiantao (xia)," *Dalu zazhi* 100.4 (2000): 21.

[73] Yang Ying, *Congzheng shilu*, pp. 164–165; Xia, *Haiji jiyao*, p. 25; *Shiliao xubian*, pp. 1022–1023; *Qing chu Zheng Chenggong jiazu Manwen dang'an yibian (er)*, TWWXHK) 1.7, p. 135.

[74] Yang Ying, *Congzheng shilu*, pp. 165–166; *Manwen dang'an 2*, p. 131.

[75] Yang Ying, *Congzheng shilu*, pp. 166–167.   [76] Xia, *Haiji jiyao*, p. 25.

[77] *Manwen dang'an 2*, p. 135.   [78] *Shunzhi shilu*, pp. 176–177.

[79] *Shiliao xubian*, pp. 1046, 1105–1106.

provinces of Zhejiang, Fujian, and Guangdong to launch an offensive on Xiamen from land and sea. Ma Fengzhi was relieved of his duties and recalled to Beijing. He would be executed for treason in 1661. Countless other suspected Zheng collaborators among the Jiangnan elites similarly faced imprisonment, beatings, and death in massive purges for their association with Koxinga and his allies.[80]

Cai Zheng, the Zheng envoy, barely escaped with his life to Xiamen. Even before his arrival in February 1660 he had forwarded news of the failure of the negotiations.[81] At this point, Koxinga decided to activate his overseas contingency plan, thanks, in part, to the persistent persuasion of He Tingbin. As it turned out, Pinqua's precarious position in Taiwan had unraveled. In February 1659, a Chinese merchant named Samsiack, either unwilling or unable to bear his heavy extralegal customs duties any longer, exposed his entire covert operation to the Dutch authorities. After detailed interrogations of some of Pinqua's fellow headmen, Governor Coyett uncovered evidence not only of Pinqua's involvement, but, to the greater alarm of the Dutch, the collusion of the other leaders of the Chinese community to keep it a secret for so long. He Tingbin was brought before the Council of Justice on charges of treason. He was convicted and stripped of his posts as headman and interpreter, and forced to pay a fine of 300 Spanish pesos.

Deprived of his sources of income, bankrupted, and hounded by creditors, Pinqua fled across the Taiwan Strait with his family in April 1659 and sought refuge at Xiamen.[82] Eager for revenge against the Dutch, he worked tirelessly to persuade Koxinga to seize Taiwan from the VOC as an alternative to what he considered a fruitless struggle with the Manchus on the mainland. He shared with Koxinga the map that he had put together from his numerous surveys, as well as information on the ocean currents and the company's secrets. He spoke of the island as a secure base "sufficient to resist the entire Middle Kingdom," while its fertile soil and resources and role as an entrepôt of maritime trade made it "truly a place for hegemons."[83]

Moved by these glowing descriptions, Koxinga convened a meeting of his main commanders to discuss an invasion of Taiwan sometime in late 1659 or early 1660. Chinese accounts uniformly indicate that the faces of his subordinates "revealed strong displeasure." His clan brother Zheng Tai expressed fear of the treacherous storms and waves in the strait and,

[80] Wakeman, *Great enterprise*, vol. II, p. 1046; *Shunzhi shilu*, pp. 176–180, 186–187.
[81] Yang Ying, *Congzheng shilu*, p. 168; Xia, *Haiji jiyao*, p. 25; *Manwen dang'an 2*, p. 162.
[82] C. E. S., *Verwaerloosde Formosa*, pp. 68, 193–194 and Cheng, *Helan Fuermosha*, p. 513.
[83] Jiang Risheng, *Taiwan waiji*, p. 191. Similar versions of Pinqua's words are found in Xia, *Haiji jiyao*, p. 27 and Peng, *Jinghai zhi*, p. 56.

citing insufficient supplies and ammunition, called for a postponement until harvest season in September. The most vocal opposition came from the division commander Wu Hao (d. 1661), who complained of the island's "bad fengshui" and diseased tropical climate. He further pointed to the strong and sturdy fortress at Zeelandia, defended by the most powerful and well-armed fleets in the world. Many ordinary soldiers simply voted with their feet. Koxinga had to specially dispatch one of his generals to patrol the seas around Xiamen to fetch back deserters.[84]

It is true that Dutch military prowess and technology struck terror into the hearts of many Chinese, including Zheng commanders and soldiers.[85] Nonetheless, these were battle-hardened veterans, who held their ground for years against tens of thousands of equally fearsome Manchu warriors. Moreover, many of them likely remembered or participated in Zhilong's epic and victorious battle against the Dutch fleets off the Fujian coast in 1633. Yet, in both cases, they were fighting on home turf for their families and livelihoods. On the other hand, Koxinga's men had performed poorly in the Yangzi River Delta, a Chinese core region far away from their native land. They were in even less of a mood to contest an island traditionally seen as a remote "barbarian" wilderness.[86]

Indeed, residents of the mainland coast looked down upon the Chinese immigrants in Taiwan, seeing them as either "arrogant and disorderly interpreters" or smugglers "greedy for the myriad profits."[87] They had lost their "Chineseness" amid long-term residence among wild aboriginal tribes and their violent, uncouth Dutch overlords, known pejoratively as "Red-Haired Barbarians" (Hongmaoyi). Koxinga reinforced this view when he banished his censor, Chang Shouning, to Taiwan in 1657 for making false accusations, and ordered Pinqua to provide for his living expenses.[88] Naturally, Koxinga's followers felt shock at his decision to send them into collective exile to a frontier deemed suitable only for criminals and other marginal elements.

Among his commanders, John Wills correctly attributes their reluctance to participate in the invasion to their "instinct of self-preservation" and refusal to abandon their "coastal trade connections" in Fujian. Chen Bisheng similarly notes that they did not want to "give up the huge profits of maritime trade" or "live a life of hardship in Taiwan." For the more idealistic bureaucrats, gentry, and Ming imperial relatives, Koxinga's

---

[84] Yang Ying, *Congzheng shilu*, p. 185; Jiang Risheng, *Taiwan waiji*, p. 192; Jacobus Anne van der Chijs (ed.), *Batavia dagregister* (1889), 1661, p. 63; C. E. S., *Verwaerloosde Formosa*, p. 83.

[85] Andrade, *Lost colony*, pp. 36–37.   [86] Teng, *Imagined geography*, p. 43.

[87] Liushiqi and Fan Xian (eds.), *Chongxiu Taiwan fuzhi*, TWWXCK, 105 (1961), p. 702.

[88] Yang Ying, *Congzheng shilu*, p. 113.

actions further amounted to an abandonment of the cause of restoration.[89] Still, it is important to point out that those most vociferously opposed to the planned invasion ironically possessed the most extensive knowledge of the island's conditions. Zheng Tai and Wu Hao once lived on Taiwan, most likely as pirates, and later handled the cross-strait trade on behalf of Zhilong. They had carefully studied the state of Dutch defenses, and continued to own land and other assets in the colony. Although Taiwan was not a *terra incognita* for them, it served as a reminder of a lowly past to which they never wanted to return. The refined luxury and exalted status they now enjoyed on the mainland coast marked not just a change in geographic setting, but also the crossing of a vast class boundary. For this reason, they and other officials only cared about Taiwan to the extent that it provided a means to acquire wealth; they could not accept making it an end goal of settlement.[90]

The reluctance of Koxinga's own followers could not contrast more sharply with the eager support for an invasion from Chinese residents on Taiwan, estimated at 50,000 in 1660.[91] Burdened with heavy taxes, they were all too eager for a change in leadership. In the countryside near Tayouan and Provintia, Dutch authorities heard reports of Han farmers inciting aborigines to revolt when they got word of Koxinga's arrival.[92] The headmen of the colony, on the other hand, were more amenable to VOC rule, having forged a prosperous civic sphere dependent upon a fragile economic cooperation between him and the company.[93] However, when bilateral tensions escalated to a point when they could no longer maintain their co-allegiance, they accepted him without question. Not only was Koxinga, like them, Chinese, but his organization also directly protected the lives and property of his fellow traders and diaspora, stood up for their interests in front of foreign governments, and tied its fate to their wellbeing. While the VOC fulfilled the same functions to a certain extent, it primarily answered not to them, but to its own employees and officials, and, ultimately, its shareholders back home in Amsterdam.

Nonetheless, in the area of ideology and class, the interests of an influential segment of Koxinga's followers based on the mainland coast

---

[89] Wills, "Maritime China," p. 227; Chen Bisheng, *Zheng Chenggong yanjiu*, p. 67.

[90] As Yeh Wen-hsin, *Provincial passages: culture, space, and the origins of Chinese communism* (Berkeley, CA: University of California Press, 1996), p. 5 shows, the stark class and cultural differences experienced in the crossing of space from periphery to core cause "the dissonance between the two worlds to be more sharply felt," and trigger a "shift of cultural allegiance from one space to another."

[91] John Robert Shepherd, *Statecraft and political economy on the Taiwan frontier* (Stanford, CA: Stanford University Press, 1993), p. 96.

[92] C. E. S., *Verwaerloosde Formosa*, pp. 72–73.

[93] Zheng (Cheng), *Taiwan shehui*, pp. 306–308.

diverged from the stance of the organization as a whole toward overseas Chinese. Their objections to an invasion of Taiwan proved difficult to overcome for the time being. Moreover, Koxinga needed to deal with the more pressing threat of the rapid Manchu advance toward his main bases. To prepare for the onslaught, he pulled back his divisions and ships from points across the littoral zone and concentrated them on the islands around Xiamen. He also relocated the family members of his officers and soldiers to adjacent Jinmen. The Qing forces under Dasu struck outside Xiamen on June 17, 1660. During a day of hard battle, Koxinga's navy decimated the inexperienced Qing fleets, killing so many men that corpses littered the bays and inlets around the twin islands. At the end of the day, Dasu gathered together his disorganized remnants and withdrew to Fuzhou. To make the Qing think twice about ever invading his bases again, an infuriated Koxinga cut off the ears and hands of over three hundred Manchu prisoners and sent them back to Dasu's camp.[94]

Despite the strong show of force, the Qing continued to pose a long-term challenge to the viability of his organization. On August 29, 1660, the Shunzhi emperor transferred Geng Jimao to a new base in Fujian, leaving Shang Kexi with exclusive administrative control over Guangdong. Both would specialize in dealing with the maritime threat. Also as part of this reshuffle, Wu Sangui was put in charge of the southwestern provinces that he had helped seize from the Yongli pretender.[95] On September 3, the emperor, determined to keep attacking until he either had Koxinga killed or forced him to surrender, ordered Manchu banner troops under the imperial clansman Loto to make a fresh attempt on Xiamen. Since the Qing now possessed most of the littoral due to Koxinga's earlier decision to withdraw his forces to defend Xiamen, it could also put teeth into its ban on maritime trade. The court approved a proposal to evacuate the residents of Haicheng and Tongan, the county to which Xiamen belonged, and relocate them into the interior.[96] The policy, aimed at physically preventing them from colluding with the Zheng organization, grew in harshness and intensity in the years to come.

Koxinga needed to do something fast; he was being cornered on several barren islands and continually threatened with a renewed Qing onslaught. For the rest of the year, he vacillated between launching a renewed restoration campaign and leaving the mainland altogether. The first option imbued his organization with legitimacy but was becoming

[94] Yang Ying, *Congzheng shilu*, pp. 178, 181; *Shunzhi shilu*, p. 179.
[95] Liu Fengyun, *Qing dai Sanfan*, pp. 111–112.   [96] *Shunzhi shilu*, pp. 178–179, 185.

increasingly unrealistic to pull off with his own men and resources. Nonetheless, he attempted to make a comeback by securing outside aid. In September, he dispatched his military officer, Zhang Guangqi, to Nagasaki with a third, and final, request to the *bakufu* for manpower and armaments.

However, the envoy arrived at an inopportune moment. In response to Koxinga's previous request for assistance, the *bakufu* had raised a massive expeditionary force consisting of scores of ships that set out for the Chinese coast during the summer of 1660. The Nagasaki-based Chinese exiles served as guides and manned the vessels. However, severe tempests forced the succor fleet to turn back.[97] Even if the journey had been smooth, it would still have arrived too late to make a difference, since Koxinga had already been defeated outside Nanjing. Toward Zhang Guangqi's renewed request, the *bakufu* understandably rejected it, citing "the losses incurred during the previous military expedition," and only granted aid in the form of armaments.[98]

Koxinga was left with the second and more pragmatic option of invading Taiwan. On two occasions in 1660, he made detailed plans to sail for the island, only to scrap them because of timely detection and heightened preparations on the Dutch side and fear on his part of the threat posed to the cohesion and legitimacy of his organization.[99] At this juncture, two major events on the Qing side hardened his resolve. In November 1660, Loto, Dasu, and the other Manchu bannermen responsible for coordinating the offensive on Xiamen were suddenly recalled to Beijing, leaving Qing naval junks docked idly by the shoreline. The Shunzhi emperor had fallen ill, and passed away shortly afterward, in February 1661. He was succeeded by his son, Shengzu (1654–1722, r. Kangxi, 1661–1722), a young boy of seven.[100]

Free of a major threat from his rear, Koxinga decisively pressed ahead with an invasion over the objection of the majority of his subordinates. To placate his critics, he reinterpreted his upcoming campaign according to the orthodoxy of Ming loyalism. According to him, Taiwan would only serve as a temporary base for his troops to recuperate free of Manchu harassment until they could enter the fight for restoration once again. He adamantly denied "coveting overseas lands to extend his own peace and happiness."[101]

---

[97] Sŏng, *Chŏngmi chŏnshinrok*, pp. 277_022a-022b.
[98] Jiang Risheng, *Taiwan waiji*, p. 190.
[99] Yang Ying, *Congzheng shilu*, p. 182; C. E. S., *Verwaerloosde Formosa*, pp. 72–73, 83, 98; *Batavia dagregisters*, 1661, pp. 62–63.
[100] Yang Ying, *Congzheng shilu*, p. 184; *Shunzhi shilu*, pp. 183–185, 188.
[101] Jiang Risheng, *Taiwan waiji*, p. 194.

Naturalizing Taiwan

On April 21, 1661, Koxinga set sail from Jinmen at the head of three hundred junks and thirteen divisions, or 11,700 men. In addition, Pinqua secretly recruited three hundred navigators from Zheng Zhilong's former base of Wankan with extensive knowledge of Taiwan's coastline to assist in a landing operation.[102] Koxinga based his plans upon a quick victory that would not overburden his men. He carried almost no grain onboard, calculating that his overwhelming numbers could handily defeat the small Dutch garrison in time to exploit Taiwan's agricultural bounty. However, soon after they set sail, a violent storm at sea forced them to encamp at Penghu. After just three days on this unproductive island chain, hunger broke out among his ranks and forced him to press ahead despite adverse weather.[103]

At the end of April, Koxinga's ships entered the narrow Lu'ermen Channel, where they received the welcome of thousands of Chinese residents, who helped his men set foot onto a sandbar lying to the north of Tayouan (Map 4.1). A small contingent of 240 Dutch troops tried to prevent the landing, but Koxinga's soldiers decimated their ranks and killed their commander, Captain Thomas Pedel (1610–1661). A similar effort led by Joan van Aeldorp also came to naught. After gathering at the sandbar, Chinese junks crossed the bay to the main island, overwhelming and scattering the Dutch ships that tried to block their way. Koxinga's men rushed to commandeer private residences and grain stores in Provintia to secure food for his famished men before the Dutch could set fire to the structures, primarily huts made out of thatched straw. The Chinese went on to surround and lay siege to Fort Provintia.[104] On May 4, 1661, with the garrison running low on potable water, its commander, Jacobus Valentijn, surrendered, leaving Koxinga in control of the main island in under a week.[105] Soon afterward, aboriginal chieftains from several villages around Provintia offered their allegiance.[106]

---

[102] C. E. S., *Verwaerloosde Formosa*, pp. 72–73, 83; Yang Ying, *Congzheng shilu*, p. 184; Blussé et al., *Zeelandia dagregisters*, Part IV, p. 520.

[103] Tonio Andrade's masterful narrative, *Lost colony*, has given a dramatic, play-by-play account of the entire campaign from the perspective of both Koxinga and the VOC. Rather than repeat what has already been covered elsewhere in brilliant and colorful detail, this chapter focuses more upon Koxinga's efforts to create the institutions and legitimacy for a new state in Taiwan.

[104] Yang Ying, *Congzheng shilu*, pp. 185–188; C. E. S., *Verwaerloosde Formosa*, pp. 101–107; and Chiang Shu-sheng (Jiang Shusheng) (trans. and annot.), *Daghregister van Philip Meij* (Taipei: Hansheng, 2003), Part II, p. 3.

[105] C. E. S., *Verwaerloosde Formosa*, p. 116.

[106] Andrade, *Taiwan became Chinese*, ch. 3.

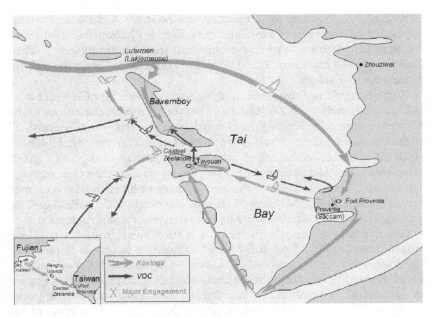

Map 4.1 Koxinga's Taiwan campaign.

However, Koxinga encountered far greater difficulties at Tayouan against Casteel Zeelandia, the residence of Governor Coyett, whose sturdy walls and access to the outside world via the sea placed it in a good position to hold out for a long time. When an overconfident Koxinga stormed the fort on May 25, the defenders repulsed the attack by unleashing a barrage of fire from their powerful muskets and heavy artillery. After sustaining heavy casualties – over a thousand killed and wounded compared to just two or three dead and a handful of injuries on the Dutch side – he ordered his junks to blockade Lu'ermen Channel and the mouths of major navigable rivers. He further instructed troops under Ma Xin to guard the narrow land passage connecting Tayouan to the rest of the island.[107] He then waited, hoping to starve the fort into submission.

This initial burst of triumph gave Koxinga the confidence to articulate a new vision for Taiwan, one more inspiring than a base for temporary exile. In the weeks after the landing, he composed a poem, which he intriguingly entitled "Recovering Taiwan" (Fu Tai), even though he himself had never set foot on the island before. The first line boasted of "opening up this land of thorns and brambles" and "expelling the Dutch

---

[107] Chiang (Jiang), *Daghregister van Meij*, Part II, p. 27.

barbarians" to "recover my forefathers' foundations." His commentary, appended to the verses, explained that Zheng Zhilong had laid those foundations when he "gathered troops and stored grain here."[108] Thus Zhilong, and by extension, his son – and not the Dutch – were the rightful possessors of Taiwan.

Koxinga reinforced this point in ultimatums to Governor Coyett and his beleaguered garrisons in Zeelandia and Provintia, and proclamations to the Chinese community. Zhilong, he claimed, lent "this land out of friendship" to the Dutch for trade and residence so long as he had no use for it. However, since his son needed the island, which "now belongs to me" by right of inheritance, they had to return it.[109] This interpretation sent a clear message not just to Taiwan but also to the vast segment of his men who had once served under Zhilong. No longer were they contesting with "barbarians" for a strange island abroad; they were fighting to recover a familial legacy.

Croizier sees Koxinga's rhetoric as a turn away from his previous commitment to the Ming in favor of "a maritime kingdom dominating the East Asian trading routes."[110] Likewise, Wills believes that Taiwan, which formed "part of his inheritance as son of his despised father," stood in diametric opposition to his legacy of "Lord of the Imperial Surname."[111] Indeed, the closing line of Koxinga's poem hints at his "inability to bear leaving" the island despite "this crucial moment of suffering," in reference to his failed campaigns against the Qing.[112] He was prepared to settle down permanently, and come to terms with a mainland under "barbarian" domination.

While Koxinga's behavior certainly pointed toward an indefinite suspension or even abandonment of Ming restoration, it did not represent a prioritization of filial piety above his carefully crafted self-image as a loyal minister. In fact, his poem referred to Zhilong by "Senior Grand Tutor to the Crown Prince" (taishi), a title conferred upon him by the Longwu emperor.[113] In surrender ultimatums to the Dutch, Koxinga became the first individual to speak of Taiwan not as a wild frontier, but an integral part of China since time immemorial. The reimagined sovereignty of Taiwan as "belonging to the government of China" complemented the legacy of his father, who had "lent" this Chinese Taiwan to the Dutch as a Ming imperial official.[114]

[108] "Yanping er wang," p. 128.
[109] Blussé et al., Zeelandia dagregisters, Part IV, pp. 352, 362.
[110] Croizier, Chinese Nationalism, p. 23.
[111] John E. Wills, Jr., Mountain of fame: portraits in Chinese history (Princeton, NJ: Princeton University Press, 1994), p. 228.
[112] "Yanping er wang," p. 128.   [113] Nantian hen, TWWXCK, 76 (1960), p. 418.
[114] Blussé et al., Zeelandia dagregisters, Part IV, p. 352.

As his men laid siege to Casteel Zeelandia, Koxinga enacted policies to make the reality on the ground conform to his discourse. On May 29 he proclaimed a new state – Dongdu Mingjing (Ming Eastern Capital) – which combined the functions of a Ming imperial capital province and autonomous kingdom within one political unit. A makeshift throne was erected at Fort Provintia, ostensibly to await the arrival of the distant Yongli pretender. The surrounding town became known as Chengtian (Receiving from Heaven) Prefecture (*fu*), which, in turn, supervised two counties (*xian*). Wannian (Ten-thousand Years) administered the area immediately south of Provintia, while Tianxing (Heavenly Renaissance), the Longwu-period name for Fuzhou, oversaw affairs in the northern vicinity. Tayouan was renamed Anping Garrison (*zhen*), after the alternate name for Anhai in Fujian. Koxinga envisioned a new headquarters for himself at Casteel Zeelandia once the Dutch surrendered.[115]

Koxinga also enacted a land development policy that divided Taiwan's entire arable acreage into three categories. A perimeter of 70 kilometers around Provintia, which comprised the most productive and intensely cultivated plots on the island under the Dutch, came under the direct jurisdiction of him and his relatives. Besides these "official fields" (*guantian*), Koxinga encouraged his civil and military officials to recruit landless peasants to open up virgin soil in "private fields" (*sitian*) farther out. The bulk of his commanders and soldiers, however, would disband and open up military colonies in the remotest parts of the island, leaving only an active force of 5,000 near Tayouan and Provintia to continue the war of attrition with the Dutch. Each soldier-farmer was given a plot of land not to exceed half a hectare, along with oxen and farming implements mostly confiscated from VOC assets. They would cultivate rice, an endeavor requiring significant long-term investments, as well as yams, which promised handsome yields within a three-month period. During the first three years of settlement, they did not have to pay taxes, but Koxinga would "borrow" upfront three-tenths of their total yield.[116]

In June, soon after his pronouncements, Koxinga organized two teams of Dutch land surveyors, who had surrendered with Jacobus Valentijn at Fort Provintia, to travel the length of the island. They were accompanied by craftsmen, lumberjacks, artists, and translators of Portuguese and aboriginal languages. They would confirm existing landholdings and set the boundaries and dimensions of new plots. In addition, the team planned cities at intervals of four hours' journey from the coast to serve

---

[115] Xia, *Haiji jiyao*, p. 1; Jiang Risheng, *Taiwan waiji*, p. 70; *Nantian hen*, p. 60.
[116] Yang Ying, *Congzheng shilu*, pp. 189–190; Jiang Risheng, *Taiwan waiji*, p. 207; Chiang (Jiang), *Daghregister van Meij*, Part 2, pp. 31, 33–34.

as regional centers and residences for civil and military officials. Frontier market towns would be established at the foot of the mountain ranges running down the center of the island for trade with aboriginal tribes and defense against raids.[117]

Opening new land and converting his soldiers into farmers became a practical necessity for Koxinga to resolve the crippling labor shortage on the island. Fundamentally, the limited number of full-time Han farmers and the slash-and-burn agricultural economy of the aborigines could hardly support his 30,000 men, who already equaled three-fifths of the largest pre-invasion Chinese population estimates! But his actions also reflected the product of a broader vision conceived, perhaps with the assistance of He Tingbin, well before the invasion of Taiwan. Koxinga was attempting to transform a "barbaric" and peripheral island into a new bastion of "civilization," in his words, "a foundational endeavor that cannot be uprooted for ten thousand generations."[118] He could abandon Ming restoration not by turning his back on "China," but by extending it to Taiwan, recentering it, and indefinitely postponing the return.

Although the transplantation promised to yield fruit in the long term, it did little to alleviate a series of pressing crises that threatened to destroy the organization. From the end of May, food shortages plagued Koxinga's troops. Requisitions only yielded sufficient quantities to last several weeks at any one time. With the military colonies still in the initial stages of cultivation, Koxinga had no choice but to import food from Xiamen to make up for the deficiency. Yet when his grain ships failed to arrive on time because of adverse winds, prices skyrocketed to such outrageous levels that most of his soldiers were reduced to a diet of barks from palm stems.[119] As the natural accompaniment to hunger, 70–80 percent of the troops, particularly those in the military colonies forced to cultivate crops in the scorching heat and humidity of summer and drink malarial water from creeks and swamps, succumbed to epidemics of tropical diseases.[120]

In a sign of growing desperation, Zheng soldiers resorted to outright extortion and plunder of the limited surplus in the surrounding country-side. The harsh exactions accompanied the steady encroachment of Han landholdings and military colonies upon aboriginal lands despite Koxinga's warnings not to do so. Tribes to the north and south of

---

[117] Chiang (Jiang), *Daghregister van Meij*, Part 2, pp. 33–35.

[118] Yang Ying, *Congzheng shilu*, p. 189.

[119] Yang Ying, *Congzheng shilu*, pp. 188, 191; Chiang (Jiang), *Daghregister van Meij*, Part 2, pp. 45, 51; Deng Kongzhao, *Ming-Zheng Taiwan yanjiu*, pp. 67–69.

[120] Ruan Minxi, *Haishang jianwenlu*, TWWXCK, 24 (1958), p. 39; Chiang (Jiang), *Daghregister van Meij*, Part 2, p. 34.

Provintia rebelled in July 1661. Under the command of powerful chieftains, the natives killed over two thousand soldiers sent to suppress them, including a key general, and sought an alliance with the VOC.[121]

Meanwhile, to Koxinga's great dismay, the Dutch did not give up easily. On August 12, a succor fleet of eleven ships and seven hundred men under Admiral Jacob Caeuw unexpectedly arrived from Batavia to reinforce the beleaguered Zeelandia garrison.[122] To make matters worse, Koxinga received word that David Harthouwer, one of Coyett's subordinates, had met with the Qing Fujian authorities. The Qing officials offered two junks and 7,000 troops to help the governor lift the siege of Zeelandia if his superiors in Batavia could send a fleet to join them in striking Koxinga's mainland bases. The news came as a complete shock to Koxinga, who held emergency councils with his generals for two consecutive days, and hastily arranged for more weapons to be forged.[123]

The hardships of settling a new frontier and the dismal progress of the campaign dampened the already low morale of the Zheng officers and soldiers. By October 1661, Koxinga had lost "eight thousand men, many of them his best soldiers" to hunger, disease, and warfare.[124] Large numbers of homesick deserters fled back to the Chinese coast on a daily basis in illegally commandeered junks. Others sneaked away or even swam across the bay to join the Dutch at Zeelandia.[125] Koxinga's closest allies in the Ming loyalist cause also openly stood against him. In the winter of 1661, Zhang Huangyan dispatched an envoy to his camp with a letter urging him to abandon the siege. Zhang reminded Koxinga that "small, inconsequential Taiwan" (ququ Taiwan) could never match "the divine land of China" (Chixian Shenzhou). If he continued to waste his energy on occupying this "barren desert," then "even if you survive, it is not wise; if you die, it is not out of loyalty."[126] He essentially accused Koxinga not only of betraying the Ming cause, but "China" and all its trappings of civilization.

---

[121] Chiang (Jiang), *Daghregister van Meij*, Part 2, p. 51.

[122] Koxinga had counted upon prevailing southern winds at the time to prevent any Dutch appeals for aid from reaching Batavia. Unknown to him, however, a small yacht named *Maria* had slipped away during the heat of battle and bravely sailed against the current for months. She miraculously arrived at Batavia with news of Koxinga's invasion. See C. E. S., *Verwaerloosde Formosa*, p. 100.

[123] See Harthouwer's account in Blussé et al., *Zeelandia dagregisters*, Part IV, pp. 579–581. Refer also to C. E. S., *Verwaerloosde Formosa*, pp. 145–149 and Chiang (Jiang), *Daghregister van Meij*, Part 2, p. 52.

[124] Chiang (Jiang), *Daghregister van Meij*, Part 2, p. 51.

[125] Yang Ying, *Congzheng shilu*, p. 191; Jiang Risheng, *Taiwan waiji*, p. 204; Chiang (Jiang), *Daghregister van Meij*, Part 2, pp. 37–39; C. E. S., *Verwaerloosde Formosa*, pp. 141, 145. For more on Chinese defectors to the Dutch, see Andrade, *Lost colony*, p. 227.

[126] Zhang Huangyan, *Zhang Cangshui shiwen ji*, TWWXCK, 142 (1962), pp. 30–31.

The Taiwan campaign had degenerated into a sheer contest for survival, for which side – Koxinga or the VOC – could hold out longest without sinking under the weight of its own problems.[127] Under these circumstances, Koxinga saw little choice but to intensify his already severe discipline to keep the organization in line. On a daily basis he executed followers and Chinese residents in due haste for the slightest crime or simply getting on his wrong side. Koxinga retaliated against Wu Hao, the most vocal opponent of the invasion, by ordering his decapitation under the convenient pretext of embezzling funds for personal use. Other victims included both the Chengtian prefect and Wannian magistrate for distributing grain with a small measure.[128] In response to complaints of his unreasonable severity, Koxinga stressed that "without a round of rectification in the initial stages of establishing a state, there will be no end of improper practices!"[129] The sheer force of his personality helped achieve a modicum of stability during the turbulent period of transition to a new frontier.

The situation began to improve during the autumn of 1661. Koxinga successfully put down the aboriginal rebellions, while retaining the loyalty of other tribes, especially the crucial native villages around Provintia.[130] On September 16, his troops handily beat back a two-pronged counterattack from the reinforced Zeelandia garrison on land and sea, killing 128 men and capturing five ships and fifty to sixty prisoners, whom he promptly executed.[131] Meanwhile, the storms in the Taiwan Strait subsided sufficiently for a fleet of twenty-four grain junks to arrive from Xiamen on October 14 with enough provisions to tide his men over until they could grow their own crops.[132] The specter of Dutch cooperation with the Qing also never actualized. Admiral Jacob Caeuw, charged with sealing the alliance with the Fujian authorities, encountered a severe storm at Penghu shortly after his departure on December 3, and sailed for Siam instead.[133] Resigned to their fates, the Dutch retreated permanently into their fortress.

---

[127] The equally serious crisis that pervaded the Dutch garrison has received extensive treatment in Andrade, *Lost colony*.

[128] Chiang (Jiang), *Daghregister van Meij*, Part 2, pp. 29–30; Yang Ying, *Congzheng shilu*, p. 185; Peng, *Jinghai zhi*, p. 60.

[129] Xia, *Haiji jiyao*, p. 29; Jiang Risheng, *Taiwan waiji*, p. 208.

[130] Ruan, *Haishang jianwenlu*, p. 38; Blussé et al., *Zeelandia dagregisters*, Part IV, p. 386.

[131] This battle is described from the Dutch side in Blussé et al., *Zeelandia dagregisters*, Part IV, pp. 532–535 and C. E. S., *Verwaerloosde Formosa*, pp. 142–144. A Chinese perspective is found in Yang Ying, *Congzheng shilu*, p. 191.

[132] Blussé et al., *Zeelandia dagregisters*, Part IV, pp. 555–556.

[133] Bitter policy disagreements within the Dutch camp over how to respond to Koxinga's invasion, compounded by personality conflicts between Caeuw and Governor Coyett, may have contributed to the former's decision to leave Taiwan and his subsequent actions. See C. E. S., *Verwaerloosde Formosa*, pp. 146–150.

Even this final haven of stability amid a hostile sea of Chinese no longer remained secure. In January 1662, Koxinga's men, acting on the advice of a German defector, stormed and occupied a strategic redoubt that overlooked Zeelandia from atop a hill. With the fort's entire defensive network now exposed entirely to Koxinga's firepower from above, Governor Coyett realized the futility of further resistance, and held talks over terms of surrender with Koxinga. After much back and forth, the two sides signed a formal treaty on February 1, ending the bitter, nine-month-long siege. Twelve days later, Coyett and his men marched to their ships decked in regalia, armed to the teeth and banners flying. They were allowed to bring along their personal possessions as they sailed away into the maritime horizon.[134] Koxinga, on the other hand, took over all of the company's assets and fortresses, and, most importantly, its colony of Taiwan.

After the Dutch left, Koxinga converted Fort Zeelandia at Tayouan, now renamed Anping, into his primary residence.[135] Besides continuing his existing policies toward Han subjects, he sought to include the aborigines within his broader vision for Taiwan. Koxinga took grand tours of their settlements with his commanders and Pinqua, a specialist in aboriginal affairs who had procured deerskins from various tribes under the Dutch and understood their languages. Koxinga showered the natives who flocked the roads to welcome him with pouches of tobacco. He feasted their chieftains at banquets and bestowed upon them Ming caps and gowns. He and his revenue official, Yang Ying, also discussed sending a Han peasant to every native village to instruct them in Chinese-style intensive farming practices and provide them with tools and oxen.[136]

Punctures to the ship

Despite the victory in Taiwan, concurrent developments across the strait posed fresh challenges to the legitimacy and cohesion of Koxinga's organization. After the Shunzhi emperor's death, four Manchu regents led by the nobleman Oboi (c. 1610–1669) ruled in the name of the young Shengzu. This cohort, unlike the recently deceased ruler, viewed Han Chinese with suspicion and pursued conservative policies aimed at

---

[134] C. E. S. *Verwaerloosde Formosa*, pp. 152–153, 160–161 and Chiang (Jiang), *Daghregister van Meij*, Part 2, pp. 49–50.

[135] Jiang Risheng, *Taiwan waiji*, p. 205.

[136] Yang Ying, *Congzheng shilu*, pp. 187–188, 193–194. This passage is the last-known reference to He Tingbin found in any source, East Asian or Western. His ultimate fate remains a mystery.

shoring up Manchu rule.[137] In late 1661, the court expanded the earlier order to vacate the counties around Xiamen to include the entire Chinese seaboard, from Liaodong in the north down to Guangdong. Actual implementation varied from place to place and across periods, depending upon the nature of the maritime threat. However, the southeastern coast, the Zheng's main sphere of activity, experienced the most systematic enforcement of the policy. Officials in southern Zhejiang, Fujian, and Guangdong oversaw the construction of walls and fortresses about 30 *li* (17.3 km) from the sea, and forcibly removed anyone living outside those boundaries. The draconian policy brought untold suffering and dislocation to coastal residents. It further brought Koxinga's commercial network to a complete standstill, as Qing soldiers, stationed every few kilometers along the boundary wall, stood ready to intercept any merchant trying to smuggle products from the interior out to sea.[138]

Since Koxinga's occupation of Taiwan as a new base shattered any hopes on the part of the Qing for a peaceful submission, Zheng Zhilong no longer had any use to the court. For some unknown reason, Zhilong also "had discord" with one of the Manchu regents, Suksaha (d. 1669), making the new leadership even less inclined to keep him around. In December 1661, the Qing finally took action. It sentenced him and his sons and servants in Beijing – a total of eleven people – to undergo the slow and painful death by slicing (or death by a thousand cuts). However, at the last minute, the court showed some mercy and commuted the punishment to decapitation. Officials also oversaw the confiscation of Zheng family land and assets, and the destruction of their ancestral graves in Quanzhou and Zhangzhou. The viciousness of the Qing toward his family caused Koxinga to suffer an emotional breakdown.[139]

The Ming loyalist cause was also on its last legs. In January 1662 Wu Sangui led Qing troops into the Myanmar capital of Ava (near present-day Mandalay), and forced the king to hand over the Yongli pretender and his entourage. In May, after bringing them back to Yunnan, Wu had him and his son strangled. Li Dingguo continued his fruitless resistance with a pitiful remnant of troops, but mounting defections from his ranks and illness soon took their toll. In August 1662 he, too, passed away in the extreme southwestern corner of Yunnan.[140]

[137] Wakeman, *Great enterprise*, vol. 2, pp. 1067–1070; Zhang Kaiyuan et al. (eds.), *Qing tongjian*, 4 vols. (Changsha, Hunan: Yuelu shushe, 2000), vol. I, p. 483.

[138] Zheng Yiju, "Zheng Chenggong zhuan," p. 21.

[139] Xia, *Haiji jiyao*, p. 28; Jiang Risheng, *Taiwan waiji*, p. 204; *Qing Shengzu shilu xuanji* (henceforth *Kangxi shilu*), TWWXCK, 165 (1963), p. 4.

[140] For a detailed account of the Yongli Emperor's flight into Myanmar and his subsequent capture and execution, refer to Struve, *Southern Ming*, pp. 170–178 and Wakeman, *Great enterprise*, vol. II, pp. 1030–1036.

Koxinga's father and the pretender had been crucial figureheads who knit together his organization and extended its authority both inward to the southeastern littoral and outward to the China Seas. Their sudden passing greatly diminished the credibility of his leadership, already under challenge because of his unpopular decision to contest Taiwan. His relatives and subordinates grew openly disobedient as 1662 progressed. In March, soon after the Dutch departed, Koxinga ordered Zheng Tai and Hong Xu, the two commanders placed in charge of Xiamen's defense, to relocate to Taiwan with their families under the pain of death. However, the two men heard reports from deserters who had fled from the island about the hunger and epidemics and Koxinga's harsh discipline. Rather than face the bleak prospects, they resorted to all manner of delaying tactics to avoid setting sail.[141]

Koxinga then learned to his dismay that his eldest son and designated successor, Zheng Jing, whom he had entrusted with Xiamen's civil affairs, had been dallying with the wet nurse of his fourth and youngest son. Two children had resulted from their illicit union. The news threw Koxinga into a fit of rage, since such liaisons were considered incest according to strict Confucian interpretations.[142] He promptly dispatched envoys to Xiamen with orders for Zheng Tai to slit Jing's throat, behead the wet nurse and illegitimate children, and execute his own wife, Madame Dong, for failure to discipline their son. Reluctant to carry out the orders, Tai and the other commanders killed only the wet nurse and children and sent their severed heads to Taiwan. Unsatisfied, Koxinga dispatched another special envoy, this time entrusting the man with his personal sword – a fearsome symbol of his power – to demand the lives of the other culpable parties. The issue became an explicit litmus test of the Xiamen commanders' loyalty. Pressed to a corner, they chose instead to openly defy him. They killed the envoy and stopped grain ships and other vessels from traveling across the strait, while detaining Koxinga's junks from Taiwan.[143] All communications between the two sides subsequently became nonexistent.

Koxinga scrambled to reassert his authority. As Wills points out, he tried to capitalize upon his adopted familial connection to the Ming imperial house to assume the throne for himself as the rightful successor

---

[141] Jiang Risheng, *Taiwan waiji*, p. 210.

[142] Xia, *Haiji jiyao*, p. 3; Jiang Risheng, *Taiwan waiji*, pp. 200–201, 210; Borao-Mateo et al., *Spaniards in Taiwan*, vol. II, p. 590. The wet nurse was considered one of the "eight mothers," and therefore, a relative of the Zheng family. See Wills, "Maritime China," p. 228.

[143] Jiang Risheng, *Taiwan waiji*, p. 210; Xia, *Haiji jiyao*, p. 30; Zheng Yiju, "Zheng Chenggong zhuan," p. 22.

of the deceased Yongli pretender.[144] At the same time, he planned to forge a new "China" among the waves that would turn back on the mainland to encompass his entire commercial network in maritime East Asia. These two aims coalesced in his expansionary designs upon the Philippines. On April 21, 1662, he wrote a pompous, arrogant letter addressed to Governor-General Manrique de Lara demanding his submission as a vassal. Koxinga emphasized that "enlightened princes chosen by heaven should be recognized with tribute by all foreign nations." If Lara complied and rendered tribute every year, he could "continue in the possession of your office and your royal city," and trade would proceed unhindered. If not, he threatened, the Spanish would suffer the same fate as the Dutch on Taiwan. His fleets would "destroy [their] armed forces, warehouses, cities, buildings, and beautiful structures, not leaving a stone unscathed."[145] Either outcome would benefit Koxinga. Compliance with his demands accorded him official foreign recognition, a major precondition for assuming the emperorship. Alternatively, an invasion would mark the next step after Taiwan in the establishment of a maritime kingdom.

In May, Koxinga dispatched the Dominican friar Vittorio Riccio as his envoy to carry the letter to Manila. The arrival of the priest, dressed in the robes of a Chinese official, caused a commotion within the Sangley community. Many Chinese, believing that a repeat of Taiwan would soon occur and that they would be freed from the harsh rule of the Spanish, rebelled on May 25. After killing several black slaves and two Spaniards, several thousand residents rushed out of the Parián and attacked the city gates. The artillery from the walls opened fire, dispersing the crowd and forcing about 1,500 of them to flee into the nearby jungles and mountains. The authorities then mobilized two hundred native Filipinos from Pampanga, northwest of Manila. These warriors hunted down all of the hideouts in the following weeks and massacred the escapees. Meanwhile, the Spanish collected as many Chinese as they could find and packed them onto ten junks in the Bay of Manila, each with up to 1,300 people. Lara forced the captains to convey them, along with a defiant written reply, to Taiwan as "tributes" of insult to Koxinga.[146]

---

[144] Wills, *Mountain of fame*, pp. 229–230.
[145] Gregorio F. Zaide (ed.), *Documentary sources of Philippine history*, 12 vols. (Manila: National Book Store, 1990), pp. 455–456.
[146] This narrative of the massacre and the Spanish response comes from two eyewitness accounts, the first from an autobiography by Vittorio Riccio written in 1665. Major excerpts can be found in Borao-Mateo et al., *Spaniards in Taiwan*, vol. II, pp. 600–609. The second source came from the hand of an unknown Jesuit priest who personally witnessed the events and recorded them in an unpublished manuscript around 1663. For a complete version, refer to Emma Blair and James Robertson, *The Philippine islands:*

Unknown to the authorities, a junk had already departed covertly from Manila on May 25, the day of the abortive uprising. Upon reaching Taiwan, its crew informed Koxinga of the news, complete with embellishments of the ensuing slaughter. However, he did not need the additional exaggeration, as the stream of refugees flooding onto the shores of Anping several weeks later provided ample evidence of what had happened. Infuriated at the brazen defiance of the Spanish, Koxinga vowed to launch an offensive on the Philippines and "destroy the islands" once and for all, "reducing to ashes its very stones."[147] He ordered soldiers to be trained and armaments and ships to be prepared for the upcoming expedition.

However, the psychological trauma caused by personal tragedy, the severe challenges to his authority from his own followers and the Qing, the burdensome administrative duties in the tropical humidity of Taiwan, and now the calculated snub from the Spanish, all wore down Koxinga's health. He first experienced a fever with chills on June 16, 1662, at his residence in the former Casteel Zeelandia. A doctor dispatched by Ma Xin to treat his illness diagnosed Koxinga with sunstroke. Unfazed, he refused the medication given to him and continued to read and observe the harbor of Anping from his castle, hoping to spot junks bearing news from Xiamen. He also discussed matters of state with his civil and military officials from his bed.[148] After much debate, he decided to adopt their advice and keep Zheng Jing as his heir despite the young man's severe moral shortcomings. Koxinga further designated his own tenth brother, Xi, as caretaker for Taiwan's affairs on Jing's behalf, and ordered his commanders to uphold them both.[149] It was his last major decision. Within days, he came down with severe bouts of delirium and insanity. On the night of June 23, a week after he first experienced adverse symptoms, Zheng Chenggong gave out a great yell, muttered a few last words, and passed away while clawing his face with his fingers and chewing his hands.[150] He was thirty-eight, still at the prime of his life.

1493–1898: explorations by early navigators, descriptions of the islands and their peoples, their histories and records of the Catholic missions, as related in contemporaneous books and manuscripts, showing the political, economic, commercial and religious conditions of those islands from their earliest relations with European nations to the close of the nineteenth century, 55 vols. (Cleveland, OH: Arthur H. Clark Company, 1906), pp. 218–250.

[147] Borao-Mateo et al., *Spaniards in Taiwan*, vol. II, p. 607.

[148] Li Guangdi, *Rongcun yulu, Rongcun xu yulu* (Beijing: Zhonghua Bookstore, 1995), p. 672; Borao-Mateo et al., *Spaniards in Taiwan*, vol. II, p. 607.

[149] Zha, *Zuiwei lu xuanji*, pp. 136–137.

[150] Jiang Risheng, *Taiwan waiji*, p. 211; Ni, *Xu Ming jishi benmo*, p. 179; *Kangxi shilu*, p. 9. Koxinga's final words varied according to the account, but mainly lamented his failure to restore the Ming, act as a filial son, or serve as a responsible family head. However, they were probably embellishments to legitimate his successors or heighten the dramatic effect of his death.

Figure 4.1 Altar to Koxinga at the shrine dedicated to his memory in Tainan, Taiwan. Photograph by author, February 2015.

Despite Koxinga's brief life, he laid the foundations for a maritime Chinese territorial state centered upon Taiwan. John Wills and Wong Young-tsu both view his decision as a desperate reaction to resource shortages caused by intensifying military pressure from the Qing and its coastal evacuation measures. Wong further contends that Koxinga aimed to establish a secure base in Taiwan in preparation for a future counterattack on the mainland.[151] Indeed, Koxinga's invasion occurred as a direct result of his defeat outside the gates of Nanjing. He had failed to revive the flagging fortunes of the Ming loyalist movement as an effective counterweight to the Manchus, or control his product sources in the Yangzi River Delta.

Nonetheless, long before 1661 Koxinga had already set his sights upon Taiwan and the Philippines for their bountiful natural resources and linkages to markets outside of maritime East Asia, the new sources of growth for the region. He had developed, in conjunction with the defector Pinqua, detailed plans for an occupation of Taiwan, ranging

[151] Wills, "Contingent connections," p. 190; Wong Young-tsu, "Security," p. 145.

from campaign logistics to the establishment of a sophisticated administrative structure. It is apparent from his actions that he was fully prepared to abandon the cause of restoration on the mainland in favor of a broader vision of recentering the Ming on Taiwan as the foundation for a maritime Chinese empire.[152] However, few of Koxinga's followers shared his farsightedness and adaptability. The unpopularity of his decision, along with the untimely demise of the organization's most important symbols of legitimacy – Zheng Zhilong and the Yongli emperor – at the hands of the Qing threatened the underpinnings of his authority. The magnitude of these challenges broke down even Koxinga's indomitable will and contributed to his sudden illness and death. However, the need to justify and institutionalize a Chinese state outside of "China" had become a necessity for the Zheng organization's continued survival, and remained a preoccupation of his successors.

---

[152] The evidence shown in this book validates, with some modifications, the perspectives of Croizier, *Chinese Nationalism*, p. 23 and Wills, *Mountain of fame*, p. 228.

5   The Zheng state on Taiwan

After ten years of encouraging the multitudes to grow, after ten years of education and nourishment, and after ten years of letting them congregate and become numerous, in thirty years, [Taiwan] can truly compete for tops with the Central Plain.

Chen Yonghua, adapting a phrase from the *Spring and Autumn Annals*, 1660s.[1]

After Koxinga occupied and administered this land, the Chinese people came one after another. I can see nothing that is not Chinese here in Anping of Dongning. Its people are the people of the Middle Kingdom, and its soil is the soil of the Middle Kingdom.

Wang Zhongxiao, "Dedication to the Dongning Shrine of Supreme Heaven," 1665.[2]

When news of Koxinga's death reached Xiamen, his commanders crafted a memorial to the Yongli emperor, informing the equally dead pretender that twenty-year-old Zheng Jing would inherit his father's ranks and titles. They then burned the document to send it to the ruler in the underworld. Henceforth, the junior Zheng referred to himself as the Inherited Feudatory (Shifan), while others called him the Crown Prince (Shizi).[3] Yet, his rule began during a precarious time when the organization just received crippling blows to its legitimacy, first from the deaths of Zheng Zhilong and the Yongli pretender, and then of Koxinga himself. Jing's own moral failings further undermined his position. Competing power centers had emerged within the organization. Taiwan came under the domination of Koxinga's second-in-command, Ma Xin, whose division boasted the largest number of soldiers in the Zheng army. The island's caretaker, Koxinga's tenth brother Zheng Xi, became a figurehead for his ambitions.[4] Zhang Huangyan, the Zhejiang and Fujian gentry, and Ming imperial descendants plotted to enthrone the prince of Lu as the Yongli

---

[1] Jiang Risheng, *Taiwan waiji*, p. 236.
[2] Wang Zhongxiao, *Wang Zhongxiao gong ji* (Nanjing: Jiangsu Ancient Texts Publishing House, 2000), p. 82.
[3] Jiang Risheng, *Taiwan waiji*, p. 213; Zheng Yiju, "Zheng Chenggong zhuan," p. 22.
[4] Li Guangdi, *Rongcun yulu*, p. 672.

146

pretender's replacement.[5] Power on the mainland bases became concentrated in the hands of Zheng Tai. All decisions at Xiamen took place through consultation in committees of civil and military powerbrokers, with Tai having the final say.[6]

Yet Zheng Jing successfully held his ground in the face of these contenders, each of whom possessed far more soldiers and resources than him, along with ensuing offensives from his vengeful Qing and Dutch enemies, to ensure the continued survival and unity of the organization. Through the creative and flexible interpretation of his father's ambiguous legacy and the employment of a cohort of bright young advisors, he succeeded in ruling longer and under more stable conditions than any before and after him. Surprisingly, compared to the extensive scholarly attention paid to the colorful and eventful lives of Zheng Zhilong and Koxinga among historians in East Asia, and, increasingly, the West, this third leader has received much scanter coverage. Yet it was under his two-decade rule that the organization completed its transformation into a territorial state, giving him a solid, prosperous base for reconstituting Zheng dominance in maritime East Asia.[7]

Zheng Jing and his opponents

Zheng Jing's character and upbringing differed markedly from that of his cosmopolitan grandfather and headstrong father. Unlike them, he had narrower horizons, having never left China and spent most of his early life along the Fujian coast. He was probably too young to clearly recall the trauma of dynastic transition, or the fate of Zheng Zhilong and his Japanese grandmother at the hands of Qing soldiers. Although, like Koxinga, Jing received a strict Confucian education that imparted within him the rigid separation of Chinese and "barbarian," his antipathy toward the Manchus assumed a less personal, but more virulently proto-racist character. His writings equate the Manchu entry into China with "the rank odor of sheep flooding the four corners of the earth." Elsewhere, he composed lyrics describing their supposedly perverse religious and sexual practices, which reinforced their image as sensual beasts.[8] His distance in time and space from any existent Ming court allowed him to equate loyalism more with an abstract allegiance to the Han ethnicity than to a particular dynastic house.

---

[5] Zhang Huangyan, *Zhang Cangshui shiwenji*, pp. 43–44; Shao, *Dongnan jishi*, p. 115.
[6] Zheng Yiju, "Zheng Chenggong zhuan," p. 22; Jiang Risheng, *Taiwan waiji*, p. 213; Borao-Mateo et al., *Spaniards in Taiwan*, vol. II, p. 614.
[7] This chapter builds, in part, upon the excellent foundational research done by Hung, "Cheng Family," pp. 175–238 and Wong Young-tsu, "Security," pp. 153–156.
[8] "Yanping er wang," p. 130.

Jing's conservative upbringing clashed with the cosmopolitan environment of Xiamen, where he could rub shoulders with people from across China and the world and access all kinds of luxury goods. As eldest son and heir to the family enterprise, he was also relatively sheltered from the wrath of his father. His earlier years saw him completely pushing aside his education and turning to a life of rebelliousness and excessive indulgence. He and his servants often commandeered private property around Xiamen and terrorized the common people at will.[9] He enjoyed, to the point of obsession, food, drink, and, especially, sex. Caught in an unhappy arranged marriage with the daughter of an eminent Ming minister, he engaged in flings with singsong boys and took a fancy toward mature women.[10] Koxinga's decision to have Jing executed for impregnating the wet nurse of a younger son represented the culmination of years of frustration and helplessness at what he perceived was the wasted promise of his designated heir.

Yet this traumatic incident, along with his father's death on Taiwan, quickly drew Jing away from his youthful waywardness. As if trying to atone for his past depravity, he readily embraced again his Confucian education. On the one hand, he made sure to strictly observe the precedents set down by Koxinga in every manner and construed all that he did as the embodiment of the will of his father, whom he referred to as the "Former King" (Xianwang).[11] At the same time, and perhaps because of his pampered past, he eased up on Koxinga's strict discipline and micromanagement of his followers. People around the fully mature Zheng Jing knew him as a benevolent and kind man, humble and respectful toward others, and willing to consult their advice. He faced fewer moral contradictions in his character compared to Koxinga. With both father and ruler out of the picture, filial piety no longer conflicted with loyalty. Jing therefore had the opportunity to take the family and organization into new directions using his imagination and flexibility.

Nonetheless, he first had to prevent becoming a pawn of other powerful interests that sought to appropriate Koxinga's legacy at his expense. Zhang Huangyan and his Zhejiang militia posed the least challenge. Their attempt to place the prince of Lu on the throne ended abruptly with the imperial descendant's death in December 1662. Zhang and his followers then left Xiamen altogether, and withdrew to a small, deserted island off Zhejiang, where they stayed for two years until the Qing captured and executed them.[12]

[9] Borao-Mateo et al., *Spaniards in Taiwan*, vol. II, pp. 592–593.
[10] Jiang Risheng, *Taiwan waiji*, p. 200; Zheng Yiju, "Zheng Chenggong zhuan," p. 22.
[11] See, for instance, Zheng Jing's edicts in "Yanping er wang yiji," pp. 133–134.
[12] Zha, *Lu chunqiu*, p. 100; Shao, *Dongnan jishi*, pp. 115–116.

A far more serious threat came from two veteran officials: Ma Xin on Taiwan and Zheng Tai in Xiamen. Soon after Koxinga's death, a bitter power struggle broke out between them. The flashpoint revolved around Tai's decision to accept a renewed invitation for talks from the Qing Fujian authorities in August 1662. Their conditions were harsh compared to Koxinga's days; Zheng followers could obtain high ranks and honors only if they evacuated their mainland coastal bases and adopted Manchu hairstyles. However, the Fujian authorities believed that they stood in a much stronger position to dictate the terms than before. They calculated that negotiations would either severely weaken the organization by exacerbating its already serious internal divisions, or, more ideally, bring about its complete collapse or submission without the use of force. Indeed, they successfully obtained the first objective and nearly achieved the second.

Bypassing both Jing and Ma Xin, Zheng Tai responded eagerly to the Qing initiative on his own accord. In his own name and those of his fellow Xiamen commanders, Tai surrendered several official seals as tokens of his sincerity. He then dispatched a trusted agent to Beijing with his letter, which actually agreed to the Qing condition of shaving the head so long as he received recognition as the organization's new leader and remained with his followers on the coast.[13] Jing could do little but play along with the talks, as he still lacked a solid power base. Yet Ma Xin, fearing that any settlement would solidify Tai's absolute leadership over the organization at his expense, cut off all contact with Xiamen and declared self-rule over Taiwan. Unknown to him, his rival was already in collusion with the aides of Zheng Xi – the figurehead caretaker – and two generals on the island. A month later, this faction launched a coup resulting in Ma's "violent death."[14] The conspirators and Tai then agreed to recognize Tai's dominance over Xiamen, while Xi could continue to run Taiwan as before (under Tai's supervision, of course). Since Zheng Jing had become redundant, they secretly plotted to assassinate him under some pretext.[15]

Ma's death removed a major obstacle to Tai's desired settlement with the Qing court. However, this initiative apparently ran into further opposition from a core of prominent civil and military officials on both

---

[13] *Tei shi kankei*, p. 2; Xia, *Haiji jiyao*, p. 31; *Shiliao sanbian*, pp. 53–54.

[14] Jiang Risheng, *Taiwan waiji*, p. 212 and Ni, *Xu Ming jishi*, p. 179 claim that Ma Xin died just days after Koxinga due to illness caused by excessive grief at his leader's passing, but this version sounds unconvincing. Qing primary records closer to the actual events more plausibly describe Ma's sudden demise as occurring several months after Koxinga and as a result of unnatural causes "without any sickness." The circumstantial evidence hints at a coup involving Zheng Tai and, possibly, carried out with the assistance of the Qing Fujian authorities. See Li Guangdi, *Rongcun yulu*, p. 672 and *Manwen dang'an 2*, p. 395.

[15] "Yanping erwang," p. 133 and Borao-Mateo et al., *Spaniards in Taiwan*, vol. II, p. 618.

sides of the strait. Their intense combined pressure forced Tai to let the talks fail by backtracking and ordering his envoy to insist upon the "Korea example" of refusing to shave the head before the Qing. Not surprisingly, the envoy returned empty handed in January 1663.[16] Tai's failure at negotiations revealed before the entire organization the limits of his authority, as well as his blatant opportunism and hunger for power at any cost.

His autocratic behavior deeply disturbed Hong Xu, the other main commander at Xiamen, who now threw his support behind Zheng Jing. In coordination with Jing's close friend and advisor, Chen Yonghua, Hong supplied the heir with ships and one thousand men to root out Tai's influence over Taiwan. In December 1662, Jing's forces landed on the island. After a brief skirmish, Zheng Xi's aides and associates in the military were killed or executed, although the caretaker himself was spared. Other officers, who had previously sat on the fence, rallied behind Jing and recognized him as the rightful head of the organization. Before the victorious troops sailed back to Xiamen in late January 1663, he discovered a stash of letters exchanged between Tai and Xi's faction plotting his assassination.[17]

Zheng Jing needed to get rid of his clan uncle or face grave danger to his own life. The opportune moment came in July, when Tai accepted an invitation to a family banquet. Chen Yonghua and Hong Xu arranged an ambush. Jing's soldiers seized Tai during the meal and locked him in a cell. His grand dreams ruined, Tai strangled himself the next day. Most of the members of his vast patronage network defected to the Qing when the news reached them. Their ranks included Tai's brother, Zheng Mingjun, and son, Zuanxu, along with their relatives and six hundred civil and military officials, 180 junks, and over ten thousand soldiers.[18] The arrival of these bitter, vengeful men with their ships, weapons, and expertise came as a timely windfall for the Qing. Having failed to bring about an implosion or submission of the Zheng through talks, the Fujian authorities decided to launch an all-out offensive against Xiamen and Jinmen.

The officials also found another willing ally in the VOC. The Dutch were deeply angered over their defeat at the hands of Koxinga. Not only did the company leave behind sizable assets and trading goods valued at

---

[16] Xia, *Haiji jiyao*, p. 31. This interpretation of the negotiations elaborates upon the narrative of Wills in *Pepper, guns, and parleys*, pp. 41–43.

[17] Li Guangdi, *Rongcun yulu*, p. 673; Jiang Risheng, *Taiwan waiji*, pp. 217–221; Xia, *Haiji jiyao*, p. 32.

[18] Xia, *Haiji jiyao*, pp. 33–34; Jiang Risheng, *Taiwan waiji*, pp. 225–226; and *Kangxi shilu*, p. 13.

400,000 guilders on Taiwan, but its surrender also struck a blow to its carefully crafted image of invincibility across maritime East Asia. The authorities at Batavia feared that all countries hostile to the Dutch in the region would now take the Zheng as an example to "raise their heads and not respect [its] power." It was imperative for the VOC to quickly avenge this humiliation. The loss of Taiwan itself, Blussé and Wills have pointed out, posed a relatively minor concern to the company. The island had gradually become less valuable over the 1650s, as it lost first its role in the intra-East Asian exchange of silk for silver, and then as a transit station for gold to India. However, for the Zheng, Taiwan's importance could not be underestimated; the island provided a strategic gateway to the depots of Southeast Asia and a linkage between the East Asian and Indian Ocean world-regions. More important than saving face, the Dutch had to prevent the organization from expanding beyond the China Seas and into areas where they traditionally exercised dominance.[19]

In the wake of Taiwan's fall, the company pursued a stringent policy of naval blockade, combined with diplomatic pressure, to expel the Zheng trading presence from markets and product sources across the Eastern and Western Oceans. Dutch ships prowled the waters, ready to intercept and plunder any junk suspected of affiliation with the Zheng.[20] As a result of rampant predation outside of Ayutthaya, the VOC successfully forced the Siamese king, Narai, to agree not to employ any Chinese on board his royal junks. Because of the importance of Chinese to Siam's economic livelihood, Narai could not fully carry out this measure, but he did secure oaths of allegiance from his merchants to serve him alone, and not the Zheng.[21] Likewise, in Tonkin, another major partner of the organization, the Trịnh lord did not completely bow to Qing and Dutch pressure to ban its activities. Nonetheless, he ordered all foreigners, with the exception of the Dutch, to move into a special quarter outside the city walls of Hanoi, where they would be placed under close supervision and heavily taxed. Any Chinese, including the Zheng merchants, who refused had to blacken their teeth and go barefoot in the Vietnamese manner. Besides these two powerful kingdoms, the Dutch set up a factory in Cambodia, and forced its ruler to grant exclusive trading rights in animal skins and other key exports.[22]

For the VOC, Koxinga's death and the ensuing succession struggle within the organization presented a golden opportunity for exterminating its rival at the source. The authorities in Batavia dispatched a naval

[19] Wills, *Pepper*, p. 32; Blussé, "No boats," p. 67.
[20] Zheng Ruiming, "Ming-Zheng yu Dongnanya," p. 76.
[21] Viraphol, *Tribute and profit*, pp. 11–12; Cheng (Zheng), *War, trade and piracy*, p. 217.
[22] Cheng (Zheng), *War, trade and piracy*, pp. 214–215.

squadron under the command of Admiral Balthasar Bort (d. 1680) to the China coast. Accompanying him was Constantijn Nobel, appointed as the VOC's main envoy to China and put in charge of negotiations with the Qing.[23] Their task was to realize the alliance with the Qing that had failed to materialize earlier during the siege of Zeelandia. After arriving at the Fujian coast in August 1662, the two men met the feudatory, Geng Jimao, and other provincial officials. Both sides agreed to an arrangement whereby the Dutch would help the Qing in its upcoming campaign to rid the Zheng from Xiamen, Jinmen, and other mainland holdouts in exchange for a second joint campaign to restore Taiwan to the VOC. The Fujian authorities offered the additional sweetener of access to Chinese products for the Japan market as a reward.

As Bort awaited official sanction from the Qing court for the alliance, he and his men conducted sporadic raids upon Zheng smuggling emporiums along the littoral. Once that approval had been secured, the Dutch returned to Fuzhou on August 29, 1663, with seventeen ships and 440 guns, 1,382 sailors, and 1,234 soldiers in preparation for the upcoming campaign against Zheng Jing. On November 19, a total of five hundred Qing junks, together with Bort's fleet, jointly attacked the Zheng navy in the narrow sea passage between Xiamen and Jinmen. Jing's four hundred ships put up a strong resistance, and even killed the Qing commander, Ma Degong, the same man who had briefly occupied and ransacked Xiamen in 1650. However, the superiority and deadly accuracy of the Dutch weapons and numerical advantage of the combined navy forced him to abandon his twin bases. Left with just a handful of tiny barren islands off the mainland coast, Zheng Jing found it increasingly difficult to maintain his troops and secure supplies. The following April of 1664, he decided to withdraw completely to Taiwan.[24]

For Jing's followers and allies, the mainland bases had represented symbols of inspiration, and kept hopes alive for a restored Ming. The loss of these final bastions of resistance presented them with two bleak choices. The first promised an indefinite exile on a "barbarian" island, while the second forced them to adopt "barbarian" customs in their native land. Enticed by offers of leniency and ranks and rewards from the Qing, the vast majority of followers chose to shave their heads and pledge loyalty to the new dynasty. On August 25, 1664, Bendai, the Manchu imperial commissioner to Fujian, estimated that surrendered Zheng personnel from 1662 to 1664 amounted to 3,985 civil and military

---

[23] Wills, *Pepper, guns, and parleys*, pp. 33–34.
[24] For a detailed narrative of the Qing-Dutch offensive, see Wills, *Pepper, guns, and parleys*, pp. 37–78.

officials, including some of Jing's most high-ranking and trusted generals, 40,962 soldiers, and nine hundred ships. This figure was one-third to a half of Jing's total troop strength in the Xiamen and Jinmen area.[25] In contrast, no more than fifty junks, two thousand officials, and four thousand soldiers chose to accompany Zheng Jing to Taiwan. They joined some 20,000 men already on the island, primarily the survivors of Koxinga's invasion and now scattered among the military colonies.[26]

An offensive on Taiwan was expected to come next. In anticipation, a Dutch fleet had already raided and seized Penghu in January 1664, just before Jing's withdrawal. From there, some ships in the fleet appeared menacingly off the waters outside Anping, while others actually landed at Tancoya (present-day Kaohsiung), farther south. Attempts by Jing to negotiate with the company, offering it islands along the mainland coast as trading posts in exchange for its neutrality, proved inconclusive. The Dutch eventually withdrew, judging that they were too low on supplies and manpower to unilaterally attack southern Taiwan, the bastion of Zheng military power.[27] However, in August 1664, another force seized and fortified Jilong, abandoned by the company during Koxinga's invasion. In this northern port, where Zheng forces had not yet penetrated, the Dutch hoped to recreate Taiwan's former prosperity as an entrepôt on the China–Japan route. The prospects looked bright, especially after the VOC received the Qing court's approval to open a factory at Fuzhou, directly facing Jilong across the Taiwan Strait.[28]

Of course, the Dutch also looked forward to the return of the entire island under their control. After much delay, the Fujian feudatory, Geng Jimao, assembled a naval squadron with three hundred junks and mostly Zheng defectors under the command of Shi Lang in preparation for an invasion of Taiwan. The VOC contributed several powerful warships to join the expedition. However, on November 27, 1664, just as the joint fleets began to depart, Shi suddenly turned his ships back to shore, citing severe typhoons in the Taiwan Strait. As a result, the expedition was postponed until December 24. On that day, however, he repeated his earlier performance.[29]

In fact, Shi Lang and Geng Jimao viewed the Dutch as a threat to their own ambitions for dominating the maritime East Asian trade. Shi and his fellow defectors, who constituted the majority of the Fujian naval

[25] Wills, *Pepper, guns, and parleys*, p. 52; Jiang Risheng, *Taiwan waiji*, p. 230; Xia, *Haiji jiyao*, p. 35. A list of the key commanders who submitted to the Qing can be found in *Tei shi kankei*, pp. 9–16.

[26] Shi, *Jinghai jishi*, p. 6; *Minhai jilue*, p. 21.

[27] Wills, *Pepper, guns, and parleys*, pp. 78–79.   [28] Ibid., pp. 90–92.

[29] Wills, *Pepper, guns, and parleys*, pp. 97–99; Cheng (Zheng), *War, trade and piracy*, p. 209.

command, a unit charged with patrolling the littoral and enforcing the coastal evacuation policy, exploited their positions to outfit junks and trade illegally abroad. They wanted Taiwan for themselves as an illicit offshore emporium for goods smuggled into and out of the zone of coastal evacuation. Their agenda received the tacit support of Geng Jimao. The feudatory possessed his own cohort of merchants who supplied the defectors with goods and also sent junks of their own, mostly to Japan. As ultimate gatekeeper over the evacuated zone, Geng hoped to fill in the vacuum left by Zheng Jing's departure to monopolize access to mainland products. With the Dutch in Fuzhou and the defectors in Taiwan, he could play them against one another to keep them both dependent upon his goodwill while bidding up the purchase price.[30]

Faced with grim prospects for recovering its lost colony, the VOC switched its emphasis toward the elimination of Zheng competition to its new Fuzhou-Jilong nexus. In the name of assisting the Qing, its ships violently and often unilaterally cleared islands along the mainland coast of Zheng smuggling bases and communities living illegally beyond the coastal evacuation boundary. The biggest raid occurred in 1665 at Putuoshan, a part of the Zhoushan Islands off Zhejiang. The Dutch ransacked a holy Buddhist pilgrimage site, killing monks, seizing hostages, and carrying off massive quantities of precious relics.[31]

As can be imagined, all of these developments dealt severe blows to the Zheng maritime enterprise. On top of everything, Zheng Jing's relations with Japan, his main ally, went downhill. As the supply of silver from mines across the country began to dwindle, along with the rise of a robust domestic economy, the Tokugawa shogunate came to view overseas trade in an increasingly unfavorable light. At the same time, the organization's settlement on Taiwan and turn away from Ming restoration dampened the *bakufu*'s ideological sympathy. By Jing's generation, the personal ties that his father once enjoyed with Japan were also starting to weaken. Despite being one-quarter Japanese, the son identified far more with the Middle Kingdom, the only cultural milieu he ever knew. Exacerbating this sense of alienation was the defection of Zheng Tai's followers, the segment of the organization that had the most extensive experience with trade at Nagasaki during the 1650s. Jing became embroiled in an acrimonious dispute with Tai's relatives over the ownership of the 300,000 taels of silver deposited at the Chinese Interpreters' Office. Both parties dispatched envoys every year to Nagasaki to plead their

[30] Cheng (Zheng), *War, trade and piracy*, p. 209 and Ho, "Sealords," p. 246.
[31] Chang Hsiu-jung, Anthony Farrington, Huang Fu-san, Ts'ao Yung-ho (Cao Yonghe), Wu Mi-tsa (Wu Micha), Cheng Hsi-fu, and Ang Ka-in (Weng Jiayin) (eds.), *The English factory in Taiwan: 1670–1685* (Taipei: National Taiwan University, 1995), p. 65.

case.[32] The intra-familial feuding sharply divided the Chinese community, with the interpreters backing Zheng Tai's claims to the money and Shichizaemon taking the side of his nephew Jing.[33]

The *bakufu* exploited these divisions and the weakened position of the Zheng to adopt measures aimed both at curbing their influence over the Chinese at Nagasaki and stemming the silver outflow. In 1664, it lifted a 1641 ban on the export of gold coins (*koban*) and encouraged them as alternatives to silver.[34] To encourage more competition with Zheng Jing, the *bakufu* dropped its previously hostile attitude toward traders from Qing territory. Accordingly, the ships of Geng Jimao and the Zheng defectors were accommodated at Nagasaki.[35] The *bakufu* further switched to a strictly neutral stance in disputes between Zheng Jing and the Dutch.[36] In what probably marked a gesture of protest, a Zheng vessel on the open sea outside Nagasaki fired four rounds from its cannon in the direction of the VOC trading post on Deshima island on October 26, 1666. The brazen act, which openly defied prohibitions against the possession of weapons in Japanese waters, precipitated an international crisis when the magistrates of the city detained and jailed the shipmaster and crew. Only the intervention of the powerful shogunal deputy, Suetsugu Heizō Shigetomo, secured their release.[37]

A new "China" abroad

In the face of these challenges on multiple levels to the organization's survival, Zheng Jing first took steps to consolidate his position on Taiwan and stabilize the volatile spirits of his remaining followers. He maintained the symbols of the Ming house, which underpinned his own legitimacy and that of his organization. In spite of the Yongli emperor's demise, everybody pretended that he was still alive, and calendars, letters, and proclamations counted the dates using his reign title. The colophon on the cover of one 1670 Yongli calendar explained that it was printed on the personal orders of Zheng Jing "as a measure of expediency," because "the

---

[32] Some examples of this back-and-forth diplomacy can be found in Historiographical Institute, *Tō tsūji*, vol. 1, pp. 14–20, 58; Hayashi Shunsai, *Ka'i hentai*, vol. 1, pp. 217–240.

[33] Ōta, *Ichiwa ichigen*, vol. 2, pp. 733–736.

[34] Yamawaki, "The great trading merchants," p. 115.

[35] Antony, *Froth*, p. 34; Historiographical Institute, *Tō tsūji*, vol. 1, pp. 22–23.

[36] Historiographical Institute, *Tō tsūji*, vol. 1, pp. 160–161; Hayashi Shunsai, *Ka'i hentai*, vol. I, pp. 237–238; Xia, *Haiji jiyao*, p. 48.

[37] This incident is documented in Historiographical Institute, *Tō tsūji*, vol. 1, pp. 74–77.

imperial calendar, proclaimed afar, has not yet arrived."[38] The former Fort Provintia became a makeshift palace for the deceased ruler. During important holidays, such as Lunar New Year, Jing and his officials, adorned in court garb, would pay homage before an empty throne.[39]

Robert Batchelor sees a "strange timeless quality" to these symbolic gestures that "both repeat and reframe the problem of sovereignty as something divorced from the rituals and instruments of the court itself."[40] Indeed, underneath the professions of loyalty to a nonexistent dynasty, Zheng Jing undertook a series of sweeping reforms that completed the transformation of his organization from a military unit of a larger empire to a territorial state in its own right. Soon after his withdrawal, he proclaimed a new official name for the island: Dongning (Eastern Pacification).[41] Whereas Dongdu, the Eastern Capital coined by his father, implied a new seat of Ming government overseas, Dongning imparted the additional connotation of abandoning the contest for restoration of the mainland in favor of a commitment to permanent settlement.

In contrast to the authoritarian leadership style of his father, Zheng Jing relied more upon consultation with an inner circle of advisors. Members included Chen Yonghua, his closest confidant, who had gone to school and played with him since childhood. Chen assumed the position of advisory staff officer (*ziyi canjun*), equivalent to a prime minister who oversaw all civil affairs on the island.[42] Others had proven their loyalty to him when they chose to accompany him to Taiwan rather than defect to the Qing. Feng Xifan (shown together with Chen and the Zheng family in Figure 5.1), whose father, a high-ranking official under Koxinga, was drowned by a bondservant during the withdrawal, controlled the military as head of the imperial bodyguard (*shiwei*). Hong Xu, a seasoned veteran of the trading lanes and numerous battles against the Qing, provided valuable advice before his death in 1666.[43] This inner core would debate and recommend key policy decisions for Zheng Jing's approval. On matters of crucial importance, Jing would bring them before a meeting of all civil and military officials for discussions to arrive at a final consensus.

The great expanse of land acquired on Taiwan naturally meant more demand for regularized revenue extraction and professional services, in

---

[38] Yang Yongzhi, *Ming Qing shiqi Tainan chuban shi* (Taipei: Taiwan Student Bookstore, 2007), pp. 15–19.

[39] Xia, *Haiji jiyao*, p. 31; Jiang Risheng, *Taiwan waiji*, p. 233.

[40] Batchelor, *London: the Selden Map and the making of a global city, 1549–1689* (Chicago: University of Chicago Press, 2014), p. 189.

[41] Xia, p. 36; Yang Ying, p. 189.

[42] For a brief biography of Chen, see Xia, *Haiji jiyao*, p. 64.

[43] Xia, *Haiji jiyao*, pp. 38, 64.

Figure 5.1 *Taiwan xingle tu* (*Portrait of seeking pleasure in Taiwan*). This painting, whose creator remains unknown, was uncovered from the private collection of the descendants of Zheng Cong, Koxinga's second son. It now belongs to the Zheng Chenggong Memorial Hall in Xiamen. According to one authoritative study, the people enjoying the natural scenery and river in the painting form the core of Taiwan's collective leadership after Koxinga's death in 1662. In the foreground, Zheng Jing,

Caption for Figure 5.1   (cont.)

dressed in the dark blue robe, stands together with Feng Xifan. Behind them, Jing's son, Keshuang, clad in light blue, is shown playing chess with Chen Yonghua. This painting, probably drawn after 1680, represents the first known piece of Chinese visual art in Taiwan.[44] *Special thanks to Professor Nie Dening of Xiamen University.*

contrast to the ad hoc seizures carried out by Zheng troops on the mainland coast. Under the supervision of Chen Yonghua, the Six Offices (Liuguan) of Works, Rites, Punishment, Revenue, Military, and Personnel became transformed into fully functional administrative organs. Civil officials acquired a status theoretically equal to their military counterparts, and both groups had the right, "as ministers," to memorialize Zheng Jing. To generate future homegrown talent, a comprehensive system of basic schools was established to promote Confucian values among residents and train examination candidates. Promising students would go on to the Imperial Academy in Chengtian, opened in 1666 and headed by Chen Yonghua. They could then sit for the triennial civil service examinations and, if successful, qualify for an official post.[45]

However, the creation of a territorial bureaucracy relied not just upon the Chinese imperial model, but also represented a further rationalization of the kinship networks of southern Fujian and the militarized hierarchy from Koxinga's time. Koxinga's former officials and the descendants of his commanders comprised most of the successful candidates who staffed the Six Offices. Hong Lei, the son of Hong Xu, took charge of the Office of Punishments. Yang Ying, a financial expert who worked for years under Zheng Tai, assumed the helm of the strategic Revenue Office, the other key bureaucratic organ.[46]

To manage the growing complexity of Taiwan's local society, Zheng Jing elevated Tianxing and Wannian counties to the status of sub-prefectures (*zhou*). Under them, he established four urban wards (*fang*) and twenty-four rural districts (*li*) in the densely settled southwestern plains, headed by captains who oversaw the Han population. Households were organized into mutual responsibility units that supervised one another and took charge of charity, firefighting, and crime prevention. Beyond the wards and districts were the military colonies, where commanders and

---

[44] Chen Jindong, "Qing *Taiwan xingle tu*," in Zhang Zhongchun and Lin Yuanping (eds.), *Taihai yizhen: Xiamen shi bowuguan guancang she Tai wenwu jianshang* (Shanghai: Academia Press, 2014).

[45] Jiang Risheng, *Taiwan waiji*, pp. 235–236; Xia, *Haiji jiyao*, p. 36.

[46] Xia, *Haiji jiyao*, pp. 38, 44; Jiang Risheng, *Taiwan waiji*, p. 238.

their rank and file farmed for their subsistence. All soldiers theoretically received training in the lax season – although this provision was probably never fully enforced – and prepared to take up arms in the event of warfare. Two divisions guarded Anping and Chengtian on a rotational basis, while permanent garrisons were based in the northern and southern frontiers for supervising the aboriginal villages and the Penghu Islands on the frontline against the Qing.[47] The aboriginal areas maintained the system of native villages (*she*), whereby chieftains enjoyed significant discretion in managing their tribes.[48]

The application of a sophisticated bureaucratic system originally intended to rule over a continent-sized empire onto a tiny island allowed the Zheng organization to enact and enforce policies at an unprecedented level of effectiveness. It could exercise administrative oversight over functions typically undertaken by gentry on a semiformal basis on the mainland.[49] Laws were rigidly and meticulously implemented and the punishments harsh. An early Qing traveler to the island in 1696, over a decade after the Zheng had surrendered, still expressed surprise at the high degree of discipline among residents, who "did not dare to steal even when the myriad goods are left unattended at the marketplace."[50]

The solid grip that Zheng Jing and his oligarchs possessed over Taiwanese society allowed them to carry out and innovate upon Koxinga's unfinished work on the island. They enacted a sliding revenue scale over the different grades of land assigned under his father. Jing and his relatives continued to monopolize the most productive "official fields" from Dutch times. Jing also encouraged his officials to expand the area of their "private fields" and disbanded more troops and placed their commanders in charge of opening new military colonies. Every three years, he dispatched surveyors to adjust the measurements and update the tax rates across the island. The leadership also retained beneficial aspects of the Dutch-era infrastructure, including the head tax on Han Chinese and aborigines and the categories of levies on different sectors of the economy. Land continued to be counted in Dutch units. The Spanish peso, rather than the Chinese tael, served as the currency of account both for internal circulation and foreign trade.[51]

---

[47] Cao Yonghe (Ts'ao Yung-ho), *Taiwan zaoqi lishi yanjiu* (Taipei: Linking, 1995), pp. 271, 285–286; Deng Kongzhao, *Ming-Zheng Taiwan yanjiu*, pp. 77–78.

[48] *Taiwan fu zhi* (*Gazetteer of Taiwan Prefecture*), ed. Jiang Yuying (Taipei: Taiwan yinhang jingji yanjiushi, 1959), 4.

[49] R. Bin Wong describes the hazy division of labor between bureaucrats and gentry in *China transformed*, pp. 113–116.

[50] Yu, *Pihai jiyou*, p. 50.

[51] See Tables 3.1 and 3.2 in Appendix 3.3 for land categorization and taxation.

Attracted in part by the reforms, some 30,000 refugees from across the strait, destitute and starving from the Qing coastal evacuation policy and the general economic downturn on the mainland, flooded into Taiwan. Zheng Jing further encouraged immigration by offering a tax remission for newcomers for their first three years. A large number of them were subsequently recruited as tenants by Zheng officials or settled in the military colonies, as greater harvests above self-sufficiency prompted commanders to lease out their land.[52] Despite the influx, there continued to be immense quantities of virgin land available outside of the south-western population centers and an acute shortage of labor. As a result, military colonies and some private fields practiced slash-and-burn agriculture, with rotation every three years among different plots.[53] Similarly, irrigation projects remained crude and limited in scale, typically involving the construction of small ponds or ditches that trapped rainwater.[54] This type of extensive farming allowed for the rapid proliferation of Han settlements, which soon stretched from the southern tip of the island to present-day Xinzhu in the north.

This expansion came largely at the expense of the aboriginal tribes. Over the 1660s, local chieftains staged numerous rebellions against perceived incursions into their land and traditional way of life. The suppression was often brutal. In one campaign, a division stationed north of present-day Taizhong obliterated the defiant Shalu tribe, leaving six people alive out of an original population of several hundred.[55]

Despite continued tensions with the aborigines, Zheng Jing and his followers largely rode out the first difficult years of settlement. By 1684, a year after the organization's demise, the entire area under cultivation had reached 45,055 *jia* (43,699.7 hectares), almost four times greater than the biggest Dutch-era figure of 12,500 hectares, reported in 1660. The sum of the annual output of the official and private fields alone equaled 53,771,335.6 kilograms of grain. Moreover, bumper harvests were recorded for 1665 and 1672.[56]

In his monumental study of land use in seventeenth-century Taiwan, sociologist John Robert Shepherd argues that the successful Zheng reforms reflected the transformation of the island's economy from the Dutch emphasis on profit maximization to the "agrarian-bureaucratic orientation" of the mainland. Under the VOC, almost 90 percent of levies were related to trade and commercial farming. On the other hand,

---

[52] Deng Kongzhao, *Ming-Zheng Taiwan yanjiu*, p. 83.
[53] Shepherd, *Statecraft*, pp. 99–102.   [54] Cao (Ts'ao), *Taiwan zaoqi lishi*, pp. 285–286.
[55] Liushiqi and Fan Xian, *Chongxiu Taiwan fuzhi*, p. 448.
[56] Jiang Risheng, *Taiwan waiji*, pp. 235, 259. *Jia* is a translation of the Dutch *morgen*. For an estimation of total yields, see Appendix 3.3.

the presence of so many hungry troops under Koxinga and Zheng Jing meant that greater priority was placed upon the rapid production of grains, such as rice and yams, to meet basic subsistence. Taxes on grain grew to almost half of the revenue sources from the island, while other levies were set at fixed quotas rather than competitive pricing at auctions, as under the Dutch. This agrarian regime, Shepherd argues, naturally led to decreased commercial potential and lower incremental revenues.[57]

However, Shepherd is only partially correct. On the eve of its demise in 1683, the Zheng organization was taking in an annual income of at least 107,546.70 taels (4,033 kg) worth of silver from Taiwan. This amount, which actually exceeds the figure given by Shepherd, was 30 percent more than the 116,513 pesos (3,145.9 kg) in Dutch revenues for 1655, at the height of VOC rule. Although unit revenues probably declined because of the massive influx of new settlers, it was hardly a sign of a diminished market economy. In fact, the main colonial extraction industries continued to expand, even if they contributed proportionally less to the overall economy. Sugar exports reached more than 20,000 piculs (1,194,000 kg) a year, exceeding the Dutch-era height of 17,300 piculs (1,032,810 kg) recorded in 1658.[58] The output of deerskin, at 100,000 pieces, remained steady.[59]

More importantly, the Zheng achieved greater economic diversification away from the profit-oriented monoculture under Dutch rule. An early Qing gazetteer identifies thirty types of basic grains, forty varieties of vegetables, and twenty kinds of fruits cultivated on the island, along with a bewildering array of seafood. There were kilns for making roof tiles, blacksmiths to forge the iron that went into plows and other agricultural tools, shipyards, and wine distilleries.[60] Techniques for refining salt underwent dramatic improvement.[61] The Zheng organization also invested in infrastructure, building roads and bridges to facilitate the transfer of surplus. Busy thoroughfares crisscrossed the commercial centers of Chengtian, Anping, and the seats of Tianxing and Wannian sub-prefectures, where markets and shops of different varieties converged

[57] Shepherd, *Statecraft*, pp. 101–103.
[58] Yao Keisuke, "Two rivals on an island of sugar: the sugar trade of the VOC and overseas Chinese in Formosa in the seventeenth century," in Leonard Blussé (ed.), *Around and about Formosa: essays in honor of Professor Ts'ao Yung-ho* (Taipei: Ts'ao Yung-ho Foundation for Culture and Education, 2003), p. 137.
[59] Andrade, *Taiwan became Chinese*, ch. 7.
[60] Jiang Yuying (ed.), *Taiwan fuzhi* (Taipei: Economic Research Office, Bank of Taiwan, 1959), pp. 69–90; Deng Kongzhao, *Ming-Zheng Taiwan yanjiu*, p. 79.
[61] Jiang Risheng, *Taiwan waiji*, p. 235.

to sell a plethora of domestic and foreign goods. Construction became a big industry, as demand for housing grew with the population.[62] These vibrant commercial activities became a major source of additional tax revenues for the organization.

The adaptation of the Chinese bureaucratic system to govern Taiwan not only proved lucrative to Zheng Jing, but also promoted balanced economic development on the island. Of course, life was still tough for the average Han peasant. A typical tenant household consisting of a husband and wife and four young children, with only the man engaged in farming, made about 2.5 taels of silver per person per year.[63] This amount compared well to life under the Dutch, when a laborer took in 3 pesos (2.16 taels) annually.[64] Crop failures, natural disasters, increased exactions, or a combination of all three could easily wipe away this meager income. Nonetheless, a commoner in Zheng Taiwan could still enjoy a modest disposable income after paying rents, taxes, and surcharges. Indeed, one contemporary observed, not without reason, that Taiwan, a place where "people once feared to go, has now become a land of happiness."[65]

Besides ensuring the continued sustenance of his organization, Zheng Jing's reforms carried the symbolic dimension of removing the stigma of Taiwan as an inhospitable frontier of exotic miasmas. In addition to what he and his advisors had already enacted, they specifically instructed commoners to replace the thatched roofs of their shops and residences – found even in urban Chengtian and Anping – with permanent houses made of baked tiles. Temples to Buddha and shrines to popular Fujianese deities, such as the sea goddess, Mazu, and the North Polar Star, were built in major centers.[66] They further dispatched teachers to the native villages to instruct the aborigines in Han customs and agricultural practices. Zheng Jing aimed to transform Taiwan into the center of a new "China" outside a mainland lost to Manchu "barbarians" and able to encompass the trading network and overseas Chinese communities of maritime East Asia.[67]

---

[62] Jiang Yuying, *Taiwan fuzhi*, pp. 127, 131–134, 153.
[63] See Appendix 3.3 for calculation of personal income.
[64] See Andrade, *Taiwan became Chinese*, "Appendix A."
[65] Ruan, *Haishang jianwenlu*, p. 44.
[66] For a list of these places of worship, including names and exact location, refer to Jiang Yuying, *Taiwan fuzhi*, pp. 119–125.
[67] In its analysis of the 1670 Yongli calendar, Batchelor, *London*, p. 188 correctly points out that Zheng Jing's transplantation of symbols of legitimacy from the mainland is "part of a larger effort to stabilize and redefine the temporal and commercial system for the benefit of Chinese merchants who had complex credit relations across East Asia from Nagasaki to Banten."

Rebuilding the enterprise

The oligarchy next set its sights upon restoring the family business to the halcyon days of Koxinga. For this project, Zheng Jing relied upon the advice of the old and wizened Hong Xu. In 1665, at Hong's suggestion, he transferred several military colonies deep into the mountains to exploit its rich forests for repairing his junks, which already rotted as they sat idly in the ports. Five years later, he could boast of possessing more than 200 long-distance junks.[68] Jing also established the Public Firm (Gongsi), which consolidated the functions of the Five Mountain and Sea Firms of his father's days. His agents, or the "King's merchants," bought and sold on behalf of him and his subordinates, and held a monopsony over the procurement of all major exports from the island. Independent traders participated by purchasing a license, but instead of a flat levy, its price now varied in increments based upon the carrying capacity of a ship's wooden beam. As before, private merchants enjoyed his armed protection on the high seas, while those vessels that did not pay became prizes of his patrol ships.[69] Shipments to Japan of sugar and deer products, Taiwan's twin exports under the Dutch, helped jumpstart his foreign trade again.

Meanwhile, Zheng Jing worked to regain dominance on the crucial China-Japan route by exploiting the growing differences within the complex and shaky alliance between the Qing center, Fujian feudatory, defectors, and the VOC. On May 29, 1665, under pressure from the court, Geng Jimao and Shi Lang organized a third expedition to Taiwan after much hesitation resulting from the previous abortive attempts. This time they hoped to seize the island without the Dutch and divide the spoils among themselves. However, soon after setting sail, a ferocious storm in the strait sunk most of their ships and forced the remainder to turn back to shore.[70]

Geng and the defectors subsequently changed their attitude toward the Zheng organization, especially in light of the new opportunities brought about by its rejuvenation on Taiwan. Although their ships continued to visit Nagasaki, most of them turned toward the lucrative smuggling of silks and cloths directly across the strait.[71] For the defectors, genuine

[68] Jiang Risheng, *Taiwan waiji*, p. 237; Hung, "Cheng Family," pp. 185–186.
[69] Xia, *Haiji jiyao*, p. 44; Chang Hsiu-jung et al., *English factory*, pp. 63–64, 69; Zheng Ruiming, "Ming-Zheng yu Dongnanya," p. 77; Liu Xufeng, "Jindai Huanan chuantong shehui zhong 'gongsi' xingtai zaikao: You haishang maoyi dao defang shehui," in Lin Yuru (ed.), *Bijiao shiye xia de Taiwan shangye chuantong* (Taipei: Taiwan History Institute, Academia Sinica, 2012), p. 232.
[70] Peng, *Jinghai zhi*, p. 71; Jiang Risheng, *Taiwan waiji*, pp. 234–235.
[71] Borao-Mateo et al., *Spaniards in Taiwan*, vol. II, p. 646.

residual attachment additionally motivated them in their pursuit of relations with the organization since almost all of them, including Shi, had relatives, comrades, friends, and old associates in Taiwan.[72] As Zheng Jing later wrote to the Fujian authorities, "those who surrendered ... could not abandon their old debts of gratitude to us merely to embrace new glory under you."[73]

Zheng agents also sailed to the Fujian coast, where they bribed coastal garrison commanders into allowing free access across the boundaries even as the guards adhered to all the outward forms of enforcing the prohibition. Traders from the organization typically infiltrated the walls under the cover of night, and carried only silver or gold with them. When "discovered," they would "run" from pursuing soldiers, actually dispatched by the commander to escort them into the interior. After obtaining their products, they bribed the lower-ranking border guards on the spot before their return. Likewise, merchants of the Fujian authorities met the Zheng agents by flocking across the boundaries, where they could sell their goods at much higher prices because of the illegal nature of the business.[74]

Although they benefited tremendously from the covert arrangement, Geng and the defectors hoped to eventually institutionalize it and obtain recognition from the court of its legality. By doing so, they could permanently justify their presence along the southeastern coast and redefine themselves away from border officials charged with the extermination of the Zheng organization toward those responsible for relations with Taiwan and ensuring its good behavior. In November 1665, about half a year after Shi Lang's abortive campaign, the feudatory sent an exploratory mission to the island to hold talks with Zheng Jing. Dutch observers concluded that "nothing came out of it" because of the high degree of mistrust on both sides.[75] However, it is clear that during these initial, lower-level exchanges, Zheng Jing gave sufficiently promising signals for Geng to persuade the court to upgrade the talks to a more formal level. The momentum on both sides of the strait began to move away from direct confrontation.

Besides Fujian, Zheng Jing formed connections with Qing officials along the entire seaboard, from Shandong to Guangdong. In 1666, through handsome bribes paid to the governor of the Nanjing area, he reestablished the foothold on Putuoshan that the Dutch had destroyed

[72] Shi, *Jinghai jishi*, p. 6. Shi Lang's eldest son remained within the organization. See Peng, *Jinghai zhi*, p. 90.
[73] Jiang Risheng, *Taiwan waiji*, p. 256.
[74] Jiang Risheng, *Taiwan waiji*, p. 57; Yu, *Pihai jiyou*, p. 48.
[75] Jacobus Anne van der Chijs (ed.), *Batavia dagregisters* (1895), 1666–1667, p. 411; Borao-Mateo et al., *Spaniards in Taiwan*, vol. II, p. 646.

earlier, and used it to secure access to supply sources in the major proto-industrial centers of the Yangzi River Delta. Jing sent official merchants from the Public Firm to live in Nanjing on a long-term basis.[76] In addition to procuring goods and supervising the trade, they could also acquire and convey valuable intelligence regarding the mainland to Taiwan.

Along with Qing officials, Zheng Jing worked with the coastal residents driven to desperation by the draconian evacuation and rampant corruption in its implementation. Many had chosen defiance rather than await death. Some fled deep into the mountains to form bands of robbers. Others settled on the deserted islands outside the evacuated boundaries. Safely out of the reach of the Qing patrols, they preyed upon villages and towns in the interior, plundered passing vessels, and otherwise maintained their former way of life. In southern Fujian, he formed an association with several thousand of the largest and most organized bandits in the South Taiwu Mountains, near Haicheng, under the command of Jiang Sheng (d. 1683).[77]

Lawless elements also congregated on the Fujian-Guangdong border and the area east and west of the Portuguese trading post of Macao, where jagged coastlines full of islands and overlapping jurisdictions facilitated their rapid proliferation.[78] Through the services of Hong Xu, who once enjoyed close commercial ties with ports in Guangdong, Zheng Jing managed to make significant inroads throughout the length of its littoral. In the Chaozhou area, Jing formed an alliance with Qiu Hui (d. 1683), a ferocious young pirate nicknamed "Stinky Red Meat (Chou hongrou)" based on the island of Dahao, near Shantou. He belonged to the Dan, a sub-ethnic caste who called the boats home, and depended upon maritime activities such as fishing and salt gathering for their livelihoods.[79] Because of their peculiar seaborne lifestyle and habits, they were ill-treated and ostracized by land residents. A huge squadron of boatpeople under his command plundered towns and cities across the province for goods and kidnapped residents for trafficking to Taiwan. Young girls, in particular, were sold as wives for the mostly single Zheng soldiers. The increased presence of women in Taiwan resulting from these admittedly perverse means alleviated the severe gender imbalance and gave the rough frontier a more settled feel.[80]

---

[76] Chang Hsiu-jung et al., *English Factory*, p. 65.
[77] Jiang Risheng, *Taiwan waiji*, pp. 238–239, 257–258; *Shiliao sanbian*, pp. 1211–1212.
[78] For a fascinating series of memorials, imperial edicts, and eyewitness testimonies that speak of piracy on the high seas and illicit collusion with Taiwan, see *Shiliao sanbian*, pp. 62–63, 66–73, 74–87.
[79] Zhou Shuoxun (ed.), *Chaozhou fuzhi* (Zhulan Bookshop, 1893), pp. 62–63.
[80] Shepherd, *Statecraft*, p. 97 estimates that under Dutch rule, "at least two-thirds of the immigrants had been adult males."

To the west of Macao lay the sphere of influence of another squadron of pirates under Chen Shangchuan (c. 1655–1720) and Yang Yandi (d. 1688) and his brothers. Since the 1650s they had operated from a base at Longmen, on the Leizhou Peninsula. After Qing soldiers under the Guangdong feudatory, Shang Kexi, defeated them in 1663, they fled to present-day Hải Dương province in Vietnam, where they sought refuge with a local strongman. From their new den, they launched raids throughout the circum-Gulf of Tonkin littoral. Around 1664, they made contact with the Zheng organization, and began to escort its vessels trading with Southeast Asia to ensure their safety from predation.[81] However, this clear passage through the gulf proved short lived. Under heavy Qing pressure, Tonkin was forced to expel Yang and his cohorts two years later. They and their ships and men then fled to Taiwan and took refuge under Zheng Jing.[82] Despite this setback, Jing's alliance with both corrupt Qing officials and anti-Qing elements gave him a renewed, albeit informal, presence on the mainland. From a strategic standpoint, these connections and coastal outposts formed a vast arc that guarded the approach to Taiwan and gave his organization a stranglehold over a large portion of China's access to the sea.

Jing could now turn his entire attention toward the Dutch, who posed a severe threat to his shipping in the Taiwan Strait and East China Sea with their base at Jilong. He was undoubtedly encouraged by the VOC's growing disagreements with Geng Jimao, primarily over the terms of trade at Fuzhou and unauthorized departures and arrivals of its ships.[83] The company had also been forced to give up its raids on all Zheng shipping en route to Japan in 1665 after its seizure of two Chinese junks traveling from Tonkin to Nagasaki prompted furious protests from both the *bakufu* and the Trịnh lord.[84] Accordingly, in February 1666 Zheng Jing dispatched envoys to Jilong, offering the Dutch a trading post on the islet of Baxemboy, which faced his headquarters at Anping from the north across the narrow channel. He further promised to provide them Chinese goods in exchange for desisting from the plunder of his ships in the future. The VOC representative, Constantijn Nobel, rudely

---

[81] Hayashi Shunsai, vol. 1, pp. 366–367; Zheng Ruiming, "Ming-Zheng yu Dongnanya," p. 80.

[82] For a fascinating biography of Yang Yandi, his cohorts, and their role in the Tonkin Gulf area during the Ming-Qing transition, see Robert Antony, "'Righteous Yang': pirate, rebel, and hero on the Sino-Vietnamese water frontier, 1644–1684," *Cross-Currents: East Asian History and Culture Review* 11 (2014).

[83] For a detailed survey of these misunderstandings, see Wills, *Pepper, guns, and parleys*, pp. 112–135.

[84] Cheng (Zheng), *War, trade and piracy*, pp. 213–214.

dismissed the terms; he claimed to have no authority from Batavia to negotiate with the organization.[85]

Zheng Jing responded by dispatching a force of 5,000 men and 60 junks to attack Jilong from the nearby port of Danshui on May 11, 1666. Jilong's renaissance fortifications, like those at Zeelandia, allowed the tiny garrison of 290 soldiers under Captain Herman de Bitter and two small ships to miraculously hold their ground through ferocious offensives. Ten days later, the Zheng forces withdrew after sustaining heavy casualties, including the death of a prominent officer. John Wills expresses admiration for the bravery and ferocity of Zheng Jing's soldiers in spite of the unsuccessful attempt. Their attack, according to him, was a powerful demonstration that their military prowess had not declined despite the recent setback at Xiamen.[86] For Tonio Andrade, on the other hand, the failure of the Zheng forces to seize this renaissance fortress meant they did not absorb what the European defectors had taught Koxinga in 1662 at Zeelandia and had regressed in their capabilities.[87] Both may be correct, albeit they examine the offensives from different angles, one from the perspective of morale, and the other in terms of tactics and techniques. It may also be true that Jing's commanders exhibited arrogance and underestimated the strength of the enemy.

Nonetheless, Jing's overall strategy, which emphasized the non-military measures from Sunzi's book that his father had so avidly read, had already borne fruit. Through deft diplomacy, he had successfully exploited divisions within the Qing-Dutch alliance to take it apart and prevent Jilong from reaching its commercial potential. Now, despite the severe setback, Zheng Jing imposed a military and economic quarantine around the outpost. Reinforcements poured into nearby Danshui from the south, while Chinese settlers continued to fill in the surrounding hinterlands over the next two years, decimating the number of aboriginal tribes that once traded with the Dutch. As the noose grew tighter over time, the lack of supplies and inability to attract business forced the company to finally abandon Jilong in 1668, demolishing its defenses and evacuating all employees to Batavia.[88]

To further put a check on the Dutch, Zheng Jing decided to take the face-saving olive branch extended by their Spanish rivals around this

---

[85] Borao-Mateo et al., *Spaniards in Taiwan*, vol. II, p. 649. Nobel also flatly refused to consider a modified offer from Jing of establishing a Chinese trading post near Jilong to do business with the Dutch. See John E. Wills, Jr., "The Dutch reoccupation of Chi-lung, 1664–1668," in Leonard Blussé (ed.), *Around and about Formosa*, pp. 284–285.

[86] Wills, "Dutch reoccupation," p. 285.   [87] Andrade, *Lost colony*, pp. 317–319.

[88] A careful study of the Dutch factory in Jilong can be found in Wills, "Dutch Reoccupation."

time. In February 1666, Diego Salcedo (r. 1663–1668), who succeeded Manrique de Lara as governor-general, dispatched a priest to Taiwan as an envoy to restore the ties that had been severed because of Koxinga's planned invasion of Manila. As preconditions, Jing ordered the Spanish to pay an annual tribute of rice and shipbuilding materials, and promise to refrain from harassing Chinese vessels in the future. He threatened to "promptly dispatch his soldiers to punish" the Philippines should it fail to comply.[89] It was unclear how the Spanish responded, especially given their fierce reaction to similar demands from Koxinga four years ago. Perhaps they agreed to the demands to appease Jing, or the envoy or a Chinese member of his entourage resorted to the same kind of deceit and double-dealing practiced by He Tingbin with the Dutch.[90] In any case, with Zheng Jing's approval, a permanent embassy of Dominicans established a church at Taiwan and served as his liaisons with Manila. Nonetheless, he kept them under strict surveillance to prevent them from proselytizing among the local populace at will and abusing their privileged positions to gather intelligence and seek access to mainland China.[91]

As before, the Spanish colony supplied American silver to the Zheng, and, along with the New World, served as a market for Chinese luxuries. In fact, this destination acquired increased importance for the organization amid growing tensions with Japan.[92] It is commonly assumed that the volume of China's total trade with Manila fell precipitously after 1640, and reached a nadir between the 1650s and 1680s. Fang Zhenzhen's brilliant new study on Zheng Jing's exchange with the Philippines during the 1660s appears to back up this claim. Based upon her meticulous analysis of the Spanish customs data, she shows that, on average, a total of 5.5 Chinese junks, of which 3.3 were from Taiwan, sailed to Manila between 1663 and 1672. The value of imports from Taiwan into Manila exceeds 10,245.14 taels. These figures represented a certain decline from the previous decade, when an average of 7.6 Chinese ships called at port. However, as Fang herself admits, the customs records are incomplete and unreliable, since junks had strong incentives to underreport their cargo or bribe Spanish officials privately.[93]

Empirical observations from contemporaries speak of a rapid recovery that contradicts the official data on revenues and ship numbers.

[89] Jiang Risheng, *Taiwan waiji*, p. 237.
[90] Borao-Mateo et al., *Spaniards in Taiwan*, vol. II, p. 654.
[91] Borao-Mateo et al., *Spaniards in Taiwan*, vol. 2, p. 656.
[92] For a complete list of exports to Manila, refer to tables 5.4–5.21 in Fang Zhenzhen, *Ming mo Qing chu Taiwan yu Manila de fanchuan maoyi (1664–1684)* (Banqiao, New Taipei City: Daoxiang, 2006), pp. 183–198.
[93] Fang, *Taiwan Manila maoyi*, pp. 61–62. For the calculation of revenues in the Manila trade, see Table 3.9 in Appendix 3.3.

According to Father Riccio, the Zheng merchants all "do big business at Manila." He reported that a galleon from Mexico in 1665 alone carried two million taels (75,000 kg) of silver to procure goods from Taiwan.[94] This figure was exactly the same as the scholarly consensus on shipments for 1688, the first available year after 1633 when data became available.[95] Therefore, it is probably accurate to say that, by the mid-1660s, the trade at Manila had walked out of the recessionary phase that had characterized the 1640s and 1650s. Still, it was a far cry from the golden age enjoyed by the colony before the 1630s.

Zheng Jing's success in restoring the family's preeminent role in the intra-East Asian trade certainly impressed many of his contemporaries. Chinese sources from the period marvel at how his profits only seemed to increase even as the enforcement of the coastal evacuation increased in stringency.[96] One group of more recent scholars concurs with their assessments.[97] Another group, however, considers the Qing measures to be ultimately effective, albeit at heavy cost, in rooting out the Zheng's bases on the mainland coast, depriving them of much-needed supplies and provisions, and constraining their ability to maintain effective commercial operations.[98] There is much truth to both sets of claims, but coastal removal should be considered less as a single factor and more as one of many contributing and shifting variables over time among the whole range of policies enacted by the Zheng organization, the Qing, and other outside players.[99] For a more concrete assessment of this interplay, it is instructive to look at quantitative data on the overall health of the Zheng trading network during a specific period.

---

[94] Borao-Mateo et al., *Spaniards in Taiwan*, vol. II, p. 639.

[95] See the table in Dennis O. Flynn and Arturo Giráldez, "Arbitrage, China, and world trade in the early modern period," *Journal of the Economic and Social History of the Orient* 38.4 (1995): 436.

[96] Yu Yonghe, *Pihai jiyou*, p. 48.

[97] Hung Chien-chao, "Cheng Family," p. 190 believes that "Taiwan's maritime trade continued to prosper even after the [Qing] strictly enforced the coastal removal policy." Likewise, Patrizia Carioti, "Zhengs' maritime power," p. 52 notes that the reign of Zheng Jing "saw the family restored to its former glory. Their maritime activity, which they had never abandoned, once more [represented] the backbone of Chinese trade and indeed international commerce as a whole."

[98] See, for instance, Ura, "Qianjieling kao," p. 118, which maintains that the coastal evacuation was probably ineffective in the short term, but gradually achieved its intended objective during the late 1670s, after almost two decades of implementation.

[99] As Wills emphasizes, the coastal evacuation policy could not defeat the Zhengs without the support of other measures, including the encouragement of defections and development of naval capabilities. As he correctly argues, "the Zheng leaders on Taiwan . . . could and did exploit every weakness in Qing control of coastal Fujian." See Wills, "Contingent connections," p. 191.

Between 1663 and 1672, incomplete estimates show that yearly commercial revenues of the family exceeded 2,818,999 taels (105,712.4 kg) worth of silver on average, equivalent to more than 60 million in 2014 US dollars. This amount is likely a serious underestimate, but even given complete information, the results would probably still indicate a decline from the days of Koxinga. One can certainly attribute it to a combination of Qing blockade and the severe military losses sustained by the organization in the early 1660s. However, as a point of reference, the Dutch East India Company, Zheng Jing's foremost competitor, witnessed a similar decrease in revenues. While the VOC realized 9,249,114 guilders over the same period – a headline increase of 702,247 guilders from the previous decade – the actual amount in silver terms declined by more than 2,000 kilograms to 104,786 kilograms because of currency depreciation relative to the metal in 1665.[100]

It is apparent that, on a fundamental level, significant shifts were taking place in the global economic structure and product mix. For one, the appeal and importance of the intra-East Asian trade, anchored in the exchange of Chinese silk for Japanese silver, was beginning to decline. Although Zheng Jing could smuggle products from the mainland coast, official Qing policy, along with the volatile attitudes of its local officials, for whom bribes were often ineffective when faced with orders from a determined court, constantly put the covert linkages in danger of interruption.[101] The protection payments required to transport the goods to Taiwan also led to higher costs. Even if the Qing did not implement the maritime ban, Chinese silk found effective competitors in their Vietnamese and Bengali counterparts.

As a result, an average of 36.8 junks from Taiwan, the mainland coast, and Southeast Asia sailed to Nagasaki each year from 1663 to 1673, half the number during Koxinga's days. The Zheng organization's mean revenues from Japan came to 1,168,180 taels (43,806.7 kg), a steep decrease of over a million taels from the previous decade. Profits declined to 662,475 taels (28,842.8 kg). In particular, the rate of return on silk fell from more than 200 percent in the 1650s to about 131 percent during the same period.[102] In contrast, the VOC's Bengal factory could market a more stable supply of silk at cheaper prices to realize comparable, if not greater, yields, as high as 192 percent for certain years.[103] Average annual

[100] See Table 3.11 in Appendix 3.3 for specific calculations.
[101] According to Wills, "Contingent connections," pp. 190–191, the China trade lay entirely at the mercy of corrupt officials and "slipped through only when [they] saw enough profit in it."
[102] See Appendixes 3.2 and 3.3.
[103] Om Prakash, *The Dutch East India Company and the economy of Bengal* (Princeton, NJ: Princeton University Press, 1985), p. 126.

revenues realized by the 7.6 Dutch ships that anchored at Nagasaki rose by more than 250,000 taels to a total of 973,530 taels (36,507.4 kg).[104] Still, growing restrictions from the Japanese side soon put a serious dent into the company's overall profit margins, which dropped from around 100 percent during the 1650s to a 1670s figure of 50 percent.[105]

The VOC's partial success with Bengali silk indicates that some components of the East Asian world-region began to be drawn in an ever-closer integration with the emerging global world system. During this initial phase, the Indian subcontinent replaced China as the world's leading manufacturer on account of its cotton textiles, including calicoes and other coarse fabrics, and silk. These items were exported in large quantities to Southeast Asia, Japan, and Taiwan. In exchange, India consumed gold, which functioned as currency, and copper, used for casting weapons and kitchenware. Meanwhile, as the Qing removed the last obstacles to its rule over the mainland, China gradually walked out of the chaos of dynastic transition. Although a full recovery from the severe economic depression of the 1650s still lay a decade or two down the road, modest growth, combined with coastal removal, generated an acute scarcity of copper coinage. In the late 1660s, its value approached and, at times, even exceeded that of silver.[106] This demand put Japan in an advantageous position as an exporter of gold and copper. Its role as a silver supplier, on the other hand, gradually became supplanted by the New World via Manila.

Within this new configuration, Southeast Asia assumed a position of crucial importance beyond being an outlet for silver surplus in the intra-East Asian luxury trade. Metals and fabric both found a ready market in its ports. At the same time, some localities in China and Japan, particularly along the littoral, began to reach the limits of their ecological capacities. To meet the resource shortages, primary products, such as rice, corn, and seafood, timber for shipbuilding, and gunpowder materials, came into great demand.[107] Of the value-added goods, pepper became a more lucrative product, as purchase prices fell from the previous decade, along with lead and tin, which fetched a hefty return of 127 percent.[108] Aside from its economic value, the region served as a mandatory conduit

---

[104] See Tables 3.4 and 3.5 in Appendix 3.3.   [105] Blussé, "No boats," pp. 69–70.

[106] According to von Glahn, *Fountain of fortune*, pp. 209–211, Qing government mints reported copper scarcity as early as the 1650s. On Taiwan, a thousand copper pieces equaled two taels (74 g) of silver during the 1670s. See Liu Xianting, *Guangyang zaiji*, p. 8. For more on copper demand in Southeast Asia and India, see Li Tana, *Nguyễn Cochinchina*, pp. 90–92.

[107] von Glahn, *Fountain of fortune*, p. 214. For a precise breakdown of these products, refer to Table 4.4 in Appendix 3.4.

[108] Cheng (Zheng), *War, trade and piracy*, p. 235.

between the China Seas and the Indian Ocean. Control over its ports and sea passages meant strategic domination over a substantial share of global trade.

For the Zheng organization, the structural shifts involved an adjustment in his trading network. Japan remained a market of primary importance. Unlike the days of his father, Jing could supplement his shipments of silk with sugar and deerskin from Taiwan, as well as Southeast Asia. These primary products made up practically his entire cargo during certain years. From Nagasaki, his ships still procured weapons, but he mostly carried gold, copper, and lead, which had substantial resale value in the mainland coast, Manila, and the Western Ocean.[109]

Zheng Jing also placed a heavier emphasis than his father upon supply sources in Southeast Asia. His irregular allies along the Guangdong littoral proved useful because of their familiarity with destinations in the Western Ocean and the strategic proximity of their bases, which could handle imports and forward them both to Taiwan or other parts of the mainland. Through their mediation, he strengthened commercial ties with the Trịnh and Nguyễn halves of Vietnam. In 1666, after a flurry of exchanges, Jing successfully demanded and received from the lord of Quảng Nam, always the friendlier party, fewer restrictions on trade at Hội An.[110]

Meanwhile, he obtained the tacit approval of the Tonkin authorities to utilize a crucial land route running along the Sino-Vietnamese border that led to Yunnan, headquarters of Wu Sangui, the biggest of the Qing feudatories. For his merit in exterminating the Yongli pretender in 1662, Wu was awarded a fiefdom encompassing four southwestern provinces. He grew increasingly powerful through control over their tax revenues and the appointments of their officials, as well as a massive personal army. He further reaped handsome profits from a monopoly over the sale of tea for horses from the neighboring Tai tribes, Myanmar, Tibet, and India. Most importantly for Zheng Jing, Wu developed mining operations to exploit the rich copper veins in Yunnan, which proved to be an attractive alternative to the Japanese variety.[111] Wu opened up a market for the mined metal north of Hekou, on the Vietnamese border. A large portion of the copper was then smuggled to the Vietnamese village of Lào Cai, across the Red River. It became an emporium where Zheng

---

[109] Chang Hsiu-jung et al., *English factory*, pp. 168, 172.
[110] van der Chijs, *Batavia dagregisters*, 1666–1667, pp. 234–235.
[111] C. Patterson Giersch, "Cotton, copper, and caravans: trade and the transformation of southwest China," in Eric Tagliacozzo and Chang Wen-chin (eds.), *Chinese circulations: capital, commodities, and networks in Southeast Asia* (Durham, NC: Duke University Press, 2011), p. 42.

Jing's agents and his Cantonese allies met with Qing merchants coming from the fiefdoms of Wu Sangui and Shang Kexi, the Guangdong feudatory.[112] It was also probably around this time that Jing established a covert line of communication with Wu.

Zheng junks paid regular visits to Siam, the biggest supplier of primary goods in the Western Ocean. Although the Dutch successfully pressured King Narai to cut off official ties with the organization, both sides continued to "enjoy a deep mutual friendship," as the ruler later recalled.[113] Bilateral trade grew unabated. For 1665 alone, out of twenty vessels in total that Zheng Jing dispatched to ports in the Western Ocean, ten docked at Ayutthaya.[114] Other ships ventured to trade farther south at Johor, Pahang, and Nakhon Si Thammarat, Siamese dependencies renowned for their rich tin deposits.[115]

In contrast to the largely peaceful trade conducted with other states, Zheng Jing resorted to violence in Cambodia to monopolize its rich supply of animal hides for the Japan market to the exclusion not just of his Dutch rivals, but also his partners from Siam and Quảng Nam. On the one hand, the resource-rich kingdom provided an ideal substitute for severed official ties with Siam. Moreover, plagued by weak rulers and internal strife, Cambodia presented an attractive target for manipulation and exploitation in its own right. Siam and Quảng Nam were already locked in a fierce competition throughout the 1650s for influence over the throne.[116]

In early 1666, Zheng Jing dispatched his Cantonese ally, Piauwja, an irregular operating in the Gulf of Tonkin, to the Mekong River Delta with a fleet of eight to nine junks. As they sailed westward down the river, traversing this liminal water world, Piauwja and his crew of fifty-six men engaged in the interception and plunder of passing ships. The following year, in February 1667, they arrived at the Cambodian capital and river port of Oudong, where they received a warm welcome from King Paramaraja VIII. He appointed Piauwja and prominent members of his crew *sabandar*, or headmen, of the several-thousand strong Chinese community.[117]

Piauwja rapidly gained influence at the court by supporting it against the growing number of Vietnamese immigrants in the Mekong River Delta. These settlers received the protection of the king's influential son and contender for the throne, Prince Ramadhipati, who, in turn, was sponsored by the Nguyễn lords of Quảng Nam. With the tacit

---

[112] Cheng (Zheng), *War, trade and piracy*, pp. 214–215.
[113] Hayashi Shunsai, *Ka'i hentai*, vol. I, p. 398.   [114] Viraphol, *Tribute and profit*, p. 45.
[115] Cheng (Zheng), *War, trade and piracy*, p. 235.   [116] Ibid., pp. 218–219.
[117] Ibid., pp. 220–221.

encouragement of Paramaraja VIII, Piauwja and his agents engineered a systematic massacre of more than one thousand Vietnamese in the spring of 1667. In exchange for this act of merit, the Chinese *sabandars* were allowed to maintain a private army and navy, and given a free hand in the country.[118]

They next plotted to destroy the VOC's exclusive privileges in Cambodia. On the fateful night of July 9, 1667, Piauwja, along with several hundred followers, robbed and burned down the Dutch trading lodge. They killed the head agent, Pieter Ketting, and several of his native servants. They also plundered the ship, *Schelvisch*, docked at the harbor, and took away massive quantities of silver and silk. Ketting's assistants fled and hid in the jungles of the Mekong for weeks, before boarding the *Schelvisch* and fleeing for Nagasaki. Under heavy Dutch pressure, King Paramaraja detained and executed Piauwja and his six coconspirators, but the move did nothing to hinder the continued growth of Zheng influence. The VOC never recovered from the devastation and, in 1670, shut down the factory because of dismal sales.[119]

These series of brilliant diplomatic maneuvers allowed Zheng Jing to solidify his foothold in the Western Ocean. However, unlike Koxinga's time, his junks could no longer sail to Batavia or other ports beneath the Malay Peninsula, areas fully within the VOC sphere of influence. The Dutch stood ready to intercept and plunder those that tried.[120] Nonetheless, Zheng Jing's average annual revenues from Western Ocean ports between 1663 and 1673 stood at 1,640,574.57 taels (61,521.5 kg) worth of silver.[121] This figure exceeded the corresponding amount for the Japan trade for the first time. Southeast Asia had become an important destination in its own right, decoupled, although still involved in, the intra-East Asian exchange.

Historians have long relegated Zheng Jing to the sidelines, and, indeed, in many ways, he lacked the charisma and forceful personality of his father and grandfather. As someone who did not have many friends or soul mates to share the ups and downs of his life, he frequently sank into depression and drank heavily to dull the pain. Under these circumstances, he relied upon his advisors as a surrogate family, inviting them to

[118] For more on this episode, see Jacobus Anne van der Chijs (ed.), *Batavia dagregisters* (1897), 1668–1669, p. 5 and Mak Phoeun and Po Dharma, "La deuxième intervention militaire vietnamienne au Cambodge (1673–1679)," *Bulletin de l'Ecole française d'Extrême-Orient* 77 (1988): 233–235.

[119] W. J. M. Buch, "La Compagnie des Indes néerlandaises et l'Indochine," *Bulletin de l'Ecole française d'Extrême-Orient* 37 (1937): 233–237.

[120] Chang Hsiu-jung et al., *English Factory*, p. 171.

[121] For details on the specific calculations, see Appendix 3.3.

sumptuous drunken feasts, taking tours of the scenic countryside, and composing verses.[122] Not without reason, contemporaries and later historians labeled him a weak-willed individual who exercised poor leadership and easily succumbed to the "obsequious flattery" of his unscrupulous retinue.[123]

Nonetheless, his approach initiated a system of consensus rule that provided a framework for institutional stability and continuity greatly needed by the organization at the time. For the first time in its existence, its adherents did not have to worry about the threat of imminent extinction at the hands of Qing forces constantly attacking a set of precarious and shifting ports. Zheng soldiers also no longer had to be fed, but could live off the land on their own. All of these factors contributed to greater retained earnings for investment in Taiwan's domestic infrastructure and rationalized bureaucratic institutions. At the same time, he restored the viability and profitability of his family's commercial network and, through diplomatic finesse, took apart the alliance of his rivals and set them off against one another. Cheng Wei-chung observes correctly that, by the late 1660s, Zheng Jing had transformed Taiwan into a hub for the exchange of "goods, information and military resources."[124] It is thus important to point out that Jing's ambitions did not just remain confined to the island. He also intended to transform it into a political center and launch pad for an expansive maritime Chinese state able to exploit the changes occurring in the regional economic and geopolitical structure. He now needed to seek new ways of legitimizing his organization before his subjects, the Qing, and Taiwan's neighbors.

---

[122] For more on Zheng Jing's personality, refer to his poems in "Zheng Jing," in Shi Yilin (ed.), *Quan Tai shi*, 5 vols. (Tainan: National Taiwan Institute of Literature, 2004), vol. I.

[123] Liushiqi and Fan Xian, *Chongxiu Taiwan fuzhi*, p. 706. For a more recent perspective, refer to Jin Chengqian, "Zheng Jing yu Ming-Zheng," *Taiwan wenxian* 23.3 (1972).

[124] Cheng (Zheng), *War, trade and piracy*, p. 223.

6   The lure of "China"

To enrich the country (*fuguo*), you must enlarge its territory. To strengthen your army (*qiangbing*), you must make your people prosperous. The one who is king must hold high the virtue of his subjects. Once you possess all three, then the royal title will follow.[1]

> Zheng Dexiao, Zheng Jing's chief secretary, advocating
> an invasion of the Philippines.

Once I heard the news, all the colors seemed to move. I was filled with happiness but also felt surprise in my heart. I want to sweep clean the camps seething with the stink of mutton, and completely recover Beijing and Nanjing.[2] We can open again the path of tributary kingdoms and rebuild the surrendered cities.[3]

> The poem "Singing joyously upon hearing of the recovery
> of the west," composed by Zheng Jing in 1674.

Chinese scholars remain polarized in their assessments of the political stance of Zheng Jing and the organization during their decade on Taiwan, which lasted until 1674, when the Rebellion of the Three Feudatories broke out against the Qing. One opinion, espoused by many historians on both sides of the strait, sees Jing carrying on his father's unfulfilled dream of Ming restoration. According to this view, his efforts to develop Taiwan and restore his trading network merely served as a means for building up a strong base of operations where he could quietly await an opportunity to counterattack the mainland.[4] Other scholars, primarily based on the

---

[1] Jiang Risheng, *Taiwan waiji*, p. 426.

[2] The "stink of mutton" (*xingshan*) refers to the foul body odor supposedly emitted by the meat-eating "barbarians."

[3] "Zheng Jing," p. 156.

[4] Zhuang Jinde reflects the classical judgment of Zheng Jing on Taiwan. He emphasizes that "time and again, Jing waited for an opportunity to command his troops in a counterattack on the mainland." See his "Zheng-Qing heyi," 28. Even those advocating a separate Taiwanese identity, such as Chen Jiahong, "Zheng shi wangchao zhi zhengzhi waijiao shixi," *Tainan wenhua* 58 (2008): 5–6, believe that the "mainland character" of Zheng Jing's value system hindered him from fully focusing upon the creation of an independent maritime kingdom on the island. Ironically, Chen's mainland counterpart, Zhu Shuangyi, agrees. He praises the younger Zheng for refusing "to rest in the small corner of Taiwan. Time and again, he thought of taking up arms to recover his native land." See Zhu

mainland, accuse Zheng Jing of plotting to found an independent state on Taiwan and secede from China.[5] Both perspectives, while containing much merit, leave many questions unanswered. Even if Zheng Jing intended to carry out the will of his father, Ming restoration only represented one of the many positions espoused by Koxinga during his lifetime. Indeed, in his final days Koxinga did not hesitate to turn his back upon it altogether. Moreover, Zheng Jing's own success in forging a viable territorial state on Taiwan gave him no pressing material motivation to recover the mainland. Yet it is also true that he ultimately did return when the Qing feudatories revolted against the court.

A more accurate picture of Zheng Jing's actions must accompany an examination of the opportunities and constraints faced by the organization in the late 1660s and early 1670s. On the one hand, he could negotiate a peaceful settlement with the Qing, leaving him free to forge a new "China" among the waves able to control the competitive new markets and relationships that his organization was forging in Southeast Asia. On the other hand, he could turn his attention to the mainland again and raise the banner of Ming restoration. Yet, in order to do so, he needed strong accomplices with dreams of wresting China from the Manchus and the ability to guarantee him part of the spoils of victory. In fact, Zheng Jing hedged his bets on both outcomes.

A question of hair and fashion

In the late 1660s, as prospects for return to a "barbarianized" mainland grew increasingly remote because of the successful consolidation of Qing rule, Zheng Jing and Chen Yonghua began to promote among their subjects an identity of being "Chinese" without a physical "China." In Jing's poems, a medium that brings out personal feelings and spontaneity in a calculated and public manner, the ritualized longing for a lost, historical "China" constituted a prominent theme. He lamented how the "mountains and rivers of my homeland ... have all changed colors, and the palaces of the old capital have turned into ashes."[6] He often portrayed himself as "a solitary Han minister from a former dynasty of old."[7] Even verses that spoke of a desire for restoration revealed hopelessness and resignation to his current plight. In one of them, after

Shuangyi, "'Zheng Jing shi Taidu fenzi' shuo zhiyi: yi *Dongbilou ji* wei zuo zheng," *Xiamen daxue xuebao: zhexue shehui kexueban* 167.1 (2005): 67.

[5] See, for instance, Lin Qian, "Kangxi tongyi Taiwan de zhanlue juece," *Qing shi yanjiu* 3 (2000) and Wang Zhengyao, *Qing shi shude* (Shenyang: Liaoning Nationalities Publishing House, 2004).

[6] "Zheng Jing," p. 130.   [7] Ibid., p. 166.

fantasizing about raising an army of brave warriors to expel the Manchu invaders, he admits, with irony, in the last line, "I look up to behold the imperial carriage, but year after year, I still cannot see it."[8] From Zheng Jing's poems, it becomes evident that the memory of the Ming and "China" in general was becoming decentered from its geographic connotations, objectified, and historicized.

References to the long flowing robes typical of Ming dress and their naturalization overseas make more frequent appearances. He noted, for instance, that "the imperial spirit is finished in the Central Plain, but [the Ming] gowns and caps survive overseas."[9] He brought up fashion again in a celebration of Taiwan's Sinicized landscape:

The Pacified Capital has been established in the eastern end of the great ocean. Thousands of mountains and hundreds of valleys stretch far into the horizon. Fragrant forests twist and turn until the edges of the blue clouds, while water turns green in the creeks. The people and houses on both shores welcome the dawn, and fishing boats throughout the rivers sail with morning winds. The ancient sages may find the place a bit difficult to describe, but the gowns and caps of the Han country are the same as all antiquity.[10]

In this manner, Ming loyalism became redefined to mean the preservation of Han ethnic markers and institutions overseas, to continue a way of life no longer existent on the mainland because of the Qing order to shave the head and adopt tight Manchu riding jackets.

At the same time, Zheng Jing drew upon tales of loyal ministers from ancient Chinese history to create a "founding legend" for his new overseas enterprise. He compared himself to Jizi, a legendary sage and minister of the fallen Shang dynasty (c. 1756–1050 BCE), who became enfeoffed in Korea by King Wu of the newly established Western Zhou (c. 1060–771 BCE).[11] He pointed to Tian Heng, "a mere commoner of Qi," who refused to serve the Western Han (202 BCE–8 CE) after the fall of Qin, and fled with five hundred of his followers to an island off the coast of Shandong, where he proclaimed himself king.[12] Like these men before him, Jing accepted the shift in the Mandate of Heaven, and went overseas to "be neighbors daily" with "mud dwellings and my soldiers" to avoid the Qing.[13]

---

[8] Ibid., p. 74.   [9] "Yanping er wang," p. 129.
[10] "Zheng Jing," p. 127. In the last line, Zheng Jing probably means that the ancient sages may have never expected an overseas island to become a place of refuge for Han people and their customs.
[11] For more on Jizi and his enfeoffment, see Sima Qian, *Xinjiaoben Shiji sanjiazhu* (Taipei: Dingwen, 1985), pp. 1609–1611.
[12] Tian Heng's biography is found in Sima Qian, *Shiji*, pp. 2646–2649.
[13] Jiang Risheng, *Taiwan waiji*, p. 257; Zheng Yiju, "Zheng Chenggong zhuan," p. 23.

Zheng Jing's redirection away from the mainland contributed to sharp divisions among his followers. On the one hand, he received the support of Chen Yonghua and other young officials within his advisory circle. Like him, they came from a generation for whom the trauma of dynastic transition remained a distant event from their infancy or early childhood. Instead, what they shared was the common experience of exile, having grown up confronted with the constant reality of "barbarian" rule over most of the mainland. For this reason, they could more readily recognize and accept a permanent peaceful settlement with the Qing. As Chen Yonghua stated, "we resolve to stay here [in Taiwan] and have no intentions toward the west [mainland]."[14]

Jing's new administration also garnered support among those immediately beneath the elite class, primarily younger generations of commoners, especially merchants, with at least a functional education. Their attitudes can be seen in conversations recorded in 1667 between Korean officials and Chen De, a twenty-four-year-old official merchant and crewmember of a Nagasaki-bound Zheng junk that had washed onto the shores of Cheju amid a storm. In one exchange, he remarked that "the Great Ming has settled among the waves ... and administers a separate land from the Qing."[15] He, along with many others, identified with the creation of a new, Taiwan-centered "China," whose territory aimed to encompass maritime East Asia.

On the other hand, the new policies ran into determined opposition from a conservative faction in the organization, spearheaded by imperial princes, some members of the exiled gentry, and key segments of the military. They saw Jing's actions as a betrayal of the Ming loyalist cause. The Zhejiang gentry Shen Guangwen (1613–1688) wrote poems bitterly satirizing him for listening to wicked advisors and "disbanding troops" into the military colonies rather than preparing for a return to the mainland.[16] This core of the old guard elite found an ally in Feng Xifan, the head of Zheng Jing's bodyguard unit, whose prestige matched Chen Yonghua in the advisory circle. Feng was undoubtedly driven by a thirst for revenge against the Manchus for causing his father's violent death during the retreat to Taiwan in 1664.[17]

Beneath the elite level, dissatisfaction was strongest among rank-and-file soldiers in the remote military colonies. Most had families on the mainland and had not married; the prospect for good wives was also much brighter on the other side of the strait. From time to time, disgruntled

---

[14] Jiang Risheng, *Taiwan waiji*, p. 238.
[15] Sŏng Haeun, *Chŏngmi chŏnshinrok*, pp. 277_012a-012b.
[16] Jiang Yuying, *Taiwan fuzhi*, pp. 216, 219–220.   [17] Xia, *Haiji jiyao*, p. 64.

men would commandeer junks and defect to the Qing.[18] Many of the more idealistic commoners, typically of an older age, continued to believe that they remained in temporary exile, and Zheng Jing would soon launch another campaign. Lin Yinguan (1623–1667), an official merchant on the same shipwrecked vessel as his crewmate, Chen De, adamantly believed that the Yongli emperor was still living and resided somewhere in south-western China. After boasting of Koxinga's glorious victories against the Manchus in former times, he took out a Yongli calendar and displayed it proudly to his Korean hosts, as tears streamed down his cheeks.[19]

However, Zheng Jing thought otherwise. Like Chen Yonghua, he believed in a negotiated settlement with the Qing as the most optimal solution, one that would free the organization to focus upon tapping into the potential of new markets, while securing its traditional interests on the mainland and preventing an attack on its rear. In January 1667, as a sign of goodwill to the Qing, he ordered the garrison commander of Penghu, on the front lines, to withdraw to Taiwan, and disbanded his men to a military colony.[20] Jing then initiated a purge of restorationists from his government. He reversed his father's deep respect for Zhu Shugui, the most prominent of the Ming imperial descendants and widely upheld among conservatives as the next occupant of a throne left vacant by the Yongli pretender. Jing cut off all financial assistance to the prince and forced him to open up new land in the countryside.[21] Evidently, his father had successfully imparted within him the lesson that the presence of a reigning emperor, even if a figurehead, posed a severe challenge to the family's autonomy and supremacy. Under similar pressure, Shen Guangwen, the most vocal opponent of Jing's policies, disguised himself as a monk and fled into the mountains, where he hid for years among local aborigines.[22]

As signs emerged that the organization would permanently withdraw from the contest for dynastic legitimacy with the Qing, the Manchu regents ruling in the name of the young Kangxi emperor backed away from an invasion of Taiwan. They had very little interest in conquering the island for its own sake, since it added little to their vast continental possessions. More than their avowed enemies, the Qing authorities had cause to view their shaky new allies with greater concern. The Dutch East

---

[18] Shi, *Jinghai jishi*, p. 6.   [19] Sŏng, *Chŏngmi chŏnshinrok*, pp. 277_007c, 277_012b.
[20] Jiang Risheng, *Taiwan waiji*, p. 238.
[21] Shen Binghu, *Chonglin yuce (The Jade Volume of Chonglin)*, *TWWXHK*, 1.1, p. 192.
[22] One of Shen's poems written in exile lamented, "I often looked toward the west [to the mainland] for good news, but I had to flee north because of my fear of alienation from the group." See "Shen Guangwen," in Shi Yilin (ed.), *Quan Tai shi*, 5 vols. (Tainan: National Taiwan Institute of Literature, 2004), p. 64.

India Company possessed powerful weapons and ships able to harass the mainland coast, while the defectors maintained independent chains of command and used their new positions of privilege to engage in smuggling and outright extortion of coastal residents. By reaching a peaceful settlement with Zheng Jing and granting him control over Chinese maritime trade, the Qing court could absorb these middlemen or cut them out altogether. As a result, a stable and prosperous boundary could emerge from this hazy coastal frontier at a far lower cost than the evacuation policy.[23]

In early 1667, the court ended the alliance with the VOC by revoking its biennial trading privileges at Fuzhou. In practice, the Dutch continued to maintain a factory without central approval, but their presence remained completely dependent upon the connivance and goodwill of Geng Jimao.[24] For the time being, however, the court left the defectors untouched. Since they possessed the most knowledge of the organization and had valuable connections with its key followers, the regents authorized them to initiate peace talks with Zheng Jing. The defectors chose Kong Yuanzhang (d. 1690), a Zhejiang native and garrison commander in the Yangzi River Delta, to head the negotiating team. A former spy who worked for Wei Geng's Ming loyalist network during the 1650s, Kong continued to maintain extensive personal contacts in Taiwan, many of them influential political figures.[25] Under him were Liu Ergong and Ma Xing, also from Zhejiang and once participants in Zhang Huangyan's militia, and Dong Shen, brother of Koxinga's wife, Madame Dong, and a maternal uncle of Zheng Jing.[26]

On July 6, 1667, after consultation with Geng Jimao and Fujian Governor-General Zu Zepu, Kong drafted a letter that implored Jing to surrender and laid out the terms and conditions of his submission. The letters relayed the Qing court's offer to bestow upon him the title of "King of Fujian" (Bamin wang), granting him control over the evacuated islands off Fujian. Like the other semi-autonomous Qing feudatories, Zheng Jing would have the power to appoint his own officials, maintain a personal army, and continue to control his commercial enterprise. However, he

---

[23] Ho, "Sealords" provides a harrowing, heart-wrenching narrative of the suffering and devastation visited upon residents of Fujian, the province hardest hit by the policy. See, in particular, pp. 200–297.

[24] Wills, *Pepper*, pp. 136–144.

[25] For a complete biography of Kong Yuanzhang, refer to He, *Qing shi conggao*, pp. 294–302.

[26] *Shiliao xubian*, p. 1158; Gu Yanwu, *Ming ji sanchao yeshi*, *TWWXCK*, 106 (1961), p. 58; Taiwan Research Institute and Number One Archives, *Tongyi Taiwan dang'an*, pp. 71–73.

must signal his submission to the new dynasty by shaving his head and abandoning Taiwan.[27]

Kong sent Liu and Ma to Taiwan with his letter. Zheng Jing treated the two envoys as guests of honor and lodged them at the spacious official guesthouse in Provintia, the former Dutch fort. A culinary staff of ten was on hand to cater delicacies to their every whim.[28] However, after a month-long wait, they received Zheng Jing's reply, which adamantly rejected the terms. He refused to shave his head and abandon the island, citing filial piety to Koxinga's will, although the stinginess of what the Qing offered proved a more compelling factor. Jing emphasized that he had already founded a new kingdom on Taiwan and established "the foundation of ten thousand generations, to the point that it cannot be transplanted." He went on to proclaim:

I have opened another universe at Dongning, outside the imperial map. Its area is thousands of *li*, and its grain can last decades. The barbarians of the four corners submit, myriad products circulate, and the living masses gather and receive education. These are enough for me to be strong on my own. . . . What have I to envy about the Central Land of China?

Now, by agreeing to the Qing terms, he would essentially have to give up the natural security of Taiwan in exchange for a fiefdom and title that would place him entirely at the mercy of a court deemed completely untrustworthy.[29]

Instead, Zheng Jing demanded recognition from the Qing as an equal and separate state, "to treat me according to the rituals of a foreign country." He pointed to Taiwan's geographic position as "neighboring Japan to the east and the Philippines to the south." These countries, like the Zheng organization, had no political ties to the Qing, in contrast to its own vassals of Ryukyu and Korea. He also hoped to legalize, or make semi-legal, the organization's regularized smuggling activities on the southeastern coast. He proposed to Kong a mutual exchange of "representatives from each country to establish friendly relations based upon commerce" in a consular-like arrangement.[30] Jing's conditions did not fundamentally conflict with his official allegiance to the Ming. An equal relationship with the Qing meant that the Manchus, like him, would both be subordinate to a world order centered upon the deceased Yongli pretender.

[27] Taiwan Research Institute and Number One Archives, *Tongyi Taiwan dang'an*, p. 70.
[28] *Qing chu Zheng Chenggong jiazu Manwen dang'an yibian (san)*, TWWXHK, 1.9, pp. 332–333.
[29] Taiwan Research Institute and Number One Archives, *Tongyi Taiwan dang'an*, pp. 69–71.
[30] Ibid., pp. 69–70.

Unable to persuade Jing in writing to agree to the Qing conditions, Kong Yuanzhang traveled to the island to make his appeal in person.[31] In October, he arrived in Taiwan to a warm welcome. Again, little substantive progress was made. The Qing held stubbornly to its condition for Jing to shave his head and return to the mainland. It did offer Zheng Jing the additional right to oversee trade along the entire Chinese seaboard, but, as a condition, he now had to send one of his sons to Beijing as a hostage to ensure his sincerity and trustworthiness. Although Jing refused as adamantly as before, he sent Kong back with an invitation to engage in future discussions over "the example of Korea," or a close relationship of subordinate vassalage to the Qing.[32]

Kong's inability to secure the Zheng organization's submission placed the future prospects of the defectors along the southeastern coast in jeopardy. As soon as he returned to Fujian, Shi Lang, head of the Fujian naval command and one of the most influential figures in the group, stabbed him in the back. In a memorial to the court, he accused Kong of incompetence, complaining that even after "our envoys went there two times," Zheng Jing still did not dispatch any officials to accompany the mission back for further consultation. Shi then clamored for another chance to lead a naval expedition against Taiwan.[33] His renewed belligerence represented a desperate strategy of survival for him and his fellow defectors. Since peace along the coast without any negotiated settlement would almost certainly render them redundant, he had to create a tense situation, while sacrificing one of their own to maintain the privileges of the entire group. Indeed, Shi's proposal struck a fatal blow to Kong Yuanzhang's leading role in the negotiations. Soon, an edict ordered the envoy back to Beijing to await his next assignment.

With his own career prospects in jeopardy, Kong retaliated by exposing Shi's illicit collusion with Taiwan, and even produced letters given to him by Zheng Jing during his mission as proof.[34] The court may previously have turned a blind eye to the smuggling, but once someone publicly brought the matter to its attention, the entire position of the defectors collapsed. On February 21, 1668, the Manchu regents ordered Shi Lang, Zheng Mingjun, and other major defectors to Beijing, giving them honorable but worthless titles and placing them effectively under

[31] Initially, Kong planned to travel together with Dong Shen, but the latter unexpectedly passed away from illness before the mission started. See Taiwan Research Institute and Number One Archives, *Tongyi Taiwan dang'an*, p. 71 and Chen Hong and Chen Bangxian, "Qing chu Pu bian xiaosheng," in Qing History Office, Historical Research Center, Chinese Academy of Social Sciences (ed.), *Qing shi ziliao* (Beijing: Zhonghua Bookstore, 1980), vol. I, p. 86.
[32] Xia, *Haiji jiyao*, p. 37 Jiang Risheng, *Taiwan waiji*, p. 239.   [33] Shi, *Jinghai jishi*, p. 3.
[34] Chen Hong and Chen Bangxian, "Pu bian xiaosheng," p. 86.

house arrest.[35] Huang Wu, too, fell under suspicion, and his nephew, Huang Yi, was reduced to commoner status.[36] The court then disbanded the entire naval establishment in Fujian, reconverting a small number of sailors into land forces, while dispatching the rest deep into the interior provinces with their families to open up military colonies.[37] War junks were grounded in Haicheng harbor, and many were eventually burned. Kong Yuanzhang, the instigator of this chain of events, was exiled to the Manchurian frontier, where he lived in isolation until his death around 1690.[38]

With the troublesome collaborators out of the way, the Qing could better coordinate its approach toward the Zheng organization. In early 1669, as the purge of personnel progressed, the court authorized a limited extension of the maritime boundaries, allowing residents to return to the evacuated areas for farming and fishing.[39] The relaxation continued despite a major palace coup in Beijing on June 14, when the fifteen-year-old Kangxi emperor ousted Oboi and his allies, and assumed personal control of the throne.[40] Faced with the daunting challenge of domestic consolidation, he continued to favor a peaceful settlement with Taiwan, but, in accordance with his ruling style, he took an active personal interest in the negotiations from the very beginning.

In July 1669, the new ruler assigned Mingju (1635–1708), secretary of the Board of Punishments, and Cai Yurong (d. 1699), assistant secretary of the Board of War, to take charge of the negotiations in conjunction with Geng Jimao and Zu Zepu.[41] The four of them agreed to send Xinghua Prefect Mu Tianyan (1624–1696) and Assistant Commander Ji Quan as envoys to Taiwan. Unlike the Zheng defectors, these imperial officials were some of the Kangxi emperor's staunchest allies. Mingju, a Manchu bannerman of the Yehe clan, enjoyed close ties to Suoetu (d. 1703), the emperor's personal bodyguard, who helped mastermind the ousting of the Oboi faction.[42] Mingju's enthusiastic patronage also allowed Cai Yurong, a Han bannerman from Liaodong, to rise to his present position. Cai, in turn, knew Zu Zepu on a personal basis, having served under his

---

[35] Shi, *Jinghai jishi*, pp. 4–5.
[36] Chen Hong and Chen Bangxian, "Pu bian xiaosheng," p. 86.
[37] Jiang Risheng, *Taiwan waiji*, p. 246; Chen Hong and Chen Bangxian, "Pu bian xiaosheng," pp. 86–87.
[38] He, *Qing shi conggao*, p. 298.
[39] Jiang Risheng, *Taiwan waiji*, p. 251; Chen Hong and Chen Bangxian, "Pu bian xiaosheng," pp. 86–87.
[40] Zhang Kaiyuan et al., *Qing tongjian*, vol. I, pp. 615–624, 608–609, 622–623.
[41] Jiang Risheng, *Taiwan waiji*, p. 251; Xia, *Haiji jiyao*, p. 22.
[42] See Mingju's biography in Zhao Erxun (ed.), *Qing shigao*, 48 vols. (Beijing: Zhonghua Bookstore, 1998), vol. XXXIII, pp. 9992–9994. For more on Suoetu's role in the overthrow of Oboi, refer to Zhang Kaiyuan, *Qing tongjian*, vol. I, pp. 616–617.

father, Zu Dashou (d. 1656), a Ming commander who surrendered to the Manchus in 1641 with his men and entire family.[43] Both Cai and Zu Zepu were close to Geng Jimao, another Liaodong bannerman. Mu Tianyan, on the other hand, represented a new generation of bureaucrats who had passed the civil service examinations during the Shunzhi period, and owed his entire career to the new dynasty.[44] Through this personal chain of ties from top to bottom, Shengzu could obtain timely and accurate information on the progress of the talks.

Mu and Ji landed on Penghu on July 9 and sent word to Zheng Jing, who dispatched a large ship that arrived several weeks later to escort them to the main island. For the upcoming talks, Jing chose two of his own high-ranking officials: Ke Ping, the officer of Punishments, and Ye Heng, head of the Rites Office and the Imperial Academy in Chengtian.[45] Both men had extensive experience with negotiations, especially with foreign powers. Ye served as Jing's envoy to northern Taiwan in 1666 in talks with the Dutch. Likewise, Ke Ping would later hammer out the details of a commercial treaty with the English East India Company.[46] The two men took responsibility for accommodating and entertaining the Qing envoys at the official guesthouse in Provintia while they arranged a date for an audience with Zheng Jing.

That meeting, which was attended by all of Taiwan's civil and military officials, occurred on August 3. The Qing representatives forwarded letters from Mingju and the others that essentially repeated the court's previous stance: accept its ranks, shave the head, and return to Fujian. Predictably, Jing flatly refused the offer. The deadlock continued despite several additional meetings. The two sides came to the point of trading insults, with Jing insinuating that he could still fight if necessary, while the Qing envoys threatened that "we do not lack war junks or soldiers."[47] A breakthrough finally occurred after two weeks, when Jing agreed to dispatch Ke and Ye to Quanzhou to meet Mingju, Cai, and Geng, who had greater latitude in deciding his requests.

The two men arrived on the mainland carrying a letter from Zheng Jing to the Qing authorities that openly stated his desire for his kingdom to "follow the example of Korea, not shaving the hair but calling ourselves your ministers and paying tribute." By adopting the Qing calendar and

---

[43] For Cai Yurong's biography, see Zhao Erxun, *Qing shigao*, vol. XXXII, pp. 9787–9791. For a detailed account of Zu Dashou and the Manchus, see Wakeman, *Great enterprise*, vol. I, pp. 180–194, 221–224. A biography of the Zu family can be found in Zhao Erxun, *Qing shigao*, vol. XXXI, pp. 9419–9429.

[44] Jiang Risheng, *Taiwan waiji*, p. 251.

[45] Xia, *Haiji jiyao*, p. 44; Jiang Risheng, *Taiwan waiji*, p. 238.

[46] Wills, "Dutch Reoccupation," p. 284; Chang Hsiu-jung et al., *English Factory*, p. 246.

[47] Jiang Risheng, *Taiwan waiji*, p. 253.

recognizing Shengzu as his suzerain, he calculated that he could acquire legitimacy from the most powerful empire in East Asia at almost no risk. Jing could legalize his illicit trade with the mainland coast and count on Qing military protection in the event of a succession crisis or rebellion. More importantly, like Korea, he would enjoy complete domestic autonomy, maintaining the Yongli calendar and Ming institutions free of interference. In fact, his letter explicitly referred to the term "serving the great" (*sadae*), which the Koreans used to characterize the Chosŏn dynasty's relationship with the Ming for more than 200 years and with the Manchus after their invasion of the peninsula in 1636.[48] This arrangement would allow Jing and his followers to continue to be "Chinese" by making themselves foreign to "China."

Still, Jing continued to strive for an equal position with the Qing. After all, the prospect of paying homage to a "barbarian" regime represented a tremendous shame, especially for someone who hated it so virulently. His letter, while polite, contained expressions that were considered arrogant and disrespectful for a prospective vassal addressing the Son of Heaven. Mu Tianyan sternly rebuked the Zheng envoys and forced them to modify or delete inappropriate passages.[49]

Moreover, on the day of the negotiations, Ke Ping and Ye Heng refused, like other Qing officials, to enter through the side gate of the compound of Mingju and Cai, and sit perpendicular to them, in the manner of ministers paying homage to the emperor, whose will these representatives embodied. The Zheng envoys instead requested treatment as foreign guests, who could use the main gate and face them directly across the room. "There are lands large and small," Ke defended his stance, "but envoys are the same." Because of the sharp differences over the preferred ceremony, the two sides refused to meet for the next few days. In the end, Mu broke the impasse by relocating the negotiations to Quanzhou's Confucian shrine. Ke and Ye would still enter through the side doors of the main hall to greet the imperial envoys.[50] Mingju and Cai could view their entry as an act of subordination to the emperor, while the Zheng envoys could claim that they were paying respects to Confucius, also an acceptable explanation to the Qing, since both sides espoused him as a great sage and upheld the Confucian value system.[51]

[48] Jiang Risheng, *Taiwan waiji*, p. 253. As Chun Hae-jong, "Sino-Korean tributary relations in the Ch'ing period," in John King Fairbank (ed.), *The Chinese world order: traditional China's foreign relations* (Cambridge, MA: Harvard University Press, 1968), p. 111 points out, close tributary relations protected the interests of both ruler and elites in the Chosŏn dynasty, partly explaining why it lasted over five centuries.

[49] Jiang Risheng, *Taiwan waiji*, p. 254.   [50] Jiang Risheng, *Taiwan waiji*, pp. 254–255.

[51] This highly convincing interpretation comes from Deng Kongzhao, *Ming-Zheng Taiwan yanjiu*, p. 119.

Some progress was made during the subsequent talks. The Qing representatives memorialized and received a formal edict from the Kangxi emperor granting Taiwan to Zheng Jing as a hereditary fiefdom. "If Zheng Jing cherishes and loves Taiwan and cannot bear to abandon it," he proclaimed, "we can concede to his desires."[52] However, he emphasized:

Korea has always been a foreign country (*waiguo*), but Zheng Jing is a man of the Middle Kingdom (*Zhongguo zhi ren*). Since he will reside on Taiwan, on what basis can we discern his sincerity in submitting if he does not shave his hair? . . . If he follows [Qing] institutions and shaves his hair, I will not hesitate to award him high ranks and honors.[53]

Although the Qing authorities agreed with him that "Taiwan did not belong to the Middle Kingdom," and could care less about this "ball of mud overseas," they considered him and his followers to be too "Chinese" to qualify for tributary status.[54] After all, they came mostly from Fujian and Guangdong, spoke their regional tongues, and practiced the same customs. As such, unlike Korea, Jing had to make Taiwan an integral part of the Qing and adopt its institutions.

Ke Ping and Ye Heng, together with Mu Tianyan and Ji Quan, returned to Taiwan to report the concessions to Zheng Jing. Jing immediately held meetings with his civil and military officials to discuss the terms, including the sensitive topic of shaving hair and changing clothing. However, the conservatives came out in adamant opposition. Zhu Shugui, the prince of Ningjing, even insinuated that he would commit suicide if the organization agreed to the deal.[55]

In the end, Jing broke off the talks, claiming that "if [the Qing] wants us to shave our heads, then I cannot change them to the point of death."[56] Besides caving into internal pressure, he realized that his entire legitimacy hinged upon the preservation of an authentic, uncorrupted Han lifestyle rather than simply control over an originally foreign island. The importance of this claim became all too apparent the moment Zheng envoys stepped foot on Quanzhou for talks with Mingju and Cai. Residents of the entire city gathered to gawk at their flowing robes and long hair, while reminiscing about the "majestic presence of the Han officials" of bygone times.[57] Without these outward markers of "Chineseness," little would distinguish his followers from the Qing, which could easily erode and

---

[52] Taiwan Research Institute and Number One Archives, *Tongyi Taiwan dang'an*, p. 85.
[53] Ibid., p. 85.
[54] Teng, *Imagined geography*, p. 3; Deng Kongzhao, *Ming-Zheng Taiwan yanjiu*, p. 122.
[55] Jiang Risheng, *Taiwan waiji*, p. 256; Chen Hong and Chen Bangxian, "Pu bian xiaosheng," p. 87.
[56] Jiang Risheng, *Taiwan waiji*, p. 256.   [57] Xia, *Haiji jiyao*, p. 37.

absorb his support base. However, the Qing simply confirmed his rights over territory, but refused recognize the uniqueness of his institutions. On the other hand, the consequences for the failure of negotiations were too low. Although the Qing held an absolute military advantage over Zheng Jing in terms of size, tax revenues, and manpower, it lacked the relative naval power to coerce him to concede. Because of the inability of both sides to bridge the wide gulf between them, the Qing recalled its officials to Beijing at the end of 1669.

Defending the monopoly

After the talks broke down, Zheng Jing eagerly anticipated another Qing delegation, but none would arrive again.[58] Nonetheless, peace largely prevailed between the two sides from 1670 to 1674, as they tacitly renounced the use of force against each other. During this time, new players were entering the scene in maritime East Asia and fundamentally challenging the heretofore dualistic competition between the Zheng organization and the Dutch East India Company. Powerful ascendant native states like Siam and the sultanate of Banten, on the western end of Java, exploited their advantageous geographic position to bind the Indian Ocean and China Seas more closely together than ever before. Chinese and Indian merchants frequented their ports and received passes from their rulers as official traders. Ships of the English East India Company, which maintained a factory at Banten, soon joined in, as did the Chinese residents and Dutch free burghers of Batavia, who were not employees of the VOC.

With the relaxation of the Qing coastal evacuation in 1669, these groups were also able to trade directly with China through the connivance of Shang Kexi at Guangzhou and Geng Jimao at Fuzhou. Some even plunged directly into the silk for silver exchange with Japan.[59] The presence of these newcomers exacerbated Japan's bullion shortage. After a major fire devastated Edo and caused prices for building materials and necessities to soar, the *bakufu* forbade silver exports altogether in 1668 and mandated gold as a substitute. Heavy pressure from Zheng merchants forced it to repeal the ban in 1671, but only for the Chinese, and not the Dutch.[60]

Cheng Wei-chung correctly argues that Jing did everything possible to shut out his new competitors from his family's traditional stranglehold

---

[58] Chang Hsiu-jung et al., *English Factory*, p. 64.
[59] Cheng (Zheng), *War, trade and piracy*, pp. 233–234, 245; Wills, *Pepper*, pp. 150–151.
[60] Totman, *Early modern Japan*, pp. 143–144; von Glahn, *Fountain of fortune*, p. 228.

over the intra-East Asian trade. When it became apparent that negotiations with the Qing could not institutionalize his presence on the mainland coast, he actively sought other ways to regularize his access to Chinese product sources. In 1669, he incorporated Jiang Sheng and his bandits, based in the chaotic evacuated zone in southern Fujian, into the Zheng military apparatus as a regular division. With the assistance of the Guangdong-based pirate, Qiu Hui, Jiang seized control of Xiamen and Jinmen from a rival band. A year later, Qiu himself, along with other Cantonese allies, formally joined the Zheng organization as military officers. Under the supervision of the new converted pirate divisions, smuggling depots along the coast were put under rationalized administration. At Xiamen, for instance, Jiang Sheng constructed straw huts as makeshift markets and enacted the strict laws of Taiwan, enforcing contracts at fair prices and prohibiting robbery and murder.[61]

However, the Qing viewed Zheng Jing's renewed overt presence on the mainland coast with trepidation. The court's anxiety precisely played into the hands of Geng Jimao, who itched for an excuse to justify his relevance in a time of relative peace. In 1671, Geng obtained permission to reestablish the Fujian naval command, and staffed it with his own clients and some of the former Zheng defectors.[62] In coordination with other fleets from Zhejiang and the Yangzi River Delta, his ships launched an attack on the organization's illicit outposts beyond the evacuated zone. By September, they had recaptured over sixty islands, killed more than 5,000 Zheng allies and smugglers, and burned down almost 3,000 makeshift buildings.[63] Although the campaign proved damaging for Jing, his main bastions at Xiamen and Dahao, guarded by thousands of troops, and the covert distribution and espionage networks in the interior, remained unaffected. With the basic infrastructure intact, smugglers could relocate to any of the thousands of other islands along the littoral. Thus, beneath the veneer of conflict, Taiwan and Fuzhou were tacitly cooperating. By maintaining controllable tensions, both Geng Jimao and Zheng Jing could boost their profit margins and corner the supply of Chinese goods between them.

Jing also took advantage of the cracks emerging beneath the monolithic veneer of Qing supremacy. Wu Sangui, the turncoat general who had led the Manchus into China, ruthlessly hunted down the last Ming pretender, and played an instrumental role in Qing consolidation, began to entertain thoughts of rebellion against his new overlords. Worried at his

---

[61] Jiang Risheng, *Taiwan waiji*, p. 239; Zheng Yiju, "Zheng Chenggong zhuan," p. 26.
[62] Taiwan Research Institute and Number One Archives, *Tongyi Taiwan dang'an*, pp. 86–88.
[63] *Kangxi shilu*, p. 36.

military and economic clout, the Kangxi emperor had gradually but steadily placed limits on his autonomy.[64] Wu, frustrated in his ambitions, probably communicated his thoughts to Zheng Jing via the smuggling networks on the Tonkin-Yunnan border. Jing responded eagerly; in March 1670, he sent an envoy to Wu's headquarters in Kunming with a reply encouraging him to rebel:

> Since I, Jing [was a young child], I had heard of your great name. Every time I read Your Highness's letters, proclamations, and drafts, I never fail to clap my hands and sigh at the intensity of your loyalty and filial piety, and am often moved to tears afterward. Looking out across the Four Seas, we all place [hope] in Your Highness. During your spare time outside of administration and military affairs, are you familiar with this solitary minister beyond the pale? ... Although my humble country is small, I have a thousand war junks and ten thousand warriors only for Your Highness to use. I await your virtuous reply from afar.[65]

For Jing, Wu promised to be the ideal ally with the formidable resources, as well as the motivation and capability to conquer China and provide him what he could not obtain from the Qing. For the time being, however, Wu's resolve wavered, as his eldest son remained a hostage in Beijing, and the emperor relaxed some of the more stringent policies toward him.[66]

On the sea routes to Japan, Zheng junks intensified their raids upon competing vessels. In one typical incident in late 1672, the *Cuylenburg*, a lightweight, richly laden Dutch *fluyt* vessel on its way back to Batavia from Nagasaki, blew off course in a storm and washed onto northeastern Taiwan. Zheng junks in the area intercepted the ship, plundered its cargo, and sunk it to the bottom of the sea. Eight sailors drowned to death, twenty-one crewmembers boarded boats and fled to Japan, while the remaining thirty-four were taken prisoner and executed.[67]

Zheng Jing further took aim at vessels belonging to the Ryukyu kingdom, a Qing vassal, which began to make regular journeys to Fuzhou, its designated port of entry, in 1663. In 1670, Zheng ships surrounded one Ryukyu ship that had lost its direction in a storm, and confiscated its goods. The crew was massacred, except for eight who were taken prisoners to Taiwan. Jing justified the act by emphasizing that Ryukyu ships "carried tribute to barbarians on barbarian soil" and thereby sold out culturally to the Manchus. Besides economic motive, the viciousness of the raid may have also signaled his jealousy and disappointment at being unable to secure the same privileges from the Qing court. At the same time, he could not fail to recognize that Ryukyu was concurrently a vassal

[64] Liu Fengyun, *Sanfan yanjiu*, pp. 138–142, 178–179.   [65] Xia, *Haiji jiyao*, p. 38.
[66] Liu Fengyun, *Sanfan yanjiu*, p. 180.
[67] Jacobus Anne van der Chijs (ed.), *Batavia dagregisters* (1899), 1672, p. 349.

of the domain of Satsuma and a key conduit for goods and intelligence from the Asian continent to Japan.[68] In this sense, his action appeared further calculated to insult the Tokugawa *bakufu* for its unfavorable policies toward the organization.

Zheng Jing's belligerent actions in the East China Sea achieved their purpose in keeping out competing Chinese junks, but they caused relations to deteriorate with Japan. On November 16, 1670, Dong Sanguan, a merchant under Geng Jimao, filed a suit against the organization before the magistrates at Nagasaki for confiscating his goods at sea. Although Dong failed to win compensation, the very decision to admit the case meant that, in the future, Jing could no longer depend unconditionally upon Japanese law to protect his commercial interests abroad.[69] Further reprisals from the *bakufu* followed suit in rapid succession. In 1671, the *bakufu* awarded the disputed silver deposits to Zheng Tai's relatives. Fortunately for Jing, the main defectors, now marginalized and kept under strict supervision in Beijing, could not send anyone to claim the prize.[70] More damaging was the *bakufu*'s decision, a year later, to replace the open competitive bidding at Nagasaki with a designated consortium of Japanese merchants specialized in purchases of imports from the Chinese and Dutch. The new regulations (*shihō shōhō*), which resembled the old silk allotment system, allowed the *bakufu* to artificially depress the exchange rate of silver, cutting deeply into the hefty profit margins enjoyed by the VOC and the Zheng organization for more than twenty years.[71]

Finally, the *bakufu* did not forget to exact revenge for Jing's seizure of the Ryukyu tribute vessel. In 1672, the Nagasaki magistrates apprehended the first Zheng ship that arrived at port, confiscated its belongings, and fined it 30,000 taels of silver. They then forwarded the cargo and payment as restitution to Ryukyu.[72] When word reached Taiwan, an infuriated Jing issued an embargo on all trade between the island and Japan. In 1673, the number of Chinese ships plying the route to Nagasaki dropped sharply to seventeen from the forty-five vessels recorded for the previous year. His junks also captured a Japanese fisherman whose vessel had blown off course into the waters around Taiwan. The unfortunate sailor was detained as a hostage at the home of a peasant family and forced to work as a slave in the fields. Jing then sent mediators to extract concessions from the *bakufu* and win back some of his lost privileges.[73]

---

[68] Hayashi Shunsai, *Ka'i hentai*, vol. I, pp. 25–30.
[69] Historiographical Institute, *Tō tsūji kaisho*, vol. I, pp. 160–161.
[70] Hayashi Shunsai, *Ka'i hentai*, vol. I, pp. 237–238, Xia, *Haiji jiyao*, p. 48.
[71] Nakamura, *Nagasaki bōekishi*, pp. 282–283.
[72] Hayashi Shunsai, *Ka'i hentai*, vol. I, p. 72.
[73] Chang Hsiu-jung et al., *English Factory*, p. 172; Tanabe, *Nagasaki jitsuroku*, pp. 56–57.

In contrast to Zheng Jing's zero-sum attitude toward the intra-East Asian luxury trade, he adopted a far more tolerant stance toward competition in the nascent global world system, which could accommodate many players with relatively little negative impact on profitability. Over the 1660s, he plunged deeper into this new realm of exchange, with an eye toward securing access to the lucrative silk and cotton goods from the Indian Ocean zone. However, Western Ocean intermediaries of such goods, such as Siam, were either too far away to achieve imports on a significant scale or located within the sphere of Dutch naval projection. Therefore, he initially improvised with substitutes from within the intra-East Asian system.

As during the days of Koxinga, the coarse fabric exported from Nagasaki, known as *cangan*, enjoyed robust demand in Taiwan and the rest of Southeast Asia. The biggest market was the Spanish Philippines. According to the rather suspect customs data at Manila, over one thousand boxes of cloth of all sorts were entering the port on average per year between 1663 and 1672. Because of brisk sales, and to cut down on costs, Jing soon moved to internalize production. Taking advantage of native place ties, he organized labor at his former familial bastion of Anhai, which enjoyed a tradition of handicraft production, to cultivate cotton and hemp, and spin and weave them into calicoes and linen. The seaside town's share of the overall quantity of shipments to Manila surpassed those from Nagasaki as the decade progressed. Moreover, the quality of its products also came to exceed the Japanese variety, as demonstrated by the increasing value realized per box. Anhai cloth soon became the second largest source of textiles sold in Manila.[74]

Zheng Jing's ties with the Philippines became further consolidated under the pro-business policies of the new governor-general, Manuel de León y Sarabia (r. 1669–1677). Through cordial relations with him, Jing acquired a foothold on Macao. The liminal status of the tiny Portuguese enclave made it a meeting ground for merchants from Siam, as well as Banten, Batavia, and other destinations where Jing could not easily reach with his own ships. Besides the typical products found in maritime East Asia, these traders provided Indian textiles for the Taiwanese, Southeast Asian, and Japanese markets. In 1670, after three-way negotiations among Zheng envoys, León's representatives, and the Portuguese, the parties agreed to open up a direct, regularized trading route among Macao, the China coast, Taiwan, and Manila. Subsequently, contemporaries noted that over thirty junks from the China coast alone visited Manila per year.[75]

---

[74] See Table 3.10 in Appendix 3.3.

[75] Blair and Robertson, *Philippine Islands*, vol. XLII, pp. 119, 151. In a sign of just how much these empirical observations diverged from the less reliable Spanish customs data,

From the early 1670s, the Portuguese authorities sheltered a sizable community of Zheng partisans in the city, sharing jurisdiction over them with Ke Gui, a naval commander dispatched from Taiwan to patrol the waters around the Pearl River Delta. Zheng Jing's allies helped the Portuguese pay heavy bribes to the Guangdong feudatory, Shang Kexi, and other Qing authorities to ensure that Macao's boundary gate, the only passageway for trading goods and food supplies from the rest of China, remained open.[76] With the connivance of Yao Qisheng (1624–1683), the magistrate of Xiangshan county, Shang's merchants slipped across the border under the cover of night to conduct business with the different mercantile groups congregated in the enclave. The atmosphere was peaceful and cordial, although transaction costs were high, since everyone had to purchase each other's permits.[77]

To further expand his area of economic influence, Jing issued a proclamation in 1668 that welcomed all merchants to trade duty-free in the areas under his control, with the exception of strategic goods under his exclusive monopoly, such as silk, deerskins, and sugar.[78] Official missions from traditional partners, such as Cambodia and Quảng Nam, congregated at his ports, as did the Siamese, even though they concurrently paid tribute to Shang Kexi at Guangzhou.[79] Also among those that responded to the call were two newly ascendant powers – the English East India Company and the sultanate of Banten. Both actively sought commercial partners and alliances able to counter Dutch designs for supremacy over Asia. Sultan Agong (1631–1695), the capable native ruler of Banten, instructed one of his royal agents, Keey Nebe Secredana, to purchase passes from Zheng Jing and placed him in charge of handling relations with Taiwan.[80] Likewise, the English delegation, led by Ellis Crispe, signed a formal treaty with the organization in July 1670. As part of the agreement, the EIC received a factory in Chengtian, housed in the same building as the Dutch-era town hall. In exchange, the company promised to pay an annual rent and provide two gunners and a skilled smith "for the King's

the latter reported no junks in 1671, while only one arrived the following year. See Table 3.9 in Appendix 3.3.

[76] For a detailed narrative of Macao's travails during this period, see John E. Wills, Jr., *Embassies and illusions: Dutch and Portuguese envoys to K'ang-hsi, 1666–1687* (Cambridge, MA: Council on East Asian Studies, Harvard University, 1984), pp. 93–99.

[77] Wu Han, *Chaoxian Li chao*, vol. IX, p. 3968.

[78] Chang Hsiu-jung et al., *English factory*, pp. 73–74.

[79] Cheng (Zheng), *War, trade and piracy*, p. 234.

[80] Chang Hsiu-jung et al., *English Factory*, p. 65; Jacobus Anne van der Chijs (ed.), *Batavia dagregisters* (1898), 1670–1671, pp. 272, 274.

service."[81] The EIC thus became a credible alternative to Japan in supplying weapons for the organization.[82]

English and Bantenese ships gave Zheng Jing direct access to the Indian Ocean network. Japanese and Chinese copper and gold were reexported to Mumbai and Surat, where they procured chintz, calicoes, and broadcloths. These, in turn, fetched high premiums in Taiwan and the Philippines. Not surprisingly, Indian textiles quickly overtook Anhai and Japanese cloth to become the leading variety sold at Manila in both quantity and value.[83] Taiwanese sugar found a receptive market in Persia.[84] The English East India Company and Banten also helped Jing break the strict Dutch naval blockade so his junks could acquire products from the resource-rich islands south of the Malay Peninsula. Keey Nebe Secredana employed skilled craftsmen to fell trees in the heavily forested eastern part of Java to construct new junks according to the Zheng organization's specifications. Zheng ships frequently traveled to insular Southeast Asia alongside their Bantenese counterparts to pick up the finished product and purchase pepper, tin, lead, and other natural resources, as well as Indian goods. To ensure the safe passage of these ships, Keey Nebe bought permits (zeebrieven) from the VOC on their behalf and secretly passed them off as his own. Zheng merchants also traveled on board the large, sturdily built English vessels, as they proved more difficult to raid than a regular junk.[85]

By 1672, Zheng Jing had overseen the transition of his organization from one fixated upon China and Japan to a more spacious, diversified economic entity oriented westward to Southeast Asia and the Indian Ocean. He used the still formidable profits from the intra-East Asian trade as capital to establish linkages to the product sources and markets that played an instrumental role in the emerging global world system. At the same time, copper from Yunnan, silver from Manila, and cloth from Anhai and India greatly decreased his reliance upon Japan. It is little wonder, then, that Zheng Jing was able to muster the confidence to impose a full-scale blockade on Nagasaki in 1673!

---

[81] Chang Hsiu-jung et al., *English Factory*, pp. 56–58, 62.   [82] Ibid., p. 62.
[83] See Table 3.9 in Appendix 3.3.
[84] Chang Hsiu-jung et al., *English Factory*, pp. 56–58, 62.
[85] van der Chijs, *Batavia dagregisters*, 1670–1671, p. 383. The Dutch company's repeated requests for Keey Nebe Secredana to promise not to harbor any Zheng vessels or crew members reveal the prevalence of the practice and the inability of the VOC to effectively curb it. See, for instance, van der Chijs, 1672, pp. 78–79, 89.

Between maritime and continent

As Zheng Jing shifted the economic gravity of his enterprise, he hoped to pick up where his father Koxinga had left off by creating a corresponding political order that would encompass his sphere of influence. An invasion of the Philippines was always on the cards, and seen as the logical next step after the successful occupation of Taiwan. Already, a shadow government loyal to the Zheng organization had taken shape by the late 1660s, just like in Dutch Taiwan. The Sangley community in Manila openly recognized Zheng Jing as "our king." Among the overseas Chinese, the laws of Taiwan also trumped their Spanish counterparts. In one typical case, Feng Xifan demanded and obtained from Governor-General León the extradition of two headmen who were incarcerated for sodomy and sentenced to burn at the stake.[86]

Chen Yonghua and his cohort of younger generals and civil officials wished to capitalize upon this advantageous position to seize the colony from the Spanish entirely. They found an excellent pretext during the winter of 1670 and 1671, when the Acapulco galleons and their shipments of New World silver failed to arrive in Manila.[87] This severe interruption caused Zheng merchants to return empty-handed to Taiwan and threatened to deprive many Chinese residents in the city of their livelihoods. Rumors spread that the Spanish purposely withheld bullion shipments to maximize their gain, undoubtedly reinforcing their image as brutal tyrants.[88]

In a persuasively drafted policy paper, Zheng Jing's secretary, Zheng Dexiao, a close friend of Chen Yonghua, played up the cruel and inhumane rule that the Sangley residents and merchants had to endure.[89] The Spanish, Dexiao stressed, did not deserve the Philippines because "they had obtained the country without trust and righteousness." He told stories of how children born to Chinese parents in Manila "were not permitted to read the books of the Middle Kingdom." If a Spaniard cursed or beat them, they could not even respond in kind. Meanwhile,

---

[86] "Carta de Manuel de León sobre embajada de Siam, cobro a sangleyes," AGI, Filipinas, 10, R.1, N.7. The Spanish records identify Feng as Pangsebuan, "Master of Camp and Governor-General of the States and Armed Forces of *Isla Hermosa* [Taiwan] and first cousin of the King." The colonial authorities found the penchant for pederasty among wealthy Chinese, known under the euphemism of "nefarious sins," abhorrent and un-Christian.

[87] Chang Hsiu-jung et al., *English Factory*, p. 117.   [88] Ibid., p. 104.

[89] Zheng Dexiao's memorial, transcribed in Jiang Risheng, *Taiwan waiji*, pp. 424–426, was written in 1683 to justify another attempt on Manila before the Qing takeover of Taiwan. However, most of its reasoning elaborates upon arguments proposed by supporters of the planned invasion during the early 1670s, when it came closest to actual implementation. See also Chang Hsiu-jung et al., *English factory*, p. 68.

Catholic priests and doctrines poisoned their minds and turned them away from the proper Confucian relations. Dexiao went on to decry the periodic massacres of the Chinese population, which left hundreds of thousands of corpses unattended across the land. Only by rescuing the Sangleyes from their miserable plight could Zheng Jing "wipe clean the hatred of our people of the Middle Kingdom."[90] An invasion of Manila thus became a moral obligation to exact retribution from the evil Spanish colonial authorities.

Dexiao went on to highlight the practical advantages of such a course of action. A tropical climate and fertile soil allowed the Philippines to readily serve as a prosperous agricultural base where crops grow year-round. The dense population provided a labor force and source of taxes, while the large Chinese community facilitated administration. From the perspective of his business network, Zheng Jing could acquire an additional foothold after Taiwan in Southeast Asia, allowing him to directly extract more of the resources that he once had to purchase. Dexiao further noted the presence of minerals, such as gold, which, he claimed, grew in abundance on the mountains. Accordingly, the expedition also promised to significantly decrease dependence upon silver from Japan and the Spanish. In sum, by "expanding the land" (*guang difang*), the organization could possess a territory with vast potential for long-term settlement that "does not fall second behind the Middle Kingdom," and supplement or outstrip Taiwan.[91]

At the same time, Dexiao articulated a broader ideological vision that clarified and expanded upon the narrative of a Chinese maritime state espoused by Chen Yonghua and his faction. Dexiao began by citing historical precedents. When "the ancient sage-kings extended their might to the four corners," he argued, "they seized power from lands overseas."[92] He further alluded to the Warring States kingdom of Qin (357–311 BCE), whose ruler adopted the advice of its leading general, Sima Cuo, to conquer the "barbarian" land of Shu (present-day Sichuan Province), instead of defending against the invading armies of the kingdom of Han. Zheng Jing, likewise, should privilege the acquisition of new territory over a contest with the Manchus for the mainland. Dexiao justified this position upon the need to bring rituals to "savage" lands and peoples afar. "When observing the movements of Heaven (*tianyun*)," he wrote, "it proceeds from north to south, forging the image of

---

[90] Jiang Risheng, *Taiwan waiji*, pp. 425–426.   [91] Ibid., pp. 259, 424.
[92] The sage-kings refer to the semi-mythical figures of Yao, Shun, and Yu, who lived in remote antiquity. According to traditional Chinese historiography, their rule represented a golden age of Chinese civilization, a utopian society to which all future generations should aspire.

civilization."[93] In this manner, "China" could become properly transformed into a mode of action, a continuous civilizing mission universal in scope and divorced from its physical milieu. Thus, Zheng Jing's very qualifications to rule hinged upon educating and providing prosperity for humankind through commercial and military expansion to the far corners of the earth, wherever his forces could reach.

Moved by this sophisticated set of arguments, Jing began making preparations for a covert attack on the Philippines. In the following months of 1670, he forged weapons and stepped up arms purchases from his trading partners, including the EIC.[94] Jing soon assembled a formidable force of "over a hundred junks, twelve to thirteen thousand soldiers ... and three to four hundred horses" mobilized from military colonies across Taiwan. The expeditionary force planned to attack Manila after the monsoon season, in early 1671. Both the Dutch and English, who followed his maneuvers closely, believed that Jing would prevail, since the tiny Spanish garrison proved ill-prepared for any external threat.[95] Before he could depart, however, staunch resistance emerged from inside his ranks. The conservative faction tried all it could to derail the invasion. When Jing received intelligence that some of his soldiers planned to commandeer his vessel at sea and deliver him into the hands of the Qing, he had no choice but to delay the expedition.[96] Without doubt, the restorationists had the greatest to gain from circulating rumors of this nature.

Unfazed, Zheng Jing prepared to launch another offensive soon after the Lunar New Year of 1672. Once again, the conservative faction came out in open opposition to the maneuvers. Feng Xifan, the influential spokesperson for the group, argued that the invasion constituted an unwise use of manpower. As a transit point for American silver, the Philippines, he argued, produced nothing of great value on its own and already sent an annual tribute of its natural resources. Moreover, any occupation would stretch the Zheng forces thin and place heavy burdens on the maintenance of garrisons. On a moral plane, "even if our soldiers set out, they would lack a good name, and lose the hearts of the people from afar." Feng concludes that "we have for years been guarding our territory here in peace, and now have the fortune of bountiful harvests. How can we recklessly raise an army of no benefit" to any side? Besides his

[93] Jiang Risheng, *Taiwan waiji*, p. 426.
[94] Chang Hsiu-jung et al., *English factory*, p. 164.
[95] van der Chijs, *Batavia dagregisters*, 1670–1671, p. 274. For more on the decrepit state of the Spanish defenses in the city, see "Carta de Lorenzo de Orella y Ugalde sobre defensa de Filipinas," AGI, Filipinas, 43, N. 39.
[96] van der Chijs, *Batavia dagregisters*, 1670–1671, pp. 271, 505.

stated reasons, Feng maintained personal business relations with the Spanish and did not want warfare to disrupt his profits.[97]

Feng's position received a huge boost when the galleon from Acapulco, aptly named *Nuestra Señora del Buen Socorro* (*Our Lady of Good Succor*), arrived at Manila in July 1671.[98] The peaceful settlement of payment to Chinese merchants for their wares removed an important *casus belli* for the organization. Meanwhile, word of the planned offensive reached the ears of the Spanish authorities, who undertook frantic defensive measures.[99] In late 1672, Governor-General León further dispatched an envoy to Zheng Jing to secure a promise from him to keep the peace between the two sides.[100] Although the momentum for an invasion stalled, fierce debates continued to plague the decision-making circles.

The sudden news of developments on the mainland in the middle of 1673 completely changed the dynamics within the organization. As the Kangxi emperor gradually stripped away at the privileges of his three feudatories, they found themselves increasingly backed into a corner. The final straw came in April 1673, when Shang Kexi sought permission to retire on the grounds of old age. The emperor not only granted his request, but also prohibited his son, Zhixin (d. 1680), from succeeding to the post, thereby abolishing the Guangdong feudatory. In response, Wu Sangui and Geng Jingzhong (d. 1682), the son and heir of the recently deceased Jimao, asked for the same "favor" of retirement to feel out the court's attitude. When the Kangxi emperor accepted their resignations, Wu Sangui promptly rose up in rebellion.[101]

Geng Jingzhong, however, continued to sit on the fence. In September 1673, he dispatched Huang Yong, a Zhangzhou native and an interpreter for the Dutch at the Fuzhou factory, as a secret envoy to Taiwan to feel out Zheng Jing's attitude. As Geng mulled over whether or not to join the rebellion, the two sides formalized their ambiguous commercial partnership and put aside any preexisting rivalries. Zheng Jing stationed one of his official merchants at Fuzhou. He and Geng further patrolled the sea lanes together, attacking and plundering ships without their passes, including another Ryukyu tributary mission to the Qing.[102]

[97] Jiang Risheng, *Taiwan waiji*, p. 259.
[98] "Cartas del Virrey Marques de Mancera," AGI, México, 46, N. 19; Blair and Robertson, *Philippine Islands*, v. XLII, p. 119.
[99] "Petición de Lorenzo de Orella y Ugalde para que se fortifique el castillo de Santiago," AGI, Filipinas, 43, N. 49; Blair and Robertson, *Philippine Islands*, v. XLII, pp. 134–135; Chang Hsiu-jung et al., *English factory*, p. 117.
[100] "Carta de Manuel de León sobre el sipuán de isla Hermosa," AGI, Filipinas, 10, R. 1, N. 28; Borao-Mateo et al., *Spaniards in Taiwan*, vol. II, pp. 658–659.
[101] Liu Fengyun, *Sanfan yanjiu*, pp. 181–206.
[102] Jiang Risheng, *Taiwan waiji*, p. 259; Hayashi Shunsai, *Ka'i hentai*, vol. I, p. 89.

In early 1674, Geng decided to join the insurgency. While Huang Yong paid further visits to Taiwan to obtain a firm commitment of support, Wu Sangui dispatched his own envoys to work out an effective mode of cooperation among all three parties. Wu proposed that Geng launch an offensive on the Yangzi River Delta from land, while Zheng Jing provided naval support. Geng would grant Jing 400 to 500 of his ships, and allow him to occupy the three prefectures of Zhangzhou, Quanzhou, and Xinghua in coastal Fujian – formerly Koxinga's main sphere of influence – as a mainland base of operations. Both feudatories also assured Taiwan in public proclamations that their uprising aimed to restore the Ming house. Wu spoke of "reviving the Ming and punishing the barbarian," while Geng called for "upholding together the civilization of the Great Ming and returning the universe to the Chinese."[103]

The outbreak of rebellion greatly strengthened the hand of the conservative faction in the organization. As long as the mainland remained securely under Qing control, Zheng Jing's plan to forge a new China among the waves could count upon the solid support of younger civil and military officials, who, for biological reasons, constituted a growing segment of the organization. Yet, once the recovery of the Ming and his followers' ancestral homes became a realistic prospect again, restoration became a potent ideological correctness able to trump any alternative legitimacy and silence all opposition. Jing agreed to the alliance, and transferred his soldiers and ships, already mobilized against the Philippines, to Penghu in preparation for crossing the strait. He concurrently assured the Spanish envoy that he had no intention of attacking Manila.[104]

In April 1674, after the necessary preparations, Jing relocated the organization's headquarters to Xiamen and Jinmen, already under his de facto control, and brought along most of his officials and soldiers to join the divisions of Jiang Sheng. Jing set up a separate branch of his Six Offices on the mainland, and implemented a regularized system of revenue collection. He implemented a monthly head tax of five silver pesos from all adult men between the ages of fifteen and fifty-nine, and recruited new soldiers from among their ranks. He also appointed commissioners to monopolize the collection and distribution of salt along the southeastern coast.[105] These methods represented a tremendous improvement over the ad hoc seizures of Koxinga's day, a testament to the rationalization of the organization's governance.

---

[103] Hayashi Shunsai, vol. 1, pp. 53, 71; Xia, *Haiji jiyao*, pp. 39–40; *Minhai jilue*, pp. 25–26, 29; Zheng Yiju, "Zheng Chenggong zhuan," p. 27; Wu Han, *Chaoxian Li chao*, vol. IX, p. 3996; Jiang Risheng, *Taiwan waiji*, pp. 262–263, 267.
[104] Borao-Mateo et al., *Spaniards in Taiwan*, vol. II, p. 660.   [105] Xia, *Haiji jiyao*, p. 44.

Feng Xifan, the same individual who had adamantly rejected an expedition on Manila in the name of peaceful development, now took charge of spearheading the military offensive. He would see his prestige within the organization increase steadily in the years to come because of his proximity to Jing. Jing also restored the honors earlier taken away from the imperial descendant Zhu Shugui, and housed him in a fabulous mansion in Xiamen.[106] The reform faction, on the other hand, who had invested their careers in Taiwan's development, remained lukewarm toward the mainland venture. Chen Yonghua chose to stay and was given the position of general director of Dongning (Dongning zongzhi) to manage affairs on the island in Jing's absence and provide logistical support for the front lines. Zheng Dexiao turned away efforts to recruit him as a military advisor on the grounds of old age.[107]

Triumphal heights

Soon after his arrival at Xiamen, Jing issued an open proclamation to the entire empire that wholly espoused the platform of restoration. Since "the Middle Kingdom views barbarians just as the cap views from high the rags of shoes," he called for "taking revenge on behalf of the country above and rescuing the people from disaster below."[108] Jing excused his previous turn away from the Ming by comparing himself to Gou Jian, ruler of the Warring States kingdom of Yue, who kept a low profile for years in order to secretly prepare for a final revenge upon his enemy, the king of Wu. Taking a page from Zheng Zhilong's old playbook, he was also careful to place his own organization on equal footing with Wu Sangui and Geng Jingzhong, characterizing the upcoming campaigns as a decentralized effort undertaken among "righteous warriors with a common cause."[109] The dramatic shift in rhetoric aimed to portray Jing as an unwavering Ming loyalist who never ceased preparations to fight against the Manchus even while in exile.

By and large, he proved tremendously successful. He not only influenced the mainstream opinion of generations of historians afterward, but his stance also gained him widespread popularity and legitimacy among his contemporaries, as Geng Jingzhong discovered all too late. At first, the feudatory severely underestimated his new ally. On the one hand, he gullibly believed the observations of his envoy, Huang Yong, who

[106] Shen Binghu, *Chonglin yuce*, p. 192.
[107] Ruan, *Haishang jianwen lu*, pp. 45–46; Xia, *Haiji jiyao*, pp. 40–41, 44.
[108] Jing adapts this passage from the Hongwu emperor, the Ming founder, who was referring to the Mongols.
[109] Hayashi Shunsai, *Ka'i hentai*, vol. I, pp. 54–55.

reported dismissively upon returning to Fuzhou from Taiwan that Zheng Jing's ships "do not amount to a hundred, while troops number less than ten thousand." These numbers fell far below Geng's expectations. Moreover, with nearly all of Fujian submitting to him with minimal resistance, the feudatory felt confident of defeating the Manchus without outside assistance. Accordingly, when Jing dispatched his rites officer, Ke Ping, to Fuzhou to seal the pact of alliance, Geng shrugged him off coldly and called for each side to "fight on his own territory." He further refused to grant the organization the promised ships and territories, and brushed off Ke's suggestion to utilize the Ming Yongli reign name as a sign of commitment to a common cause.[110] To add insult to injury, the feudatory reinstated the Qing maritime ban and terminated their economic cooperation.[111]

Yet a substantial number of feudatory soldiers in Fujian had once served under Jing, having been spared the plight of exile that had befallen most of their comrades in the naval forces in 1668.[112] Besides residual sentiments, his return made him, a Minnanese who shared their cultural outlook, a far more attractive alternative to Geng, a coarse bannerman from the Liaodong frontier. Even among those with little prior connection to the organization, Jing's unabashed embrace of the Ming gave him a sounder ideological platform than the feudatory, who betrayed both the Ming and Qing courts and remained ambiguous about his commitment toward restoration. Under pressure from subordinates and soldiers, commanders across Minnan soon switched their allegiances to the Zheng camp. Both the Quanzhou and Zhangzhou garrison heads killed the Geng-appointed prefects and handed their cities over to Jing. Defections swelled Zheng Jing's ranks to 70,000 men and 700 ships within several months.[113] Geng, on campaign in southern Zhejiang, became increasingly nervous about Jing's growing power at his rear. In October 1674, the feudatory ordered his men to attack Quanzhou. However, the Zheng forces under Liu Guoxuan successfully repulsed Geng, and seized more territory and troops from him.

Bilateral relations became so estranged that, in January 1675, Wu Sangui had to dispatch a special envoy to mediate between the two men and exhort them to make up their differences or risk becoming "the laughingstock of the enemy country." After a series of difficult negotiations marked by

---

[110] Geng continued to utilize the traditional Chinese sexagenery roots and stems, based upon the lunar calendar, to mark the dates in his proclamations.

[111] Xia, *Haiji jiyao*, p. 40; Jiang Risheng, *Taiwan waiji*, p. 266.

[112] Hayashi Shunsai, *Kai'i hentai*, vol. I, pp. 71, 97 and Beizhuan ji *zhu shu youguan Yao Qisheng deng zhuanji*, *TWWXHK* 2.9, p. 101.

[113] Jiang Risheng, *Taiwan waiji*, pp. 270–271; Xia, *Haiji jiyao*, pp. 41–42.

heated exchanges, Geng took advantage of a New Year's greeting to back down from his previously haughty stance. He lifted the ban on trade with Xiamen and the coastal areas, and rewarded Zheng Jing with five huge war junks as a token of his sincerity. Both sides renewed their friendship, and set a ceasefire boundary at the town of Fengting, in Xinghua prefecture, promising never to attack each other again.[114]

Even as he earned, through feat of arms, the respect of his peers and allies, Zheng Jing infused his movement with symbolism to impart a more inspiring ideological vision for the anti-Qing resistance than a marriage of convenience among warlords. Like a model filial son, he avenged past insults to his father, Koxinga. In mid-1675, he unleashed his fury upon the descendants of Huang Wu, the turncoat who had handed over the strategic supply depot of Haicheng to the Qing two decades earlier. Huang himself had submitted to Geng Jingzhong after the rebellion broke out but soon died of a malicious carbuncle on his spine. His son, Fangdu, and nephew, Yi, in turn, surrendered their garrison assignment at Zhangzhou to Jing after his rise to power in the province. In secret, however, they appealed for aid from the Qing at the same time. When their plot was discovered, Zheng Jing laid siege to Zhangzhou. Although the defenders held out stubbornly for four months, a top subordinate betrayed them and opened the city gates. Rather than face the certain retribution awaiting him, Huang Fangdu drowned himself in a well. After entering, Jing's men retrieved the deceased's body and dug up the corpse of his father, Huang Wu, mutilated them in public, and displayed their severed heads on the ramparts. Huang Yi and other close followers were taken to Haicheng and decapitated in full view of the town.[115]

In April 1675, Zheng Jing further enshrined prominent heroes in the Minnan region who had bravely chosen martyrdom for the Ming rather than surrender to the enemy amid the tumultuous dynastic transition. Meanwhile, he ordered his subordinates to tear down Qing-erected shrines to turncoats, such as Hong Chengchou (1593–1665), who played an enormous role in helping the new dynasty consolidate its hold on power. Hong's entire clan of over a hundred members was rounded up and exiled to Jilong and Longiou, on the extreme northern and southern end of Taiwan. Most would perish from tropical epidemics. On the other hand, Jing exhibited generosity to those who never wavered from the beginning in their loyalty to the Qing, either facilitating their passage to enemy territory if living or erecting shrines in their memory if dead.[116]

---

[114] Xia, *Haiji jiyao*, pp. 41–43, 45; Jiang Risheng, *Taiwan waiji*, pp. 289–290.
[115] Xia, *Haiji jiyao*, p. 47; Jiang Risheng, *Taiwan waiji*, pp. 297–299.
[116] Xia, *Haiji jiyao*, p. 45; Jiang Risheng, *Taiwan waiji*, p. 291.

Zheng officials, dispatched to administer the newly occupied territories in coastal Fujian, were put to work updating the gazetteers compiled under the previous Qing administrators that detailed the geography, people, customs, and history of each locality. In Ningyang county, in the mountainous western frontier of Zhangzhou prefecture, the magistrate, Jin Ji, meticulously supervised the revision of its gazetteer and published it in 1675. The introduction, written by him, spoke of "purging the corrupt, wicked barbarian influences" from the text and "restoring the old institutions of our Ming dynasty."[117] Although the volume largely inherited the Qing version intact, the compilers made sure to append a character for "fake" (*wei*) before any references to the Manchus, and add information on how the lives of the common people had improved because of "the Great Ming's restoration" (*Da Ming zhongxing*) spearheaded by Zheng Jing.[118]

The sophisticated use of propaganda in a remote outpost of Zheng-held territory demonstrated once again the effectiveness of the organization's reach and governance as perfected over the previous decade on Taiwan. Jin Ji and other officials placed in charge of Ningyang represented a new generation of administrators who owed their careers entirely to the organization. The gazetteer describes Jin as originally from Zhangzhou but "belonging to the registers of Dongning," which shows that Taiwan, at the time, constituted a separate unit of administration from Jing's mainland possessions. The child of a deceased commander, Jin had received his education at Koxinga's Hall for Nourishing Descendants and passed the civil service examinations in Taiwan. He had worked within the Personnel Office before assuming his position as Ningyang magistrate.[119] Zheng Jing thus had a large corps of competent administrators like Jin Ji able to capably meet the local demand for law and order.[120]

Jing's renewed commitment to the mainland also allowed him to finally achieve the unquestioned leadership over his clan that had eluded him since the bitter succession struggles of the early 1660s. In a stunning turnaround, he regained the support not just of relatives who unwillingly defected in the wake of Xiamen's fall in 1664, but also the majority of Zheng Tai's wing, once his most hostile rivals. Perhaps because of the

[117] Jin Ji, *Yongli Ningyang xianzhi*, pp. 693–694.   [118] Ibid., pp. 557, 693–694.
[119] Ibid., p. 694.
[120] According to Wills, "Contingent connections," p. 185, the key to Qing victory along the Fujian littoral lay in the dynasty's ability to utilize officials with commitment to the wellbeing of local society, facilitating "the rapid emergence of a longed-for condition of stable 'law and order.'" Wills is largely correct. However, as Jin Ji's example shows, both the Zheng and the Qing competed, often neck and neck, in the provision of this crucial service. At least during the mid-1670s, the outcome remained contingent and dependent upon conditions in the broader war fought between the two sides.

mistrust and severe restrictions that they endured at the hands of their new Qing masters, their impression of Jing greatly improved. In contrast to the wayward youth of a decade ago, they saw him as a "benevolent, compassionate" ruler in his maturity. Although the main figures of Tai's wing, including Zheng Zuanxu, remained under strict house arrest in Beijing, they secretly instructed their relatives, dependents, and agents still in Fujian to rejoin the organization.[121]

Their submission allowed Jing to regain the services of a highly skilled group of merchants with significant experience in foreign trade. They proved especially valuable in helping him mend estranged relations with Japan. Because of their intervention, the two sides successfully stepped away from further escalation. Zheng Jing released the Ryukyu prisoners and the Japanese castaway, provided them with silver and provisions, and had his junks escort them to Nagasaki. The *bakufu*, pleased by his gesture and his renewed commitment to the anti-Qing resistance, returned the favor by compensating him the value of the cargo it had seized earlier. Jing refused the money out of courtesy and lifted the economic blockade.[122] Meanwhile, he secured an amicable resolution to the decade-long dispute over Tai's silver deposits at Nagasaki. The Zheng relatives in Beijing instructed for the bullion, awarded to themselves by the *bakufu* in 1671, to be transferred to Jing. In the summer of 1675, Gong Chun and Huang Xiongguan, their representatives, sailed to Nagasaki and received the money from the Chinese interpreters in the presence of Jing's official ships from Xiamen, Taiwan, and Guangdong.[123]

The successful resolution of disputes within the family and with Japan allowed bilateral trade to gradually pick up again, especially after traditional smuggling routes to the silk production bases of the Yangzi River Delta became cleared from the initial disruption related to warfare. Zheng Jing's ships increased their imports of cannon, swords, and other armaments from Nagasaki. Samurai were once more recruited in large numbers to support his war effort. In fact, he specially reserved an island off the northern Taiwan port of Jilong to house the Japanese mercenaries, as well as merchants coming to the island for trade. An imposing, abandoned Spanish fortress overlooked the Japanese quarter, known as Fuzhou Street, where Zheng agents flocked to conduct business and obtain information on developments in Japan.[124]

---

[121] Hayashi Shunsai, *Kai'i hentai*, vol. I, p. 188.
[122] Hayashi Shunsai, *Ka'i hentai*, vol. I, p. 73.
[123] Hayashi Shunsai, *Ka'i hentai*, vol. I, pp. 188, 244–245; Xia, *Haiji jiyao*, p. 48.
[124] Hayashi Shunsai, *Ka'i hentai*, vol. I, p. 194; Liushiqi and Fan Xian, *Chongxiu Taiwan fuzhi*, p. 30.

In addition to the legalized framework of exchange, Tai's network of associates used their close ties with the Nagasaki hierarchy, along with the additional sweeteners of bribes and gifts, to bypass the *bakufu*'s strict quota on silver exports. With the assistance of city officials, Zheng merchants continued to exchange their products at far more attractive rates than those mandated in the *bakufu*'s provisions. To avoid drawing suspicion, the magistrates had the cargo on board the first two ships of each year transferred to four small boats that sailed for Kyoto and Osaka at separate times, thereby diluting the shipment.[125]

The Zheng merchants went as far as to outfit ships in Taiwan, probably in Jilong, on behalf of the shogunal deputy, Suetsugu Heizō Shigetomo. Shigetomo transported his retainers onboard these vessels, along with sulfur, maps, and armaments, to trade with China and Cambodia. His activities went well beyond the semi-private aid allowed to the Zheng organization and directly threatened Edo's exclusive right to regulate trade, immigration, and the export of strategic materials abroad. In March 1676, when a shocked *bakufu* discovered what he was doing, it ordered him and his entire family exiled to a remote island. Many of his retainers were imprisoned or put to death.[126] Despite the crackdown, illicit collusion between the Zheng and the Nagasaki authorities continued. The Dutch complained bitterly that the two magistrates of the port city "only care for the Koxinga Chinese daily from afar."[127]

However, the combination of legitimate and illicit transactions could not stem the long-term decline in both the volume and value of trade with Japan despite relatively fewer hindrances to the acquisition of mainland luxury sources. On average, 25.2 Chinese junks from the China coast, Taiwan, and Southeast Asia visited Nagasaki per year between 1673 and 1683, over eleven fewer than in the previous decade. Annual revenues of the Zheng stood at 925,788 taels (34,717 kg) worth of silver, a slight decline from the previous decade. Significant volatility also appeared to characterize the exchange. In 1675, for instance, Zheng junks achieved a value of 1,503,618 taels, while the figure dropped sharply to 665,989 taels in 1676. On the bright side, Zheng Jing appears to have captured a greater proportion of the Japan trade, as much as 90 percent, if not more. Moreover, the value of exports sold at Nagasaki continued to exceed that of the VOC, which registered an even steeper decline. Its 4.3 ships realized 644,021.90 taels (24,150.8 kg) worth of silver over the same

[125] Cai Yuping, "Zheng shi shiqi Taiwan dui Ri maoyi zhi yanjiu," unpublished MA thesis, National Chenggong University, 2005, pp. 51, 58; Cheng (Zheng), *War, trade and piracy*, p. 241.

[126] Tanabe, *Nagasaki jitsuroku*, p. 345; Hayashi Shunsai, *Ka'i hentai*, vol. I, p. 190.

[127] Cai Yuping, "Dui Ri maoyi," pp. 51, 58; Cheng (Zheng), *War, trade and piracy*, p. 241.

period, down more than 300,000 taels from the previous decade. Jing's efforts to exclude others from the intra-East Asia exchange had evidently borne fruit.[128]

Jing continued to expand commercially in Southeast Asia despite abandoning his plans for military conquest. Because of his formal military alliance with Geng Jingzhong, a peaceful reconciliation gradually took shape between Jing and the Dutch East India Company, a partner of the feudatory. Dutch predation on Zheng ships largely came to a halt, and they received official licenses from Batavia guaranteeing safe passage south of the Malay Peninsula. Total revenues and profits from the Western Ocean remain unknown for the bulk of the 1670s. However, it is estimated that Jing dispatched twenty-three ships there in a typical year, reflecting robust growth.

The Philippines remained an important destination for Zheng ships. According to the official customs data, the number of Chinese junks sailing to Manila between 1673 and 1683 totaled 5.7 on average per year, a slight increase over the previous decade. Since the Rebellion of the Three Feudatories made possible fully open access to the China coast, Taiwan lost its role as a transit point for the mainland. Moreover, the island's own products mostly overlapped with the Philippines. For these reasons, Taiwanese ships visiting Manila declined over the decade to just two per year on average, and the value of exports to the port fell sharply to 4,744.10 taels (177.9 kg) worth of silver.[129] Most likely, this loss was compensated well by mainland junks, although the scale of their business remains unknown. Indian textiles continued to constitute a source of growth in Manila, while the Japanese variety disappeared completely.[130] Shipments of Anhai cloth may have continued from the mainland coast, although a new source of export production for cotton goods was located along the Guangdong littoral and in the Yangzi River Delta.[131]

The Zheng officials on Taiwan exercised primary oversight over these commercial operations. Chen Yonghua controlled the Gongsi (Public Firm) in conjunction with Koxinga's widow, Madame Dong. He also conducted significant trade on his own ships. English merchants viewed the two as the main points of contact for business transactions, and frequently showered them with expensive presents on special occasions, such as their birthdays or the Lunar New Year.[132] In addition, Zheng Jing threw open Xiamen as a duty-free port in 1675, and exempted both Chinese and foreign merchants from impositions and duties for three

---

[128] See Tables 4.1 and 4.2 in Appendix 3.4.   [129] See Table 4.5 of Appendix 3.4.
[130] See tables 5.4–5.7 of Fang Zhenzhen, *Taiwan Manila maoyi*, pp. 183–191.
[131] Chang Hsiu-jung et al., *English factory*, pp. 235, 351.   [132] Ibid., pp. 218–220.

years. That year, thirteen ships arrived from Banten, Cambodia, Batavia, and other Western Ocean ports. Moreover, the EIC received permission to establish a second factory at Xiamen in exchange for supplying armaments and gunpowder for his soldiers on the frontlines. Feng Xifan took charge of supervising the trade along the mainland coast. Through his initiative, Xiamen soon became home to a large foreign mercantile community engaged in trade for the long term.[133]

Since Zheng Jing had shelved his plans for a maritime Chinese state, domination over ports in Guangdong became the next best alternative for him to maintain his economic influence over Southeast Asia and the Indian Ocean on account of their strategic proximity to these areas. As 1676 began, he decided to work together with Wu Sangui to either subjugate or expel the feudatory, Shang Kexi, and his son, Zhixin, who still sat on the fence in terms of their loyalties.[134] In the spring, Zheng forces under Liu Guoxuan rapidly penetrated into the Pearl River Delta from their traditional power bases along coastal Chaozhou prefecture, in the eastern part of the province. Meanwhile, Wu's forces overran Qing resistance in Guangxi and came in from the west through Zhaoqing. As the two armies converged on the provincial capital of Guangzhou, Shang Zhixin convinced his ailing father, Kexi, to surrender. Their submission linked the rebel groups of central and south China together into a unified bloc that presented an unprecedented menace to the Qing court. Zheng Jing emerged as the biggest winner of the campaign, since Wu ordered the Shang family to grant him all territory east of Dongguan, just fifty kilometers from Guangzhou, to demonstrate their commitment to the new alliance.[135]

After the spectacular successes in Guangdong, Zheng Jing and Geng Jingzhong, at Wu Sangui's initiative, stood ready to launch the joint push into the Yangzi River Delta that had been put off because of their earlier infighting. However, before the campaign got off the ground, Jing again turned his weapons against Geng. In the summer of 1676, Liu Yingling, the feudatory garrison commander of Tingzhou, dissatisfied at leaving his comfortable strategic outpost in the mountains of southwestern Fujian to join the northern expedition, offered to hand it over to Jing. Jing readily accepted the commander's submission in flagrant violation of the earlier armistice agreement.[136] Perhaps he had grown overconfident from his victories over the previous year. The seizure of Tingzhou would also lay a

[133] Xia, *Haiji jiyao*, p. 46; Chang Hsiu-jung et al., *English factory*, pp. 218–220; Hayashi Shunsai, *Ka'i hentai*, vol. I, pp. 192–193.

[134] Hayashi Shunsai, *Ka'i hentai*, vol. I, pp. 77, 106.

[135] Xia, *Haiji jiyao*, p. 48; Jiang Risheng, *Taiwan waiji*, p. 304.

[136] Xia, *Haiji jiyao*, p. 49; Jiang Risheng, *Taiwan waiji*, pp. 305–307.

solid foundation for the takeover of all of Fujian, which would enhance the image of him as a filial descendant recovering his family's territorial patrimony, certainly a greater priority than the Yangzi River Delta. Finally, he could use this chance to get rid of Geng, a potential competitor for the spoils of victory, incorporate the feudatory's soldiers, and join forces with Wu Sangui for the final northward push.[137]

In retrospect, the move was incredibly shortsighted. The seizure of Tingzhou came on top of a series of dismal defeats that befell Geng in southern Zhejiang and Jiangxi at the hands of Manchu banner forces under Giyešu, the Prince Kang (d. 1697). News of Liu Yingling's defection severely shook the morale of the feudatory's core commanders and their commitment to the anti-Qing resistance. In August 1676, two rebel generals surrendered to the Qing and secretly guided Giyešu's men across the strategic mountainous entryway from Zhejiang into Fujian. Manchu troops then quickly overran the northwestern corner of the province. With no hope for relief on the horizon, another corps of officials turned against Geng and held him hostage in Fuzhou as they initiated contacts with the Qing of their own accord. Cornered from three sides by the Manchus, an uncooperative Zheng Jing, and his subordinates, Geng had no choice but to welcome the Qing into Fuzhou in November 1676. Both the Kangxi emperor and Giyešu treated him with generosity and forgiveness, allowing him to retain his feudatory position and soldiers, and giving him a chance to redeem himself through victory.[138]

In the short term, however, many of Geng's commanders refused to join him in surrender and swelled the Zheng ranks. They handed over to Zheng Jing the prefectures of Xinghua, north of Quanzhou, and Shaowu, in the northwest, allowing his troops to take positions along the Wulong River, within striking distance of Fuzhou.[139] The fortunes of the organization now reached a pinnacle; Zheng Jing possessed seven prefectures in Fujian and Guangdong, controlled Taiwan, maintained outposts along the entire mainland coastline, and enjoyed a sphere of influence extending from Japan to the Indian Ocean. Never before did it rule over so much territory, not even in the days of Zhilong and Koxinga. His popularity among his subjects also reached unprecedented heights. As the crew of a junk at Nagasaki reported to the Japanese authorities, the "people admire and look up to him, and everyone says that he is a great general whose benevolence and compassion are unmatched in recent years."[140]

[137] Jiang Risheng, *Taiwan waiji*, p. 306.   [138] Liu Fengyun, *Sanfan yanjiu*, p. 271.
[139] Xia, *Haiji jiyao*, pp. 50–51; Jiang Risheng, *Taiwan waiji*, pp. 312–315.
[140] Hayashi Shunsai, *Ka'i hentai*, vol. I, p. 192.

Cheng Wei-chung portrays Zheng Jing during the Rebellion of the Three Feudatories as desperately struggling to hold onto the momentum of his shrinking monopoly over the China-Japan route. Ultimately, the organization lost out because of the emergence of competitors in the South China Sea zone, such as the feudatories, Siam, Banten, the EIC, and the VOC, which provided attractive alternatives for Chinese merchants, especially access to the Indian Ocean.[141] While there is much truth to this perspective, it overlooks the fact that, during the 1660s, Zheng Jing had already anticipated the decline of the traditional intra-East Asian exchange and tried to squeeze as much as possible from it for use in an emerging global trading system. He forged highly cooperative ties with the other trading conglomerates to successfully tap into new product sources and markets in Manila, the Western Ocean, and the Indian Ocean. In addition, Jing engaged in the import substitution of textiles to control the means of production, a potential first step in transforming the organization from wholesaler to manufacturer.

Seen in this light, Jing's participation in the Rebellion of the Three Feudatories represented, first and foremost, a political, and not economic, decision. Indeed, his mainland campaign reaped significant initial benefits in the reunion of his family, the mending of the generational divide in his organization between reformists and conservatives, better relations with Japan, and widespread popularity among his subjects. His return to the platform of Ming restoration allowed him to acquire a level of legitimacy unprecedented since the days of his father. Certainly, economic considerations also figured into the strategy. His campaigns in Guangdong and Fujian aimed at securing hinterlands and strategic ports that could provide unhindered access to the new, global world system. But the same effect could be more readily achieved from a purely economic standpoint by establishing a maritime Chinese state able to control the sea lanes as far as the Indian Ocean and directly extract resources on site. Originally, Jing had precisely this intention in mind with his plan to invade the Philippines in the early 1670s. As it turned out, his renewed prioritization of Ming restoration proved incredibly fragile; once the Qing began its counterattack, everything came crashing down.

---

[141] Cheng (Zheng), *War, trade and piracy*, p. 243.

7   A contingent destruction

Why do you not lay down your weapons and rest your men, bring all your carriages and armor to protect Taiwan, and count yourself among the overseas guest ministers? As for receiving ranks and titles, it is only at your wish. If you do not wish to do so, you do not have to receive them. How can our Dynasty regret granting a remote and impoverished corner of the seas for your rulers and ministers to preserve their names and rituals?

Letter from the Manchu noblemen Lahada and Giohoto to Zheng Jing, 1677.[1]

The maritime bandits resemble an ailment of scabies, but Taiwan is merely a ball of mud. If we obtain it, it does not add any value. If we do not obtain it, nothing is lost.   Kangxi emperor, 1683.[2]

Possessing bountiful land and resources, the three feudatories overwhelmed the Qing forces and swept across the southwest, southeast, and northwest. In early 1676, well over half the empire came under rebel control. Zheng Jing, too, chalked up incredible gains through military campaigns and funded them with continued economic expansion. It appeared highly likely that he could finally achieve the unrealized goal of his grandfather and father: to control Taiwan, the three southeastern provinces of Zhejiang, Fujian, and Guangdong, and a commercial network whose reach encompassed maritime East Asia and into the Indian Ocean. Nonetheless, his gains proved fragile and ultimately unsustainable. Under the skillful direction of the Kangxi emperor, Qing forces stemmed the rebel gains and began to push back. By 1677, Zheng Jing came to face the entire might of the Qing by himself. Nonetheless, and more than any other time in the past, he possessed significant bargaining power to secure recognition and guarantees for the future stability of his organization through a peaceful settlement with the court.

[1] Jiang Risheng, *Taiwan waiji*, pp. 328–329.   [2] *Kangxi shilu*, p. 129.

Stalemate without settlement

By the end of 1676, Zheng forces had reached the Wulong River, within striking distance of Fuzhou, the provincial capital. All of Fujian appeared to be within their grasp. So far, however, they had only seen action against feudatory troops. Zheng Jing's men were thus in for a rude awakening when the more powerful and mobile Manchu cavalry forded across the river one snowy night in January 1677 and charged into their camp. Already ill-adjusted to the abnormally bitter weather, Zheng soldiers fled in disarray before the terrifying neighs of the swiftly advancing horses. The rout spread rapidly. Within weeks, Tingzhou was abandoned without a fight, while Giyešu's men exploited the dissension among commanders of the Xinghua garrison to easily take the city. The Manchus continued their advance southward, with Quanzhou and Zhangzhou prefectures falling with little resistance in March. Zheng Jing and his advisors, based in Zhangzhou, hastily boarded their junks and returned to Xiamen, abandoning the strategic outpost of Haicheng along the way. His defeat, along with Geng Jingzhong's defection, profoundly impacted neighboring Guangdong. Shang Zhixin, additionally threatened by the Qing advance into Jiangxi from the south, submitted to the Qing in April under the same favorable terms as Geng. The Zheng commander in eastern Guangdong followed suit in July.[3]

By the middle of 1677, all of the gains made by Zheng Jing over the previous three years had dissipated overnight. Highly discouraged, he and his advisors initially planned to abandon the mainland altogether. However, the residents of Xiamen and Jinmen obstructed their departure by collectively falling on their knees and wailing. Under heavy pressure, he and his advisors decided to take another stand. He calmed the panicked mood and regrouped his fleeing generals, assigning them to defend the key approaches to Xiamen. He also beheaded the main commanders responsible for the recent fiasco and ordered the families of generals not native to the southeastern coast to relocate to Taiwan.[4] For the rest of the year, he avoided direct engagement, giving his troops time to recuperate from the disaster.

Meanwhile, the Qing offensive sputtered to a halt, as Manchu forces found it almost impossible to maneuver among the islands and jagged coastline surrounding Xiamen and Jinmen. Giyešu ordered the construction of war junks at shipyards along the littoral. However, the Zheng defectors, the ones with the expertise in naval matters, had largely been demobilized or rejoined the organization. It would take time before the

---

[3] Jiang Risheng, *Taiwan waiji*, pp. 312–319; Xia, *Haiji jiyao*, pp. 50–53.
[4] Xia, *Haiji jiyao*, pp. 51–52; Jiang Risheng, *Taiwan waiji*, pp. 317–320.

Qing could separately commission and train qualified personnel. The prince further faced a rebellion in the newly retaken areas of southern Fujian. Cai Yin, a fortuneteller and martial arts practitioner, amassed a huge following by proclaiming himself the missing third son of the late Ming Chongzhen emperor. Known as the White-headed Bandits for the color of their turbans, they joined forces with defeated Zheng remnants to overrun counties in Quanzhou, and, at one point, enter the city itself.[5] In the rest of the empire, Qing forces had gone on the offensive, pushing deep into Wu Sangui's strongholds in central China, but progress was slow, and territory changed hands frequently.[6]

Faced with these challenges, Giyešu decided to try the same strategy that had worked so successfully with Geng Jingzhong and Shang Zhixin and with other enemies in the past: offer Zheng Jing ranks and titles in exchange for his submission. Success in this effort would lead to the isolation of Wu Sangui, allowing the Qing to focus all its energies upon his extermination. As the emperor's elder cousin and an expeditionary general, the prince could unilaterally negotiate and reach accords on the ground before reporting to the court. Accordingly, in April 1677, Giyešu dispatched two envoys to Xiamen, where they received a warm welcome from Zheng Jing and his officials. However, in reply to their offer, Jing insisted that the duty for any "loyal minister and righteous official" involved the "strict delineation of 'Chinese' and 'barbarian'."[7] Instead, he demanded a relationship with the Qing based upon the tributary model of Korea, the same terms as he proposed in 1669, which did not involve the need for him and his subjects to shave their heads in the Manchu style.

Giyešu found Jing's reply infuriating, arrogant in tone and full of gross exaggerations. Nonetheless, as the stalemate between the two sides dragged on with no apparent end in sight, he took the time to carefully study the demands in greater detail. He even pored through the Qing court records, where he learned, apparently for the first time, the long history of negotiations with the organization, and, specifically, the latest talks held in 1669. Armed with a more precise contextual knowledge, Giyešu appointed four men to head a second mission to Xiamen whose scale and prestige exceeded all other negotiators to date. Zhang Zhongju and Bian Yongyu, the Quanzhou and Xinghua prefects, represented a new generation of Liaodong bannermen who passed the civil service

---

[5] Xia, *Haiji jiyao*, p. 56; Jiang Risheng, *Taiwan waiji*, pp. 321–323.
[6] Liu Fengyun, *Sanfan yanjiu*, pp. 286–288.
[7] Jiang Risheng, *Taiwan waiji*, p. 321; *Minhai jilue*, p. 41.

examinations under the Qing and enjoyed the full trust of the court.[8] Two Quanzhou gentry, Huang Zhimei and Wu Gonghong, would accompany and assist the officials on account of their extensive local knowledge and ties with key figures from the Zheng organization.[9] Giyešu's mission thus combined the bureaucratic formality of the 1669 talks with reliance upon the informal networks of southern Fujian that characterized Kong Yuanzhang's endeavor in 1667.

From the end of 1677 to the early months of 1678, the four envoys met with Zheng Jing several times in the presence of all his key civil and military officials. They transmitted the prince's willingness to grant him Taiwan in perpetuity given that he retreated from the mainland coast and shaved his head. Zheng Jing and Feng Xifan, however, refused both conditions and demanded, in addition, four prefectures in Minnan to feed and supply their troops. Since these requests went beyond what the Qing envoys could authorize by themselves, they returned to seek further instructions from Giyešu. At this point, the prince decided to take the unprecedented step of approving the Zheng family's long-standing request for tributary relations along the Korean model. While not ideal, this option appeared to be the most effective way for the Qing to persuade him to leave the mainland voluntarily while sparing the heavy loss of lives involved in a protracted campaign. Giyešu ordered his subordinate, the Manchu bannerman Lahada, to draft a letter to Zheng Jing. Since Lahada's command of Chinese was imperfect, the letter underwent editing at the hands of Giohoto, a grand secretary at the imperial court.[10] The close coordination with Beijing clearly shows the Kangxi emperor's support of the new terms, at least as "feelers."

The letter opened by complaining that "envoys have traveled back and forth for years in fruitless discussions about surrender and tribute to the extent that our tongues are broken and lips become rotten." Because of the Zheng family's stubborn but futile resistance against the Qing to restore the Ming, countless suffering befell residents of the southeastern Chinese coast. Yet, Lahada and Giohoto went on to argue, Jing should not direct his ire against the Manchus; after all, the Ming fell to Han Chinese rebels. Far from being usurpers, the Qing had entered China to revenge the usurpers and restore order. The Shunzhi emperor "paid a

---

[8] For more on Zhang Zhongju, see Huai Yinbu (ed.), *Quanzhou fuzhi xuanlu*, *TWWXCK*, 223 (1967), p. 111. The entry on Bian Yongyu is found in Jiang Liangqi, *Donghualu xuanji*, *TWWXCK*, 262 (1969), p. 287.

[9] Wu Gonghong, for instance, served under both Geng Jingzhong and Zheng Jing before defecting to the Qing. He even helped Jing arrange for the defection of a prominent general from Geng's camp during the bitter internecine conflict between the two men. See *Minhai jilue*, p. 27.

[10] Jiang Risheng, *Taiwan waiji*, p. 326; *Minhai jilue*, p. 43.

personal visit to the Chongzhen emperor's tomb with tears in his eyes, and honored him with an imperial edict."[11] The letter further spoke about the Kangxi emperor's project to compile a comprehensive history of the Ming, one that Giohoto himself was supervising at the time.[12] In sum, the Qing rightfully inherited the Mandate of Heaven, which the former dynasty had lost of its own accord.

At the same time, Lahada and Giohoto recognized that the Zheng's defiance emanated out of a desire to "defend the sanctity of Ming institutions. For thirty years, you did not forget your former ruler." This steadfast adherence differs "from Wu Sangui ... who betrayed two dynasties." The Qing was abandoning its decades-old view of the Zheng as pirates and rebels, and put them, as Ming loyalists, in a class above the turncoat feudatories. Lahada and Giohoto explained that previous envoys failed to exhibit sufficient sensitivity to those residual ties. They admitted:

If you follow the orders to "shave your head" and "return to the mainland," it causes you to submit to our Dynasty at the expense of abandoning your former emperors. It not only destroys the reputation of your ruler [Zheng Jing] and ministers as symbols of righteousness, but it also harms our effort to encourage loyalty for over a thousand generations.[13]

The Qing realized that its previous policies had proven inflexible and fallen short of overcoming the suspicions of the Zheng and, instead, prolonged their resistance.

Based on this assessment, Lahada and Giohoto put two options on the table before Jing. He could continue the struggle, but they left him no doubt as to which side would emerge victorious. After all, "how can two tiny islands match the vastness of the Four Seas? How can a crowd of rabble compete with the majesty of ironclad cavalry? How can salt and fish of the sea compare to tribute from fields across China?" On the other hand, Zheng Jing could abandon his acquisitions in Fujian and return to Taiwan. As long as he withdrew his soldiers from the mainland coast, the letter promised him, the Qing could accept whatever political arrangement he desired on Taiwan, even if it meant not paying tribute. The two sides could also initiate regular trading relations once peace returned. The letter concludes by appealing to their shared sense of Confucian morality:

---

[11] Jiang Risheng, *Taiwan waiji*, p. 327.

[12] The *Ming History* would be completed in 1735 under the direction of the scholar Zhang Tingyu (1672–1755) during the reign of the Kangxi emperor's successor, Yongzheng (r. 1722–1735).

[13] Jiang Risheng, *Taiwan waiji*, p. 327.

To preserve the country and its rituals marks the height of loyalty. To protect your ancestors and lineage marks the height of filial piety. To keep your entire body far away from harm marks the height of wisdom. To rest your troops and comfort the people marks the height of benevolence. When you can gather all four advantages with just one move, what difficulties do your rulers and ministers have that prevent you from accepting them?[14]

Giohoto and Lahada thus appropriated Jing's previous negotiating position, holding him to the same standards that he had set for himself in 1669. This recognition of the Zheng organization's political and ideological legitimacy offered Jing a practical and face-saving way out of further confrontation with East Asia's largest empire.

Confident of forging an agreement, Giyešu sent Wu Gonghong to Xiamen with the letter in hand. However, during the envoy's meeting with Zheng civil and military officials, Feng Xifan came out in opposition to the offer. To his shock, not only did Feng argue against a withdrawal, but he imposed the additional condition of control over all islands off the Chinese coast. This proposal, moreover, received backing from Zheng Jing. When they heard about the counter-terms, the Manchu officials wondered whether Jing and Feng had gone crazy.[15] What had motivated them to reject a plan that granted most of what they desired based upon a realistic assessment of the capabilities and limitations on both sides?

Indeed, most Zheng officials recognized that prospects for a Ming restoration had grown suddenly remote in the wake of recent setbacks and the surrender of two key feudatory allies. In April 1678, Zheng Jing learned, to his further dismay, that Wu Sangui had proclaimed himself the founding emperor of a new Zhou dynasty. Jing remarked satirically that "Wu's age had made him foolish and arrogant to the point of usurping the throne. With heroes disillusioned, I fear [his cause] cannot last long."[16] The enthronement removed the very ideological reasoning that underpinned the rebellion, with its powerful appeal to the Ming legacy. Jing also could not fail to notice that accepting the Qing offer would leave him free to concentrate upon the more realistic option of asserting political control over his sphere of commercial influence in the sea lanes.

Yet, on the other hand, Zheng Jing felt confident that, compared to a decade ago, he held better cards against the Qing because of his renewed presence on the mainland coast. He could at least use the talks to salvage some of the territory lost in previous campaigns. He and his officials must have equated the mere conferral of his rights to Taiwan to the

---

[14] Jiang Risheng, *Taiwan waiji*, pp. 327, 329.
[15] *Minhai jilue*, p. 43; Jiang Risheng, *Taiwan waiji*, p. 330.
[16] Jiang Risheng, *Taiwan waiji*, p. 346.

abandonment of a cause in which they had invested years of effort. In particular, his pro-restoration advisors, centered upon Feng Xifan, not only felt ideologically disinclined to accept the offer, but they also feared losing their dominant role at Zheng Jing's side to Chen Yonghua if they returned to Taiwan. Moreover, Jing's withdrawal would be construed as a cold-hearted betrayal by his numerous new followers on the mainland coast. Fundamentally, these considerations emanated from the confidence that the organization's elites had in Taiwan's absolute security from an invasion, betting upon the Qing's inability to field an effective naval force able to cross the treacherous strait.

It was precisely this assurance that gave Zheng Jing the audacity to renew his confrontation with the Qing all on his own after the talks broke down. He received additional affirmation for his hardline stance when Cai Yin and the White-headed Bandits submitted to his leadership, while reinforcements under Liu Guoxuan arrived at Xiamen from Guangdong. Impressed by Liu's ability to execute a bloodless and orderly withdrawal from what was already enemy territory, Zheng Jing appointed him field commander of the Zheng armies. At Jing's orders, the newly reconstituted forces launched a full-scale offensive from Xiamen. Initially, they encountered stunning success, overrunning Qing positions across Quanzhou and Zhangzhou prefectures. In June, they surrounded Haicheng, Xiamen's strategic gateway, successfully entrapping a sizable contingent of Manchu banner forces. After a siege of eighty-three days in which the garrison was reduced to starvation, Liu's men stormed and seized the town. More than 30,000 defenders perished, including the Fujian military commander, who hung himself from the main gate. Zheng troops captured several thousand Qing officers and soldiers, both Manchu and Han, and sent most of them to Taiwan to open up new fields.[17]

As the fiasco at Haicheng unfolded, an infuriated Kangxi emperor sacked the governor-general and governor of Fujian and replaced them with two junior officials. Yao Qisheng was the same magistrate of Xiangshan county who had played an active role in smuggling and collusion with Macao during the 1660s. He had been removed from office for his illicit activities. Nonetheless, his rich experience with maritime affairs and the Zheng organization, as well as his demonstration of loyalty in recruiting a volunteer force to fight Geng Jingzhong from his own funds, convinced the Kangxi emperor to use him again, this time as governor-general. In contrast, Wu Xingzuo (1632–1698), the new governor, distinguished himself in a more conventional manner in hard-fought battles

[17] Xia, *Haiji jiyao*, pp. 53–56.

against feudatory forces.[18] The ruler cultivated close personal ties with Yao and Wu as counterweights to Giyešu, whose handling of warfare and negotiations left much to be desired. Moreover, the prince came under suspicion, rightly, as it turned out, of abusing his discretionary powers to illicitly trade with the Zheng organization and extort bribes from Dutch merchants at Fuzhou.[19]

Still, Yao and Wu were, for the moment, powerless to stem the rapid progression of events. After taking Haicheng, Liu Guoxuan's forces continued their rampage and surrounded the Quanzhou prefectural city. To the court's relief, the siege went poorly in the face of courageous resistance from residents organized under the prefect, Zhang Zhongju.

Figure 7.1 Entrance gate of the Dongshi stockade, in present-day Jinjiang, Quanzhou. Built in 1677, this was one of the numerous defensive fortifications used by Liu Guoxuan to repel a potential Qing invasion on Xiamen. The characters above the entrance gate read, "Gate to Suppress the Seas." Photograph by author, July 2009.

---

[18] For more on Yao Qisheng's early career, refer to *Beizhuan ji*, pp. 93–94. For Wu Xingzuo, see Xia, *Haiji jiyao*, p. 55.
[19] Wills, *Pepper*, pp. 156, 162–163.

A Qing counterattack in August forced Liu, whose troops were already seriously overextended, to abandon his offensive. He ordered the construction of a heavily fortified network of mountainous stockades around Haicheng, maintaining a defensive line that blocked further Qing advancement, one example of which is seen in Figure 7.1.[20]

Faced with this impasse, Governor-General Yao dispatched a young military advisor, Zhang Xiong, to Xiamen in November to reinitiate talks with Zheng Jing.[21] During meetings with Jing and his officials, the envoy went as far as to refer respectfully to Koxinga as the "Former King" (Xianwang), the title frequently used by his son to appeal to his memory. The Qing once again demonstrated its willingness to recognize Jing as a vassal if he withdrew to Taiwan. However, the talks failed again when he and Feng insisted upon keeping Xiamen and Jinmen as main bases, and Haicheng as their gateway.[22]

After Zhang returned empty-handed, Yao settled down to a war of attrition. In January 1679, at his recommendation, the court tightened the coastal evacuation policy, ordering the construction of a continuous wall running the entire length of Fujian from north to south. Once again, hundreds of hectares of fields beyond a heavily guarded boundary became a vast wasteland. Unlike the policymakers of the 1660s, Yao anticipated the potential fallout and tried his best to minimize the suffering of the common people. He lowered or eliminated taxes, prevented soldiers from entering homes at will or abusing the local population, and operated soup kitchens for the destitute.[23]

In the face of the severe sanctions, the economic fundamentals of the Zheng organization remained sound. As before, illicit smuggling across the boundaries flourished, occurring with the connivance of Giyešu and the Qing commanders.[24] The mean trading value realized by the thirty-two Chinese junks traveling to Japan in 1679 and 1680 stayed at around one million taels worth of silver.[25] Connections with Southeast Asia continued to intensify on account of the steady demand for English armaments, Indian Ocean products, and grain. Although Zheng Jing had lost Guangdong, he dispatched Yang Yandi and Chen Shangchuan back to their pirate den on the Leizhou Peninsula in 1677. Over the following year, they helped Jing secure a base of operations across the

---

[20] Xia, *Haiji jiyao*, p. 58.

[21] Zhang Xiong's biography can be found in Luo Qingxiao (ed.), *Zhangzhou fuzhi xuanlu*, *TWWXCK*, 232 (1967), p. 73.

[22] Xia, *Haiji jiyao*, pp. 58–59; Jiang Risheng, *Taiwan waiji*, pp. 350–351.

[23] Xia, *Haiji jiyao*, p. 59; *Min song huibian*, *TWWXHK* 2.1, pp. 85–107.

[24] For one typical case of smuggling, see Yang Jie, *Ping Min ji*, *TWWXCK*, 98 (1961), pp. 357–358.

[25] See Table 4.1 in Appendix 3.4.

length of the Cantonese littoral and Hainan Island that provided trading goods from farther south and offered Zheng ships protection through the Gulf of Tonkin.[26] In 1679, Yang and Chen further led 3,000 men and fifty ships to the port of Hội An. They secured the approval of the Nguyễn lord for some of the troops to open up new land in the fertile Mekong River Delta, traversing the Quảng Nam-Cambodia boundary to grow grain for the organization.[27]

However, coastal evacuation worked brutally against the organization in one respect: its ability to secure reliable food supplies. After the loss of Jing's early territorial acquisitions in the interior of Fujian and Guangdong, the remaining strip of coastline under his control proved unable to feed his heavily concentrated troops. While imports from the Mekong Delta, Siam, and Manila could augment the granaries to a certain extent, overseas shipments took time to arrive and remained subject to fluctuations in volume. Moreover, they diverted funds better used to purchase weapons and other resources, causing shortages in those areas as well. Meanwhile, Taiwan, Jing's primary supplier of grain, suffered from a shortage of labor to work the fields, since most soldiers from the military colonies had left to fight on the mainland.[28] To continue the massive transfers to Zheng Jing's troops, more taxes had to be levied on fewer people on the island and upon every item imaginable; even, for instance, on the number of rooms in houses.[29]

In 1679, Zheng Jing, out of desperation, ordered his soldiers to revert to the involuntary "voluntary contributions" and outright grain seizures of Koxinga's day. Wealthy gentry and merchants suffered the most, but common coastal residents also increased their regular tax contributions to twenty liters of rice per year, twice the amount previously.[30] The Zheng conformed ever more closely to the Qing portrayal of them as a band of ruthless pirates only interested in plunder. Hungry and demoralized, commanders and soldiers began defecting en masse, at a rate of several hundred per day, to the Qing. To encourage this trend, Yao Qisheng established a "Hall for Reform and Return" (Xiulaiguan) on the outskirts of Zhangzhou in late 1678 that advertised monetary rewards, food, and official ranks for any of Jing's followers who submitted. Due in part to his efforts, fifteen major commanders, five hundred officials, and more than

---

[26] Antony, "'Righteous Yang'," 20.   [27] Ibid., 1.   [28] Ruan, *Haishang jianwenlu*, p. 47.
[29] Many residents destroyed part of their dwellings to avoid this onerous exaction. See Xia, *Haiji jiyao*, p. 73.
[30] For more on the increasingly desperate measures to secure provisions, see Xia, *Haiji jiyao*, pp. 59–60; Ruan, *Haishang jianwen lu*, p. 52; Zheng Yiju, "Zheng Chenggong zhuan," p. 32.

30,000 soldiers had come over to the Qing by 1680.[31] In addition, when Yao uncovered Zheng spies in his ranks, he not only did not punish them, but recruited them instead to conduct counterespionage or released them after supplying them with false rumors.[32]

In the spring of 1679, Yao Qisheng felt that he had weakened Zheng Jing enough to launch a fresh attack against his positions. However, an attempt to storm a stockade at Tongan, on the opposite shore of Xiamen, resulted in a humiliating rout at the hands of Liu Guoxuan's forces. The defeat gave Giyešu, who felt threatened by Yao's position in Fujian, an opportunity to reassert his influence. In August, the prince dispatched his secretary, Su Kuang, and Kuang's brother, a local gentry named Su Cheng, to Xiamen to restart negotiations with Zheng Jing. This time, the two sides made significant progress. They agreed to put aside their differences and follow the Korean example of tributary ties. They even talked of fixing a boundary in the Taiwan Strait near Penghu and initiating normal commercial relations.[33]

Unlike the previous occasions, Jing dispatched Fu Weilin (d. 1681), the Director of Honored Guests, to Fuzhou to continue the negotiations with Giyešu and Yao in person.[34] However, heavy pressure from Feng Xifan's restoration faction once again derailed the positive momentum. As a compromise to the infighting, Fu was asked to raise additional demands at the meeting. Besides keeping control over Xiamen and Jinmen, he requested the conversion of Haicheng into a free trade zone under joint administration (*gongsuo*). According to this innovative arrangement, which surprisingly resembled the treaty port system imposed upon the Qing by the Western powers in the nineteenth century, Zheng Jing would pay a rent of 60,000 taels of silver per year to the court for this privilege. He would fund the proceeds by supervising the collection of duties at Xiamen. Fu's additional demands shocked Giyešu, the organization's biggest potential advocate, and strengthened the hardline position of Yao Qisheng. Yao could then confidently retort that "every inch of land belongs to our Emperor. Who dares to convert an integral territory of this realm into a jointly ruled zone?"[35] Since, unlike Taiwan, Fujian's status as an inseparable part of the empire made it nonnegotiable, the two officials promptly dismissed the Zheng envoy.

---

[31] Zheng military commanders would be guaranteed an equivalent rank in the Qing bureaucracy. Moreover, the Qing offered all Zheng followers gifts of silver along the following pay scale: "3 taels for long hair, 1.5 for half-long, 0.8 for short." The length of the hair supposedly marked the years of service under the Zheng organization. See Wills, "Contingent connections," p. 195.

[32] Peng, *Jinghai zhi*, pp. 89–90.   [33] Jiang Risheng, p. 358.

[34] Fu Weilin's biography is found in Huai, *Quanzhou fuzhi*, pp. 127–128.

[35] Xia Lin, *Haiji jiyao*, pp. 60–61; Jiang Risheng, *Taiwan waiji*, pp. 358–359.

Defeat and flight

Yao Qisheng realized that passive measures, such as coastal evacuation, negotiations, and the encouragement of defectors could weaken the organization but proved unable to eliminate its presence from the mainland coast.[36] Final victory could only be achieved through a direct attack from a strong, well-trained navy. From a near-complete void since the disbandment of the Fujian navy in 1668, the Qing could boast a fleet of 240 junks and fifty supporting boats after years of frantic construction. Nonetheless, it still lacked personnel with the knowhow to operate them.[37]

In the winter of 1679, the court dispatched an embassy to Batavia in the hopes of restoring the alliance with the VOC, banking upon Dutch naval prowess to repeat the successful cooperation that had driven Zheng Jing from the mainland coast in 1663. However, the Dutch refused to spare any of their men and ships this time around. Besides being preoccupied with campaigns in Sumatra and Java, they had fundamentally grown disillusioned in their attempts to control the China market over the past fifty years. Moreover, they and the Chinese merchants under them already enjoyed illicit lucrative smuggling arrangements along the Guangdong coast, mainly with Zheng partisans. The Dutch thus no longer saw Taiwan as a transit point for Chinese goods worth fighting for. The VOC also tired of the "Tartar perfidy," or what it saw as treacherous and deceitful behavior from Qing rulers and officials that made any deals between them meaningless because of their lack of sincerity.[38]

With VOC assistance not forthcoming, Yao Qisheng turned to the former Zheng followers whose defections he had helped secure. Although their knowledge of naval matters and conditions in the opposing camp made them valuable assets, there was always a risk that they would change sides again. Nonetheless, the Kangxi emperor overcame his own suspicions and overruled objections from more conservative advisors to throw his full support behind Yao's project. Soon, defectors made up the majority of the 50,000 sailors in the province.[39] In late 1679, the emperor further authorized the appointment of Wan Zhengse (d. 1691) as head of the Fujian naval command. Born in Quanzhou, Wan possessed that rare combination of naval expertise, native knowledge, and

---

[36] John Wills likewise points out the limitations of the passive measures in "Contingent connections," p. 191.

[37] Chen Zaizheng, *Taiwan haijiangshi yanjiu* (Xiamen: Xiamen University Press, 2002), pp. 58–59.

[38] A detailed account of the mission can be found in Wills, *Pepper, guns, and parleys*, pp. 179–187.

[39] Chen Zaizheng, *Taiwan haijiangshi yanjiu*, pp. 58–59.

unwavering loyalty to the throne. An early defector from the Zheng organization, Wan served with valor in battles against Wu Sangui's rebels. His defining moment came in 1678, when he led a naval contingent that crushed Wu's fleets on Lake Dongting, paving the way for the complete Qing occupation of Huguang.[40]

Wan wasted no time after assuming his new post in Fujian. On March 6, 1680, his ships directly confronted the main Zheng fleets at their naval base at Haitan Island, off the coast of Xinghua prefecture. When the smoke cleared, the Qing navy, once seen as inexperienced and utterly incompetent, carried the day. Keeping up the momentum, Wan routed another Zheng detachment on March 20 in the waters outside Chongwu, off Quanzhou, the only major island blocking the southward advance to Xiamen.[41]

At this point, the Zheng organization's war effort, already buffeted by defections, resource shortages, and low morale, dramatically imploded. When news of the defeat reached Xiamen, panic engulfed the city. Commanders could not discipline their troops, and watched helplessly as they plundered and raped at will in the following weeks. Yao Qisheng lost no time exploiting the chaos within the Zheng ranks. Through covert bribes, he secured the collusion of a fifth column of several hundred men, the most prominent among them being Shi Hai (d. 1680), one of Zheng Jing's closest confidants and surprisingly, a close relative of Shi Lang. The conspirators plotted to capture Jing onboard his ship during a scheduled inspection tour of the maritime defenses, and turn him over to the Qing. Yao calculated that, with the leader gone, he could secure the submission of the entire organization without having to launch a separate campaign on Taiwan. However, the plot was uncovered by Liu Guoxuan, and the conspirators were put to death. Another effort by Yao to have Jing's cook poison him also proved unsuccessful.[42]

Although Jing managed to survive, he could not stem the collapse occurring around him at an increasing velocity. By the end of March, towns around Xiamen had surrendered to the Qing. Liu Guoxuan, with his rear suddenly in disarray, was forced to withdraw from the frontlines, abandoning his stockades and Haicheng to rescue the twin islands. The situation continued to spiral out of control, as top officials boarded their junks and fled to Taiwan. Fearing mutiny, Zheng Jing, too, burned down his palace and pleasure grounds and sailed away on March 26. Two days later, the Xiamen garrison commander surrendered to the Qing. Yao

---

[40] Wan Zhengse's biography is found in Huai, *Quanzhou fuzhi*, pp. 148–151. See also *Minhai jilue*, pp. 57–58.

[41] Xia, *Haiji jiyao*, p. 62.

[42] Ding Rijian, *Zhi Tai bigao lu*, *TWWXCK*, 17 (1959), p. 77; Peng, *Jinghai zhi*, p. 90.

Qisheng, Wu Xingzuo, and Wan Zhengse led their men into the city in an orderly fashion, taking pains to prevent harm to local residents. In March 1681, the Kangxi emperor ended the harsh coastal evacuation and opened the boundaries for residents to farm and fish.[43]

In the rest of the country, too, the tide had turned decisively in favor of the Qing. Wu Sangui passed away from dysentery in late 1678. His grandson and successor, Wu Shifan (d. 1681), lacked the capability to rejuvenate the lagging spirits of his forces, which gradually retreated into his southwestern strongholds after losing the strategic province of Huguang. In March 1681, Qing forces pushed into the final rebel bastion of Yunnan and besieged Kunming. They took the city at the end of the year, and executed Wu Shifan and his officials. Several months earlier, in September 1680, the court had forced Shang Zhixin to commit suicide. In 1682, it removed the last vestiges of the feudatory legacy by putting Geng Jingzhong through the slow and painful execution of slicing.[44] The Rebellion of the Three Feudatories, which lasted seven long and bitter years, came to an end.

Abortive state building

Zheng Jing returned to Taiwan with only several thousand troops. His mother, and Koxinga's widow, Madame Dong, severely castigated his "lack of talent" and wondered aloud whether his mainland venture was worth the needless suffering inflicted upon the common people.[45] Liu Guoxuan felt similarly disillusioned with Jing's leadership; he had done most of the tough fighting, yet Jing remained closer to Feng Xifan and shut him out of the inner circles of power. After the debacle at Xiamen, Liu refused to return to Taiwan. Instead, he sailed with his men for the Guangdong coast and attacked Macao and nearby ports in attempts to seize a new base of operations on the mainland. If successful, Liu had plans to capture Taiwan and install Jing's younger brother, Kuan, who was accompanying him, as the organization's new leader.[46] Crushed and forlorn by these developments, Zheng Jing ran away from reality. He built

---

[43] Xia, *Haiji jiyao*, pp. 62–63; *Kangxi shilu*, p. 112.
[44] Liu Fengyun, *Sanfan yanjiu*, pp. 295, 307–308, 315–325.   [45] Xia, *Haiji jiyao*, p. 63.
[46] VOC 1362: 1011–1054v, Fuzhou to Batavia, 3 and 9 March 1681, at 1011–1015v, citation found in the upcoming monograph of John E. Wills, Jr. Dutch sources refer to this brother of Jing as Laxia. Wills correctly identifies him as the Zheng Lushe mentioned in Zheng Da, *Yeshi wuwen*, *TWWXCK*, 209 (1965), p. 168. The clan genealogies do not list any brother of Jing by that name, but he is almost certainly Zheng Kuan, Koxinga's sixth son and the only one who did not surrender to the Qing or die beforehand. See Zheng Yuhai et al., *Zheng shi zongpu*, *TWWXHK* 1.9, p. 16.

a pleasure garden on the outskirts of Chengtian and whiled away his days intoxicated with wine and women.[47]

Despite the widespread malaise that pervaded the organization in the wake of its defeat, its fundamentals still held. Chen Yonghua's capable administration and keen commercial management on Taiwan had minimized the disruption to the island's residents throughout the rebellion. He also prepared for future contingencies. In 1679, at Chen's persuasion, Zheng Jing named his eldest son, the fifteen-year-old Kezang (d. 1681), as heir. Chen groomed the young man in administrative duties during his father's absence. Jing further boosted Kezang's status after his return by giving his own sword and seals of authority to his designated successor, allowing the young man to exercise power in his name.[48]

The Zheng trading network did take a hit in the short term from the newly ascendant Qing navy, which attacked shipping and illicit depots suspected of collusion with Taiwan in the waters around Fujian and Guangdong as part of the coastal removal policy.[49] As a result, the trading value realized by nine Chinese junks at Nagasaki for 1681 fell to an unprecedented low of 147,756 taels worth of silver.[50] Yet the raids must have also driven Liu Guoxuan away from the Guangdong coast. He and his men presently arrived in Taiwan.

Then, halfway through 1680, the Qing court relaxed the maritime restrictions. The fleets and coastal garrisons, led and staffed primarily by Zheng defectors, immediately turned a blind eye to the smuggling in exchange for a cut of the profits.[51] In 1682, twenty-six vessels sailed to Japan and, according to incomplete estimates, saw a jump in revenues to more than 952,940 taels. Estimates of the value realized in the Western Ocean derive entirely from severely incomplete data available only in 1684, a year after the organization surrendered and when its business network had all but collapsed. Three junks belonging to Liu Guoxuan and Hong Lei arrived at Xiamen with cloth, spices, and grain from Siam. An examination of Liu's vessel alone revealed a cargo valued at more than 13,000 taels if sold on the China coast.[52]

In fact, the total average annual revenues of the organization between 1673 and 1683 can only be extrapolated, in part, upon the inventory of this one junk. During the decade, the Zheng raked in more than

[47] Jiang Risheng, *Taiwan waiji*, p. 376.
[48] Xia, *Haiji jiyao*, pp. 60, 64, 67; Jiang Risheng, *Taiwan waiji*, p. 376.
[49] Hayashi Shunsai, *Ka'i hentai*, vol. 1, pp. 329, 339, 342.
[50] Cai Yuping, "Dui Ri maoyi," p. 58.
[51] Dutch observers spoke of business as usual in "the smuggling between the long-haired and short-haired people" at Xiamen and Jinmen. Quoted in Zheng Weizhong (Cheng Wei-chung), "Shi Lang 'Taiwan guihuan Helan' miyi," *Taiwan wenxian* 61.3 (2010): 42.
[52] See Table 4.4 in Appendix 3.4.

1,524,830 taels (57,181.1 kg) worth of silver. This figure lagged behind the Dutch, who realized some 8,369,030 guilders (89,668.2 kg) over the same period.[53] Yet, the VOC, too, saw a heavy decline of almost a million guilders from the previous decade. Leaving out the factor of political instability and military defeat on the part of the Zheng, it appears that the long-term decline of the Japan trade played a bigger role in denting revenues on both sides. In sum, although the Zheng organization took heavy losses, its foreign trade earnings were still considerable enough to prop up its vast operations and, at the very least, to maintain Taiwan.

Indeed, Zheng Jing had sufficient faith in the fundamental security of Taiwan to leave its strategic gateway of Penghu undefended in the wake of his retreat. Moreover, he could spurn another overture for negotiations from Giyešu. In the fall of 1680, Jing received from a Qing envoy a letter from Laita (d. 1684), a banner general under the prince. In the letter, Laita reasoned that since Taiwan lies "outside the domain of the Middle Kingdom," Zheng Jing and his followers could keep it as a hereditary possession. No longer did he need to concede anything tangible in exchange; he simply had to promise not to harass the mainland coast ever again. More so than any previous round of talks, the Qing terms had reached their most lenient and generous extent. However, and again to Giyešu's consternation, Zheng Jing continued to obstinately demand Haicheng as a jointly ruled zone. Upon reading the reply, a disgusted Yao Qisheng forced Laita to abandon the talks.[54] The governor-general became convinced that only a campaign against Taiwan could rid the Qing of this persistent menace. Yao would have a freer hand to carry out his designs in the province at the end of 1680, when Laita left the southeastern coast to exterminate Wu Shifan's remnants in Yunnan, while Giyešu was recalled to Beijing by the emperor.[55]

Renewed political turbulence on Taiwan presented a golden opportunity for Yao. During the rebellion, Chen Yonghua's faction had controlled the island's bureaucracy, and, as Kezang's father-in-law, could be assured of continued influence over Taiwan after Jing's death. On the other hand, Feng Xifan and the restorationist faction had suffered a huge blow to their reputations because of their poor performance against the Qing. Fearing the complete dominance over the island's affairs and his marginalization by Chen, Feng decided to recruit Liu Guoxuan into the inner decision-making circle. Apparently, the two men reached a deal. Feng would relinquish his oversight of all Zheng military forces to Liu in

---

[53] See Table 4.6 in Appendix 3.4.   [54] Ni, *Xu Ming jishi*, p. 194.
[55] For more on Laita, see Li Huan, *Qing qixian leizheng xuanbian*, *TWWXCK*, 230 (1967), pp. 425–431. Giyešu's entry can be found in pp. 343–346.

exchange for Liu's support for him in seizing control over civil administration. The biggest obstacle to their goal was, of course, Chen Yonghua, but, fortunately for them, his division was outnumbered by the massive forces at their disposal. Under this implicit threat of violence, Feng forced Chen to retire. Nature also intervened in favor of the two men. Late in 1680, a pestilence struck southern Taiwan and claimed the life of Chen Yonghua, along with two key reformist officials, Ke Ping and Revenue Officer Yang Ying. In the early winter of 1681, Zheng Jing himself suddenly died of alcohol overdose and sexual exhaustion at his palace on the outskirts of Chengtian at the age of 39.[56]

The demise of the patriarch and major pro-reformist figures removed the institutional bases of support for Kezang. As soon as Jing died, Feng and Liu conspired to get rid of the heir and enthrone his younger brother and Feng's son-in-law, the twelve-year-old Keshuang. They convinced Zheng relatives and Madame Dong that Kezang had been adopted into the family at a young age and thereby did not qualify as a legitimate successor.[57] The matron bought into the story and had him strangled to death in March 1681. Keshuang then assumed the hereditary titles of his grandfather and father and took over the official sword and seals. After Madame Dong's death from illness several months later, Feng and Liu acquired total dominance over Taiwan's affairs. They exercised influence through Feng's in-law relationship and the newly appointed regent, Koxinga's second son Zheng Cong, a weak and pliant figure who was obedient to their will.[58]

Kezang had enjoyed widespread popularity on account of his sound policies and strict discipline, reminding many of a younger version of Koxinga. His downfall added to the profound disillusionment across the island. When news of the crisis reached Yao Qisheng, he decided to take advantage of the Zheng organization's disunity to exterminate it. He and the other Fujian-based officials initiated another wave of ship construction and troop mobilization and successfully persuaded the Kangxi emperor to throw his weight behind a campaign on Taiwan. In the summer of 1681, the ruler brought Shi Lang out of confinement and

---

[56] Xia, *Haiji jiyao*, pp. 64, 67; Jiang Risheng, *Taiwan waiji*, pp. 373–374.

[57] Zheng Jing's primary wife, Lady Tang, failed to produce any offspring. Although he had many concubines, all of them initially gave birth to daughters. According to a widespread rumor at the time, Jing's retinue arranged to have the daughter of one concubine replaced with a baby boy surnamed Li, who later became Kezang. This matter was kept strictly confidential, especially from Zheng Jing, who was fond of the boy. Feng and Liu must have presented highly credible evidence to convince Madame Dong and other relatives of Kezang's origins. See Xia, *Haiji jiyao*, p. 67; Zheng Yiju, "Zheng Chenggong zhuan," p. 35; Jiang Risheng, *Taiwan waiji*, pp. 380–381.

[58] Xia, *Haiji jiyao*, p. 68; Jiang Risheng, *Taiwan waiji*, p. 383.

reappointed him to his old post as head of the Fujian Navy, replacing Wan Zhengse, who took over the infantry.[59]

While waiting for the preparations to be completed, Yao utilized the same informal channels for smuggling with Taiwan to promote a different breed of illicit products: fear, disinformation, and intimidation. On the one hand, he encouraged terrorism and sabotage against military and civilian targets. In early 1683, an arson-induced fire at Chengtian burned down more than 1,600 homes and storefronts. Yao also reestablished contact with Fu Weilin, Zheng Jing's former envoy in charge of negotiations at Fuzhou in 1679. Despite the failure of those talks, the two had struck up a cordial friendship. Fu was already thoroughly embittered by Feng Xifan's seizure of power. It did not take much for Yao to persuade him to join forces in plotting against Taiwan's leaders and handing over the island to the Qing. Fu and a small circle of friends kept Yao apprised of their progress through junks operated by their official merchants. They received handsome gifts of silver as a reward for their services. However, the plot was discovered in November 1681 after one of the conspirators confessed, leading to a massive roundup of the traitors by Liu Guoxuan's forces. Fu Weilin and his cohort were sentenced to die by slicing.[60]

The failure of this conspiracy gave the organization another opportunity to bounce back. Feng Xifan played a crucial role in this respect; where he had failed as a military commander, he proved surprisingly competent as a civil administrator. With his internal enemies eradicated, he turned toward harnessing the island's energies toward the prevention of an external Qing attack. With Liu Guoxuan's cooperation, he ordered new war junks constructed and grouped one out of every ten male tenants from the official and private fields into a reserve force that underwent regular training. Liu led two hundred ships and 20,000 men to garrison the previously undefended Penghu Islands, while another contingent went to Jilong and Danshui in the north. Feng also appointed younger officials to top administrative posts, engineering a smooth generational transition.[61]

With prospects for Ming restoration now remoter than ever in the wake of the mainland debacle, Feng pushed aside his ideological stance and unambiguously embraced what he had once vociferously opposed: the establishment of an outwardly oriented maritime state. Elements of the military, perhaps with the support of Liu Guoxuan, had already taken

---

[59] *Kangxi shilu*, p. 113; Ni, *Xu Ming jishi*, p. 195.
[60] Xia, *Haiji jiyao*, pp. 69, 70–71, 74; Jiang Risheng, *Taiwan waiji*, pp. 386–392.
[61] Xia, *Haiji jiyao*, pp. 64, 71–74.

matters into their own hands.[62] The followers of Chen Shangchuan and Yang Yandi appeared to be building upon the precedent set by the Zheng agent Piauwja in the late 1660s to expand Chinese influence over the frontier of Quảng Nam and Cambodia and set it up for eventual seizure by their forces. Meanwhile, sometime in the middle of 1681, a group of Zheng generals in Taiwan rekindled the long-buried proposal to invade the Philippines. In a petition filed through the grand secretary, Zheng Dexiao, they presented the fertile archipelago as an ideal solution to the resource shortages and overpopulation on Taiwan resulting from the return of massive numbers of Zheng soldiers from the mainland. Feng Xifan enthusiastically embraced this plan, most likely another brainchild of Liu Guoxuan. The two men and the generals set out to organize a contingent of sturdy junks to spearhead the campaign. To boost morale, the soldiers' family members were permitted to accompany them on the expedition.[63]

Feng further infused these ambitious expansionary efforts with a larger symbolic purpose. In May 1681, under his direction, Keshuang enshrined Koxinga as the martial king (Wuwang) and Jing as the civil king (Wenwang). Their temple names were conscious allusions to Kings Wen and Wu, sagely founders of the Zhou dynasty, considered a golden age of Chinese antiquity. Likewise, Keshuang honored his ancestors as founders of a reconstituted "China" overseas that would recreate the glorious conquests and benevolent rule of these cultural heroes. Given the traditional superiority of civil arts over military prowess, Zheng Jing's role in opening Taiwan to Chinese administration thus gave him a higher place in the pantheon than Koxinga, who secured the island by force. Keshuang further proclaimed a new dynastic name of Chao for his domain, after a title conferred upon his grandfather by the Yongli emperor in 1660.[64] Koxinga had rejected the honor out of calculated modesty, but it now became the final step toward the formalization of the Zheng organization as a hereditary kingdom among the waves.

---

[62] Special thanks to John E. Wills, Jr. for highlighting Liu Guoxuan's connections to the overseas ventures in the final years of the Zheng organization.

[63] According to Chinese accounts, such as Xia, *Haiji jiyao*, p. 77 and Jiang Risheng, *Taiwan waiji*, p. 426, plans to invade the Philippines only began in the fall of 1683 as a desperate last-minute ploy to save the organization from destruction. Although this rendering certainly heightens the dramatic effect of the narrative, discussions and preparations began much earlier, as confirmed by Western sources. A letter to the Spanish king dated June 11, 1681, from the governor-general at Manila, Juan de Vargas (d. 1690), already mentioned rumors that the Zheng would attack. See Borao-Mateo et al., *Spaniards in Taiwan*, vol. 2, p. 662. The Dutch sources used by Wills in his upcoming monograph on Sino-Western relations reported the same rumors of an invasion.

[64] Xia, *Haiji jiyao*, pp. 30, 70; Ruan, *Haishang jianwen lu*, p. 25.

As the situation in Taiwan stabilized, the momentum toward a Qing invasion stalled as well. Bitter disagreements broke out between Yao Qisheng and Shi Lang soon after the latter's arrival at Fuzhou in November 1681. The governor-general wanted him to act immediately, taking advantage of the northerly winter winds to directly seize Taiwan, followed by Penghu. Shi, on the other hand, opted to wait until summer for the gentler southerly winds to take the navy to Penghu before attacking the main island. The deadlock lasted for an entire year, until the Kangxi emperor issued an edict that granted Shi exclusive authority over military decisions, while relegating Yao and other officials in Fujian to logistical support on the sidelines.[65]

To stem his shrinking influence over the Taiwan campaign, which he had come to see as his pet project, Yao Qisheng reversed his uncompromising stance toward the Zheng organization. In February 1683, he sent Fuzhou vice-garrison commander Huang Chaoyong, a former general under Geng Jingzhong and an old friend of Liu Guoxuan, to Taiwan with a letter repeating the terms proposed by Laita three years ago. This time, Feng Xifan adopted a more pragmatic stance, dispatching two envoys across the strait with instructions to accept the proposal without preconditions. Although they met with Yao Qisheng, Shi Lang refused to see the two men, claiming that negotiations in the past had never made the "sea bandits" submit. Only force could bring peace to the coastal areas. Unable to resolve their differences, the strong-willed Qing officials referred the matter to the Kangxi emperor for arbitration. On June 17, they received an imperial rescript that strongly backed Shi's position. The emperor proclaimed that the people on "Taiwan are all Fujianese. They cannot be compared to Ryukyu or Korea." As ethnic Han, they did not qualify for tributary status and must signal their submission by shaving their hair. If the Zheng envoys refused to accept these conditions, Shi Lang and the Qing navy should launch an offensive without delay.[66] The directive ended all further official attempts at negotiations.

Surrender

Meanwhile, severe grain shortages on Taiwan contributed to renewed destabilization within the organization. The shortfall had long-term causes. The mobilization of troops from the military colonies to join the Rebellion of the Three Feudatories over the 1670s had led to a sharp

---

[65] Shi, *Jinghai jishi*, pp. 12–17; *Kangxi shilu*, pp. 121–123.
[66] *Kangxi shilu*, p. 123; Shi, *Jinghai jishi*, p. 25; Jiang Risheng, *Taiwan waiji*, pp. 404–405; Li Zhifang, *Li Wenxiang gong zoushu yu wenyi*, *TWWXCK*, 285 (1970), pp. 295–296.

decline in the farming population. Even so, Taiwan continued to bleed massive amounts of grain, especially as severe setbacks increasingly confined the Zheng to barren coastal outposts on the mainland. Now, the return of these soldiers overwhelmed what remained of the island's capacity. To make matters worse, a drought afflicted Taiwan in 1681 and devastated the harvest.[67]

Overseas grain imports carried in lieu of other goods temporarily kept food consumption in balance. However, in early 1682, a Qing naval campaign in Guangdong drove Yang Yandi and Chen Shangchuan from their Longmen base into permanent exile in their Mekong colony. They had previously ensured stable access to Western Ocean grain producers. Now food supplies on Taiwan became volatile, driving prices sky high. In March 1682, famine broke out. Many starved to death or fell victim to disease, such as an outbreak that claimed over half of the soldiers at the Jilong garrison. Taxes and military duties became unbearably onerous, forcing many to sell wives and children to make ends meet. Unmoved, the officials imposed more levies to maintain defenses in the event of a Qing attack.[68] Even so, Liu Guoxuan's garrison at Penghu did not receive rations for over a month. In September 1682, aboriginal porters impressed to supply the Danshui and Jilong garrisons, overburdened under the famine conditions, killed their abusive Han overseers, and rebelled. Native villages across northern Taiwan rose up in support, murdering Chinese interpreters and seizing grain stores before troops suppressed the revolt.[69]

Nonetheless, observing the frontlines from Penghu in the summer of 1683, Liu Guoxuan had good reason to feel confident in Taiwan's security. The high frequency of typhoons in the strait until late autumn meant little chance for a Qing invasion, he thought. Similar storms had hampered previous efforts, and he believed that Shi would not be foolish to risk his men and reputation again. Given another year, the organization would have weathered the crisis after the decommissioned soldiers settled down and renewed the cultivation of their fields.

Liu miscalculated spectacularly. With the Kangxi emperor's blessing, Shi's expeditionary force, consisting of three hundred ships and 21,000 soldiers, most of them Zheng defectors, set out from the Fujian coast on July 7, 1683. Two days later, they appeared in the waters around Penghu, catching the defenders by surprise. At this point, Liu could have made the sensible decision to abandon his positions and withdraw to Taiwan, preserving his strength while drawing the Qing fleets to engage near the

[67] Jiang Liangqi, *Donghualu xuanji*, p. 265.
[68] Hayashi Shunsai, *Ka'i hentai*, vol. I, p. 357; Xia, *Haiji jiyao*, pp. 73–75.
[69] Xia, *Haiji jiyao*, pp. 73–74; Jiang Risheng, *Taiwan waiji*, pp. 408–409.

much better-defended main island. They would then be an isolated force deep within hostile territory. Instead, Liu took the risky gambit of pitting his men and ships, in effect the bulk of the Zheng navy, against Shi in an epic showdown. Liu was primarily considering his own future rather than that of the organization. He figured that, regardless of the outcome, a climactic battle would enhance his status at the expense of Feng Xifan. If he won, he could gather enough popular support on the ground to dominate the inner decision-making circle, and eventually replace Keshuang with his favorite Zheng member, Kuan. If Liu lost, however, he could surrender to the Qing on the best possible terms, receiving the highest ranks and honors for voluntarily dismantling the organization and ending the prolonged carnage.[70]

But to achieve these contingencies, Liu had to fight hard and fight smart. This he did, with the aim of ensuring a victory which would grant him the largest subsequent freedom of action. A detachment of his ships led a courageous frontal charge that beat back an initial attack, causing Shi to flee south to some of Penghu's remoter islands. Liu brushed aside calls from subordinates to pursue and eliminate Shi. He feared that overly heavy demands placed upon his famished soldiers could invite mutiny. Instead, he counted upon the frequent storms that plagued the Taiwan Strait during this time of the year to wreck the Qing fleet. Even though ominous clouds hovered on the horizon, none came.[71]

Instead, a healthy southerly wind prevailed. A week later, on July 17, the swift currents it generated carried the Qing fleets back. They swooped down on the Zheng defenders with a vengeance. Several hours of intense combat ensued, with cannons and muskets roaring, ships ramming against each other, and soldiers locked in combat, with blood spilling and mixing with the salty seawater that periodically sprayed upon them. Once calm returned, only Shi Lang's naval forces remained to claim victory, after losing two commanders, several ships, and 329 troops. On the other hand, they almost decimated some of the Zheng organization's most well-trained and well-equipped military units, sinking 169 junks and 12,000 soldiers. Forty-seven top commanders, including the ferocious pirates Jiang Sheng and Qiu Hui, perished in the conflict. More than 4,000 others surrendered to Shi. Liu Guoxuan and a handful of followers hastily boarded several small vessels and barely escaped with their lives.[72]

---

[70] John E. Wills, Jr., personal communication, December 15, 2014.
[71] Xia, *Haiji jiyao*, p. 76; Jiang Risheng, *Taiwan waiji*, pp. 411–412; Chen Zaizheng, *Taiwan haijiangshi yanjiu*, p. 86.
[72] Several narratives of the battle, in varying detail, are found in Xia, *Haiji jiyao*, p. 76; Jiang Risheng, *Taiwan waiji*, pp. 406–423; Ruan, *Haishang jianwenlu*, pp. 60–61; Shi, *Jinghai jishi*, pp. 26–37.

The ominous news they brought along with them sent shockwaves throughout Taiwan, and shattered the myth of its natural security and Zheng naval superiority. Moreover, Shi Lang treated the captives with respect and leniency, arranging medical care for the wounded and sending them back with plenty of rations. Upon arrival, they spread word of their favorable experience while in Qing hands. Residual morale crumbled on the famine-stricken island. Key commanders at Danshui, Jilong, and other strategic coastal frontiers of the north and south openly disobeyed orders and returned with their soldiers to Chengtian. Some even secretly sent envoys to Shi Lang, offering their support in the event of a Qing invasion.[73]

Amid the chaos, Feng Xifan, together with a group of generals, pushed forward with an invasion of Manila. They planned to establish an administration loyal to Keshuang under Koxinga's third son, Zheng Ming. In case Taiwan fell, Keshuang could relocate and "create another country for preserving the Zheng line." However, before they could implement the plan, widespread rumors that the troops would plunder and abandon Taiwan drove many commoners to the verge of rebellion. There were also fears that the underpaid and underfed crew would mutiny and kill their commanders along the way.[74] It is highly likely that Liu Guoxuan was the mastermind behind these rumors, or at least fanned their flames. He may have advocated overseas offensives before, but doing so now would harm his personal interests, ensuring that he may never have another chance to gain the initiative over Feng.

Whatever his private agenda, he openly went against Feng and called for a halt to the campaign during a major meeting on July 27, 1683. Instead, Liu stressed that, given the military defeat at Penghu, the enveloping panic and chaos, and the crumbling legitimacy of the organization, its cause was already lost; no course of action remained other than surrender on the most favorable terms possible. Since Liu controlled most of the military divisions, Feng had no choice but to go along after a series of heated exchanges. The two men then forced the young Keshuang, who lacked any independent decision-making power, to send a negotiation team to meet Shi Lang at Penghu. When the two sides met, the Zheng envoys begged him to allow Keshuang to remain on Taiwan as its hereditary ruler, and promised that all of its officials and residents would shave their heads in the Manchu style in exchange. Shi coldly rebuffed them and laid out stringent conditions for submission. Besides shaving their hair, top officials on Taiwan had to return to the

[73] Shi, *Jinghai jishi*, p. 44; Jiang Risheng, *Taiwan waiji*, pp. 426–427.
[74] Xia, *Haiji jiyao*, p. 77; Jiang Risheng, *Taiwan waiji*, p. 426.

mainland and individually accept honors and ranks. If they refused to wholly comply, Shi would not hesitate to launch an invasion on the main island.[75]

Feng Xifan and Liu Guoxuan reluctantly but quickly accepted the terms, and persuaded Keshuang to do the same. On August 26, Chief Secretary Zheng Dexiao wrote a proclamation of surrender on behalf of the young ruler. To demonstrate their sincerity, Feng and Liu dispatched their brothers as envoys to carry it to Penghu. Shi Lang received them cordially and dispatched representatives of his own to Taiwan to supervise the transition. Under the watchful eyes of the Qing envoys, Zheng Keshuang handed over his seals and other symbols of authority that had tied the family's destiny to the defunct Ming and Yongli court. In the meantime, the Kangxi emperor gave his official approval to the terms of surrender. On September 8, the young Keshuang shaved his head, along with his ministers and practically all Han Chinese subjects on the island, including commoners, officials, gentry, and the Ming imperial descendants.[76]

Only two people refused to comply. Zheng Kuan strongly opposed Keshuang's decision to submit. Aside from ideological conviction, he did not seem to get along with Jing's wing of the family, probably also explaining why he joined forces with Liu to contest the leadership. Kuan closely followed the progress of talks with the Qing through his friend, Zhu Shugui, the prince of Ningjing. One day, the prince handed him a scroll with the cryptic words, "the wind has blown, and the bamboo has replied" (feng lai zhu you sheng). The message implicitly informed him that Keshuang had agreed to the surrender terms and Qing troops would soon arrive. As soon as Kuan read it, he and his son fled north with the scroll in hand. They settled down on an obscure island called Dongboshe and farmed for the rest of their lives.[77] For generations after Kuan's death, their descendants hid their identities as Koxinga's progeny out of self-protection.[78]

---

[75] Xia, Haiji jiyao, pp. 77–78; Jiang Risheng, Taiwan waiji, pp. 427, 429; Shi, Jinghai jishi, pp. 43–44.

[76] Shi, Jinghai jishi, pp. 43–45; Jiang Risheng, Taiwan waiji, p. 437; and Ruan, Haishang jianwenlu, pp. 61–62.

[77] Zheng Da, Yeshi wuwen, p. 168. The location of the island remains unidentified. It could be in northern Taiwan, deep in what was then aboriginal territory. Another place could be the Guangdong coast. There is a Dongbo neighborhood committee in Chaonan district of Shantou. Apparently, Kuan's wife did not accompany him and surrendered to the Qing, since the Zheng genealogies list her as being buried in Beijing. See Zheng Yuhai et al., Zheng shi zongpu, p. 16.

[78] Through meticulous research and fieldwork, Japanese scholars during the early twentieth century successfully identified and tracked down Kuan's mainline descendants in Tainan. The scroll given by Zhu Shugui was also discovered at their home. Subsequent

The other person was, of course, Zhu Shugui, the prince of Ningjing. After the defeat of the mainland offensive, the prince had returned to Taiwan and retired to his rural estate. Yet, heavy requisitions for troops soon deprived him of his tenants and plunged him into abject penury and depression, a condition compounded by the death of his beloved wife. Upon hearing news of the surrender, the prince arranged for Zheng Kuan's flight. Then, he and his five concubines hung themselves in a final, dramatic act of martyrdom for the Ming cause.[79] Although Zhu's tragic plight generated widespread sympathy, his death could no longer rekindle the fire of loyalist resistance. For everyone else, the Mandate had irrevocably passed to the Manchu Qing.

On October 3, 1683, Zheng Keshuang, along with Feng Xifan, Liu Guoxuan, and the rest of the oligarchy, welcomed Shi Lang and the Qing navy at Lu'ermen, the narrow and winding entryway into Taiwan. As soon as Shi set foot, he proclaimed a general amnesty and prohibited his men from harming the local populace. He bestowed Manchu garments and caps upon the civil and military officials, and distributed food and gifts liberally to Han and aboriginal residents. On October 22, Shi visited Koxinga's shrine, where he paid respects to his former overlord as tears streamed down his cheeks. He hoped to convey through this dramatic act a sense of closure to a bitter conflict that lasted almost forty years and most tragically, pitted fathers, sons, brothers, and fellow countrymen across the southeastern coast against each other.[80] Soon afterward, the entire elite stratum, from Zheng family members, commanders, and officials to Ming imperial princes and gentry, packed up and sailed for the mainland. The Zheng organization's resistance ended, completing the redefinition of "Chineseness" according to Manchu ethnic characteristics.

Epilogue

Scholars in mainland China and Taiwan attribute the Zheng organization's defeat to relentless Qing military offensives and blockades, which gradually wore down its cohesion and morale.[81] This view also has wide

---

tests have confirmed that the calligraphy did, in fact, come from the hand of the Ming prince. See Yang Yihong, "Zheng Chenggong di jiu dai sun Taiwan shengen," *China Times Weekly Magazine* 1534 (July 17, 2007).

[79] Shen Binghu, *Chonglin yuce*, p. 192.

[80] Shi, *Jinghai jishi*, pp. 51–56; Jiang Risheng, *Taiwan waiji*, pp. 441–444; Peng, *Jinghai zhi*, p. 98.

[81] Representative views include Chen Jiahong, "Zheng shi wangchao," pp. 14–15 and Chen Bisheng, *Lishi yanjiu*, pp. 242–259.

resonance in Western scholarship.[82] Cheng Wei-chung, on the other hand, has offered a refreshing corrective from the perspective of maritime trade. As he shows, the organization in its final years lost competitiveness and market share to the Dutch, ascendant English, and native Southeast Asian networks, all of whom demonstrated greater capability in advancing the interests of Chinese merchants.[83] This crucial economic factor was just as responsible as the Qing, if not more so, in bringing down the Zheng. These arguments are sound, but they overemphasize the role of outsiders and external forces in causing the organization's demise. It is almost as if the Zheng, as helpless victims, had no say in their own destiny.

Although the organization suffered drastic military reversals at the hands of the Qing, at every stage during the later years of the Rebellion of the Three Feudatories, possibilities existed for a mutually beneficial settlement. During at least five rounds of negotiations, the Qing not only gave the Zheng plenty of room to execute a face-saving withdrawal to Taiwan, but it also promised them official recognition as an independent kingdom and control over trade along the mainland coast. The generous terms remained in place even after their defeat and flight to Taiwan in 1680. Although the Zheng organization did lose market share to competitors, the setbacks were temporary and closely correlated with the decline in military fortunes. During the times when it could get its act together, it performed decently in the traditional intra-East Asian trade, while maintaining a healthy transition toward the global world system. In sum, the last years of the Zheng organization held significant contingencies, both positive and negative, for continued survival. One can only blame its leaders and officials for their own intransigence, hubris, and short-sightedness for engineering a course of events that led to the worst possible outcome: the ultimate destruction of the family enterprise from within and without.

Then again, perhaps one need not be too harsh on the Zheng, since these qualities also applied to many of their enemies and competitors. In fact, with the exception of the English, a rather minor player in maritime East Asia at the time, none of them proved flexible or adaptable enough to remain economically viable. To take the example of the Dutch East India Company, rather than open up new product sources and markets in the Indian Ocean and Southeast Asia, it fought tooth and nail to preserve its established mix of products, centered upon Bengali textiles and Indonesian spices. In a series of wars throughout the 1670s, around the time of the Rebellion of the Three Feudatories, the company spent most

---

[82] See, for instance, Wills, "Contingent connections," pp. 190–195.
[83] Cheng (Zheng), *War, trade and piracy*, pp. 242–246.

of its energy trying to destroy any potential challengers, usually through violence whenever and wherever it can. In the most part, the VOC achieved its objectives, pulling off a series of significant victories.[84]

However, as Derek Massarella argues, what the Dutch actually succeeded in doing was to acquire absolute control over "the prizes of yesterday's battles."[85] Om Prakash shows that demand among consumers in Japan, and, in the long term, Western Europe, for spices, silk, and other luxuries had begun to decline in the mid-1670s.[86] By focusing its entire attention upon preserving them, the VOC left the handling of dynamic new sources of growth, such as the trade in tea, tin, gold, and opium, in the hands of the Chinese merchants. Profits from these goods became so entrenched in their hands that any major structural reforms would prove devastating for the urban economy of Batavia, whose entire livelihood depended upon its Chinese mercantile residents. As the eighteenth century progressed, rampant smuggling and corruption within the company ranks further created severe agency problems among its employees that began to eat away at its rigid monopoly from within. The VOC was finally dissolved in 1799.[87]

The Zheng family's other arch-nemesis, Shi Lang, tried to inherit and recreate the organization's commercial network for his own benefit, having failed to do so in the early 1660s. After Shi returned in triumph from his Taiwan campaign in 1683, a huge debate erupted in Beijing over whether the Qing should incorporate the island into the empire. Many influential Manchu and Han officials at court advocated abandoning it altogether and moving all its Chinese residents back to the mainland.[88] The Kangxi emperor was initially amenable toward this plan. Shi saw in the debate a grand opportunity for him to exploit his knowledge of local conditions in Fujian and Taiwan to dominate maritime East Asian trade.

After Shi landed on Taiwan, he discovered that the English continued to operate their factory on Taiwan, and that there were still Dutch prisoners surviving from the time of Koxinga's invasion. He released the Dutchmen on the condition that they forward a secret letter to Batavia

---

[84] For a detailed narrative of these contests, see Boxer, *Dutch merchants*, pp. 343–386; Blussé, "No boats," p. 72; and Wills, *Pepper*, pp. 150–151.

[85] Derek Massarella, "Chinese, Tartars and 'thea' or a tale of two companies: the English East India Company and Taiwan in the late seventeenth century," *Journal of the Royal Asiatic Society*, 3rd series, 3.3 (1993): 425.

[86] Prakash, *Dutch and Bengal*, pp. 131–135, 201.

[87] Massarella, "Chinese, Tartars and 'thea,'" 425; Julia Adams, "Principals and agents, colonialists and company men: the decay of colonial control in the Dutch East Indies," *American Sociological Review* 61.1 (1996): 12–13.

[88] Deng Kongzhao, *Ming-Zheng Taiwan yanjiu*, p. 154. Even if implemented, the removal of all Han Chinese settlers on Taiwan would have been an impossible task, as the population had reached about 120,000 by 1682.

offering to return Taiwan to VOC control. He also invited both the English and the Dutch to establish trading posts at Xiamen.[89] Then, on February 7, 1684, he memorialized the Qing court, urging it to keep the island and pointing to the same English and Dutch as potential threats to coastal security if it did not station troops on a permanent basis.[90] If all went according to plan, Shi, like Zheng Zhilong, could develop Xiamen and Taiwan as commercial entrepôts for the China-Japan exchange, and force all merchants on that route to purchase his passes. On the other hand, if the court refused to annex Taiwan, he could still arrange for the VOC to retake the island. In any scenario, the Dutch and English would become his intermediaries to Southeast Asian product sources and markets. In the meantime, the continued presence of these foreigners at China's shores would ensure that the Kangxi emperor maintained the maritime prohibitions.[91]

At first, all appeared to go according to plan. His confidence in the scheme received a boost in January 1684 when Governor-General Yao Qisheng, the biggest obstacle to his perceived hegemony, passed away.[92] On March 6, the Kangxi emperor, persuaded by Shi's memorial, decided in favor of annexation. Taiwan formally became incorporated as a prefecture of Fujian and divided into three counties and garrisoned by 11,000 troops under Shi's command. However, the other parts of his plan failed to come together. The VOC, already committed to the Indian Ocean, lacked enthusiasm for a renewed occupation of Taiwan and only made half-hearted efforts in responding to Shi's invitation. Since the "threat" from the evil "barbarians" did not materialize, the emperor rescinded the decades-long maritime ban on November 24, opening China to relatively unrestricted private trade.[93] Shi's dream of cornering the exports of Chinese products was shattered for good, as ships from his ports now had to face stiff competition from traders across the empire, especially neighboring Guangdong.

Shi and his family continued to own significant property and exercise some administrative rights in Minnan and Taiwan. However, they had lost much of even that residual influence by the time of his death in 1696.[94] Shi Lang had pursued an outdated dream of monopoly and

---

[89] Zheng (Cheng), "Taiwan guihuan Helan," pp. 39, 53–57.
[90] The memorial, entitled "Gongchen Taiwan qiliu shu" ("Memorial on my opinion on the abandonment or keeping of Taiwan"), is found in Shi, *Jinghai jishi*, pp. 62–63.
[91] Zheng (Cheng), "Taiwan guihuan Helan," pp. 67–68.
[92] Wong Young-tsu, "Security," p. 189.
[93] Zheng (Cheng), "Taiwan guihuan Helan," pp. 59–61, 67–69; Wong Young-tsu, "Security," p. 191.
[94] Wills, "Maritime China," pp. 229–230.

Figure 7.2 Zheng family tomb, Shuitou, Nan'an, Quanzhou. The remains of Koxinga and Zheng Jing were moved here from Taiwan in 1696, on the order of the Kangxi emperor. After Zheng Keshuang's death in 1717, he, too, was interred together with his father and grandfather.

territorial autonomy no longer possible to replicate under a Qing that was reaching the height of its political power. Compared to him and the Dutch, the Zheng proved far more sensitive and adaptable to changes in the broader economic and geopolitical climate.

And so what became of the main leaders of the Zheng organization? In 1699, on the orders of the Kangxi emperor, the graves of Koxinga, Jing, and other clan members were transferred from their original location at the organization's official cemetery in Zhouziwei, on the outskirts of Tainan, to the Zheng ancestral home of Shijing, where they remain to this day (see Figure 7.2).[95] A wary court ignored the requests of Zheng Keshuang and his brothers to reside near the deceased in their native land, and assigned them instead to the Eight Banners far away in

---

[95] Wang Bichang and Lu Dingmei (eds.), *Chongxiu Taiwan xianzhi*, *TWWXCK*, 113 (1961), p. 544.

Beijing, where they lived out the remainder of their lives. Their descendants served in military positions across the empire until the end of the Qing. Nonetheless, the Beijing Zheng maintained close ties to clan members in the Quanzhou area, and, with their assistance, acquired large tracts of land and carried on an extensive trade along the southeastern coast. After the collapse of the Qing in 1911, most of the bannermen returned to Fujian.[96] In the early twenty-first century, the Zheng clan retains local influence in Nan'an and Anhai. Many members still hold bitter feelings toward their equally prominent Shi neighbors in Jinjiang. Even though many generations have passed since that fateful day when Shi Lang abandoned Koxinga for the Qing, their descendants still refuse to intermarry.[97]

In Japan, Koxinga's half-brother, Shichizaemon, never forgot his sentiments toward the native land of his father. He made preparations on several occasions to immigrate to China, but the plans all failed to materialize. In the end, he passed away a disillusioned man at Nagasaki. In memory of Shichizaemon's attachment to China and his connection to the illustrious Koxinga, his son changed the family surname from Tagawa to Zheng. In the early 1700s, Zheng Daoshun, as he became known, moved to Edo, where he practiced medicine for a living until his death.[98] Several of his descendants would enter the historical stage once again during the nineteenth century. One of them opened up Japan's premier coffee joint, while another became a Chinese specialist, and authored the country's first comprehensive textbook for teaching the language. Quite a number of them became diplomatic representatives of the Meiji government to China, and played an important role in facilitating early Japanese imperial expansion in East Asia.[99]

However, the person who benefited the most from the Zheng organization's surrender by far was Liu Guoxuan. His earlier gamble paid off handsomely when he was appointed garrison commander of Tianjin, responsible for the maritime defense of nearby Beijing. He held the position until his death in 1693. Although overshadowed by his earlier fame (or notoriety) as a rebel, he also proved to be a brilliant scientist and innovator at his new post. He constructed an irrigation network around

[96] Lu Zhengheng, "Qi yu min, hai yu lu: cong xin faxian de Zheng shi Manwen zuolingce tanqi," *Dongya haiyu jiaoliushi yanjiu* 1.1 (forthcoming). The upcoming monograph of John E. Wills, Jr. also contains some fascinating tidbits from Zheng Keshuang's later life.

[97] Professor Deng Kongzhao, Xiamen University, personal communication, Xiamen, Fujian, June 27, 2006; Professor Zheng Guangnan, Fujian Normal University, personal communication, Fuzhou, Fujian, July 15, 2009.

[98] Kawaguchi, *Tei shi kiji*, p. 8.

[99] Qin Jiu, *Chuan wang Zheng Zhilong* (Taipei: Shixue, 2002), pp. 314–319.

the capital and undertook the successful transplantation of southern rice crops for cultivation in the harsher northern climate, no mean accomplishment in itself.[100] Feng Xifan, that other protagonist during the last days of the Zheng, joined the Eight Banners with Keshuang. His ultimate fate remains a mystery.

[100] Personal visit to the Changting County Museum, Changting, Longyan, Fujian, June 2009.

8   Conclusion

The Zheng organization emerged along the southeastern Chinese coast during the waning years of Ming dynastic power. It inherited both the legacy of multinational smugglers and pirates of the sixteenth and early seventeenth centuries who sailed abroad in violation of the official Chinese ban on overseas trade, and the semiofficial mercenary forces organized to suppress them. The robust growth of the intra-East Asian trade, centered upon the exchange of prized luxuries from China for silver in Japan, melded the forces of law and illegality into quasi-legal alliances in a common pursuit of profit. The ambitious young Zheng Zhilong became the catalyst for their transformation into an autonomous military unit and commercial enterprise through cooperation and competition with gentry and merchants from Quanzhou and Zhangzhou, and Japanese and European networks. He then obtained recognition for it through an official post from the Ming.[1]

Zheng Zhilong and his descendants followed a trajectory similar to John L. Anderson's conception of a "piracy cycle." As Anderson points out, successful piracy, or, in the context of the China Seas, the hazy continuum ranging from quasi-legal trade to smuggling and, at the most extreme end, predation, usually results in more sophisticated forms of political organization. Groups starting out as evaders of control gradually implement their own systems of control when their power bases begin to expand and their accumulated assets grow. He notes that "with further success the pirates' strength becomes such as to make them a virtually independent power." They could then join recognized states and become an official military force. If unsuccessful, they would disintegrate back into outlaw status or risk extermination from other powers.[2]

---

[1] Cheng Wei-chung argues, convincingly, that the Zheng organization represented the outgrowth of a "defensive monopoly" organized by the Ming state in the face of domestic disorder and the looming threat of the "aggressive monopolies," such as the Dutch East India Company. See Cheng (Zheng), *War, trade and piracy*, pp. 247–249.

[2] John L. Anderson, "Piracy and world history: an economic perspective on maritime predation," in C. R. Pennell, *Bandits at sea: a pirates reader* (New York: New York University Press, 2001), pp. 88–89.

Zheng Zhilong represented the culmination of many similar "macro-parasites" who preceded him in exercising influence over the maritime frontier of East Asia. Yet what differentiated the Zheng from Li Dan and Lin Feng before them is that Zhilong and his descendants came closest to achieving sustained political control over the zone of their commercial activities. The family was a participant in a broader process of state building and the delineation of boundaries across Eurasia during the seventeenth to eighteenth centuries. Peter Perdue and C. Patterson Giersch have examined Qing expansion into Inner Asia and southwestern China, and the meticulous classification and fine tuning of policies toward its multiethnic subjects.[3] Michael Laver and Adam Clulow portray the Tokugawa maritime restrictions in Japan as a product of the *bakufu*'s desire to impose ideological conformity and eliminate potential challenges to its supremacy from daimyo and other local and foreign players.[4] Victor Lieberman documents the emergence of modern Myanmar, Siam, and a unified Vietnam, each characterized by coherent administrations and increasingly uniform cultures. The excellent scholarship on this topic has also uncovered remarkable parallels with more familiar state-building processes in Russia and Western Europe, placing them in a global context.[5]

However, in treating the East Asian maritime frontier, the literature often assumes that it formed a vast, stateless zone, while the Chinese merchants and junks roaming its sea lanes constituted a stateless people. Both were just waiting for outsiders, such as the Dutch East India Company, to control and exploit them. As Wang Gungwu argues, "it was astonishing how many disparate groups of Chinese, compatriots as well as competitors, managed to devise ways to serve foreign rulers, powerful mercantile companies as well as themselves, even while European powers consolidated control over new colonial states."[6] Indeed, this scenario largely rings true, especially for the nineteenth century.

Nonetheless, it overlooks the contingency that Chinese living along the maritime littoral could construct durable institutions for governance in their own right and on their home turf. In fact, the Zheng family fulfilled just such as role. Zheng Zhilong and his son Koxinga took advantage of

---

[3] Perdue, *China Marches West*, p. 42; C. Patterson Giersch, *Asian borderlands: the transformation of Qing China's Yunnan frontier* (Cambridge, MA: Harvard University Press, 2006), pp. 207–217.

[4] Laver, *Sakoku edicts*, p. 5; Clulow, *Company and Shogun*.

[5] Lieberman, *Strange Parallels* (2009), vol. II: mainland mirrors: Europe, Japan, China, South Asia, and the islands.

[6] Wang Gungwu. "Foreward," in Eric Tagliacozzo and Chang Wen-chin (eds.), *Chinese circulations: capital, commodities, and networks in Southeast Asia* (Durham, NC: Duke University Press, 2011), p. xiii.

the Manchu entry into China in 1644 and the onset of a severe worldwide economic depression to transform their commercial organization into a pro-Ming resistance force. They acted as a largely independent authority along the southeastern coast, answering only nominally to a pretender far away in the southwestern provinces. Their activities, in the words of Wong Young-tsu, "politicized the entire region."[7]

After Koxinga seized Taiwan from the Dutch in 1662, a civil administration took shape, complete with a sophisticated bureaucracy and rationalized system of revenue extraction. Leadership by forceful and colorful personalities gave way, under Zheng Jing, to collective rule in which decisions resulted through consensus among members of a powerful advisory body. By the 1680s, before the organization's downfall, elites in Taiwan had proclaimed a dynastic name and honored Koxinga and his son as kings. As Carioti has argued, the Zheng organization's control over territory, people, and economic policy after 1662 certainly meets the definition of a state.[8] In fact, the degree of penetration of their authority in Taiwan exceeded that of the land-based Ming and Qing empires, whose administration was stretched thinly or became altogether nonexistent beneath the county level.

Cheng Wei-chung, however, sees little difference between this state and the other short-lived regional warlord fiefdoms that flourished in past periods of dynastic eclipse in China. Because of the complex international background of the seventeenth century, it merely took on a form more akin to a trade-based Malay port principality. Once global trading patterns shifted and the Manchus had completed their consolidation over the mainland, the Zheng polity quickly disintegrated.[9] Such a categorization, while illuminating, does not sufficiently address the far-reaching impact of the Zheng on maritime East Asian and global history.

Here, it would be instructive to compare the organization to the Dutch East India Company, its partner, and, more often, competitor on the sea lanes. Since the two entities embodied the political, social, and economic systems of their home countries as transplanted and adapted to a different spatial context, this framework would allow, by proxy, a broader juxtaposition between Chinese institutions and their Western counterparts. Indeed, a sound basis for comparison exists; the VOC and the Zheng organization were both formed to resist foreign invasion, monopolized the overseas trade of their mother countries, and evolved along a similar trajectory toward rationalized institutions and expansive territorial states. It is true that significant differences characterized the composition and

[7] Wong Young-tsu, "Security," p. 133.   [8] Carioti, "Zhengs' maritime power," p. 51.
[9] Cheng (Zheng), *War, trade and piracy*, pp. 251–252.

structure of their organizations and the external opportunities and challenges that they faced, but, on balance, they canceled each other out. The Zheng had some advantage operating on their home turf in the China Seas. On the other hand, the VOC had a head start of almost half a century before Zheng Zhilong's business network reached its mature form during the 1640s. The company also enjoyed strong state support compared to the lukewarm or downright hostile attitude from Chinese dynasties toward him and his descendants.

Within this context, the state forged by the Zheng can be rightfully characterized as one based upon capitalized coercion.[10] Zhilong and his descendants used the Ming imperial system and Confucian ideology to formalize the once informal lineage networks and debt obligations of Chinese merchants, and the pirate bands and semi-official mercenary forces that characterized society and economic life in maritime East Asia. This combination violated most textbook preconditions for a rationalized, modern enterprise in its complete lack of separation between public and private, official and nonofficial, and management and capital.[11] Nonetheless, the application of these powerful agrarian continental institutions to a more compact and sparsely populated maritime frontier zone proved just as effective as, if not more than, the European joint-stock corporations in advancing mercantile interests. Like the Dutch, Zhilong and his descendants incorporated merchants and militarists into their governance and used the latter to actively protect and promote the former's interests and property at home and abroad. They further pursued relations with foreign countries to enhance their own political and economic power rather than trying to order the world according to a Sinocentric-style tributary hierarchy.

In fact, the Zheng consistently matched or outperformed the VOC in revenues and profitability for most of their time in power, and proved more adaptable to changes in the structure of trade. Beginning in the late 1650s, faced with mounting barriers to the intra-East Asian exchange from both the Qing and Tokugawa *bakufu*, the Zheng used their declining profits to buy into an ascendant global world system centered upon Indian textiles, Southeast Asian tropical goods, and the minerals of

---

[10] Charles Tilly defines a state based on capitalized coercion as one that uses its coercive power, i.e., military, police, and legal systems, not simply to extract resources from the economy but to promote and enforce market mechanisms able to generate and reinvest capital. For more on the roles and interaction of capital and coercion in state building, see Charles Tilly, *Coercion, capital, and European states: AD 990–1992* (London: Wiley, 1992), p. 30.

[11] As Gipouloux, *Asian Mediterranean*, p. 143 argues, "Chinese merchants were not capable of directing their capital towards 'spheres of public interest protected by law and encouraged by the state.'"

copper, gold, and tin. The organization increasingly operated from bases in Taiwan and Guangdong, which provided more convenient access to Western Ocean ports. The Zheng further formed new partnerships with key intermediaries in the new circulation network, such as the English and Sultanate of Banten. This cooperation with rulers and officials outside the Chinese cultural zone proved highly beneficial for the organization, in stark contrast to the VOC's often disappointing alliances with various Chinese middlemen in its ill-fated attempt to gain a foothold in China.

The solid economic performance of the Zheng compared to the Dutch validates the observations of Rosenthal and Wong that "different institutions can work as near substitutes in different circumstances."[12] It can also put to rest any notions of Europeans somehow introducing "advanced" business practices to "backward" and "traditional" East Asian economies.[13] Admittedly, a large part of the Zheng organization's capital became sunk into prolonged warfare against the Manchu Qing. However, this situation was not unique. Much wealth in Europe and the joint-stock corporations abroad went into similarly destructive activities, since the pace of capital accumulation exceeded the growth in the number of productive investment outlets.[14] Indeed, the comparability here to the European case indirectly demonstrates the ability of the Zheng organization to raise tremendous amounts of capital and to grow it by means of profit maximization. Moreover, a substantial sum did flow into regenerative investments, such as land development in Taiwan and the cloth export industry of Anhai.

Another key weakness of the Zheng lay in their relative military disadvantage to the superior ships, weaponry, and fortress designs of the Dutch East India Company and other Western colonial enterprises. Nonetheless, as Tonio Andrade has shown, the gap between them was still small enough to be bridged relatively quickly. Using the expertise of a defected German sergeant, Koxinga's forces mastered the technical knowhow to score a decisive victory over the VOC in 1662. Moreover, the Zheng made up for the shortfall in military hardware with "softer" competencies, such as capable commanders, highly disciplined soldiers, and efficient logistics.[15] Yet, aside from the military realm, the

---

[12] Rosenthal and Wong, *Beyond divergence*, p. 8.

[13] Hamashita Takeshi has convincingly challenged this notion in *Kindai Chūgoku no kokusai teki keiki: Chōkō bōeki shisutemu to kindai Ajia* (Tokyo: Tokyo University Press, 1990), p. 6, as have Dennis O. Flynn and Arturo Giráldez, "Born with a 'silver spoon': the origin of world trade in 1571," *Journal of World History* 6.2 (1995): 205–206. As Flynn and Giráldez argue, the Portuguese, Spanish and the East India Companies functioned as important, "but potentially disposable" middlemen, and faced fierce competition from Japanese and Chinese merchants in the region.

[14] Pomeranz, *Great divergence*, p. 77.   [15] Andrade, *Lost colony*, p. 16.

organization's main officials also proved to be master strategists gifted with long-term planning. Their diplomatic initiatives and commercial acumen allowed them to acquire significant geopolitical advantages in maritime East Asia with a minimum of violence, and often at the expense of the VOC, despite its earnest attempts to sabotage their efforts through blockades and raids, and a shaky alliance with the Qing court.

The successful transition of the Zheng organization into a fully functional state by the 1660s raises the realistic possibility of a durable institutional framework involving two independent Chinese polities or a unified Chinese empire with an autonomous maritime dependency. The momentum came from both sides of the Taiwan Strait. On the one hand, the Zheng organization's trajectory bore striking resemblances to modern notions of nationalism. Initially, and similar to other early modern states, nominal sovereignty was vested in a ruler – the Yongli emperor – who received divine sanction as the Son of Heaven over an unlimited, universal Ming dominion. The neo-Confucian ethical system, in turn, reinforced a theoretical social order that was, in the words of Victor Lieberman, "implacably hierarchic, anti-entropic, obsessed with innumerable particularities of status and privilege determined by one's distance from the sovereign."[16] Within this context, the conflict between the Zheng organization and the Qing still took the form of a dispute over the "correct" universalism to implement over a common imperial space.

However, by the 1660s, this vertical, class-based ideal began to give way to more horizontal associations, as the Zheng recentered their organization on Taiwan and the Yongli emperor's death led to a permanent vacancy on the throne. With prospects for a recovery of the mainland growing ever more remote, the Zheng leadership and many followers came to divorce "China" from its geographic and dynastic context and equate it with more abstract markers, including its rich history and cultural practices. Most important among these symbols were the long hair and flowing robes of the Ming that had disappeared on the mainland because of the Manchu haircutting order. Likewise, Confucian universal values became appropriated to serve a more limited project of ethnic differentiation vis-à-vis a Qing state seen to have corrupted and "barbarianized" the mainland.[17] In fact, a new generation of Zheng subjects too young to fully remember the dynastic transition already conceived of Taiwan as constituting the nexus of a separate maritime Chinese kingdom. These sentiments cut across class lines, reaching at least to

---

[16] Lieberman, *Strange parallels* (2003), vol. I: integration on the mainland, p. 41.
[17] Prasenjit Duara, *Rescuing history from the nation* (Chicago: University of Chicago Press, 1995), pp. 58–59.

the level of semi-literate merchants. Ironically, on an island considered foreign to China, a common experience of exile, loyalty to a defunct dynasty, and shared Han roots contributed to a more popularly held identity as "Chinese" than on the mainland.

The Qing, on the other hand, proved increasingly willing to tolerate the existence of the Zheng. Although the two sides confronted one another violently in major campaigns and countless other skirmishes, they also held negotiations on almost twenty separate occasions from the 1640s to the 1680s, meaning that, on average, one round of talks took place every two years. Moreover, the Qing bottom line gradually relaxed over time. Starting from a position of duplicity, using talks as a means to liquidate the main Zheng leaders, it moved to an offer of limited territorial rights in a few Minnanese prefectures, and finally to formal recognition of Taiwan as a hereditary kingdom. In the 1670s, it went even further and acquiesced to their desire for a Korean-style tributary relationship and the preservation of their hair and dress.

This behavior runs counter to R. Bin Wong's generally sound claim that the Qing state prioritized the maintenance of internal stability and prevention of social unrest, rather than alliances with ascendant mercantile groups.[18] It had good reason to view merchants engaged in overseas trade like the Zheng with suspicion. Since their accumulation of wealth and influence occurred largely outside state supervision, they could harass the coastline or ally with hostile domestic and foreign forces to subvert its rule. This attitude differed markedly from the active support of mercantile-oriented states like the Netherlands, which allowed the Dutch East India Company to remain a durable institution until the end of the eighteenth century.

However, as Ng Chin-keong and Zhao Gang have effectively argued, the Kangxi emperor and key Qing officials, many with significant experience in the coastal provinces, believed that a peaceful realm could be achieved precisely by legalizing and encouraging private overseas trade. These measures would improve the local economy and living standards, and remove incentives to cause trouble.[19] Here, the organization promised to become part of the solution rather than the problem. The Qing could outsource the regulation and policing of a large group of otherwise scattered merchants to the sophisticated commercial mechanisms of an intermediary authority dependent upon its legitimation. The

---

[18] R. Bin Wong, *China transformed.*

[19] See Ng Chin-keong, *Trade and society: the Amoy network on the China coast, 1683–1735* (Singapore: Singapore University Press, 1983), p. 221. Zhao Gang, *The Qing opening to the ocean: Chinese maritime policies, 1684–1757* (Honolulu: University of Hawai'i Press, 2013).

organization's powerful navy would further ensure the security of the mainland coast from foreign threats. These were precisely the biggest weaknesses of the continental-oriented regime. Thus, the Qing could reap the biggest benefits from foreign trade at the lowest possible administrative cost. Apparently, the Qing, at the height of its power, had already learned what the Ming only realized the hard way during its decline.

At the same time, the mercantile orientation of the Zheng would be protected from direct interference because of separate jurisdictions, leaving them free to forge an expansive new China among the waves. Indeed, one can argue that Koxinga's invasion and occupation of Dutch Taiwan constituted the initial stage of a broader ambition to control Southeast Asia, along with its rich natural resources and strategic access to new product sources in the Indian Ocean. An expedition to the Philippines was always next on the cards. Although the plan never materialized, it remained a credible option for the family under the leadership of Koxinga and his descendants Zheng Jing and Keshuang whenever mainland affairs did not distract their attention.

Since the Zheng and Qing had shared worldviews and culture, and a similar ethnic majority of Han Chinese, at least some competition would also take place between the two. Each could thereby hold up a mirror for the other to look into to gauge the advantages and shortcomings of its own bureaucracy and social system. If the scenario of a mutual compromise played out, and it very likely would have, both sides would have been more likely to draw each other into an active diplomatic, economic, and cultural engagement with the rest of the increasingly interconnected world. In many ways, the dynamic would have resembled the role of Hong Kong and Taiwan vis-à-vis the Chinese mainland in the late twentieth and early twenty-first centuries.

Of course, the hypothetical scenarios belong to the shaky realm of counterfactual history, and no more shall be spoken of it. The Zheng organization, despite numerous contingencies for a peaceful settlement, ultimately perished at the hands of a Qing military campaign in 1683. It lost not just because of grain shortages, declining competitiveness, and defeats on the battlefield, but also in its inability to institutionalize its autonomy in a manner befitting their actual sphere of control. If judged according to Benedict Anderson's criteria of a nation-state, Zheng subjects had acquired a definite sense of ethnic community, but notions of sovereignty over a limited space, while in development, remained an unsettled matter.[20] In other words, the precise limits of their territory

---

[20] Benedict Anderson, *Imagined communities: reflections on the origin and spread of nationalism* (London: Verso Press, 1983), pp. 15–16.

among the waves remained hazily defined and in flux, while they could not manage to set "hard" boundaries between themselves and the physical, geographic "China."

The Zheng were constrained not so much by a hostile empire like the Qing or competitors at sea, but by the internalization of their professed loyalty to the Ming. Instead of focusing upon the creation of a maritime state able to institutionalize and support their mercantile activities, they constantly turned back to shore in efforts to bring back a defunct dynasty whose agrarian-centered policies actually had the potential to harm their commercial orientation. Their behavior becomes even more incomprehensible when one considers that the rump Ming court and its pretender had little, if any, administrative control over what the organization did, and became a mere fiction after 1662. Yet, once any contingency of internal disorder and rebellion broke out on the mainland, the loyalist ideal proved powerful enough to trump other courses of action, no matter how sensible or practical.

Admittedly, the Zheng benefited greatly from waving the banner of restoration in the short term. Ranks and titles from the Ming pretenders certified Zhilong and his descendants as loyal Confucians charged by the rulers to expel the "barbarian" Manchu from China. The discourse, in turn, legitimated their leadership over a diverse following of merchants, soldiers, Qing defectors, fishermen, peasants, gentry, and bureaucrats, giving them a common voice and aspiration. The Ming imperial system could be readily adapted to bolster the organization's own governance. Ideally, the Zheng hoped to contribute a reasonable share to assist other pro-restoration players with larger imperial ambitions, such as the Longwu court under Zhilong, the Yongli court during Koxinga's days, and Wu Sangui under Jing. In exchange, the family could receive official recognition of their autonomous rights over the maritime zone.

However, just as Ming restoration served as a useful instrument to enhance their power, it also formed an overarching matrix of political correctness that limited the scope of their actions. The Zheng frequently found themselves forced to preserve their image as loyal ministers in front of their followers, even when doing so appeared unrealistic or suicidal. Thus, Koxinga invaded the Yangzi River Delta when Ming resistance elsewhere on the mainland was crumbling, and Zheng Jing continued his offensive in Fujian despite his own admission that Wu Sangui could not win. Any other course of action would generate severe opposition from an influential contingent of Ming imperial princes, gentry, key military commanders, and homesick soldiers. Indeed, they viewed Koxinga's invasion of Taiwan as a betrayal, and unified into a powerful faction to block further attempts to take the Philippines. If the Zheng insisted, they faced the specter of mass defections among disenchanted followers to the opposing side, which proved all too happy to welcome them with open arms.

The story of the organization's rise and fall forces a reassessment of the role of institutions, ideologies, and culture in historical development. Recent scholarship has moved beyond Ray Huang's pioneering study, which faults China's bureaucratic system and Confucian orthodoxy for leading the country down a path of stagnation.[21] As Rosenthal and Wong correctly retort, China continued to remain dynamic on all fronts – politically, socially, intellectually, and economically – until well into the nineteenth century. Indeed, the trajectory of Chinese institutions, like those of other civilizations, represented the evolving "products of choices made in response ... to diverse ecological and environmental conditions."[22] Still, it is important to note that the very same institutions also acted to restrict and standardize the range of options, and hinder innovative adaptations despite profound changes in the conditions on the ground. Of course, political structures, and the cultural and intellectual foundations underlying them, by no means constituted a closed system. Contingencies always existed for the introduction of new avenues of thought or even an "exit strategy" to transform the entire order altogether.

As seen in the case of the Zheng organization time and again, it possessed the credible option of securing a peacefully negotiated settlement with the Qing. Its leaders and many of its followers genuinely desired this outcome. Yet they refused to sacrifice anything while asking for everything in return. Besides the powerful pull of their worldview, this intransigence emanated from a fundamental confidence in the superiority of their navy and the natural security of Xiamen and Taiwan. They believed that even if the talks failed, they could always withdraw to the safety of their bases and try something else, or come back to attack the mainland again. Their unfounded hubris forced the Qing to take the most hostile stance possible, constructing a navy from scratch and employing Zheng defectors to exterminate the organization in 1683. This victory, achieved despite serious financial difficulties, additionally demonstrates that, in the seventeenth century, the agrarian Chinese empire was still more productive and could mobilize more resources than states founded upon a dynamic mercantile sector. Since the Zheng compared quite well to their Western counterparts in almost every respect, European states likewise lacked the means to challenge China's political, economic, and

[21] Ray Huang, *1587*.   [22] Wong and Rosenthal, *Beyond divergence*, p. 7.

military primacy, at least in East Asia. The tipping point would only come at some point in the eighteenth century.

Legacies

Although the Zheng organization faded from the historical stage, its multiple legacies continue to generate profound repercussions across maritime East Asia and beyond. The global world system that it had participated in forging would reach maturity during the eighteenth century. Once precarious linkages between Asia and Europe via the Cape of Good Hope, and Manila and the New World via the Pacific, now became densely circuited lifelines. Within this framework, Western Europe, in addition to Southeast Asia, emerged as a leading consumer market for textiles produced in the Indian Ocean zone. By the end of the century, the Europeans would successfully employ mechanized processes to produce their own textiles for export, while the subcontinent switched to the cultivation of opium.[23]

The Qing, meanwhile, experienced economic recovery starting from the 1680s; commercialization accompanied by rapid population growth stimulated a voracious demand for basic necessities that made it more dependent than ever before upon overseas imports.[24] China became, once again, a giant sink for silver from Europe and the Americas, as well as an importer of cotton and woolen goods and, later, opium. Its traditional consumption of natural resources and tropical goods now expanded from Southeast Asia to include the entire Pacific Rim. Like before, Southeast Asia held strategic significance as a transit point for these exchanges. Moreover, it provided minerals; not only tin, but also local gold and copper became so profitable that they stimulated a surge of Chinese immigration to work the mines. In exchange, China continued to sell luxury goods, such as silk and porcelain, but their importance soon became overshadowed by massive shipments of tea for the rapidly expanding European market. By the nineteenth century, British textiles, Chinese tea, and Indian opium had beat out the competition to become the leading commodities that defined the world system.[25]

---

[23] Prakash, *Dutch and Bengal*, pp. 257–258; de Vries, "Connecting Europe and Asia."
[24] Ramon H. Myers and Wang Yeh-chien, "Economic developments, 1644–1800," in Willard J. Peterson (ed.), *The Cambridge history of China* (Cambridge, UK: Cambridge University Press, 2002), part IX.1: the Ch'ing empire to 1800, pp. 563–564.
[25] Cranmer-Byng and Wills, "Trade and diplomacy," pp. 216–222; Leonard Blussé, "Junks to Java: Chinese shipping to the Nanyang in the second half of the eighteenth century," pp. 222–223 and Reid, "Mining Frontier," pp. 22–23, both in Eric Tagliacozzo and Chang Wen-chin (ed.), *Chinese circulations: capital, commodities, and networks in Southeast*

Until the middle of the eighteenth century, coastal Fujian remained integrated with global trading networks. Xiamen, Quanzhou, and other ports handled an extensive trade with Southeast Asia. However, its business was soon overshadowed by Guangzhou because of the latter's more strategic location at the intersection of China and the new commercial opportunities to the south. Guangzhou's position received a further boost in 1759, when the Qing restricted all private foreign trade to the city and shut down customs houses elsewhere. Fujian's integration as a peripheral maritime province of the Qing, once a contingent connection, had finally solidified.[26]

The East Asian world-region continued its gradual decline as a coherent unit during this period. The Qing tributary system, like its predecessors, still provided a framework for trade and political legitimacy, especially for Southeast Asian kingdoms such as Siam and Sulu. However, it no longer had universal applicability. For one, tribute trade had to coexist with the bustling, albeit heavily regulated, private exchange at Guangzhou that already integrated crucial segments of the world-region into the global world system. Moreover, centrifugal tendencies emerged within the Sinocentric world order. For instance, although Korea remained, on the outside, a loyal vassal of the Qing until 1895, it continued to pride itself as a repository of the institutions of the lost, authentic "China" of the Ming. Domestically, it retained the use of the calendar and the long hair and flowing robes of the previous dynasty. Only the Ming qualified as the "Imperial Dynasty" (Huangchao), while the Koreans officially referred to their new overlords by the neutral term of "Qing people" (Qing ren) and, in private, the pejorative "northern barbarians" (lu).[27]

In fact, the Zheng organization figured prominently in the collective memory of the Chosŏn elites. It was through conversations with the shipwrecked Zheng agent Lin Yinguan and his crew at Cheju in 1667 that the Koreans learned for the first time, and with great excitement, of a Ming loyalist resistance under the Yongli emperor, some five years after it had ended in failure. However, under intense pressure from the Qing court, Korea was forced to hand over the castaways to Manchuria, where the men faced certain execution. Because the merchants were "subjects of the Imperial Dynasty," intense discussions and debates raged among Confucian scholars for generations afterward over the morality of this course of action. To assuage their collective guilt and remorse, many

Asia (Durham, NC: Duke University Press, 2011); Matt Matsuda, *Pacific worlds: a history of seas, peoples, and cultures* (New York: Cambridge University Press, 2012), pp. 176–196.
[26] Viraphol, *Tribute and profit*, pp. 70–139; Wills, "Contingent connections," pp. 197–198.
[27] Sun, *Da Ming qizhi*, pp. 226–255.

within the ruling circles in Seoul called for an alliance with Zheng Jing and
Wu Sangui during the Rebellion of the Three Feudatories. Although a
cautious court rejected the appeal, it did erect a shrine to the shipwrecked
sailors much later, in 1784. Situated at the border outpost of Ŭiju, directly
across the Yalu River from Manchuria, it reinforced Korea's separation
from the Qing in physical, ideological, and chronological space.[28]

Japan effectively declared its independence from the Sinocentric tributary system by forging its own, Japanocentric world order. From the
Japanese perspective, the demise of the Zheng represented the final act
in the drawn-out disintegration of the Ming. From then on, in the words
of Hayashi Shunsai (1618–1688), a historian and Confucian scholar at
the shogun's court, the authentic China was no more and had "transformed into a barbarian state."[29] Accordingly, Qing subjects no longer
embodied a superior civilization worthy of emulation, but were foreigners
of the lowest kind, slaves who bore the shame of their subjugation
outwardly in their shaven pates and long queues, imposed under the
pain of death by their Manchu rulers. As Ronald Toby's groundbreaking
study argues, Chinese merchants at Nagasaki now occupied the lowest
rung of "barbarian" in the *bakufu*'s hierarchy of partners. They ranked
below Korea, which the *bakufu* dealt with on the basis of status parity,
followed by Ryukyu and the organized commercial entity of the VOC,
both regarded as subordinate vassals.[30]

Ironically, instead of facilitating commercial linkages, the decline and
fragmentation of the China-centered tributary system ultimately caused
their scale to shrink. Even as the Kangxi emperor opened the Qing to
private overseas trade, Japan turned away from the sea lanes and began to
encourage domestic handicraft production. Without the Zheng organization around to protect the interests of Chinese traders and overseas
diaspora at Nagasaki, the *bakufu* gradually stripped away the extraterritorial privileges that they had previously enjoyed. In 1684, it restored
the silk allotment guild, artificially reducing the silver price of imports to
unprecedented depths.[31] In 1686, the *bakufu* further ordered all Chinese
traders deprived of their mobility, and confined them to a walled compound (*Tōjin yashiki*) in the middle of Nagasaki, similar to their Dutch
counterparts at Deshima. The final act of consolidation came in 1715,
when the value of imports was capped at a million taels per year, with
600,000 taels divided among seventy junks from different regions of
China, and 400,000 taels for the Dutch. Some silk, silver, and copper

---

[28] Sun, *Da Ming qizhi*, pp. 226–255; Sŏng, *Chŏngmi chŏnshinrok*, pp. 299_058a–299_060a.
[29] Hayashi Shunsai, vol. I, p. 1.   [30] Toby, *State and diplomacy*, p. 226.
[31] Totman, *Early Modern Japan*, pp. 144–145.

continued to be exchanged via Nagasaki, as well as through Korea and Ryukyu, but better substitutes were now found in Southeast Asia, Europe, and the New World.

The constituent parts of the East Asian world-region thus demarcated clear ideological and territorial boundaries that discouraged trade with each other. The advent of the Guangzhou system in 1759 further compressed access to the global world system to a small, heavily regulated window. The defensive characteristics of the tributary system, already apparent in the early Ming, now reached their full articulation for the Qing and its neighbors.[32] Amid the restrictive climate, Taiwan lost its position as an entrepôt in the intra-East Asian exchange and shrunk back into the Greater Fujian maritime space. The island became an outlet for immigrants from its crowded and destitute neighbor, and a supplier of grain and other resources. Otherwise, it remained a largely neglected frontier until the nineteenth century, when incursions from Western powers and Japan forced the Qing to place renewed importance in its development.[33]

Former adherents of the Zheng organization took the skills and experiences that they had acquired in Taiwan elsewhere. In the wake of the island's fall, they formed the vanguard of a massive wave of immigrants to Southeast Asia. Yang Yandi, Chen Shangchuan, and their followers governed their satrapy on the Mekong River Delta until 1717. They developed Saigon into a bustling regional port and opened up its hinterlands to intensive rice agriculture. Meanwhile, at Hà Tiên, along the present-day Vietnam-Cambodia border, a Cantonese immigrant named Mo Jiu (1655–1736) founded a long-lived dynasty that lasted until the 1780s. He and his son, Mạc Thiên Tứ (1718–1780), profited tremendously from exploiting the rich fisheries in the Gulf of Siam and selling natural resources to China.[34] Anthony Reid believes that the memory of a defunct Ming among these exiles made them less willing to become absorbed into native Southeast Asian society, as was the case with previous generations.[35] Indeed, both domains continued to enforce Ming systems of governance among their subjects.

The Zheng further left behind durable institutions for the effective organization and mobilization of Chinese abroad. After Zheng Jing

---

[32] Cranmer-Byng and Wills, "Trade and diplomacy," pp. 252–253.

[33] Taiwan's role as a Qing frontier has received extensive treatment in Shepherd, *Statecraft*.

[34] For more on the Chinese regimes in the Mekong River Delta, see Yumio Sakurai, "Eighteenth-century Chinese pioneers on the water frontiers of Indochina," in Nola Cooke and Li Tana (eds.), *Water frontiers: commerce and the Chinese in the lower Mekong region, 1735–1880* (Lanham, MD: Roman and Littlefield, 2004).

[35] Reid, *Age of commerce*, vol. II: expansion and crisis (1993), pp. 314–315.

withdrew to Taiwan in 1664, he modified the monopoly firms of Koxinga's day, characterized by interlocking debt obligations and a hierarchy of agents and adopted sons, and renamed it Gongsi (Public Firm). The earliest known reference to the term appeared in the memorial of a Korean official in 1667 in reference to the different categories of cargo on board the shipwrecked vessel of Jing's agent.[36] After the organization's fall, adaptations of this model proliferated rapidly in Southeast Asia, and not just among Zheng refugees, but also a new wave of legal Qing immigrants, primarily from Fujian and Guangdong, who benefited from the Kangxi emperor's legalization of private overseas trade. Besides pooling capital and mobilizing labor for economic ventures, these new *gongsi* took on the role of surrogate lineage networks. They provided entertainment, religious services, and welfare for immigrants from the same provinces, prefectures, or counties, depending on the density of settlement by people of a particular native place. Some even organized militias for self-defense.[37]

Because of their sophisticated organization, *gongsi* had the potential to become completely self-governing entities. In southwestern Borneo, Minnanese and Hakka gold-mining *gongsi*, with the help of dissident Qing refugees, united to form the Lanfang republic in 1777, a full decade before the signing of the US Constitution. It was led by presidents and exercised power in consultation with popular assemblies that debated and decided all issues by majority vote.[38] As already shown, the roots of these seemingly surprising exercises in democracy and egalitarian associations of community could be traced back to the days of the Zheng organization. They further point to the as of yet understudied contributions of maritime Chinese to modern conceptions of nationalism and republicanism in China itself.

At the same time, the collapse of the Zheng meant that Chinese in maritime East Asia could no longer collectively coordinate their actions under a unified authority. Just as some immigrants forged their own states, many more actively used their formidable organizational skills to assist the imperial projects of others. Chinese co-colonizers, in large part, made possible the British domination of Malaya and Singapore, Dutch

---

[36] Liu Xufeng has done meticulous philological work on this topic in his "'Gongsi' xingtai zaikao," pp. 231–233.

[37] For more on the *gongsi*, see Carl A. Trocki, "Boundaries and transgressions: Chinese enterprise in eighteenth- and nineteenth-century Southeast Asia," in Ong Aihwa and Donald M. Nonini (eds.), *Ungrounded empires: the cultural politics of modern Chinese transnationalism* (London: Routledge, 1997).

[38] A concise study of the rise and fall of Lanfang and other *gongsi* on Borneo is Yuan Bingling, *Chinese democracies: a study of the* kongsis *of west Borneo (1776–1884)* (Leiden: Leiden University Press, 1999).

rule in Indonesia, and the consolidation of modern Vietnam, Thailand, and the Philippines. The solidification and articulation of these coherent Southeast Asian states and colonies led to the decline and ultimate demise of the autonomous *gongsi* federations in the nineteenth century. With the concurrent onset of the Industrial Revolution, Chinese mercantile networks found new niches subordinate to a Western-centered global supply chain. As scholars have shown, they became key intermediaries coordinating between raw material extraction and labor-intensive manufacturing across East Asia, and the importation of technology and capital from Europe, Japan, and the United States.[39] It is from then that the Chinese term *gongsi* came to designate a commercial firm in the modern sense.

Zheng remnants in China helped solidify Qing hegemony and contributed to its commercial development. Zheng soldiers repatriated from Taiwan and Fujian acquitted themselves with valor against the Zunghar Mongols in Xinjiang and used their naval expertise in the rivers of Manchuria to fight the Russians.[40] The mercantile spirit continued to flourish in the family's traditional bastions along the southeastern coast. Ng Chin-keong has examined the role played by Minnanese merchants in the transformation of Xiamen into a flourishing hub for coastal shipping and trade with Southeast Asia.[41] After 1684, many merchants once operating under Zheng auspices also relocated to Guangzhou. In fact, they and their fellow Fujianese compatriots owned the bulk of the officially sanctioned monopoly firms (Co-Hong) responsible for dealing with European traders.[42] Even the notorious pirates of this period who leeched off the Guangzhou trade came from Fujian, with many claiming descent from the subordinates of Koxinga.[43]

In large part, the court's policies aimed to regulate and encourage these overseas linkages, while curtailing the predatory behavior that threatened to harm them.[44] However, as Angela Schottenhammer correctly argues, the Qing always subordinated overseas trade to the needs of maritime defense.[45] Far from being "lulled into a false sense of security" and confidence in its superiority to the rest of the world, the Qing vigilantly

---

[39] Philip Kuhn, *Chinese among others: emigration in modern times* (Lanham, MD: Rowman and Littlefield, 2008), pp. 3–4; "Historical capitalism, east and west," in Arrighi, Hamashita, and Selden (eds.), *The resurgence of East Asia: 500, 150, and 50 year perspectives*, London: Routledge, 2003.

[40] *Kangxi shilu*, p. 135.   [41] Ng, *Trade and society*, pp. 56–58.

[42] Leonard Blussé, *Visible cities*, p. 5.   [43] Antony, *Like froth*, pp. 43–47.

[44] Ng, *Trade and society*, pp. 190–192; Zhao Gang, *Qing opening*.

[45] Angela Schottenhammer, "Characteristics of Qing China's maritime trade policies, *Shunzhi* through *Qianlong* reigns," in Schottenhammer (ed.), *Trading networks in early modern East Asia* (Wiesbaden, Germany: Otto Harrassowitz, 2010), pp. 143–144.

followed the latest developments in the coastal zone and the world beyond.[46] The court viewed with trepidation the high concentration of dissident activity among overseas Chinese, especially Ming loyalist holdouts and secret societies in Southeast Asia, and the growing presence of Western warships at China's doorstep.[47] After the British incursion into China during the Opium War (1839–1841), the philologist Wei Yuan (1794–1856) wrote in his famous treatise on coastal defense:

How do the Zheng sea bandits' demands for Zhangzhou and Quanzhou, and requests for Haicheng to become a joint zone of administration, differ from the Western barbarians' calls to open up treaty ports? How do the sea bandits' encroachment into [Zhejiang] and invasion of Nanjing differ from the barbarians' incursions into the interior?[48]

He and other Qing literati could thus readily allude to the past experience of the Zheng as a point of reference for contemporary policymakers in dealing with the new Western menace.

Ironically, this focus upon security automatically placed a cap upon the upward mobility of mercantile groups. Without the Zheng organization to provide an institutionalized voice on their behalf as a collective whole, the court never saw a need to incorporate them into government, work with them to secure the littoral, or locate new sources of capital expansion abroad. To seek better protection and guarantees for their property and more lucrative channels of wealth, many Chinese joined Western firms as compradors or left the country altogether. Yet any individual or group able to succeed through such avenues might also translate their accumulated fortunes into the subversion of the dynasty. Fearing this outcome, the court used extortion and a quarantine of foreign trade to Guangzhou to limit the influence of the Co-Hong traders.[49] In 1717, it also issued a ban on immigration, characterizing overseas Chinese as subjects who had abandoned their ancestral land (qimin). As a result, Pomeranz asserts, the Qing proved unable to fully tap into the natural bounty beyond China to break out of the population pressures and ecological shortages of its agrarian economy.[50]

A change in trajectory was not impossible but grew increasingly difficult over time. Most of the Qing political, military, and economic resources remained entrenched in the management of the Inner Asian land frontier.[51] Any expansion of state capacity to the benefit of maritime

---

[46] Fairbank, *Trade and diplomacy*, p. 38.
[47] Wills, "Introduction," p. 17; Cranmer-Byng and Wills, "Trade and diplomacy," p. 223.
[48] Ding Rijian, *Bigao lu*, p. 71.
[49] Ng, *Trade and society*, pp. 185–187; Matsuda, *Pacific worlds*, pp. 178–183.
[50] Pomeranz, *Great divergence*, pp. 201–205.   [51] Perdue, *China marches west*, p. 564.

affairs ran into the practical barriers of a thinly stretched bureaucracy, a Confucian commitment – no matter how nominal – to an agrarian base and minimal interference in people's livelihoods, and ethnic tensions between Manchu and Han. This combination of strong market and weak state, according to Deng Gang's model, translated into steep opportunity costs for change. Even after the onset of Western and Japanese imperialist penetration into China, the Qing enacted reforms slowly, and ultimately lost the race to maintain a say in the country's future. In the meantime, China began a painful, agonizing transition into an economic periphery. Its role declined dramatically from a producer of high-quality industrial luxuries to processing primary goods for mass consumption, such as tea.[52] In contrast, the compact European nation-states, locked in fierce competition with one another, harnessed the resources and techniques to lead the world in achieving a breakthrough to a mechanized industrial order.

However, one cannot, for this reason, write off larger, continental empires like China as inherently inefficient and conservative. As Andrade notes, growing evidence points to a long-term convergence characterized by similar processes on both sides of Eurasia beginning around the late sixteenth century.[53] While Western Europe won the first round of the race, industrial modernity could only fulfill its maximum potential through the vast markets and economies of scale provided by imperial-sized units.[54] Indeed, China began to realize this potential during the latter half of the twentieth century by combining elements from the rubble of the old imperial system with the imported frameworks of nationalism and Marxist class struggle to achieve an unprecedented level of penetration over local society.[55]

As scholars have shown, the People's Republic has, with its enormous state capacity, almost entirely inherited the legacy of the Qing Inner Asian frontier.[56] Yet, the PRC also embraces, to a great extent, the maritime China as defined and articulated by the Zheng organization. It incorporates merchants and militarists into its national vision, encourages commercial expansion abroad, and welcomes foreign investment. The interpenetration between state and capital, with Communist Party officials and relatives owning majority shares in corporations and private individuals accumulating fortunes through Party connections, is also reminiscent of the Zheng trading structure. This arrangement has not

---

[52] Deng Gang, *Maritime sector*, pp. 57, 222–224.   [53] Andrade, *Lost colony*, p. 15.
[54] Rosenthal and Wong, *Beyond divergence*, p. 221.
[55] Philip Huang, *The peasant family and rural development in the Yangzi Delta, 1350–1988* (Stanford, CA: Stanford University Press, 1990), p. 165.
[56] Perdue, *China marches west*, p. 4.

impeded, and perhaps even facilitated, the rapid growth in productivity and living standards that has propelled China to the position of the world's second largest economy in 2011, or some sixty years after the communists took power.[57]

Moreover, the PRC takes an interest in categorizing and setting boundaries around its maritime frontier. Its position on Taiwan surprisingly echoes Koxinga's, the first person to proclaim that the island belongs to China since antiquity. After 2009, Beijing has set its sights farther upon actualizing its territorial claims to the disputed, uninhabited islets of the East and South China Seas. This strategic and resource-rich maritime space, stretching from the shores of Japan to the Strait of Melaka, overlaps entirely with the Zheng sphere of influence in the seventeenth century. Like the Zheng, the China of the early twenty-first century maintains a navy of growing sophistication to defend the smooth circulation of its industrial exports and imports of primary goods via these waterways, and integrate East Asia and the rest of the world via a new maritime Silk Road. The PRC has also become more proactive in protecting the interests of overseas Chinese, and nurturing within them an attachment to their ancestral land.[58]

Other aspects of the Zheng organization's legacy live on in Taiwan, its territorial base after 1662, and Hong Kong, one of the many coastal outposts utilized by its Cantonese allies. Their rise to prominence in the seventeenth century reflected the interplay among Manchu, Japanese, and European economic and military expansion. Likewise, Hong Kong and Taiwan in the early twenty-first century form liminal zones of contestation and negotiation among Chinese and Western – especially Anglo-American – interests. The hegemony exercised by the United States, the Asia-Pacific's preeminent outside power, since the end of the Second World War has enforced an uncomfortable but peaceful status quo.

Accordingly, the political legitimacy of both territories and the identity of their residents remain ambiguous. The special administrative region of Hong Kong resembles a cross between a tributary vassal and Qing-style feudatory fiefdom of the PRC, while the government on Taiwan is not officially recognized by most of the world's nation-states and continues to claim nominal rule over all of China – not just the island. Both populations remain deeply divided over the sovereignty and spatial limitations of their communities, especially over the question of whether or not to exclude the PRC. For the nativist faction in Taiwan, Zheng Jing's

---

[57] Jennifer Y. J. Hsu and Reza Hasmath, *The Chinese corporatist state: adaptation, survival, and resistance* (London: Routledge, 2012).

[58] Bertil Lintner, "China's third wave," *Asia Times* (April 17, 2007).

emphasis that the island did not belong to the Middle Kingdom in his letters to the Qing court constitutes an effective claim to an identity and destiny separate from the mainland.

Nonetheless, the mainland, Hong Kong, and Taiwan have all benefited from their existence as separate entities. Just as in the seventeenth century, when Zhilong and his descendants controlled the arbitrage among the Qing, Japan, and European colonial powers, Hong Kong and Taiwan have profited as intermediaries for the production of export goods on the mainland to Western consumer markets. On the other hand, Taiwanese and Hong Kong capital and commercial expertise introduced modern management practices and contributed to rapid industrialization on the mainland. The future of the two territories will hinge upon the changing power balances in the Asia-Pacific region, whether it continues to remain under US hegemony or gravitate again toward a China-centered order. To remain as distinct, viable entities, they will both have to take calculated risks and settle upon a relationship with the Chinese mainland that most accurately predicts its future geopolitical position.[59]

The Zheng organization, despite its own failed attempts at maritime state creation, thus remains crucial to an understanding of modern China. It was an anomaly simply because it was too far ahead of its time, when the broader political, social, and economic environment still lacked the maturity to adapt accordingly. However, in the early twenty-first century, many of the same institutional elements once developed in maritime East Asia have reappeared on a continental scale after a prolonged and difficult state-building experience. Had Zheng Zhilong and Nurhaci lived under the PRC, perhaps they and their descendants might not become the bitter enemies as they had during the seventeenth century. They would, in all likelihood, have found camaraderie in a shared vision of a China marching west via highways and high-speed rail, and sailing east and south among the waves on container vessels and aircraft carriers.

---

[59] Chietigj Bajpaee, "Hong Kong, Taiwan wilt in the dragon's glare," *Asia Times* (August 16, 2007).

Appendix 1 Romanization of East Asian languages

For the transcription of Chinese, this work primarily utilizes the Pinyin system, the official Romanization standard of the People's Republic of China. Exceptions to this rule include instances of a more popularly accepted spelling or a Chinese name listed in a non-Chinese source whose Chinese equivalent could not be located. Thus, Taipei vs. Taibei, Koxinga vs. *Guoxingye*, and Sausinja (characters unknown). Another exception occurs when an author utilizes his or her own orthographic variation in an article or book published in a non-Chinese medium (Wong Young-tsu instead of Wang Rongzu). If the same author also writes in Chinese, both Pinyin and the alternate spelling will be listed. For his or her Chinese-language work, the Pinyin is used with his or her variation in parentheses, and vice versa for his or her non-Chinese work. So, for instance, Cheng Wei-chung (Zheng Weizhong), *War, trade and piracy* and Zheng Weizhong (Cheng Wei-chung), *Taiwan shehui*.

Japanese terms utilize the Revised Hepburn system except for words commonly used in English without its diacritical marks (Sunpu and *aitai shōbai*, but daimyo instead of daimyō, shogun instead of shōgun). Korean follows the McCune-Reischauer method of transcription other than for the spelling of the capital city, Seoul (Sŏul). Vietnamese words will be presented in their original form, complete with diacritics, unless an alternative spelling has gained wide currency in English. So Quảng Nam, but Vietnam instead of Việt Nam, and Hanoi instead of Hà Nội. East Asian names, places, and other terms, with the exception of those commonly used in English (i.e., samurai, Ming, and Beijing), are listed together with their Chinese-character equivalents in Appendix 4.

Appendix 2   Measurements and currency conversions

The following are the primary units of measurement found in this work, and their rates of conversion among one another and with corresponding present-day metric units.

Weight:	1 *dan* (picul) = 1 *shi* = 100 *jin* (catties) = 59.7 kg
Area:	1 *jia* = 1 *morgen* = 0.96992 hectares
	1 *mu* = 0.06667 hectares
Distance:	1 *li* = 150 *zhang* = 0.576 km
	1 *zhang* = 3.84 m

A dizzying array of metals and coins circulated throughout the world during the seventeenth century. There are often no standard units, and the same coin would experience drastic variations in value at different places and over time. Further complicating the picture, they often get debased as a result of government policy or the activities of private merchants. The conversions given below represent a rough approximation of exchange rates current as of the 1660s and standardized based upon grams of silver.

1 Japanese *kan* = 100 Chinese taels (*liang*) = 3,750 g

1 Chinese tael (*liang*) = 2.85 pre-1665 Dutch guilders = 3.5 post-1665 Dutch guilders = 37.5 g[1]

1 Spanish *real de a ocho* or peso = 0.72 Chinese taels = 27 g[2]

1 Dutch guilder = 13.2 g (pre-1665) = 10.7 g (post-1665)

1 *shi* of unhusked grain = 0.3 taels

---

[1] von Glahn, *Fountain of fortune*, p. 133; Shepherd, *Statecraft*, p. 471 n. 63; Suzuki Yasuko, *Japan-Netherlands trade, 1600–1800: the Dutch East India Company and beyond* (Kyoto: Kyoto University Press, 2012), p. 109.

[2] Shepherd, *Statecraft*, p. 471 n. 63.

Appendix 3 Zheng market share, revenues, and profitability, 1640–1683

One can get a sense of the overall scale of the Zheng organization primarily by quantifying its multidirectional trade flows among mainland China and, after 1662, Taiwan, and Japan and the Western Ocean – the main sphere of its commercial activities.[1] The Zheng also participated in alternative routes. Haphazard documentation exists for the trade between mainland China, Japan, and Taiwan and Manila, which is sometimes counted in the calculations. Others, including the China coast and VOC Taiwan; Vietnam and Japan; and the Indian Ocean zone via Macao, Banten, and the English East India Company; remain poorly understood and are thus excluded. In general, the most comprehensive estimates for the Zheng organization are only possible for the years from 1650 to 1662. More fragmented information survives from 1640 to 1646, during Zheng Zhilong's days, and from 1663 to 1683, the final two decades of the organization.

Still, some guesswork is necessarily involved in the calculations for every period. Any extrapolations make sure to employ a conservative approach. Whenever possible, lower-bound figures are adopted when given a range of estimates, and all results are rounded down. For profits, the highest unit purchase price and lowest sale price are used unless indicated otherwise. When the scale of a particular exchange remains unknown, it is excluded from calculations or assumed to have zero value.

The final totals, if available, are juxtaposed to those of the Dutch East India Company over a similar period to place them in a more understandable context. Unlike the Zheng, most of the Dutch records have survived intact. They contain meticulous information on total mean annual revenues and gross profits realized by the entire enterprise, whose concerns stretched from Japan to the Middle East and to Western Europe. They also indicate the average annual income generated

---

[1] Yang Yanjie, "1650 zhi 1662 nian Zheng Chenggong haiwai maoyi de maoyi'e he lirun'e gusuan," in Academic Division of the Zheng Chenggong Scholarly Discussion Group (ed.), *Zheng Chenggong yanjiu lunwen xuan xuji*, Fuzhou: Fujian People's Publishing House, 1984, pp. 222–223.

Table 1.1 *Scale of Zheng Zhilong's trade at Nagasaki*[2]

Year	Total Chinese junks	Zheng junks	Zheng trading value (kan)	Zheng trading value (kg)
1640	74	2	2,000[*]	7,500[*]
1641	89	6	5,614[*]	21,052.5[*]
1642	32	3	5,000[*]	18,750[*]
1643	34	7	8,500[*]	31,875[*]
1644	–	6	2,780	10,425
1645	–	1	–	–
1646	–	>3	250	937.5
TOTAL	229	>28	24,144	90,540
MEAN	57.3	>4	4,024	15,090

* Value of Chinese silk sold, not counting other exports to Japan.

by the VOC through trade and colonial revenues in Asia, a more direct comparison with the Zheng, although it still includes a vaster area of operations.

1.   1640–1646

Japan. A rough picture of Zheng Zhilong's trade with Japan can be gleaned based upon data provided by the VOC factory records at Nagasaki. The trading values are denominated in *kan*, a unit of Japanese silver coin (see Appendix 2 for conversions).

As Table 1.1 shows, Zheng Zhilong's personal ships, excluding traders carrying his passes, realized an average of 4,024 *kan*, or 402,400 taels of silver between 1640 and 1646. He contributed, at the very least, to 7 percent of all Chinese shipping in maritime East Asia. These values are most likely severe underestimations. Besides the lack of complete information, the data are distorted by the chaos and warfare accompanying the dynastic transition in Fujian during 1645 and 1646. Ishihara estimates that, at the height of Zheng Zhilong's power, in 1642, junks under his name accounted for over a quarter of Chinese shipping and took 80 percent of cargoes.

Manila. The total number of Chinese junks arriving at Manila is listed below. However, the figures, based upon official Spanish customs data, are grossly inaccurate because so much of the trade escaped official channels through corruption, bribes, and evasion.

[2] Based upon Ishishara, *Nippon kisshi*, pp. 272–305; table 8.2 in Cheng (Zheng), *War, trade and piracy*, p. 122.

Table 1.2 *Chinese junks visiting*
Manila, 1640–1646[3]

Year	Chinese junks[*]
1640	7
1641	8
1642	34
1643	30
1644	8
1645	11
1646	17
TOTAL	115
MEAN	16.4

[*] Counts only junks from mainland China.

Data are lacking as to the proportion of these ships affiliated with Zheng Zhilong, as well as the quantity of his commerce at Manila. He also had close ties with Macao and the Western Ocean, the extent of which likewise remains poorly understood.

2.   1650–1662

Japan. Koxinga's total revenues from Japan are derived from the value of products from China and Southeast Asia sold in Japan, and Japanese goods in China. A compendium of foreign relations documents arranged by the Confucian scholar and diplomat Hayashi Akira (1800–1859) during the nineteenth century has preserved the Nagasaki customs data on Chinese and Dutch ships entering the port. It contains a precise breakdown of the silver value of goods brought to Japan by both groups of traders from 1648 to 1673. Tables 2.1 and 2.2 display these data for the Chinese and the VOC, but delay the starting date to 1650, when Koxinga gained ascendancy, and stop at 1662, the year of his death. The following section continues with 1663 until 1672. The monetary values are denominated in Japanese *kan* (see Appendix 2 for conversions).

Koxinga's share of Chinese trade with Japan can be imperfectly derived from the number of ships belonging personally to him or his subordinates, and those that procured affiliation through his passes. A Dutch account

[3] Adapted from Series 13, tables 3 and 4 in Pierre Chaunu, *Les Philippines et le Pacifique des Ibériques (XVIe, XVIIe, XVIIIe siècles): introduction méthodologique et indices d'activité* (Paris: S.E.V.P.E.N., 1960), pp. 161, 164.

Table 2.1 *Scale of Chinese trade at Nagasaki, 1650–1662*[4]

Year	Chinese junks	Silver value of procured Japanese goods[*]	Silver from official purchase[**]	Silver imported from Japan	Silver retained in Japan	Total value of exports by Chinese junks[***]
1650	70	5,293.53	58.02	6,827.71	3,178.17	15,357.44
1651	40	3,208.12	23.22	4,749.43	1,660.03	9,640.80
1652	50	6,165.82	36.27	5,867.30	1,917.40	13,986.79
1653	56	9,304.67	113.52	3,517.44	2,281.20	15,216.82
1654	51	7,070.07	147.94	8,181.17	3,829.35	19,228.53
1655	45	6,651.18	130.97	4,655.05	627.50	12,064.69
1656	57	7,440.30	94.10	5,241.11	1,535.52	14,311.02
1657	51	6,568.11	262.25	2,449.75	1,348.44	10,628.56
1658	43	4,364.71	173.35	11,028.54	1,035.93	16,602.54
1659	60	5,621.42	248.91	19,400.90	930.75	26,201.97
1660	45	2,448.80	184.27	20,151.29	1,206.76	23,991.12
1661	39	2,711.07	170.65	25,769.44	833.22	29,484.37
1662	42	3,335.04	230.18	12,942.65	2,581.50	19,089.37
TOTAL	649	70,182.82	1,873.65	130,781.78	22,965.77	225,804.02
MEAN	49.9	5,398.68	144.13	10,060.14	1,766.60	17,369.54

* All trading values denominated in *kan*.
** Mandatory sale of products destined for the private collection of the shogun and the imperial court (*gyobutsu*). Out of respect for the authorities, the original calculation for the total Chinese revenues purposely excludes the commercial value of these goods.
*** Includes value realized from the forced official purchases.

notes that in 1657, at the height of his power, forty-seven of his junks arrived in Nagasaki. Twenty-eight came from Anhai, eleven from Cambodia, three from Siam, two from Quảng Nam, two from Pattani, and one from Tonkin.[5] This figure amounted to more than 90 percent of the total of fifty-one ships recorded at the port for that year. Thus, one can assume that Koxinga captured roughly 90 percent of all trade on the sea lanes to and from Japan.

Accordingly, Koxinga's share of the export value realized by all Chinese junks at Nagasaki can be determined by taking 90 percent of the total amount. During the 1650s, silver constituted the vast majority of outbound cargoes from Japan. It was consumed as official currency in Zheng-held

[4] Based upon Hayashi Akira, *Tsūkō ichiran* (1912), vol. IV, pp. 323–325. See also Iwao Seiichi, "Kinsei Nisshi bōeki ni kansuru sūryōteki kōsatsu," *Shigaku zasshi* 62.11 (1953): 12–13 and Yamawaki, "Trading Merchants," p. 111. Note that total revenue is calculated by adding up the figures given by the individual categories. Thus, they may not accord completely with the sums found in the book.
[5] Cheng, *Helan Fuermosha*, pp. 490–491.

Table 2.2 *Scale of VOC trade at Nagasaki, 1650–1662*[6]

Year	VOC Ships	Silver value of procured Japanese Goods*	Silver imported from Japan	Silver retained in Japan	Total value of exports by VOC
1650	7	1,025.09	3,940.60	506.86	5,472.54
1651	8	1,294.43	4,895.60	466.13	6,656.16
1652	9	1,062.02	5,538.90	451.35	7,052.27
1653	5	786.76	6,190.20	446.96	7,423.92
1654	4	900.32	3,848.20	442.25	5,190.78
1655	4	703.97	4,011.50	387.12	5,102.59
1656	8	1,668.75	6,190.25	576.48	8,435.48
1657	8	2,017.37	3,444.24	411.69	5,873.30
1658	9	1,811.94	5,640.55	509.35	7,961.83
1659	8	1,422.05	5,960.40	683.92	8,066.36
1660	5	1,715.56	4,268.39	561.32	6,545.26
1661	11	2,958.17	5,543.59	626.93	9,128.69
1662	8	2,068.04	5,960.01	1,176.04	9,204.09
TOTAL	**94**	**19,434.46**	**65,432.41**	**7,246.40**	**92,113.27**
MEAN	**7.2**	**1,494.96**	**5,033.26**	**557.42**	**7,085.64**

* All trading values denominated in *kan*.

territories and the rest of China, or used to purchase Southeast Asian products. Other items consisted of copper, shipbuilding materials, and weapons primarily for use on the mainland coast against the Qing. Yang Yanjie estimates from sixteenth-century Ming records that Japanese arms could fetch a rate of return of approximately 80 percent if sold in China.[7] Assume that 90 percent of Japanese products went to China during this period, and that war-related materials constituted the entire share of these shipments. The category "Silver Value of Procured Japanese Goods" in Table 2.1 is thus multiplied by 90 percent to estimate the value of Japanese products bound for China. An additional 90 percent is taken to reflect the Zheng contribution. Adding the result, in turn, to Koxinga's share of the export value of his ships at Nagasaki yields his total revenues from the Japan trade. Table 2.3 displays these figures in both *kan* and kilograms.

The calculation of Koxinga's gross profits from the Japan trade involves taking the difference between the purchase and sale prices. The cost of Japanese goods handled by him and bound for China, estimates of their price in China, and the value of exports to Nagasaki are already listed in

[6] Based upon the data presented in Hayashi Akira, *Tsūkō ichiran*, vol. IV, pp. 332–334. Note that total revenue is calculated by adding up the figures given by the individual categories. Thus, they may not accord completely with the sum found in the book.
[7] Yang Yanjie, "Zheng Chenggong maoyi," pp. 229–230.

Table 2.3 *Total revenues of Koxinga from the Japan trade, 1650–1662*

Year	Total value of exports by Chinese junks in Japan *	Zheng export value in Japan ** (i)	Silver value of procured Japanese goods	Zheng share of procured Japanese goods ***	Zheng value of Japanese goods to China +	Zheng import value of Japanese goods in China ++ (ii)	Total Zheng revenues (i+ii)	Total Zheng revenues (kg)
1650	15,357.44	13,821.69	5,293.53	4,764.18	4,287.76	7,717.97	21,539.66	80,773.7
1651	9,640.80	8,676.72	3,208.12	2,887.31	2,598.58	4,677.44	13,354.16	50,078.1
1652	13,986.79	12,588.11	6,165.82	5,549.24	4,994.32	8,989.77	21,577.88	80,917
1653	15,216.82	13,695.14	9,304.67	8,374.20	7,536.78	13,566.20	27,261.34	102,230
1654	19,228.53	17,305.68	7,070.07	6,363.06	5,726.76	10,308.16	27,613.84	103,551.8
1655	12,064.69	10,858.22	6,651.18	5,986.06	5,387.45	9,697.41	20,555.64	77,083.6
1656	14,311.02	12,879.92	7,440.30	6,696.27	6,026.64	10,847.96	23,727.88	88,979.5
1657	10,628.56	9,565.70	6,568.11	5,911.30	5,320.17	9,576.30	19,142.00	71,782.5
1658	16,602.54	14,942.28	4,364.71	3,928.24	3,535.42	6,363.75	21,306.04	79,897.6
1659	26,201.97	23,581.77	5,621.42	5,059.27	4,553.35	8,196.02	31,777.80	119,166.7
1660	23,991.12	21,592.01	2,448.80	2,203.92	1,983.53	3,570.35	25,162.36	94,358.8
1661	29,484.37	26,535.94	2,711.07	2,439.96	2,195.96	3,952.73	30,488.67	114,332.5
1662	19,089.37	17,180.43	3,335.04	3,001.54	2,701.38	4,862.49	22,042.92	82,660.9
TOTAL	225,804.02	203,223.62	70,182.82	4,764.18	56,848.09	102,326.56	305,550.18	1,145,813
MEAN	17,369.54	15,632.59	5,398.68	2,887.31	4,372.93	7,871.27	23,503.86	88,139.4

* All trading values denominated in *kan* unless indicated otherwise.

** "Total value of exports by Chinese junks in Japan" × Zheng proportion (90%).

*** "Silver value of procured Japanese goods" × Zheng proportion (90%).

+ "Zheng share of procured Japanese goods" × 90%

++ "Zheng value of Japanese goods to China" × (1+80% rate of return).

Table 2.4 *Koxinga's gross profits from the Japan trade, 1650–1662*

Year	Profits from exports to Japan*	Japan rate of return**	Profits from Japanese goods in China***	Total profits (kan)	Total profits (kg)	Total rate of return+
1650	9,821.69	245.54	3,430.21	13,251.90	49,694.6	151.2
1651	4,676.72	116.92	2,078.86	6,755.58	25,333.4	98.0
1652	8,588.11	214.70	3,995.45	12,583.57	47,188.3	131.7
1653	9,695.14	242.38	6,029.42	15,724.56	58,967.1	127
1654	13,305.68	332.64	4,581.40	17,887.08	67,076.5	172.6
1655	6,858.22	171.46	4,309.96	11,168.18	41,880.6	111.8
1656	8,879.92	222.00	4,821.32	13,701.24	51,379.6	128
1657	5,565.70	139.14	4,256.13	9,821.83	36,831.8	99.1
1658	10,942.28	273.56	2,828.33	13,770.62	51,639.8	173.6
1659	19,581.77	489.54	3,642.68	23,224.45	87,091.6	256.3
1660	17,592.01	439.80	1,586.82	19,178.83	71,920.6	309.1
1661	22,535.94	563.40	1,756.77	24,292.71	91,097.6	377.2
1662	13,180.43	329.51	2,161.11	15,341.54	57,530.7	219.1
TOTAL	**151,223.62**	–	**45,478.47**	**196,702.09**	**737,632.8**	–
MEAN	**11,632.59**	**290.81**	**3,498.34**	**15,130.93**	**56,740.9**	**181.1**

* "Total Zheng revenues" from Table 2.3 – 400,000 taels or 4,000 *kan* estimated cost.
** ("Profits from exports to Japan" / 4,000 *kan*) × 100.
*** "Zheng import value of Japanese goods in China" – "Zheng value of Japanese goods to China" from Table 2.3.
+ "Total profits" / ("Zheng value of Japanese goods to China" + 4,000 *kan*).

Table 2.3. The next step is to figure out the mainland cost of what his ships sold at Nagasaki. According to a Qing memorial, Zeng Dinglao, head of the Five Mountain Firms, obtained 250,000 taels of silver to purchase silk and other items from the Yangzi River Delta at the beginning of 1654. The next year, he received two further payments of 50,000 taels in June and 100,000 taels in December from the Revenue Office.[8] If the reasonable assumption is made that Koxinga forwarded all these amounts to Zeng and his agents three times in a single year, and all of the money went toward the purchase of goods, then the cost totals 400,000 taels, or 4,000 *kan*. The sum of Koxinga's earnings from Japan and the sale of Japanese goods in China equal the total gross profit. Table 2.4 provides a breakdown of the figures, along with rates of return.

Western Ocean. Junks in the Western Ocean traveled along two sets of routes. The first involved sailing directly from ports in China and then back. Ships on the second, or triangular, route went from the mainland coast to Western Ocean destinations and then Nagasaki before returning,

[8] *Shiliao sanbian*, pp. 4–5.

or the other way around. An examination of Dutch and Japanese records reveals the extent of Zheng involvement in both. In 1655, Koxinga was documented to have dispatched twenty-four junks to Southeast Asia. It is also known that nineteen out of the forty-seven Zheng vessels headed for Nagasaki two years later came from Western Ocean ports, and, ultimately, from the China coast. Assuming that, in 1657, Koxinga sent the same number of ships to the Western Sea, nineteen out of twenty-four, or about 80 percent of them, would participate in the triangular trade. More typically, according to Yang Yanjie, sixteen to twenty junks went annually to Southeast Asia. Participants on the direct route thus ranged from three to four vessels.

Calculations of revenues and profits involve adding the value of goods from China and Japan at the Western Ocean ports to those from the Western Ocean in China. A rough approximation of the first is derived from Koxinga's demand for reparations from the Dutch in 1657 for confiscating two of his ships around Johor and Pattani.[9] The amounts come to 80,000 and 100,000 taels, respectively. Presumably, the value of the cargoes came from earlier sales of Chinese and Japanese goods at these Western Ocean destinations for a similar amount. Assume that this range represents the value of exports by each of Koxinga's junks in any given year. Multiplying the lower-bound estimates of 80,000 taels by the sixteen junks sent to ports in the Western Ocean yields a total of 1,280,000 taels, or 48,000 kilograms.

The profits realized by Zheng exports to the Western Ocean involve a bit of extrapolation from available estimates on unit prices. Although Japan sold weapons and copper to both of the warring parties in Vietnam, the amount remains undetermined and likely did not constitute a significant share of total shipments. Raw silk constituted the main source of exports from the China coast. According to Wills, the Chinese price amounted to 240–250 taels per picul on the eve of the Qing coastal evacuation policy, presumably from the 1650s.[10] The sale price at Banten given in the English factory records in 1670 stood at 400 Spanish pesos (288 taels) per picul, yielding a rate of return of at least 15.2 percent. Assume that raw silk constituted the entire value on all shipments from China, and that Chinese exports accounted for 90 percent of the total cargo onboard Zheng ships, with the remainder yielding zero in returns. Based upon the mean revenue of 1,280,000 taels, the profit equals 152,000 taels worth of silver.[11]

---

[9] Cheng, *Helan Fuermosha*, p. 511.   [10] Wills, *Pepper*, p. 82.
[11] Profit = Revenue − Cost. Cost can be obtained from rate of return with the formula: Rate of Return = (Revenue − Cost) / Cost = Revenue / Cost − 1. Thus, 1 + Rate of

The second source of income comes from the sale of tropical goods from the Western Ocean in China and Japan.[12] The Japanese market has already been included in the total export value realized by Chinese junks at Nagasaki. To avoid overlap, all Zheng ships on the triangular route are excluded for the purposes of this calculation, even if many of them had the mainland coast as their final destination. Hence, at the risk of undercounting, only the lower-bound estimate of the three ships on the direct route between China and the Western Sea is counted. At 80,000 taels per ship, the silver value of goods procured in the Western Sea amounted to 240,000 taels.

Pepper constituted one of the most valuable items on board the China-bound ships. The Southeast Asian price was 6.25 pesos (4.50 taels) per picul during the decade.[13] For China, Wills shows that, in the 1660s, the Dutch offered pepper at 13 taels per picul to Qing merchants, who countered with a bid of 7 taels.[14] Since the VOC would naturally ask for a high sale price and the Qing would use its administrative privileges to acquire it at below-market rates, taking the middle ground of 10 taels more accurately approximates a fair value. This figure leads to a rate of return of 122 percent. Now, assume that the three junks on the direct route had 70 percent of their cargoes filled with pepper. Of course, Zheng ships carried many other goods, including sappanwood, ivory, and rice, but they are considered, for the purposes of this calculation, to have zero value. With a modified return of 85.4 percent, the value of exports from Western Sea ports to the mainland coast amounts to 444,960 taels, which translates into a profit of 204,960 taels.[15]

The Zheng organization realized 1,724,960 taels, or 64,686 kilograms, in annual average revenues from the Western Ocean.[16] Mean profits add up to 356,960 taels, or 13,386 kilograms worth of silver.[17]

Manila. Pierre Chaunu has estimated the total number of Chinese junks arriving at the port over this period, given in Table 2.5. As during Zhilong's days, data are lacking as to how many of these ships were affiliated with Koxinga, and the value of his business at Manila.

Return = Revenue / Cost. So in this case, 1,280,000 − (1,280,000 / 1.152) = 168,888.89 taels. Taking 90% of this sum yields 152,000 taels.

[12] Chang Hsiu-jung et al., *English factory*, p. 74.

[13] See table 3.6 in David Bulbeck, Anthony Reid, Cheng Tan Lay, and Wu Yiqi (ed.), *Southeast Asian exports since the fourteenth century: cloves, pepper, coffee, and sugar* (Singapore: Institute of Southeast Asian Studies, 1998), p. 84.

[14] Wills, *Pepper*, p. 97.

[15] Taking 70% of 122% = 85.4%. Then, 240,000 taels * (1 + 85.4%) = 444,960 taels.

[16] Value of exports from China to the Western Sea (1,280,000 taels) + value of imports from Western Sea to China (444,960 taels) = 1,724,960 taels.

[17] Gross profit on exports from China to the Western Sea (152,000 taels) + gross profit on imports from Western Sea to China (204,960 taels) = 356,960 taels.

Table 2.5 *Chinese junks visiting Manila, 1650–1662*[18]

Year	Chinese junks[*]
1650	10
1651	9
1652	4
1653	8
1654	8
1655	3
1656	0
1657	0
1658	16
1659	11
1660	12
1661	11
1662	8
TOTAL	**100**
MEAN	**7.6**

[*] Counts only mainland China and Japan.

Table 2.6 *Mean annual revenues and gross trading profits of Koxinga vs. VOC, 1650–1662*

	Revenues (currency)	Revenues (kg)	Revenues (USD)[***]	Profits (currency)	Profits (kg)	Profits (USD)
Koxinga	>4,075,346 taels[*]	>152,825.4	>91,695,285	>1,870,053 taels[+]	>70,126.9	>42,076,192
VOC[**]	ƒ8,546,867	112,458.8	67,475,266	ƒ6,014,955	79,144.1	47,486,641
VOC (Asia)				ƒ4,114,123	54,133.2	32,479,918

[*] 1,724,960 taels from Western Ocean + (23,503.86 *kan* × 100) from Japan.
[**] Guilders first converted to taels at 2.85 guilders per tael and then multiplied by 37.5 g. For details on the specific calculations for the VOC, see J. P. de Korte, *De jaarlijkse financiële verantwoording in de VOC, Verenigde Oostindische Compagnie* (Leiden: Martinus Nijhoff, 1984), pp. 31, 60–61, *Bijlage* 9A-9B, *Bijlage* 13A.
[***] US$600/kg on September 15, 2014. See http://silverprice.org for real-time updates.
[+] 356,960 taels from Western Sea + (15,130.93 *kan* × 100) from Japan.

Totals. Table 2.6 lists the total average yearly revenues and profits of the Zheng organization and the VOC between 1650 and 1662, both in

[18] Adapted from Series 13, tables 4 and 5 in Chaunu, *Philippines et Pacifique*, pp. 161, 164.

their respective currencies and more uniform standards based upon kilograms of silver and present-day US dollars. Note that profits for the Zheng organization remain grossly incomplete for the Western Ocean.

3.　　1663–1672

Taiwan. Zheng Jing largely inherited Koxinga's trading network. However, he now possessed Taiwan, and obtained revenues and incurred costs in administering it. Gazetteers of the island and guidebooks for Qing officials, the majority of them published in 1684, in the wake of Taiwan's occupation, allow scholars to piece together data on land use, taxes, duties, and even per capita income. Table 3.1 lists the different categories of land, the quality of the soil, rates of rent and taxation, and area of cultivation. The levy of the official fields (*guantian*) consists of rent paid in kind to Zheng Jing and his relatives. In exchange, they provided agricultural implements and animals for the tenants and constructed and maintained dikes for irrigation. In private fields (*sitian*), operated by

Table 3.1 *Land categories, soil quality, rates, and area of cultivation in Taiwan*[19]

Land quality	Official fields (guantian)	Output (shi)	Rent %	Private fields (sitian)	Output (shi)	Tax %	TOTALS
Tian High[*]	18	65	27.7	3.6	55	6.5	
Tian Middle	15.6	50	31.2	3.12	45	6.9	
Tian Low	10.2	35	29.1	2.04	30	6.8	
Yuan High	10.2			2.04			
Yuan Middle	8.1			1.62			
Yuan Low	5.4			1.08			
Total area (*jia*)	**9,783**			**20,272**			**30,055**
Total revenue (*shi*)	**84,921**			**41,403**			**126,324**
Total revenue (taels)	**25,476.30**			**12,420.90**			**37,897.20**

[*] All rent and tax rates in *shi* per *jia*.

[19] Derived from Jiang Yuying, *Taiwan fu zhi*, pp. 145–146, 148–149 and Ji Qiguang, *Dongning zhengshiji*, *TWWXHK*, 4.2, pp. 224–228.

select civil and military officials, rent charges and investments were arranged on an individual basis. The landlord only needed to pay a tax on the property. Official and private fields on Taiwan varied according to two classes of fertility: *tian* and *yuan*. Each, in turn, was subdivided into three subcategories of quality and valued at different rates.[20]

Based upon the calculations for the official and private fields, a rough estimate of total agricultural output on Taiwan, in other words, a gross national product (GNP), can be calculated. Official fields charged a rent, on average, at 29.1 percent of total output, while private fields levied a tax at 6.8 percent. Zheng revenues for each category are then divided by these percentages to yield 270,207.70 taels, or 900,692.3 *shi* in total agricultural output, translating to 53,771,335.6 Kilograms.[21] The military colonies, which constituted the majority of landholdings, are left out of the calculations for GNP. Deng Kongzhao estimates that the total area under cultivation could not fall fewer than 15,000 *jia* (14,550 hectares). However, the rate of taxation remains unknown.[22]

All of the sources of revenue from Taiwan in an average year are listed in Table 3.2. Besides rents and taxes on land in areas of Han settlement,

Table 3.2 *Zheng revenue structure in Taiwan*[23]

Revenue sources	Revenues in kind (shi)	Revenues in silver (taels)	Revenues in silver (kg)
Han land taxes	126,324	37,897.20	1,421.1
Aboriginal land taxes	11,868	3,560.40	133.5
Han head tax		18,320	687
Aboriginal head tax		19,288.80	723.3
Mills and carts		2,622	98.3
Storefronts		3,888	145.8
Fishing		840	31.5
Shipping		2,042.70	76.6
Salt		3,680	138
Import duties		13,000	487.5
Miscellaneous land revenues		703	26.3
Penghu		1,704.60	63.9
TOTAL	**138,192**	**107,546.70**	**4,033**

[20] See Jiang Yuying, *Taiwan fu zhi*, p. 145.
[21] Total output modified from Jian, "Ming-Zheng haiwai maoyi," pp. 25–27.
[22] Deng Kongzhao, *Ming-Zheng Taiwan yanjiu*, pp. 77–78.
[23] Based upon table 4.1 in Shepherd, *Statecraft*, p. 102 and Ji Linguang, *Dongning zhengshiji*, pp. 227–238.

eight aboriginal tribes in Wannian sub-prefecture practiced Chinese-style agriculture and paid a portion of their output in kind. In Penghu, which, unlike the main island, did not use the Dutch system, everything was levied in cash, including on land. Taiwanese exports, such as deerskin and sugar, are considered a part of the Zheng commercial network and are excluded from the calculations.

A rough calculation of personal income can be derived from these figures. It assumes a tenant household of the official fields consisting of a husband and wife and four young children, with only the man engaged in farming. Their field, of *tian* middle quality, produces 50 *shi* of grain annually in a decent harvest year. If sold on the market, this quantity can generate 15 taels of silver, or earnings of 2.50 taels per person. A family of six required 30 *shi* to maintain basic subsistence, based upon the Qing standard of 7 *shi* for each of the two adults and 4 *shi* for each of the four children. The household would also have to pay rent of 15.6 *shi*. After subtracting these from the 50 *shi* of grain production from the field, the result comes to 4.4 *shi*, or 1.32 taels. Further deducting a head tax of 0.38 taels and housing tax of 0.62 taels leads to a disposable income of 0.32 taels, or 0.05 taels per person.[24]

Japan. Tables 3.3 and 3.4 list the annual trading values for the Chinese and VOC in Nagasaki during this period.

Information is lacking on the Zheng organization's share of the Chinese trade with Japan during this decade. Zheng Jing started out from a much weakened position compared to his father. The Qing blockade cut off direct access to production sources in the Yangzi River Delta. He also faced competition from the Zheng defectors and Geng Jimao. After the Qing maritime prohibitions relaxed during the late 1660s, independent private merchants also joined the game. Nonetheless, within several years, Jing strengthened his grip over the sea lanes. His naval vessels in the East China Sea caught and confiscated many junks found without the organization's passes. He also entered into cooperative arrangements with most of his competitors. English records further show that Zheng Jing monopolized the supply and purchase of silk, deerskins, and sugar in Taiwan.[25] Hence, his strong rebound more than made up his initial position of weakness. On average, while he and his affiliated merchants may not have controlled 90 percent of the Japan trade as his father did, about 80 percent appears to be a reasonable, conservative estimate.

---

[24] Modified from Jian, "Ming-Zheng haiwai maoyi," pp. 25–27 and Ji Linguang, *Dongning zhengshiji*, pp. 235–237.

[25] Chang Hsiu-jung et al., *English factory*, pp. 73, 151.

Table 3.3 Scale of Chinese trade at Nagasaki, 1663–1672[26]

Year	Chinese junks*	Silver value of procured Japanese goods**	Silver from official purchase	Silver value of gold from official purchase	Silver imported from Japan	Silver value of gold imported from Japan	Silver retained in Japan	Silver value of gold retained in Japan	Total value of exports by Chinese junks+
1663	29 (30)	1,968.15	3,710.27	–	5,411.35	–	179.44	–	11,269.21
1664	38	2,751.27	1,425.80	–	16,663.68	29.92	37.25	–	20,907.92
1665	36 (31)	2,764.82	1,883.76	–	8,041.99	–	91.45	–	12,782.02
1666	37 (33)	3,866.41	1,736.18	–	7,235.51	251.60	34.79	–	13,124.49
1667	30 (27)	2,937.09	1,843.29	–	4,547.01	826.88	3.13	–	10,157.40
1668	43 (31)	4,246.28	335.38	1,650.69	3,415.04	7,894.09	0.00	–	17,541.48
1669	38 (27)	4,192.99	–	2,175.39	–	10,040.00	0.02	9.88	16,418.29
1670	36 (31)	2,187.59	–	2,866.20	394.75	8,833.62	2.05	–	14,284.20++
1671	38 (37)	3,934.34	–	2,610.71	950.12	6,930.97	0.00	–	14,426.14
1672	43 (45)	8,972.75	–	3,353.26	2,756.16	–	0.00	–	15,082.17
TOTAL	368 (330)	37,821.68	10,934.70	12,656.25	49,415.60	34,807.08	348.12	9.88	145,993.31
MEAN	36.8 (33)	3,782.17	1,822.45	2,531.25	5,490.62	4,972.44	34.81	9.88	14,599.33

* Alternate figures for Chinese junk numbers from Iwao, "Nisshi bōeki," pp. 12–13 in parentheses.

** All trading values denominated in kan.

*** Mandatory sale of products destined for the private collection of the shogun and the imperial court (gyobutsu). Out of respect for the authorities, the original calculation for the total Chinese revenues purposely excludes the commercial value of these goods.

+ Includes value realized from the forced official purchases.

++ Original total of 15,282.38, but figures do not add up.

26 Based upon the data presented in Hayashi Akira, Tsūkō ichiran, vol. IV, pp. 325–327. Note that total revenue is calculated by adding up the figures given by the individual categories, and converting from gold to Japanese monetary units, where necessary. Thus, they may not accord completely

Table 3.4 *Scale of VOC trade at Nagasaki, 1663–1672*[27]

Year	VOC ships	Silver value of procured Japanese goods[*]	Silver imported from Japan	Silver value of gold imported from Japan[**]	Silver retained in Japan	Silver value of gold retained in Japan	Less head tax	Total value of exports by VOC ships[***]
1663	6	2,259.85	3,671.40	–	479.74	–	0.00	6,410.99
1664	9	4,138.79	5,602.47	–	1,272.97	–	56.83	10,957.39
1665	12	2,573.85	7,045.60	–	1,001.09	–	61.52	10,559.01
1666	7	1,995.61	–	2,040.00	876.86	–	55.19	4,857.28[+]
1667	8	2,145.15	6,978.84	–	1,306.34	–	62.91	10,367.43
1668	9	1,879.15	–	8,890.28	0.01	650.44	71.87	11,348.01
1669	5	2,045.41	–	8,089.98	0.01	318.47	61.84	10,392.04
1670	6	3,497.87	–	7,695.79	0.00	681.85	71.67	11,803.84
1671	7	2,887.71	–	8,047.79	0.00	0.00	0.00	10,935.50
1672	7	3,501.52	–	6,219.98	0.00	0.00	0.00	9,721.50
TOTAL	76	26,924.90	23,298.31	40,983.82	4,937.02	1,650.76	441.82	97,353.00
MEAN	7.6	2,692.49	5,824.58	6,830.64	493.70	330.15	44.18	9,735.30

* All trading values denominated in *kan*.
** Gold is converted into *kan* at 1 tael to 5.80 taels (.058 *kan*) in 1671 and 1 tael to 6.80 taels (.068 *kan*) in 1672.
*** Less taxes.
\+ Original total of 15,282/37/5, but figures do not add up.

Table 3.5 displays the Zheng share of annual revenues from the Japan trade in *kan* and kilograms. The figures represent 80 percent of the total Chinese export value from mainland China, Taiwan, and Southeast Asia to Nagasaki. Japanese goods flowed in the other direction as well. Zheng Jing and his affiliates carried large quantities of silver for use as currency at home or consumption in the Western Ocean. In contrast to Koxinga's time, when other imports consisted almost exclusively of armaments, they now also included greater quantities of non-silver metals, such as gold and copper, items with more intrinsic commercial value. However, until 1672, the official price for gold in Japan ranged from 5.40 to 5.80 taels of silver per piece. This rate was unprofitable in Taiwan, where it sold for 5.50 pesos (3.96 taels). Likewise, the cost of copper, the other main export item, was not competitive. The purchasing price stood at 12.40

[27] Based upon the data presented in Hayashi Akira, *Tsūkō ichiran*, vol. IV, pp. 334–335. Note that total revenue is calculated by adding up the figures given by the individual categories, and converting from gold to Japanese monetary units, where necessary. Thus, they may not accord completely with the sum found in the book. Major discrepancies beyond reasonable allowance for rounding are noted.

Table 3.5 *Total revenues of Zheng Jing from the Japan trade, 1663–1672*

Year	Total value of exports by Chinese Junks (kan)	Total Zheng revenues from Japan (kan)[*]	Total Zheng revenues from Japan (kg)
1663	11,269.21	9,015.37	33,807.6
1664	20,907.92	16,726.34	62,723.7
1665	12,782.02	10,225.62	38,346
1666	13,144.49	10,515.60	39,433.4
1667	10,158.27	8,126.61	30,474.8
1668	17,541.81	14,033.45	52,625.4
1669	16,408.48	13,126.79	49,225.4
1670	14,302.15	11,441.72	42,906.4
1671	14,426.01	11,540.81	43,278
1672	15,082.17	12,065.74	45,246.5
TOTAL	**146,022.54**	**116,818.03**	**438,067.6**
MEAN	**14,602.25**	**11,681.80**	**43,806.7**

[*] Total value of exports by Chinese junks × Zheng proportion (80%)

taels per picul in the 1660s, while in the early 1670s, it sold for 16 pesos (11.52 taels) in Taiwan.[28] Most of the metals were thus retained for another round of purchases at Nagasaki or sent to the English or the Western Ocean. Hence, at the risk of underestimation, only the Zheng share of export value to Nagasaki is calculated in the revenues.

Gross trading profits from the Japan trade during this decade is based upon the sum of price differentials among the three biggest exports to Nagasaki: silk, sugar, and deerskin. Cheng Wei-chung shows that silk prices in Japan averaged 472.50 taels per picul on average from 1668 to 1670. The purchase price for silk at Taiwan in 1670, according to an English account, comes to 255 pesos (183.60 taels) per picul. The return amounts to 157 percent. The volumes of silk fluctuated but averaged 94,966 *jin* (56,695 kg) using available data from 1663 to 1665 and in 1671. Taking 80 percent of the amount to reflect the Zheng share yields 75,972.8 *jin* (45,355.7 kg). Silk thus netted 304,829.62 pesos in profits annually for the organization.[29]

White sugar can be purchased at 3 pesos per picul in Taiwan and sold at 8 pesos at Nagasaki, a 167 percent rate of return. If processed into rock candy, the revenue would rise even further to 12 pesos, or a 300 percent rate of return. English observers pointed out that the island exported

[28] Chang Hsiu-jung et al., *English factory*, p. 153; Cheng (Zheng), *War, trade and piracy*, p. 235.
[29] 472.50 taels − 183.60 taels = 288.90 taels, which converts to 401.25 pesos. This amount is then multiplied by 75,972.8 *jin*, or 759.7 piculs, to arrive at 304,829.62 pesos.

some 10,000 piculs (597,000 kg) for export per year. Assume that all sugar shipments consist solely of white sugar. The result equals a profit of 50,000 pesos (1,350 kg).[30]

Some 200,000 pieces of deerskin were produced in Taiwan per year. Bucks were valued at 20 pesos, while does went for at 16 pesos, each per hundred skins. In Japan, they sold anywhere from 60 to 70 pesos, yielding a rate of return of 200 percent. Utilizing the higher purchasing price and the lower sale price, annual exports of deerskin come to 80,000 pesos.[31]

For the purposes of this calculation, exclusively silk, sugar, and skins are considered. They are assumed to occupy 80 percent of the cargo on board Zheng junks sailing for Japan, with the rest of the shipment having zero value.[32] A weighted average can then be taken of the yields of raw silk (157 percent), deerskin (200 percent), and sugar (167 percent), based upon their respective contributions to earnings. Out of a total value of 434,829.65, silk made up 70 percent of the sum, while deerskin came in second at 18 percent, and sugar, 11 percent. Their mean rate of return totals 166.2 percent. The result is further weighted to assume an 80 percent contribution. The rate of return on the entire annual Zheng shipment to Nagasaki comes to 131 percent.[33] Table 3.6 provides a calculation of total profits during this decade.

Western Ocean. Revenues from this leg comprise the sum of the values realized by Zheng junks transporting goods from mainland China, Taiwan, and Japan to the Western Ocean, and imports from the Western Ocean to mainland China and Taiwan. Since Japan-bound shipments have already been counted in the exports at Nagasaki, this figure is excluded to avoid overlap. In all, Zheng Jing dispatched twenty trading ships to Western Ocean ports in 1665. The proportion of vessels engaged in the triangular trade is derived from Japanese records, which indicate a total of seventeen junks arriving at Nagasaki that year from the Western Ocean. Assume that 80 percent of them, or fourteen, belonged to Zheng Jing. The remaining six ships thus sailed exclusively between Southeast Asia and mainland China and Taiwan. In other words, 30 percent of junks went on the direct route, while 70 percent opted for the triangular trade.[34]

---

[30] (8 pesos − 3 pesos) × 10,000 piculs.   [31] (60 pesos − 20 pesos) × 2,000 hundred skins.

[32] *The English Factory in Taiwan*, ed. Chang Hsiu-jung et al., 65, 69, 159 and Zhu Delan, "Qing chu Qianjieling shi Zhongguo hanghai shang maoyi zhi yanjiu," in *Zhongguo haiyang fazhan shi lunwenji*, 10 vols. (Taipei: Three People's Principles Research Institute, 1986), vol. II, pp. 147–148.

[33] 70% (157%) + 18% (200%) + 11% (167%) = 164%. 80% of 164% = 131%.

[34] Viraphol, *Tribute and profit*, 45.

Table 3.6 *Zheng Jing's gross profits from the Japan trade, 1663–1672*

Year	Total Zheng revenues from Japan (kan)	Total gross profits (kan)[*]	Total gross profits (kg)[*]
1663	9,015.37	5,112.61	19,172.2
1664	16,726.34	9,485.50	35,570.6
1665	10,225.62	5,798.94	21,746
1666	10,515.60	5,963.39	22,362.7
1667	8,126.61	4,608.60	17,282.2
1668	14,033.45	7,958.36	29,843.8
1669	13,126.79	7,444.20	27,915.7
1670	11,441.72	6,488.60	24,332.2
1671	11,540.81	6,544.79	24,542.9
1672	12,065.74	6,842.47	25,659.2
TOTAL	**116,818.03**	**66,247.45**	**248,427.9**
MEAN	**11,681.80**	**6,624.75**	**24,842.8**

[*] Total Zheng revenues from Japan − Total Zheng revenues from Japan / (1 + 131%).

Table 3.7 calculates the value and profitability of select exports from Japan to the Western Ocean. Copper had a purchase price of 12.40 taels in Japan and was marketed in Southeast Asia at 26 pesos (18.72 taels) for a rate of return of 50 percent. Eighty percent of the total quantity of copper recorded to have shipped onboard Chinese vessels is taken to reflect the Zheng share of the trade at Nagasaki. It is assumed that gold was exchanged in Japan at the most unfavorable rate before 1672, or 5.80 taels of silver per piece. Its sale price came to 8.50 pesos (6.12 taels) in the Western Ocean, or a 5.5 percent yield.[35] Since 70 percent of the twenty Zheng junks sent to Southeast Asia relied upon the triangular trade, it is safe to assume that 56 percent of the gold obtained in Japan (70 percent × 80 percent) went to the Western Ocean.

The estimated value of Chinese exports to the Western Ocean comes from the cargo of a Zheng junk seized by the Dutch off the coast of Java in 1671, a typical trading year. The ship was traveling from Taiwan to Banten, and contained 5,000 pieces of gold, 250 piculs of copper, and 100 *ton* (a Dutch colloquial term for 100,000 guilders) worth of goods.[36] If one assumes a price for gold at 8.50 pesos (6.12 taels) at Banten, and copper at 18.72 taels per picul, the two metals would sell at 35,280 taels of

[35] *The English Factory in Taiwan*, ed. Chang Hsiu-jung et al., 74–75 and Cheng (Zheng), *War, trade and piracy*, p. 235.

[36] van der Chijs, *Batavia dagregisters*, 1670–1671, p. 273. Because of the location of the ship within the Indonesian archipelago, the copper most likely came from China, perhaps the mines of Yunnan. Although the gold originated in Japan, it constitutes the portion retained in Taiwan and is thus not counted among the Japanese exports to the Western Ocean.

Table 3.7 *Revenues and gross profits on exports from Japan to the Western Sea, 1663–1672*

Product/year	Quantity	Zheng share	Purchase (taels)*	Sale (taels)**	Profit (taels)
	(taels)	Quantity × 56%	1 tael of gold = 5.80 taels of silver	1 tael of gold = 6.12 taels of silver	
Gold					
1664	470	263.2	1,526.56	1,610.78	84.22
1666	3,700	2,072	12,017.60	12,680.64	663.04
1667	12,160	6,809.6	39,495.68	41,674.75	2,179.07
1668	120,818	67,658	392,416.86	414,067.45	21,650.59
1669	180,026.1	100,814.6	584,724.77	616,985.45	32,260.68
1670	152,340.1	85,310.4	494,800.64	522,099.99	27,299.35
1671	119,499.2	66,919.5	388,133.40	409,547.66	21,414.26
1672	125	70	406	428.40	22.40
MEAN	**73,642.3**	**41,239.6**	**239,190.19**	**252,386.89**	**13,196.70**
Copper	(picul)	Quantity × 80%	12.40 taels per picul	18.72 taels per picul	
1664	2,838	2,270.4	28,152.96	42,501.89	14,348.93
1665	3,437	2,749.6	34,095.04	51,472.51	17,377.47
1666	5,264	4,211.2	52,218.88	78,833.66	26,614.78
1667	7,482	5,985.6	74,221.44	112,050.43	37,828.99
1672	11,581	9,264.8	114,883.52	173,437.06	58,553.54
MEAN	**6,120.4**	**4,896.3**	**60,714.37**	**91,659.11**	**30,944.74**
TOTAL			**299,904.56**	**344,046**	**44,141.44**
AVERAGE					

* Unit purchase price × quantity.
** Unit sales price × quantity.

silver.[37] The 100,000 guilders convert to 28,571.42 taels at a rate of 3.50 guilders to a tael. The sum of all three equals 63,851.42 taels. All of the twenty junks sent to the Western Ocean, both on the triangular and direct routes, likely carried a similar mix of goods. A multiplication of the value of the seized vessels by twenty yields 1,277,028.57 taels, or 47,888.5 kilograms. Sufficient information is still lacking to determine the profitability of these exports.

An overall picture of import value and profits of Western Ocean goods bound for Taiwan and Mainland China remains elusive, but detailed information is available on unit prices and quantities for select items from one product source: Nakhon Si Thammarat. The records reveal that pepper continued to enjoy a sizable market in China during this period. Costs had fallen to 4.38 pesos (3.15 taels) per picul, while 10 taels remain reasonable as a sale price. The rate of return amounts to 217.4 percent.[38] One new item with growing demand in China was tin, bought for 6.60 taels per picul and sold for 15 taels per picul, a yield of 127.2 percent.[39] Table 3.8 calculates the average annual value and profit of both goods. Note that the figures apply to just Nakhon Si Thammarat. The Zheng organization doubtless had extensive ties with other parts of Southeast Asia. Information on them, however, remains insufficient to serve as a basis for calculating the overall revenue and profitability of imports from the Western Ocean.

Adding together the export and incomplete import values realized in the Western Ocean yields a total of 1,640,574.57 taels, or 61,521.5 kilograms in revenues.[40] Profitability remains even patchier. It certainly exceeds the 55,623.94 taels generated with the available data.[41]

Manila. Fang Zhenzhen has calculated the total number of ships and value of exports from Zheng-held Taiwan to Manila over the decade based upon a meticulous scrutiny of the Spanish customs records. Cheng Wei-chung has converted the currency into taels. Table 3.9 is based upon his modified version. Moreover, the ship numbers are juxtaposed with Chaunu's figures for total Chinese junks visiting Manila during this period.

---

[37] 6.12 taels × 5,000 pieces of gold + 18.72 taels × 250 piculs of copper = 35,280 taels.

[38] Bulbeck et al., *Southeast Asian exports*, p. 84.

[39] Quantities of gold derived from yearly shipments out of Japan in Hayashi Akira, *Tsūkō ichiran*, vol. IV, pp. 325–327. Copper comes from table 6 in Zhu Delan, "Qing chu Qianjieling," p. 150. For pepper and tin, see table 14.11 in Cheng (Zheng), *War, trade and piracy*, p. 235.

[40] Value of exports from Japan to the Western Sea (344,046 taels) + value of exports from mainland China and Taiwan to the Western Sea (1,277,028.57 taels) + value of imports from Western Sea to mainland China and Taiwan (19,500 taels) = 1,640,574.57 taels.

[41] Gross profits on exports from Japan to the Western Sea (44,141.44 taels) + value of imports from Western Sea to mainland China and Taiwan (11,482.5 taels) = 55,623.94 taels.

Table 3.8 *Revenues and gross profits on select imports from Nakhon Si Thammarat, 1663–1672*

Product/year	Quantity (piculs)	Purchase (taels)*	Sale (taels)**	Profit (taels)
Pepper		3.15 taels per picul	10 taels per picul	
1668	450	1,417.50	4,500	3,082.50
1669	450	1,417.50	4,500	3,082.50
MEAN	**450**	**1,417.50**	**4,500**	**3,082.50**
Tin		**6.6 taels per picul**	**15 taels per picul**	
1668	900	5,940	13,500	7,560
1669	1,500	9,900	22,500	12,600
1672	600	3,960	9,000	5,040
MEAN	**1,000**	**6,600**	**15,000**	**8,400**
TOTAL AVERAGE		**8,017.50**	**19,500**	**11,482.5**

* Unit purchase price × quantity.
** Unit sales price × quantity.

Table 3.9 *Value of Taiwanese exports to Manila, 1663–1672*[42]

Year	Junks from Taiwan	Chinese junks*	Taiwanese exports to Manila
1663		2	
1664	1	6	
1665	5	15	>9,035.50
1666	2	5	>2,626.20
1667	2	3	>3,634.50
1668	4	4	>16,166.50
1669	3	5	
1670	8	8	>28,411.50
1671	1	1	>3,197.40
1672	4	6	>8,644.40
TOTAL	**30**	**55**	**>71,716**
MEAN	**3.3**	**5.5**	**>10,245.14**

* Counts only ships from mainland China, Taiwan, Macao, and Japan.

These data almost certainly underestimate the actual scale of trade with Manila. Besides the rampant evasion, they do not count the sale of products from the Philippines and New World in Taiwan and mainland China, or the

[42] Based upon table 5.23 in Fang Zhenzhen, *Taiwan Manila maoyi*, p. 200; table 14.9 in Cheng (Zheng), *War, trade and piracy*, p. 229; Series 13, tables 5 and 6 in Pierre Chaunu, *Philippines et Pacifique*, pp. 165, 168.

value realized by Zheng ships from outside Taiwan. Still, the data provide intriguing information regarding the types of goods exported to Manila. The quantities and values of cloth, one of the most prominent items marketed at the port, and the fluctuating contributions of its three largest providers – Anhai, India, and Japan – over the decade are shown in Table 3.10.

Totals. Table 3.11 lists the total average revenue and profit of the Zheng organization between 1663 and 1672. Similar to the previous decade, they are juxtaposed to the corresponding figures from the Dutch East India Company. Note that documentation for the organization's profits remains grossly incomplete for the Western Ocean and cannot serve as a meaningful basis for comparison. Moreover, the earnings from Taiwan are only counted in the "Profits" columns to match with the Asian trade and colonial income of the VOC.

4.   1673–1683

Japan. In 1677, all but two of the twenty-nine junks that sailed to Nagasaki, or 90 percent, belonged to the Zheng organization.[43] There is good reason to believe that this proportion held steady throughout the decade. It is true that the Zheng faced competition from private merchants in Southeast Asia. Nonetheless, the organization's return to mainland China in 1674 realized a reunion with the part of the family that had earlier defected to the Qing, among them many with seasoned experience in dealing with Japan. Zheng agents also secretly colluded with the local authorities of Nagasaki, who allowed them to sell at a greater profit than mandated by law.

Table 4.1 displays the number of Chinese junks at Nagasaki, their export values, and the estimated Zheng share during this decade as juxtaposed to the VOC.

As in the previous decade, gold and copper brought out of Japan fetched little value in mainland China and Taiwan. On the other hand, the sale of war materiel likely picked up because of renewed warfare along the southeastern Chinese coast, but the scale of these imports remains unknown. Hence, only the Zheng share of export value to Nagasaki is calculated in the revenues.

Gross profits from the Japan trade are derived from estimates of the rates of return on silk, sugar, and deerskin, and their combined proportion of total cargo value. Available data in 1674 and 1676 and between 1680 and 1683 reveal that, on average, 955,188 *jin* (570,247.2 kg) of silk went to Nagasaki. A Zheng contribution of 90 percent comes to 859,669.2 *jin* (513,222.5 kg). The cost of silk remained at 255 pesos per picul in Taiwan. Due to restrictive government policies and an increased supply

---

[43] von Glahn, *Fountain of fortune*, p. 226.

Table 3.10 *Origins, quantity, and proportion of cloth exports to Manila, 1663–1672*[44]

Year	Anhai quantity (boxes)*	India quantity*	Japan quantity*	Total quantity	Anhai value (pesos)**	India value**	Japan value**	Total value
1665	140 (20.1)	60 (8.6)	265 (38.1)	695	1,070 (11.1)	210 (2.2)	6,805 (70.5)	9,660
1666	80 (21.3)	0 (0)	175 (46.7)	375	180 (16)	0 (0)	618.8 (54.8)	1,128.8
1667	0 (0)	0 (0)	73 (78.5)	93	0 (0)	0 (0)	2,150 (81.1)	2,650
1668	240 (50.5)	60 (12.6)	97 (20.4)	475	6,005 (37.2)	360 (2.2)	2,988.8 (18.5)	16,166.3
1670	1,050 (27.7)	1,840 (48.6)	530 (14)	3,790	7,135 (26.6)	12,895 (48)	4,230 (15.8)	26,847.5
1671	130 (24.1)	280 (51.9)	130 (24.1)	540	652.5 (19.9)	1,860 (56.8)	495 (15.1)	3,277.5
1672	340 (18.8)	560 (30.9)	230 (12.7)	1,810	1,585 (22)	2,430 (33.7)	1,130 (15.7)	7,215
TOTAL	1,980	2,800	1,500	7,778	16,627.5	17,755	18,417.60	66,945.10
MEAN	282.9	400	214.3	1,111.1	2,375.4	2,536.40	2,361.10	9,563.60

* Proportion of total quantity in % in parentheses.
** Proportion of total value in % in parentheses.

[44] Based upon the sums of quantities and prices in tables 5.4–5.7 of Fang Zhenzhen, *Taiwan Manila maoyi*, pp. 183–191, and then converted into Spanish pesos. Note that figures are missing entirely for 1669.

Table 3.11 *Mean annual revenues and gross trading profits of Zheng Jing vs. VOC, 1663–1672*

	Revenues (currency)	Revenues (kg)	Revenues (USD)[***]	Profits (currency)	Profits (kg)	Profits (USD)
Zheng Jing	>2,818,999 taels[*]	>105,712.4	>63,427,477	>825,645 taels[+]	>30,961.7	>18,577,026
VOC[**]	ƒ9,249,114	104,786	62,871,621	ƒ6,112,964	69,465.5	41,679,298
VOC (Asia)				ƒ5,692,238	64,684.5	38,810,710

[*] 1,640,574.57 taels from Western Sea + 10,245.14 from Manila + (11,681.80 *kan* × 100) from Japan.

[**] Until 1665, guilders converted to taels at 1 tael to 2.85 guilders. After that year, the Dutch currency depreciated to 1 tael to 3.50 guilders. This means that for three out of ten years, the first rate held, while in the remaining seven, the second rate was used. Taking a weighted average of 30% × (2.85) + 70% × (3.5) = 3.31 guilders to 1 tael. This rate is then multiplied by 37.5 g. For details on the specific calculations for the VOC, see de Korte, *Jaarlijkse financiële verantwoording*, pp. 31, 60–61, *Bijlage* 9A-9B, *Bijlage* 13A.

[***] US$600/kg on September 15, 2014. See http://silverprice.org for real-time updates.

[+] 55,623.94 taels from Western Sea + 107,546.70 taels from Taiwan + (6,624.75 *kan* × 100) from Japan.

Table 4.1 *Scale of Chinese trade at Nagasaki and the Zheng share vs. the VOC, 1673–1683*[45]

Year	Chinese junks	Chinese exports[*]	Zheng exports[**]	VOC ships	VOC exports[***]
1673	17	1,152,198.30	1,036,978	6	890,346.70
1674	21	1,827,031.40	1,644,328	6	774,983.40
1675	31	1,670,687	1,503,618	4	547,401.40
1676	26	739,988	665,989	4	483,739.60
1677	29	959,988.20	863,989	3	553,575.80
1678	27	1,277,997.70	1,150,198	4	466,821.10
1679	36	956,820.90	861,139	4	549,352.50
1680	29	1,142,857	1,028,571	4	686,2710
1681	9	147,756	132,980	4	819,557.10
1682	26	952,940	857,646	3	481,529.70
1683	27	486,929.10	438,236	5	830,662.20
TOTAL	**278**	**11,315,193.60**	**10,183,672**	**47**	**7,084,240.50**
MEAN	**25.2**	**1,028,653.90**	**925,788.40**	**4.3**	**644,021.90**

[*] All values in taels of silver.

[**] Chinese exports × 90% Zheng share.

[***] Converted from gold at a rate of one tael = 6.80 taels of silver.

[45] Based upon the data presented in table 14.13 in Cheng (Zheng), *War, trade and piracy*, p. 241 and Hayashi Akira, *Tsūkō ichiran*, vol. IV, pp. 336–337.

Table 4.2 *Zheng organization's gross profits from the Japan trade, 1673–1683*

Year	Zheng revenues at Japan (taels)	Zheng revenues at Japan (kg)	Total gross profits (taels)	Total gross profits (kg)*
1673	1,036,978	38,886.6	326,742.45	12,252.84
1674	1,644,328	61,662.3	518,112.97	19,429.24
1675	1,503,618	56,385.6	473,776.52	17,766.62
1676	665,989	24,974.5	209,847.15	7,869.27
1677	863,989	32,399.5	272,235.17	10,208.82
1678	1,150,198	43,132.4	362,417.05	13,590.64
1679	861,139	32,292.7	271,337.16	10,175.14
1680	1,028,571	38,571.4	324,093.48	12,153.51
1681	132,980	4,986.7	41,900.80	1,571.28
1682	857,646	32,161.7	270,236.54	10,133.87
1683	438,236	16,433.8	138,084.22	5,178.16
TOTAL	**10,183,672**	**381,887.7**	**3,208,783.50**	**120,329.38**
MEAN	**925,788.40**	**34,717**	**291,707.59**	**10,939.03**

* Total Zheng revenues – (Total Zheng revenues / 1 + 45.8%).

of the luxury, however, its Nagasaki price fell to 307 pesos in 1675, achieving a rate of return of 20.4 percent, or earnings of 447,027.98 pesos.[46] While silk now came out of Xiamen and other ports on the mainland coast, Taiwan exclusively exported sugar and deerskin. Production of both held steady, with yields of 167 percent, or a profit of 50,000 pesos, and 200 percent, or 80,000 pesos, respectively.[47] Suppose that a junk sets out from Xiamen, makes a stop in Taiwan, and then sails for Nagasaki. Out of a total cargo worth 577,027.98 pesos, silk contributes 78 percent, while deerskin constitutes 14 percent, and sugar, 8 percent. Assuming that the goods in these proportions make up 80 percent of the total value of the ship, with the remainder contributing nothing to profits, the rate of return in Japan is estimated at 45.8 percent.[48] Table 4.2 displays the results.

Western Ocean. A mean of 12.1 Chinese junks from Southeast Asian ports visited Nagasaki each year from 1673 to 1683.[49] Assuming 90 percent of them belonged to the Zheng, the number of ships would be 10.8. Japanese records also note the arrival of thirteen ships from Western Sea ports at Zheng-held Xiamen in 1675.[50] Thus, one can use twenty-three ships (10.8 + 13) as a ballpark figure for the total number of Zheng

[46] (307 pesos – 255 pesos) × 859,662.2 *jin* or 8,596.6 piculs = 447,024.34 pesos.
[47] Chang Hsiu-jung et al., *English factory*, p. 218; table 3 in Zhu Delan, "Qing chu Qianjieling," p. 146.
[48] 78% (20.4%) + 14% (200%) + 8% (167%) = 57.2%. 80% of the result yields 45.8%.
[49] Table 2 in Cai Yuping, "Dui Ri maoyi," p. 51.
[50] Hayashi Shunsai, *Ka'i hentai*, vol. I, pp. 192–193.

Table 4.3 *Revenues and profits on copper exports from Japan to the Western Sea, 1673–1683*

Year	Quantity (piculs)	Zheng share*	Purchase (taels)**	Sale (taels)***	Profit (taels)
1673	10,966.5	9,870	122,386.14	177,657.30	55,271.16
1674	10,326	9,293	115,238.16	167,281.20	52,043.04
1675	19,354	17,419	215,990.64	313,534.80	97,544.16
1676	10,442	9,398	116,532.72	169,160.40	52,627.68
1677	12,000	10,800	133,920.00	194,400	60,480
1678	18,000	16,200	200,880.00	291,600	90,720
1679	18,477.7	16,630	206,211.13	299,338.74	93,127.61
1682	32,839.2	29,555	366,485.47	531,995.04	165,509.57
1683	28,253.5	25,428	315,309.06	457,706.70	142,397.64
MEAN	**17,850.9**	**16,066**	**199,217.04**	**289,186.02**	**89,968.98**

* Quantity × 90%
** 12.40 taels × Zheng share.
*** Banten price of 25 pesos (18 taels) × Zheng share.

ships operating in the Western Ocean in a given year. It remains unclear which participated in the triangular trade and which took the direct route.

A similarly imperfect picture of revenues and profitability emerges by tracing the flow of goods from Japan to the Western Ocean and then to China. Table 4.3 calculates the value and profits realized by the sale of Japanese copper in Southeast Asia.[51] The purchase price of 12.40 remained the same in Japan, while the Banten price fell by one peso to 25 pesos (18 taels). The Zheng organization's share is derived by taking 90 percent of the recorded quantity. Gold, the other mainline export, was no longer profitable. In 1672, the *bakufu* mandated that one piece must exchange for 6.80 taels of silver.[52]

Numerical estimates of Western Ocean imports into China are derived from a fascinating Qing memorial that contains fragments of an inventory of the goods on board one of Liu Guoxuan's vessels. The *Dongbenniao* junk followed a triangular route, setting sail from Xiamen in July 1683 for Japan. After several months at Nagasaki, it left again for the port of Ayutthaya, where it arrived in January 1684. There, the junk sold its cargo for 8,312.78 taels, aside from 175 piculs of copper, worth 3,150 taels at the Banten rate of 18 taels per picul. Thus, the total initial value of the ship amounted to 11,462.78 taels. This amount is then used to buy local products. Table 4.4 displays the goods procured by the *Dongbenniao*

---

[51] Chang Hsiu-jung et al., *English factory*, p. 257; table 6 in Zhu Delan, "Qing chu Qianjieling," p. 150.
[52] Suzuki, *Japan-Netherlands trade*, p. 110.

Table 4.4 *Inventory of the Zheng junk* Dongbenniao, *1684*[53]

Product	Quantity	Purchase unit price	Cost of purchase (taels)	Projected sale unit price	Projected value (taels)	Rate of return (in %)
Lead	264.8 piculs	10 ticals[54]	1,161.48	8.50 pesos[55]	1,620.58	39.5
Sapanwood	1,450 piculs	0.60 taels	870	>2 taels[56]	>2,900	233.3
Tin	495 piculs	6.60 taels	3,267	15 taels[57]	7,425	127.2
Superior gum benzoin[58]	4.5 piculs	8 pounds sterling[59]	123.12	12 pounds sterling	184.68	50
Inferior gum benzoin	400 catties	7 pounds sterling	95.76	10.50 pounds sterling	143.64	50
Pepper	13 piculs	3.85 pesos[60]	36	9 pesos[61]	84.24	133.8
Nutmeg	50 catties					
2 Elephant teeth	>1 picul	16 taels	>16	25 pesos	>18	12.5
3 Elephant teeth	3.96 piculs	14 taels	55.44	25 pesos	71.28	28.5
7 Elephant teeth	1.72 piculs	6 taels[62]	10.32	25 pesos[63]	30.96	200
2 Full bird's nests	188 catties					
3 Half bird's nests	153 catties					
2 Black bird's nests	126 catties					
Colored coarse Western cloth	80 pieces			2.50 pesos	144	

53 *Shiliao sanbian*, pp. 218–219.
54 John Anderson, *English intercourse with Siam in the seventeenth century* (London: K. Paul, Trench, Trübner, and Co., Ltd., 1890), p. 423. One tael equals approximately 2.28 ticals.
55 Chang Hsiu-jung et al., *English factory*, p. 221.
56 John Anderson, *English intercourse*, p. 423. Sapanwood normally sold in Siam at 0.60 taels. When prices in China rose in 1677, however, the king's merchant decided to increase the price to two taels. Therefore, the consumer price in China in normal years probably came to at least this amount.
57 Cheng (Zheng), *War, trade and piracy*, p. 235.
58 Chang Hsiu-jung et al., *English factory*, p. 488.
59 One pound sterling equals 4.75 pesos, or 3.42 taels.
60 Bulbeck et al., *Southeast Asian exports*, p. 84.
61 Chang Hsiu-jung et al., *English factory*, p. 221.
62 All unit purchase prices for elephant teeth come from John Anderson, *English intercourse*, p. 423.
63 All projected unit sales prices for elephant teeth come from Chang Hsiu-jung et al., *English factory*, p. 67.

Table 4.4 (cont.)

Product	Quantity	Purchase unit price	Cost of purchase (taels)	Projected sale unit price	Projected value (taels)	Rate of return (in %)
White coarse Western cloth	76 pieces			5.50 pesos[64]	300.96	
Corn	25 piculs					
Shrimp	15 piculs					
Acronychia pedunculata	10 piculs					
Sandalwood	15 piculs			14 pesos[65]	151.20	
Woolens	4 pieces			17 taels[66]	68	
Green dye	2 pieces			20 taels	40	
Wooden red dye	2 pieces			20 taels[67]	40	
Pahang Rattan	12 piculs			5 pesos[68]	43.20	
Peacock tails	17 tails					
TOTAL			>5,635.08		>13,265.74	

[64] Prices for cloths found in Chang Hsiu-jung et al., *English factory*, p. 157. The lowest prices are used as the basis for calculation.
[65] Chang Hsiu-jung et al., *English factory*, p. 158. [66] Ibid., p. 565.
[67] Prices for dyes found in Ibid., p. 519. [68] Ibid., p. 68.

in Siam, and, where available, the local purchase price and potential value in the Chinese home market.

The revenue of 13,265.74 taels earned by the *Dongbenniao* almost certainly represents an underestimation, since its activities took place amid the destruction of the Zheng organization and thus more accurately depict the situation in the early 1680s. Nonetheless, assuming that its cargo was typical of the other twenty-two ships, on average, that operated in Southeast Asia in a given year, total imports into China from the Western Ocean would amount to at least 305,112.02 taels, or 11,441.7 kilograms of silver. To calculate profits, a cost of purchase of 8,312.78 taels is used. This figure is the original amount of silver realized through the sale of products from Japan, and all of it is assumed to have been spent on buying goods from Ayutthaya. Taking the difference of the projected value and cost of purchase over twenty-three ships yields a profit of more than 113,918.06 taels, or 4,271.9 kilograms, for a 59.6 percent rate of return.[69]

From the calculations provided above, one can determine that the total mean revenue for the Western Ocean trade comes to at least 594,298.02

Table 4.5 *Value of Taiwanese exports to Manila, 1673–1683*[70]

Year	Junks from Taiwan	Chinese junks[*]	Taiwanese exports to Manila[**]
1673	4	6	>11,417.20
1674	3		>5,477.70
1675	1	3	>2,159.80
1676	2	9	>3,241.80
1677	1	10	5,067
1678	1	4	1,101.60
1679	1	6	
1680	1	5	
1681	4	3	
1682	2		
1683	2	6	
TOTAL	**22**	**52**	**>28,465.10**
MEAN	**2**	**5.7**	**>4,744.10**

* Counts only mainland China, Taiwan, Macao, and Japan.
** Converted to taels.

[69] Profits are determined through the following calculation: 305,112 taels − 8,312.78 taels × 23 ships = 113,918.06 taels. For rate of return: [113,918.06 taels / (8,312.78 taels × 23 ships)] − 1.

[70] Based upon tables 4.1 and 5.23 in Fang Zhenzhen, *Taiwan Manila maoyi*, pp. 111, 200 and Series 13, table 6 in Pierre Chaunu, *Philippines et Pacifique*, p. 168.

Table 4.6 *Mean annual revenues and gross trading profits of the Zheng vs. VOC, 1673–1683*

	Revenues (currency)	Revenues (kg)	Revenues (USD)***	Profits (currency)	Profits (kg)	Profits (USD)
Zheng organization	>1,524,830 taels*	>57,181.1	>34,308,686	>603,141 taels+	>22,617.7	>13,570,679
VOC**	ƒ8,369,030	89,668.2	53,800,907	ƒ6,815,650	73,024.8	43,814,893
VOC (Asia)				ƒ5,686,641	60,928.3	36,556,978

* 594,298.02 taels from Western Sea + 4,744.10 from Manila + 925,788.40 taels from Japan.

** Converted to taels at 1 tael to 3.5 guilders. For details on the specific calculations for the VOC, see J. P. de Korte, *Jaarlijkse financiële verantwoording*, pp. 31, 60–61, *Bijlage* 9A–9B, *Bijlage* 13A.

*** US$600/kg on September 15, 2014. See http://silverprice.org for real-time updates.

+ 203,887.04 taels from Western Sea + 107,546.70 taels from Taiwan in Table 3.2 + 291,707.59 taels from Japan.

Table 5.1 *Lifetime mean annual revenues and gross trading profits of the Zheng vs. VOC*[71]

1650–1683	Revenues (currency)	Revenues (kg)	Revenues (USD)[***]	Profits (currency)	Profits (kg)	Profits (USD)
Zheng organization[*]	>2,880,665 taels	>118,535.4	>71,121,240	>1,152,990 taels[+]	>43,237.1	>25,942,294
VOC	ƒ8,695,874[**]	102,828.7	61,697,199	ƒ6,302,830[++]	74,317.7	44,590,620
VOC (Asia)				ƒ5,087,030[+++]	59,434.9	35,660,940

[*] (13/34) × 4,075,346 taels + (10/34) × 2,818,999 taels + (11/34) × 1,524,830 taels.

[**] Currency amount: (13/34) × ƒ8,546,867 + (10/34) × ƒ9,249,114 + (11/34) × ƒ8,369,030 kg amount: (13/34) × 112,458.8 + (10/34) × 104,786 + (11/34) × 89,668.2.

[***] US$600/kg on September 15, 2014. See http://silverprice.org for real-time updates.

[+] (13/34) × 1,870,053 taels + (10/34) × 825,645 taels + (11/34) × 603,141 taels.

[++] Currency amount: (13/34) × ƒ6,014,955 + (10/34) × ƒ6,112,964 + (11/34) × ƒ6,815,650 kg amount: (13/34) × 79,144.1 + (10/34) × 69,465.5 + (11/34) × 73,024.8.

[+++] Currency amount: (13/34) × ƒ4,114,123 + (10/34) × ƒ5,692,238 + (11/34) × ƒ5,686,641 kg amount: (13/34) x 54,133.2 + (10/34) x 64,684.5 + (11/34) x 60,928.3.

[71] Obtained by taking the weighted average of the three periods of 1650–1662 (Table 2.6), 1663–1672 (Table 3.11), and 1673–1683 (Table 4.6) based upon a total of thirty-four years.

taels, or 22,286.1 kilograms worth of silver.[72] Profits stood at a minimum of 203,887.04 taels, or 7,645.7 kilograms.[73]

Manila. Table 4.5 lists the total estimated number of Chinese junks visiting Manila, Taiwan's share of the shipping, and the value of Taiwanese exports to the port during the decade based upon the official Spanish customs data.

Totals. Table 4.6 lists a very rough estimate of the average yearly revenue and profit of the Zheng organization in its final decade. Because of the lack of data, crucial gaps exist in the calculations, especially for the value and profitability of Chinese exports to the Western Ocean, undoubtedly a sizable sum. Therefore, the results cannot serve as reliable indicators of the organization's scale. Nonetheless, similar to before, the numbers for the Dutch East India Company are also listed as a broad framework of reference.

5.   Lifetime revenues and profits, 1650–1683

Table 5.1 lists the total mean annual revenue and profit achieved over the lifetime of the Zheng organization, or 1650 to 1683, when the availability of data allow for a comprehensive estimate, albeit with many missing gaps and imperfect extrapolations. They are compared to the figures for the VOC during the same period.

---

[72] Value of exports from Japan to the Western Sea (289,186.02 taels) + value of imports from Western Sea to mainland China and Taiwan (305,112.02 taels) = 594,298.02 taels.

[73] Gross profits on exports from Japan to the Western Sea (89,968.98 taels) + value of imports from Western Sea to mainland China and Taiwan (113,918.06 taels) = 203,887.04 taels.

Appendix 4 Glossary of Chinese characters

aitai shōbai	–	相對商賣
Anhai	–	安海
Anping	–	安平
Arima Harunobu	–	有馬晴信
ashigaru	–	足輕
Bamin wang	–	八閩王
bakufu	–	幕府
baoshui	–	報水
Bendai	–	貴岱
Bian Yongyu	–	卞永譽
Binge	–	斌哥
bu Qing bu Ming	–	不清不明
bushidō	–	武士道
Cai Yin	–	蔡寅
Cai Yurong	–	蔡毓榮
Cai Zheng	–	蔡政
Chayan si	–	察言司
Chang Shouning	–	常壽寧
Changting	–	長汀
Chao	–	潮
Chaonan	–	潮南
Chaozhou	–	潮州
Cheju	–	濟州
Chen De	–	陳德
Chen Jin	–	陳錦
Chen Shangchuan	–	陳上川
Chen Yonghua	–	陳永華
Chen Zhenguan	–	陳軫官
Chengtian	–	承天
Chikamatsu Monzaemon	–	近松門左衛門
Chikan	–	赤嵌
Chixian Shenzhou	–	赤縣神州
Chongming	–	崇明

Chosŏn	–	朝鮮
Chongzhen	–	崇禎
Chongwu	–	崇武
Chou hongrou	–	臭紅肉
Dahao	–	達豪
Da Ming zhongxing	–	大明中興
Dasu	–	達素
daikan	–	代官
dan	–	擔
Dan	–	疍
Danshui	–	淡水
Deshima	–	出島
Dong, Madame		
(Dong *furen*)	–	董夫人
Dongbenniao	–	東本鳥
Dongboshe	–	東波社
Dongdu Mingjing	–	東都明京
dongfan	–	東番
Dongguan	–	東莞
Dongli	–	東里
Dongning	–	東寧
Dongning zongzhi	–	東寧總制
Dong Sanguan	–	董三官
Dong Shen	–	董申
Dongting, Lake	–	洞庭
Dorgon	–	多爾袞
fan	–	藩
fang	–	坊
Fangdu, Huang	–	黃芳度
feng lai zhu you sheng	–	風來竹有聲
Fengting	–	楓亭
Feng Xifan	–	馮錫範
fu	–	府
fuguo	–	富國
Fu Weilin	–	傅為霖
Fujian	–	福建
Fu Tai	–	復臺
fu zongbing	–	副總兵
Fuzhou	–	福州
Fukumatsu	–	福松
Geng Jimao	–	耿繼茂
Geng Jingzhong	–	耿精忠

Giohoto	–	覺霍拓
Giyešu	–	傑書
"Gongchen Taiwan qiliu shu"	–	恭陳臺灣棄留疏
Gong Chun	–	龔淳
Gongsi	–	公司
gongsuo	–	公所
Gou Jian	–	勾踐
Gulang Island (Gulang *yu*)	–	鼓浪嶼
Guazhou	–	瓜洲
guanshang	–	官商
guantian	–	官田
guang difang	–	廣地方
Guangdong	–	廣東
Guangxi	–	廣西
Guangzhou	–	廣州
Guizhou	–	貴州
Guo Huaiyi	–	郭懷一
Guoxingye	–	國姓爺
gyobutsu	–	御物
Hà Tiên	–	河仙
Haicheng	–	海澄
Hải Dương	–	海陽
haijin	–	海禁
Hainan	–	海南
Haitan	–	海壇
Hai wushang	–	海五商
Hamada Yahyōe	–	濱田彌兵衛
Han	–	韓
hang	–	行
Hangzhou	–	杭州
hatamoto	–	旗本
Hayashi Akira	–	林輝
Hayashi Shunsai	–	林春齋
Hekou	–	河口
He Tingbin	–	何廷斌
Hirado	–	平戶
Hội An	–	會安
Hong Chengchou	–	洪承疇
Hongguang	–	弘光
Hongkui, Zheng	–	鄭鴻逵

Hong Lei	–	洪磊
Hongmao yi	–	紅毛夷
Hongwu	–	洪武
Hong Xu	–	洪旭
Huguang	–	湖廣
Huang	–	黃
Huangbo	–	黃檗
Huangchao	–	皇朝
Huang Chaoyong	–	黃朝用
Huang Cheng	–	黃程
Huang Wu	–	黃梧
Huang Xiongguan	–	黃熊官
Huang Yi	–	黃翼
Huang Yong	–	黃鏞
Huang Zhimei	–	黃志美
Huizhou	–	惠州
Ietsuna, Tokugawa	–	德川家綱
Ieyasu, Tokugawa	–	德川家康
Ingen	–	隱元
itowappu	–	絲割符
Jidu	–	濟度
Jilong	–	雞籠
Ji Quan	–	季佺
Jizi	–	箕子
jia	–	甲
Jiayi	–	嘉義
Jiang Sheng	–	江勝
Jiangxi	–	江西
jin	–	斤
Jin Ji	–	金基
Jinjiang	–	晉江
Jinmen	–	金門
juan	–	卷
kaikin	–	海禁
kan	–	貫
Kang, Prince	–	康親王
Kangxi	–	康熙
Kaohsiung (Gaoxiong)	–	高雄
Ke	–	柯
Ke Gui	–	柯貴
Ke Ping	–	柯平
koban	–	小判

Kōfukuji	–	興福寺
Kong Yuanzhang	–	孔元章
Koryŏ	–	高麗
Kuan, Zheng	–	鄭寬
Kunming	–	昆明
Lahada	–	喇哈達
Laita	–	賚塔
Lanfang	–	蘭芳
Lào Cai	–	老街
Lê	–	黎
leshu	–	樂輸
Leizhou	–	雷州
li	–	里
Li Dan	–	李旦
Li Dingguo	–	李定國
Li Feng	–	李鳳
Li Guozhu	–	李國助
Li Maochun	–	李茂春
Limin ku	–	利民庫
Li Zicheng	–	李自成
liang	–	兩
Liaodong	–	遼東
Lin Daoqian	–	林道乾
Lin Feng	–	林鳳
Lin Huanguan	–	林環官
Lin Jinwu	–	林金武
Lin Xingke	–	林行可
Lin Yinguan	–	林寅官
Liubu	–	六部
Liu Ergong	–	劉爾貢
Liuguan	–	六官
Liu Guoxuan	–	劉國軒
Liu Xiang	–	劉香
Liu Yingling	–	劉應麟
Loto	–	羅託
Longmen	–	龍門
Longwu	–	隆武
Longyan	–	龍岩
lu	–	虜
Lu	–	魯
Lu, Prince of (Lu *wang*)	–	魯王
Lu'ermen	–	鹿耳門

Ma Degong	–	馬得功
Ma Fengzhi	–	馬逢知
Ma Xin	–	馬信
Ma Xing	–	馬星
Mazu	–	媽祖
Mạc Thiên Tứ	–	鄭天賜
Matsuura	–	松浦
Min River (Min *jiang*)	–	閩江
Minbei	–	閩北
Mindong	–	閩東
Minnan	–	閩南
minzu yingxiong	–	民族英雄
Mingju	–	明珠
Mito	–	水戶
Mo Jiu	–	鄭玖
Motohakatachō	–	本博多町
mu	–	畝
mufu	–	幕府
Mu Tianyan	–	穆天顏
Murayama Tōan	–	村山東庵
Nan'an	–	南安
Nan'ao	–	南澳
Nguyễn	–	阮
Nguyễn Phúc Tần	–	阮福瀕
Ningbo	–	寧波
Ningjing, Prince of (Ningjing *wang*)	–	寧靖王
Ningxia	–	寧夏
Ningyang	–	寧洋
Nurhaci	–	努爾哈赤
Ōbaku	–	黃檗
Oboi	–	鼇拜
paixiang	–	牌餉
Pan Mingyan	–	潘明巖
Penghu	–	澎湖
Putian	–	莆田
Putuoshan	–	普陀山
Qi	–	齊
Qi Jiguang	–	戚繼光
qimin	–	棄民
Qian Qianyi	–	錢謙益
Qian Zuanzeng	–	錢纘曾

qiangbing	–	強兵
Qing ren	–	清人
Qiu Hui	–	邱輝
Qiuran	–	虬髯
quliang	–	取糧
ququ Taiwan	–	區區臺灣
Quanzhou	–	泉州
Quảng Nam	–	廣南
rōjū	–	老中
rōnin	–	浪人
sadae	–	事大
Sakai	–	堺
Sansheng wang	–	三省王
Satsuma	–	薩摩
seii taishōgun	–	征夷大將軍
Sen, Zheng	–	鄭森
seppuku	–	切腹
Shacheng	–	沙埕
Shalu	–	沙轆
Shandong	–	山東
Shantou	–	汕頭
Shan wushang	–	山五商
Shang Kexi	–	尚可喜
Shaowu	–	邵武
she	–	社
Shen Guangwen	–	沈光文
Shengzu, Qing	–	清聖祖
shi	–	石
Shibiao, Zheng	–	鄭士表
Shichizaemon	–	七左衛門
Shifan	–	世藩
Shi Hai	–	施亥
shihō shōhō	–	市法商法
Shijing	–	石井
Shi Lang	–	施琅
Shimabara	–	島原
Shimazu	–	島津
shiwei	–	侍衛
Shizi	–	世子
Shizu, Qing	–	清世祖
Shizuoka	–	靜岡
Shu	–	蜀

shuin	–	朱印
Shuangyu	–	雙嶼
Shuitou	–	水頭
Shun	–	舜
Shunzhi	–	順治
Sichuan	–	四川
Sima Cuo	–	司馬錯
Siming	–	思明
sitian	–	私田
Sizong, Ming	–	明思宗
South Taiwu Mountains (Nan Taiwu shan)	–	南太武山
Su Cheng	–	蘇呈
Su Kuang	–	蘇鑛
Suksaha	–	蘇克薩哈
Suzhou	–	蘇州
Suetsugu Heizō Masanao	–	末次平蔵正直
Suetsugu Heizō Shigetomo	–	末次平蔵茂朝
Sun Kewang	–	孫可望
Sunpu	–	駿府
Sunzi	–	孫子
Suoetu	–	索額圖
Tagawa Matsu	–	田川マツ
Tainan	–	台南
taishi	–	太師
Taiwan xingle tu	–	臺灣行樂圖
Taizhou	–	台州
Taizhong	–	台中
Tang, Lady (Tang *shi*)	–	唐氏
tian	–	田
Tian Heng	–	田橫
Tianhuang	–	天潢
Tianjin	–	天津
Tianxing	–	天興
tianyun	–	天運
tieren	–	鐵人
Tingzhou	–	汀州
Tōjin yashiki	–	唐人屋敷
Tō tsūji kaisho	–	唐通事會所
Tongan	–	同安
toshiyori	–	年寄
Toyotomi Hideyoshi	–	豐臣秀吉

Trịnh	–	鄭
Trịnh Tráng	–	鄭柲
Ŭiju	–	義州
waiguo	–	外國
Wannian	–	萬年
Wan Zhengse	–	萬正色
Wang Yunsheng	–	汪雲升
Wang Zhongxiao	–	王忠孝
wei	–	偽
Wei Geng	–	魏耕
wei-suo	–	衛所
Wei Zhongxian	–	魏忠賢
Wei Yuan	–	魏源
Wen, King (Wen wang)	–	文王
Wenzhou	–	溫州
wokou	–	倭寇
Wu	–	吳
Wu, King (Wu wang)	–	武王
Wu Gonghong	–	吳公鴻
Wu Hao	–	吳豪
Wulong River (Wulong *jiang*)	–	烏龍江
Wu Sangui	–	吳三桂
Wu Shifan	–	吳世璠
Wu Xingzuo	–	吳興祚
Xi, Zheng	–	鄭襲
Xiamen	–	廈門
xian	–	縣
Xianwang	–	先王
Xiangshan	–	香山
Xiangyu, Zheng	–	鄭翔宇
Xinzhu	–	新竹
Xinghua	–	興化
xingshan	–	腥膻
Xiong Wencan	–	熊文燦
Xiulaiguan	–	修來館
Xu Fuyuan	–	徐孚遠
Xu Xinsu	–	許心素
Xuyuan	–	旭遠
Yalu River (Yalu *jiang*)	–	鴨綠江
Yamato damashii	–	大和魂
Yan Siqi	–	顏思齊

Yangshan	–	陽山
Yang Yandi	–	楊彥迪
Yang Ying	–	楊英
Yao	–	堯
Yao Qisheng	–	姚啓聖
Ye	–	葉
Yehe	–	葉赫
Ye Heng	–	葉亨
yeshi	–	野史
Yiguan	–	一官
Yinyuan	–	隱元
Yongle	–	永樂
Yongli	–	永曆
Yongzheng	–	雍正
youji	–	遊擊
Yu	–	禹
Yu Dayou	–	俞大猷
Yuguo ku	–	裕國庫
Yuzhouguan	–	育胄館
Yu Zigao	–	俞諮皋
yuan	–	園
Yue	–	越
Yuegang	–	月港
Yunnan	–	雲南
Zeng Dinglao	–	曾定老
Zeng Ruyun	–	曾汝雲
zhang	–	丈
Zhang Guangqi	–	張光啟
Zhang Huangyan	–	張煌言
Zhang Mingzhen	–	張名振
Zhang Tingyu	–	張廷玉
Zhang Xiong	–	張雄
Zhang Zhongju	–	張仲舉
Zhangzhou	–	漳州
Zhejiang	–	浙江
Zhaoqing	–	肇慶
Zhaotao dajiangjun	–	招討大將軍
zhen	–	鎮
Zhenjiang	–	鎮江
Zheng	–	鄭
Zheng Cai	–	鄭彩
Zheng Cong	–	鄭聰
Zheng Chenggong	–	鄭成功

Zheng Daoshun	–	鄭道順
Zheng Dexiao	–	鄭德瀟
Zheng He	–	鄭和
zhenggong	–	正供
Zheng Jing	–	鄭經
Zheng Keshuang	–	鄭克塽
Zheng Kezang	–	鄭克臧
Zheng Lian	–	鄭聯
Zheng Lushe	–	鄭祿舍
Zheng Ming	–	鄭明
Zheng Mingjun	–	鄭鳴駿
Zheng Shaozu	–	鄭紹祖
Zheng Tai	–	鄭泰
Zheng Yongchang	–	鄭永常
Zheng Zhilong	–	鄭芝龍
Zhiwan, Zheng	–	鄭芝莞
Zhixin, Shang	–	尚之信
Zhongguo	–	中國
Zhongguo zhi ren	–	中國之人
zhou	–	州
Zhou	–	周
Zhou Hezhi	–	周鶴芝
Zhoushan	–	舟山
Zhouziwei	–	洲仔尾
Zhu	–	朱
Zhu Di	–	朱棣
Zhu Shugui	–	朱術桂
Zhu Shunshui	–	朱舜水
zhuxiang	–	助餉
Zhu Yihai	–	朱以海
Zhu Youlang	–	朱由榔
Zhu Yujian	–	朱聿鍵
Zhu Yousong	–	朱由崧
Zhu Yuanzhang	–	朱元璋
ziyi canjun	–	諮議參軍
zongbing	–	總兵
Zou	–	鄒
Zou Weilian	–	鄒維璉
Zu Dashou	–	祖大壽
Zuguan	–	祖官
Zu Zepu	–	祖澤溥
Zuanxu, Zheng	–	鄭纘緒

Bibliography

Abbreviations of archival collections and series

AGI, Filipinas – Archivo General de Indias, Audiencia de Filipinas (General Archive of the Indies, Audience of the Philippines).

AGI, México – Archivo General de Indias, Audiencia de México (General Archive of the Indies, Audience of Mexico).

NBS – *Nagasaki bunken sōsho* 長崎文獻叢書 (*Nagasaki historical documents collectanea*), Nagasaki: Nagasaki bunken, 1973–Ongoing.

TWWXCK – *Taiwan wenxian congkan* 臺灣文獻叢刊 (*Taiwan historical documents collectanea*), Taipei: Economic Research Office, Bank of Taiwan, 1957–1972.

TWWXHK – *Taiwan wenxian huikan* 臺灣文獻匯刊 (*Compendium of Taiwan historical documents*), Beijing: Jiuzhou, 2004.

Primary sources

East Asian languages

Beizhuan ji *zhu shu youguan Yao Qisheng deng zhuanji* 《碑傳集》諸書有關姚啓聖等傳記 (*Biographical records related to Yao Qisheng and others found in the* Collection of biographies inscribed in stone tablets *and various works*), *TWWXHK* 2.8, 2004.

Chen Hong 陳鴻 and Chen Bangxian 陳邦賢, "Qing chu Pu bian xiaosheng 清初莆變小乘" ("Minor account of the changes in Putian during the early Qing"), in Qing History Office, Historical Research Center, Chinese Academy of Social Sciences (ed.), *Qing shi ziliao* 清史資料 (*Documents on Qing history*), Beijing: Zhonghua Bookstore, 1980, vol. I.

Chen Lunjiong 陳倫炯, *Haiguo wenjianlu* 海國聞見錄 (*Record of things heard and seen in the maritime kingdoms*), *TWWXCK*, 26, 1958.

Cheng Shaogang 程紹剛 (trans. and annot.), *Helan ren zai Fuermosha* 荷蘭人在福爾摩莎 (*The Dutch in Formosa*), Taipei: Linking, 2000.

Ding Rijian 丁日健, *Zhi Tai bigao lu* 治台必告錄 (*A record of what must be transmitted in governing Taiwan*), *TWWXCK*, 17, 1959.

Du Guangting 杜光庭, "Qiuran ke zhuan 虯髯客傳" ("Biography of the Bearded Warrior"), in Zhang Youhe 張友鶴 (ed.), *Tang-Song chuanqi zhuan* 唐宋傳奇傳

(Legendary biographies of the Tang and Song periods), Beijing: People's Literary Publishing House, 1962.

Ehara Uji 江原氏, *Nagasaki mushimegane* 長崎蟲眼鏡 (*Spectacles of Nagasaki*), *NBS*, 1.5, 1975.

Fujian sheng li 福建省例 (*Regulations of Fujian province*), *TWWXCK*, 199, 1964.

Gu Yanwu 顧炎武, *Ming ji sanchao yeshi* 明季三朝野史 (*The wild history of three courts during the last days of the Ming*), *TWWXCK*, 106, 1961.

Haidong yishi 海東逸史 (*Historical record of the eastern seas*), *TWWXCK*, 90, 1961.

Hayashi Akira 林輝, *Tsūkō ichiran* 通行一覽 (*A glance at commerce and navigation*), 8 vols., Tokyo: Kokusho kankōkai, 1912–1913.

Hayashi Shunsai 林春齋 and Ura Ren'ichi 浦廉一 (eds.), *Ka'i hentai* 華夷變態 (*The metamorphosis from Chinese to barbarian*), 2 vols., Tokyo: Tōyō bunko, 1958–1959.

Historiographical Institute, Tokyo University (ed.), *Tō tsūji kaisho nichiroku* 唐通事會所日錄 (*Daily records of the Chinese Interpreters' Office*), *Dai Nihon kinsei shiryō* 大日本近世史料 (*Historical sources of modern Japanese history*), bk. 3, 7 vols., Tokyo: Tokyo University Press, 1955, vol. I.

Huai Yinbu 懷蔭布 (ed.), *Quanzhou fuzhi xuanlu* 泉州府志選錄 (*Excerpts from the Gazetteer of Quanzhou Prefecture*), *TWWXCK*, 223, 1967.

Huang Zongxi 黃宗羲, *Cixing shimo* 賜姓始末 (*An account of the Imperially Bestowed Surname from beginning to end*), *TWWXCK*, 25, 1958.

Ji Liuqi 計六奇, *Ming ji beilue* 明季北略 (*Brief account of the final days of the Ming in the north*), *TWWXCK*, 275, 1969.

Ming ji nanlue 明季南略 (*Brief account of the final days of the Ming in the south*), *TWWXCK*, 148, 1963.

Ji Qiguang 季麒光, *Dongning zhengshiji* 東寧政事集 (*Collection of administrative documents from Dongning*), TWWXHK, 4.2, 2004.

Jiang Liangqi 蔣良騏, *Donghua lu xuanji* 東華錄選輯 (*Selections from the Records of the Donghua Gate*), *TWWXCK*, 262, 1969.

Jiang Risheng 江日昇, *Taiwan waiji* 臺灣外記 (*An unofficial record of Taiwan*), *TWWXCK*, 60, 1960.

Jiang Yuying 蔣毓英 (ed.), *Taiwan fuzhi* 臺灣府志 (*Gazetteer of Taiwan prefecture*), Taipei: Economic Research Office, Bank of Taiwan, 1959.

Jin Ji 金基 (ed.), *Yongli Ningyang xianzhi* 永曆寧洋縣誌 (*Yongli-era gazetteer of Ningyang county*), *Riben cang Zhongguo hanjian difangzhi congkan xubian* 日本藏中國罕見地方誌叢刊續編 (*Continued collectanea of rare Chinese local gazetteers stored in Japan*), 10, Beijing: Chinese Library Press, 2003.

Kawaguchi Chōju 川口長孺, *Taiwan kakkyoji* 臺灣割據志 (*History of an autonomous Taiwan*), *TWXXCK*, 1, 1958.

Taiwan Tei shi kiji 臺灣鄭氏記事 (*A record of Taiwan's Zheng regime*), *TWWXCK*, 5, 1958.

Li Guangdi 李光地, *Rongcun yulu, Rongcun xu yulu* 榕村語錄、榕村續語錄 (*Written records of Rongcun and continued written records of Rongcun*), Beijing: Zhonghua Bookstore, 1995.

Li Huan 李桓, *Qing qixian leizheng xuanbian* 清耆獻類徵選編 (*Edited selections from the categorized summaries of Qing ancestral worthies*), *TWWXCK*, 230, 1967.

Li Zhifang 李之芳, *Li Wenxiang gong zoushu yu wenyi* 李文襄公奏疏與文移 (*Memorials and correspondences of the honorable gentleman Li Wenxiang*), *TWWXCK*, 285, 1970.

Lian Heng 連橫, *Taiwan shihui zawen chao* 臺灣詩薈雜文鈔 (*Copies of Taiwanese poetry, art, and miscellaneous jottings*), *TWWXCK*, 224, 1966.

Liushiqi 六十七 and Fan Xian 范咸 (eds.), *Chongxiu Taiwan fuzhi* 重修臺灣府志 (*Revised edition of the gazetteer of Taiwan prefecture*), *TWWXCK*, 105, 1961.

Liu Xianting 劉獻廷, *Guangyang zaji xuan* 廣陽雜記選 (*Selections from the random thoughts of Guangyang*), *TWWXCK*, 219, 1965.

Luo Qingxiao 羅青霄 (ed.), *Zhangzhou fuzhi xuanlu* 漳州府志選錄 (*Selections from the Gazetteer of Zhangzhou Prefecture*), *TWWXCK*, 232, 1967.

Minhai jillue 閩海紀略 (*Brief record of the Fujian seas*), *TWWXCK*, 23, 1958.

Min song huibian 閩頌匯編 (*Edited compilation of Fujianese laudatory compositions*), *TWWXHK* 2.1. 2004.

Ming shilu *Minhai guanxi shiliao* 明實錄閩海關係史料 (*Historical records related to the Fujian seas in the* Ming Veritable Records), *TWWXCK*, 296, 1971.

Nantian hen 南天痕 (*Scar in the southern sky*), *TWWXCK*, 76, 1960.

Ni Zaitian 倪在田 (ed.), *Xu Ming jishi benmo* 續明紀事本末 (*Continued record of the rise and fall of the Ming*), *TWWXCK*, 133, 1962.

Nishikawa Joken 西川如見, *Nagasaki yawasō* 長崎夜話草 (*Rough draft of a night talk on Nagasaki*), Nagasaki: Nagasaki Municipal Government, 1926.

Ōta Nanpo 太田南畝, *Ichiwa ichigen* 一話一言 (*Word by word*), 2 vols., Tokyo: Yoshikawa kōbunkan, 1928.

Peng Sunyi 彭孫貽, *Jinghai zhi* 靖海志 (*Account of the pacification of the sea*), *TWWXCK*, 35, 1959.

Qing chu Zheng Chenggong jiazu Manwen dang'an yibian (er) 清初鄭成功家族滿文檔案譯編(二) (*Edited translations from the Manchu language archives related to Zheng Chenggong and his family during the early Qing: part 2*), *TWWXHK*, 1.7, 2004.

Qing chu Zheng Chenggong jiazu Manwen dang'an yibian (san) 清初鄭成功家族滿文檔案譯編(三) (*Edited translations of the Manchu language archives related to Zheng Chenggong and his family during the early Qing: part 3*), *TWWXHK*, 1.9, 2004.

Qing Shengzu shilu xuanji 清聖祖實錄選輯 (*Selections from the Veritable Records of Emperor Shengzu of the Qing*), *TWWXCK*, 165, 1963.

Qing shi liezhuan xuan 清史列傳選 (*Selections from the Qing history biographies*), *TWWXCK*, 274, 1968.

Qing Shizu shilu xuanji 清世祖實錄選輯 (*Selections from the Veritable Records of Emperor Shizu of the Qing*), *TWWXCK*, 158, 1963.

Ruan Minxi 阮旻錫, *Haishang jianwenlu* 海上見聞錄 (*Record of things seen and heard on the sea*), *TWWXCK*, 24, 1958.

Sekisai Ugai 石齋鵜之, *Min Shin tōki* 明清鬪記 (*Record of the struggle between Ming and Qing*), Rare books collection, National Taiwan University Library.

Shao Tingcai 邵廷采, *Dongnan jishi* 東南紀事 (*Records of the southeast*), *TWWXCK*, 96, 1961.

Shen Binghu 沈冰壺, *Chonglin yuce* 重麟玉冊 (*Jade volume of Chonglin*), *TWWXHK*, 1.1, 2004.

"Shen Guangwen 沈光文," in Shi Yilin 施懿琳 (ed.), *Quan Tai shi* 全臺詩 (*Complete collection of Taiwanese poems*), 5 vols., Tainan: National Taiwan Institute of Literature, 2004.

Shen Yourong 沈有容, *Minhai zengyan* 閩海贈言 (*Admonitions on the Fujian seas*), *TWWXCK*, 56, 1959.

Shen Yun 沈雲, *Taiwan Zheng shi shimo* 臺灣鄭氏始末 (*An account of the Zheng Family on Taiwan from beginning to end*), *TWWXCK*, 15, 1958.

Shi Lang 施琅, *Jinghai jishi* 靖海紀事 (*A record of the pacification of the sea*), *TWWXCK*, 13, 1958.

Sima Qian 司馬遷, *Xinjiaoben Shiji sanjiazhu* 新校本史記三家注 (*Records of the Grand Historian: new annotated edition with commentaries from three schools*), Taipei: Dingwen, 1985.

Sŏng Haeun 成海應, *Chŏngmi chŏnshinrok* 丁未傳信錄 (*Record of correspondences in the Chŏngmi year* [1667]), in Hanguk gochŏn bŏnyŏkwon 韓國古典翻譯館 (Institute for the translation of Korean classics) www.itkc.or.kr/MAN/index .jsp, 2007.

Taiwan Research Institute of Xiamen University and China Number One Archives (eds.), *Kangxi tongyi Taiwan dang'an shiliao xuanji* 康熙統一臺灣檔案史料選集 (*Selections of historical documents from the archives on Kangxi's unification of Taiwan*), Fuzhou: Fujian People's Publishing House, 1983.

Zheng Chenggong dang'an shiliao xuanji 鄭成功檔案史料選集 (*Volume of selected historical archival materials on Zheng Chenggong*), Fuzhou: Fujian People's Publishing House, 1985.

Tanabe Mokei 田邊茂啓, *Nagasaki jitsuroku taisei* 長崎實錄大成 (*Compendium of the Veritable Records of Nagasaki*), *NBS*, 1.2, 1973.

Tei shi kankei bunsho 鄭氏関係文書 (*Documents related to the Zheng family*). *TWWXCK*, 69, 1960.

Wang Bichang 王必昌 and Lu Dingmei 魯鼎梅 (eds.), *Chongxiu Taiwan xianzhi* 重修臺灣縣志 (*Revised edition of the Gazetteer of Taiwan county*), *TWWXCK*, 113. Taipei, 1961.

Wang Zhongxiao 王忠孝, *Wang Zhongxiao gong ji* 王忠孝公集 (*Collections of the gentleman Wang Zhongxiao*), Nanjing: Jiangsu Ancient Texts Publishing House, 2000.

Wu Han 吳晗 (ed.), *Chaoxian Li chao shilu zhong de Zhongguo shiliao* 朝鮮李朝實錄中的中國史料 (*Historical documents on China found within the Chosŏn Yi dynasty Veritable Records*), 12 vols., Beijing: Zhonghua Bookstore, 1980.

Wu Weiye 吳偉業, *Luqiao jiwen* 鹿樵紀聞 (*Jottings from the Deer Wood Studio*), *TWWXCK*, 127, 1961.

Xia Lin 夏琳, *Haiji jiyao* 海紀輯要 (*A summary of records of the sea*), *TWWXCK*, 22, 1958.

Xu Xingqing 徐興慶 (ed.), *Xinding Zhu Shunshui ji buyi* 新訂朱舜水集補遺 (*Newly compiled additions to the collections of Zhu Shunshui*), Taipei: Taiwan University Press Center, 2004.

"Yanping er wang yiji 延平二王遺集" ("Surviving collections of the two Princes of Yanping"), in *Zheng Chenggong zhuan* 鄭成功傳 (*Biographies of Zheng Chenggong*), *TWWXCK*, 67, 1960.

Yang Jie 楊捷, *Ping Min ji* 平閩紀 (*Account of the pacification of Fujian*), *TWWXCK*, 98, 1961.

Yang Ying 楊英, *Congzheng shilu* 從征實錄 (*Veritable record of accompanying the expeditions*), *TWWXCK*, 32, 1958.

Yu Yonghe 郁永河, *Pihai jiyou* 郫海紀遊 (*Small sea travels*), *TWWXCK*, 44, 1959.

Zha Jizuo 查繼佐, *Lu chunqiu* 魯春秋 (*Annals of the Prince of Lu*), *TWWXCK*, 118, 1961.

   Zuiwei lu xuanji 罪惟錄選輯 (*Selections from the confessions of my guilt*), *TWWXCK*, 136, 1962.

Zhang Huangyan 張煌言, *Zhang Cangshui shiwen ji* 張蒼水詩文集 (*Collection of Zhang Huangyan's poems and writings*), *TWWXCK*, 142, 1962.

Zhang Xie 張燮, *Dongxiyang kao* 東西洋考 (*Account of the Eastern and Western Oceans*), Beijing: Zhonghua Bookstore, 1981.

Zhao Erxun 趙爾巽 (ed.), *Qing shigao* 清史稿 (*A draft Qing history*), 48 vols., Beijing: Zhonghua Bookstore, 1998.

Zheng Da 鄭達, *Yeshi wuwen* 野史無文 (*An unspoken wild history*), *TWWXCK*, 209, 1965.

Zheng Dayu 鄭大郁 and Zheng Zhilong 鄭芝龍 (eds.), *Jingguo xionglue* 經國雄略 (*Grand strategy for ordering the country*), Harvard Univeristy Yenching Library (ed.), *Meiguo Hafo daxue Yanjing tushuguan cang Zhongwen shanben huikan* 美國哈佛大學圖書館藏中文善本彙刊 (*Compendium of Chinese rare books in the Yenching Library Collection of Harvard University in the United States*), vols. XIX–XX, Beijing: Commercial Press, 2003.

"Zheng Jing 鄭經," in Shi Yilin 施懿琳 (ed.), *Quan Tai shi* 全臺詩 (*Complete collection of Taiwanese poems*), 5 vols., vol. I, Tainan: National Taiwan Institute of Literature, 2004.

Zheng shi shiliao sanbian 鄭氏史料三編 (*Historical materials of the Zheng regime, part 3*), *TWWXCK*, 175, 1963.

Zheng shi shiliao xubian 鄭氏史料續編 (*Historical materials of the Zheng regime, continued*), *TWWXCK*, 168, 1963.

Zheng Yiju, "Zheng Chenggong zhuan 鄭成功傳" ("Biography of Zheng Chenggong"), in *Zheng Chenggong zhuan* (*Biographies of Zheng Chenggong*), *TWWXCK*, 67, 1960.

Zheng Yuhai 鄭玉海 et al., *Zheng shi zongpu* 鄭氏宗譜 (*Ancestral genealogy of the Zheng family*), *TWWXHK* 1.9, 2004.

Zhou Shuoxun 周碩勳 (ed.), *Chaozhou fuzhi* 潮州府志 (*Gazetteer of Chaozhou prefecture*), Zhulan Bookshop, 1893.

Zhu Zhiyu 朱之瑜, *Zhu Shunshui ji* 朱舜水集 (*Collections of Zhu Shunshui*), Taipei: Hanjing, 2004.

Western languages

Anderson, John, *English intercourse with Siam in the seventeenth century*, London: K. Paul, Trench, Trübner, and Co., Ltd., 1890.

Blair, Emma and James Robertson, *The Philippine islands: 1493–1898: explorations by early navigators, descriptions of the islands and their peoples, their histories and records of the Catholic missions, as related in contemporaneous books and manuscripts, showing the political, economic, commercial and religious conditions of those islands from their earliest relations with European nations to the close of the nineteenth century*, 55 vols., Cleveland, OH: Arthur H. Clark Company, 1906.

Blussé, Leonard, M. E. van Opstall, and Ts'ao Yung-ho (Cao Yonghe 曹永和) (eds.), *De dagregisters van het Kasteel Zeelandia, Taiwan (The daily registers of Zeelandia Castle, Taiwan)*, 4 vols., The Hague: Institute for the History of the Netherlands, 1986–2000.

Borao Mateo, José Eugenio, Pol Heyns, Carlos Gómez, and Anna Maria Zandueta Nisce (eds.), *Spaniards in Taiwan: documents*, 2 vols., Taipei: SMC Publishing, 2002.

Archivo General de Indias, "Carta de Lorenzo de Orella y Ugalde sobre defensa de Filipinas" ("Letter from Lorenzo de Orella y Ugalde on the defense of the Philippines"), AGI, Filipinas, 43, N. 39.

Archivo General de Indias, "Carta de Manuel de León sobre embajada de Siam, cobro a sangleyes" ("Letter of Manuel de León on the embassy of Siam, pardon of the Sangleyes"), AGI, Filipinas, 10, R.1, N.7.

Archivo General de Indias, "Carta de Manuel de León sobre el sipuán de isla Hermosa" ("Letter from Manuel de León about Zheng Jing of Formosa Island"), AGI, Filipinas, 10, R. 1, N. 28.

Archivo General de Indias, "Cartas del Virrey Marques de Mancera" ("Letters from the Viceroy Marquis of Mancera"), AGI, México, 46, N. 19.

Archivo General de Indias, "Petición de Lorenzo de Orella y Ugalde para que se fortifique el castillo de Santiago" ("Petition of Lorenzo de Orella y Ugalde for fortifying the castle of Santiago"), AGI, Filipinas, 43, N. 49.

C. E. S., *'t Verwaerloosde Formosa, of Waerachtig verhael: Hoedanigh door verwaerloosinge der Nederlanders in Oost-Indien, het Eylant Formosa, van den Chinesen Mandorijn ende Zeeroover Coxinja, overrompelt, vermeestert, ende ontweldight is geworden (The neglected Formosa, or the true story: how, through the neglect of the Netherlanders in East India, the island of Formosa has been invaded, subdued, and conquered by the Chinese Mandarin and pirate Koxinga)*, annot. G. C. Molewijk, Zutphen, The Netherlands: Walburg Pers, 1991.

Chang Hsiu-jung, Anthony Farrington, Huang Fu-san, Ts'ao Yung-ho (Cao Yonghe 曹永和), Wu Mi-tsa (Wu Micha 吳密察), Cheng Hsi-fu, and Ang Ka-in (Weng Jiayin 翁佳音) (eds.), *The English factory in Taiwan: 1670–1685*, Taipei: National Taiwan University, 1995.

Chiang Shu-sheng (Jiang Shusheng 江樹生) (trans. and annot.), *Daghregister van Philip Meij (The daily register of Philip Meij)*, 2 pts., Taipei: Hansheng, 2003.

De missiven van de VOC-gouverneur in Taiwan aan de Gouverneur-generaal te Batavia (Letters from the VOC governor in Taiwan to the governor-general at Batavia), 1 vol., Taipei: SMC Publishing, 2007–Ongoing.

Colenbrander, H. T., Jan Ernst Heeres, Jacobus Anne van der Chijs, J. de Hullu et al. (eds.), *Dagh-register gehouden int Casteel Batavia vant passerende daer ter plaetse als over geheel Nederlandts-India (Daily register kept in Batavia Castle of the happenings at places throughout Netherlands East India)*, 31 vols., The Hague: Martinus Nijhoff, 1887–1931.

Coolhaas, Willem Phillippus (ed.), *Generale missiven van gouverneurs-generaal en raden aan Heren XVII der Verenigde Oostindische Compagnie* (*General reports from the governors-general and councils to the Gentlemen 17 of the United East India Company*), 11 vols., The Hague: Martinus Nijhoff: 1960–Ongoing.

Díaz, Casimiro, *Conquistas de las islas Filipinas: la temporal, por las armas del señor don Phelipe Segundo el Prudente; y la espiritual, por los religiosos del orden de nuestro padre San Augustin: fundacion, y progressos de su provincia del santissimo nombre de Jesus* (*Conquest of the Philippine islands: the temporal by virtue of King Phillip II, the Prudent, and the spiritual by the religious of the order of our father Saint Augustine: and the development of the province of the holy name of Jesus*), 2 vols., Valladolid, Spain: L.N. de Gaviria, 1890.

Huber, Johannes, "Relations between Cheng Ch'eng-kung and the Netherlands East India Company in the 1650s," in Leonard Blussé (ed.), *Around and about Formosa: essays in honor of Professor Ts'ao Yung-ho*, Taipei: Ts'ao Yung-ho Foundation for Culture and Education, 2003.

Zaide, Gregorio F., *Documentary sources of Philippine history*, 12 vols., Manila: National Book Store, 1990.

Scholarly resources

East Asian languages

Cai Yuping 蔡郁蘋, "*Zheng shi shiqi Taiwan dui Ri maoyi zhi yanjiu* 鄭氏時期臺灣對日貿易之研究" ("*Research on Taiwan's trade with Japan during the Zheng period*"), unpublished MA thesis, National Chenggong University, 2005.

Cao Yonghe 曹永和 (Ts'ao Yung-ho), *Taiwan zaoqi lishi yanjiu* 臺灣早期歷史研究 (*Studies in early Taiwanese history*), Taipei: Linking, 1995.

Chao Zhongchen 晁中辰, *Ming dai haijin yu haiwai maoyi* 明代海禁与海外贸易 (*The Maritime Prohibitions during the Ming and overseas trade*), Beijing: People's Publishing House, 2005.

Chen Bisheng 陈碧笙, *Zheng Chenggong lishi yanjiu* 郑成功历史研究 (*Historical research on Zheng Chenggong*), Beijing: Jiuzhou, 2000.

Chen Guodong 陳國棟, *Taiwan de shanhai jingyan* 臺灣的山海經驗 (*The experience of Taiwan's mountains and seas*), Taipei: Yuanliu, 2006.

Chen Jiahong 陳佳宏, "*Zheng shi wangchao zhi zhengzhi waijiao shixi* 鄭氏王朝之政治外交試析" ("Attempt at analysis of the politics and diplomacy of the Zheng kingdom"), *Tainan wenhua* 台南文化 (*Tainan culture*) 58 (2008).

Chen Jiexian 陳捷先, *Bu titou yu Liangguo lun* 不剃頭與兩國論 (*Not shaving hair and the Two-States Theory*), Taipei: Yuanliu, 2001.

Chen Jindong 陈进东, "*Qing Taiwan xingle tu* 清《台湾行乐图》" ("Qing-period *Painting of seeking pleasure in Taiwan*"), in Zhang Zhongchun 张仲淳 and Lin Yuanping 林元平 (eds.), *Taihai yizhen: Xiamen shi bowuguan guancang she Tai wenwu jianshang* 台海遗珍：厦门市博物馆馆藏涉台文物鉴赏 (*Treasures from Taiwan: appreciation of the collections related to Taiwan stored at the Xiamen City Museum*), Shanghai: Academia Press, 2014.

Chen Xiyu 陈希育, *Zhongguo fanchuan yu haiwai maoyi* 中国帆船与海外贸易 (*Chinese junks and overseas trade*), Xiamen: Xiamen University Press, 1991.

Chen Zaizheng 陈在正, *Taiwan haijiangshi yanjiu* 台湾海疆史研究 (*Historical research on the Taiwan maritime frontier*), Xiamen: Xiamen University Press, 2002.

Deng Kongzhao 邓孔昭, *Zheng Chenggong yu Ming-Zheng Taiwan shi yanjiu* 郑成功与明郑台湾史研究 (*Study of Zheng Chenggong and Taiwan History during the Ming-Zheng period*), Beijing: Taihai, 2000.

Fang Zhenzhen 方真真, *Ming mo Qing chu Taiwan yu Manila de fanchuan maoyi* 明末清初臺灣與馬尼拉的帆船貿易 (*1664–1684*) (*The junk trade between Taiwan and Manila between the end of the Ming and beginning of the Qing: 1664–1684*), Banqiao, New Taipei City: Daoxiang, 2006.

Hamashita Takeshi 浜下武志, *Kindai Chūgoku no kokusai teki keiki: Chōkō bōeki shisutemu to kindai Ajia* 近代中国の国際的契機：朝貢貿易システムと近代アジア (*Modern China's global opportunity: the tributary trading system and modern Asia*), Tokyo: Tokyo University Press, 1990.

Han Zhenhua 韩振华, "Zheng Chenggong shidai de haiwai maoyi he haiwai maoyi shang de xingzhi: 1650–1662 郑成功时代的海外贸易和海外贸易商的性质" ("The character of overseas trade and overseas trading merchants during the Zheng Chenggong era: 1650–1662"), in Xiamen University History Department (ed.), *Zheng Chenggong yanjiu lunwen xuan* 郑成功研究论文选 (*Selection of research articles on Zheng Chenggong*). Fuzhou: Fujian People's Publishing House, 1982.

He Lingxiu 何龄修, *Wukuzhai Qing shi conggao* 五库斋清史丛稿 (*Collected drafts on Qing history from the Five-Treasury Study*), Beijing: Xueyuan, 2004.

Huang Dianquan 黃典權, *Zheng Chenggong shishi yanjiu* 鄭成功史事研究 (*Historical research on Zheng Chenggong*), Taipei: Taiwan Commercial Press, 1975.

Huang Yuzhai 黃玉齋, "Ming Zheng Chenggong deng de kang Qing yu Riben 明鄭成功等的抗清與日本" ("The anti-Qing resistance of Zheng Chenggong and other Ming loyalists and Japan"), *Taiwan wenxian* 臺灣文獻 (*Taiwan historica*) 9.4 (1958).

Inagaki Kigai 稻垣其外, *Tei Seikō* 鄭成功 (*Zheng Chenggong*), Taipei: Taiwan keisei shinpōsha, 1929.

Ishihara Michihiro 石原道博, *Min matsu Shin sho Nippon kisshi no kenkyū* 明末清初日本乞師の研究 (*Research on the requests for soldiers from Japan during the late Ming and early Qing periods*), Tokyo: Fuzanbō, 1944.

Iwao Seiichi 岩生成一, "Kinsei Nisshi bōeki ni kansuru sūryōteki kōsatsu 近世日支貿易に関する数量的考察" ("An investigation of the trading figures between China and Japan during the early modern era"), *Shigaku zasshi* 史学雑誌 (*Journal of historical studies*) 62.11 (1953).

"Ming mo qiaoyu Riben Zhinaren Jiabidan Li Dan kao 明末寓日本支那人甲必丹李旦考" ("Study of Li Dan, China Captain living in Japan during the late Ming"), in Xu Xianyao 許賢瑤 (ed. and trans.), *Helan shidai Taiwan shi lunwen ji* 荷蘭時代臺灣史論文集 (*Collection of papers on Dutch-era Taiwan history*), Yilan, Taiwan: Foguang renwenshe, 2001.

"Ming mo qiaoyu Riben Zhina maoyishang Yiguan Augustin Li Guozhu zhi huodong 明末寓日本支那貿易商一官Augustin李國助之活動" ("The activities of Augustin Iquan, or Li Guozhu, a Chinese merchant living in Japan during the late Ming"), in Xu Xianyao 許賢瑤(ed. and trans.), *Helan shidai Taiwan shi lunwen ji* 荷蘭時代臺灣史論文集 (*Collection of papers on Dutch-era Taiwan history*), Yilan, Taiwan: Foguang renwenshe, 2001.

Nanyō Nihonmachi no kenkyū 南洋日本町の研究 (*Research on the Japantowns of the Southern Ocean*) Tokyo: Iwanami Bookstore, 1966.

Jian Huiying 簡惠盈, "*Ming-Zheng shiqi Taiwan zhi haiwai maoyi ji qi zhuanyun diwei zhi yanjiu* 明鄭時期臺灣之貿易及其轉運地位之研究" (*"Research on the overseas trade of Taiwan during the Ming-Zheng period and its position as a hub"*), unpublished MA thesis, National Taipei University, 2000.

Jiang Renjie 江人傑, *Jiegou Zheng Chenggong: Yingxiong, shenhua yu xingxiang de lishi* 解構鄭成功：英雄、神化與形象的歷史 (*Deconstructing Zheng Chenggong: History of a hero, mythmaking, and images*), Taipei: Sanmin Bookstore, 2006.

Jin Chengqian 金成前, "Zheng Jing yu Ming-Zheng 鄭經與明鄭" ("Zheng Jing and the Ming-Zheng regime"), *Taiwan wenxian* 臺灣文獻 (*Taiwan historica*) 23.3 (1972).

Li Shunping 李順平, "Zheng Chenggong zusun sandai jingying Taiwan de qian-hou 鄭成功祖孫三代經營臺灣的前後" ("Account of the management of Taiwan over three generations by Zheng Chenggong and his descendants"), *Taibei wenxian zhizi* 臺北文獻 (*Taipei historical documents*) 38 (1976).

Liao Hanchen 廖漢臣, "Zheng Zhilong kao: shang 鄭芝龍考：上" ("A study of Zheng Zhilong: part 1"), *Taiwan wenxian* 臺灣文獻 (*Taiwan historica*) 10.4 (1959).

Lin Qian 林乾, "Kangxi tongyi Taiwan de zhanlue juece 康熙統一台湾的战略决策" ("The Kangxi emperor's strategic decision to unify Taiwan"), *Qing shi yanjiu* 清史研究 (*Studies in Qing history*) 3 (2000).

Lin Renchuan 林仁川, "Shi lun zhuming haishang Zheng shi de xingshuai 试论著名海商郑氏的兴衰" ("Preliminary investigation into the rise and fall of the renowned Zheng family of merchants"), in Academic Division of the Zheng Chenggong Scholarly Discussion Group (ed.), *Zheng Chenggong yanjiu lunwen xuan xuji* 郑成功研究论文选续集 (*Selection of research papers on Zheng Chenggong, second part*), Fuzhou: Fujian People's Publishing House, 1984.

Liu Fengyun 刘凤云, *Qing dai Sanfan yanjiu* 清代三藩研究 (*Study of the Three Feudatories during the Qing period*), Beijing: Renmin University Press, 1994.

Liu Xufeng 劉序楓, "Jindai Huanan chuantong shehui zhong 'gongsi' xingtai zaikao: You haishang maoyi dao defang shehui 近代華南傳統社會中'公司'形態再考：由海上貿易到地方社會" ("Reinvestigation of the state of 'Gongsi' within the traditional society of south China during the modern period: from maritime trade to local society"), in Lin Yuru 林玉茹 (ed.), *Bijiao shiye xia de Taiwan shangye chuantong* 比較視野下的臺灣商業傳統 (*Commercial traditions in Taiwan: a comparative perspective*), Taipei: Taiwan History Institute, Academia Sinica, 2012.

Lu Zhengheng 盧正恒, "Guan yu zei zhijian: Zheng Zhilong baquan ji 'Zheng bu' 官與賊之間：鄭芝龍霸權及'鄭部'" ("Between bureaucrat and bandit: Zheng Zhilong's maritime hegemony and 'Zheng Ministry'"), unpublished MA thesis, National Tsinghua University, 2013.

"Qi yu min, hai yu lu: cong xin faxian de Zheng shi Manwen zuolingce tanqi 旗與民、海與陸：從新發現的鄭氏滿文佐領冊談起" ("Banner and commoner, maritime and continent: speaking from the newly discovered Manchu-language banner company records on the Zheng family"), *Dongya haiyu jiaoliushi yanjiu* 東亞海域交流史研究 (*History of monsoon Asia*) 1.1 (forthcoming).

Nagazumi Yōko 永積洋子, "Helan de Taiwan maoyi 荷蘭的臺灣貿易" ("Dutch trade at Taiwan"), in Xu Xianyao 許賢瑤 (trans.), *Helan shidai Taiwan shi lunwen ji* 荷蘭時代臺灣史論文集 (*Collection of papers on Dutch-era Taiwan history*), Yilan, Taiwan: Foguang renwenshe, 2001.

Nakamura Tadashi 中村質, *Kinsei Nagasaki bōekishi no kenkyū* 近世長崎貿易の研究(*Research on the history of Nagasaki's foreign trade during the early modern era*), Tokyo: Yoshikawa kōbunkan, 1988.

Ni Lexiong 倪乐雄, "Zheng Chenggong shidai de haiquan shijian dui dangdai Zhongguo de yiyi 郑成功时代的海权实践对当代中国的意义" ("The significance of the sea power experience of Zheng Chenggong's era on contemporary China"), *Huadong shifan daxue xuebao zhexue shehui ban* 华东师范大学学报哲学社会版 (*East China Normal University journal philosophy and social sciences edition*) 44.2 (2012).

Nie Dening 聂德宁, "Ming-Qing zhi ji Zheng shi jituan hai shang maoyi de zuzhi yu guanli 明清之际郑氏集团海上贸易的组织与管理" ("The Zheng organization's management and control of maritime trade during the Ming and Qing"), in Xiamen University History Department (ed.), *Zheng Chenggong yanjiu lunwen xuan* 郑成功研究论文选 (*Selection of research articles on Zheng Chenggong*), Fuzhou: Fujian People's Publishing House, 1982.

Qin Jiu 秦就, *Chuan wang Zheng Zhilong* 船王鄭芝龍 (*The ship magnate Zheng Zhilong*), Taipei: Shixue, 2002.

Sakuma Shigeo 佐久間重男, *Nichi-Min kankeishi no kenkyū* 日明関係史の研究 (*Research on the history of relations between the Ming and Japan*), Tokyo: Yoshikawa kōbunkan, 1992.

Su Junwei 蘇軍瑋, "*Qing chao yu Ming-Zheng hezhan hudong celue jianlun qi dui liang'an guanxi de qishi* 清朝與明鄭和戰互動策略兼論其對兩岸關係的啟示" ("The strategic interaction between the Ching dynasty and Ming-Cheng: Implications for cross-strait relations"), unpublished MA thesis, National Taiwan University, 2008.

Sun Weiguo 孙卫国, *Da Ming qihao yu xiao Zhonghua yishi: Chaoxian wangchao zun Zhou si Ming wenti yanjiu* 大明旗号与小中华意识：朝鲜王朝尊周思明问题研究, *1637–1800* (*The banner of the Great Ming and the mini-Middle Kingdom worldview: research on the topic of the Chosŏn kingdom's respect for the Zhou and commemoration of the Ming, 1637–1800*), Beijing: Commercial Press, 2007.

Tang Jintai 湯錦台, *Kaiqi Taiwan di yi ren: Zheng Zhilong* 開啟臺灣第一人：鄭芝龍 (*Zheng Zhilong: the first person to open Taiwan*), Taipei: Guoshi, 2002.

Ura Renichi 浦廉一 and Lai Yongxiang 賴永祥 (trans.), "Qing chu Qianjieling kao 清初遷界令考" ("Investigation of the Order to Shift the Boundary in the early Qing"), *Taiwan wenxian* 臺灣文獻 (*Taiwan historica*) 6.4 (1955).

Wang Zhengyao 王政尧, *Qing shi shude* 清史述得 (*Narrative of Qing History*), Shenyang: Liaoning Nationalities Publishing House, 2004.

Weng Jiayin 翁佳音 (Ang Ka-in), *Helan shidai Taiwan shi de lianxuxing wenti* 荷蘭時代臺灣史的連續性問題 (*The question of continuity in the history of Taiwan's Dutch period*), Taipei: Daoxiang, 2008.

Wu Micha 吳密察, "Zheng Chenggong zheng Tai zhi beijing: Zheng shi zhengquan xingge zhi kaocha 鄭成功征臺之背景: 鄭氏政權性格之考察" ("The background of Zheng Chenggong's conquest of Taiwan: a study of the nature of the Zheng's political administration"), *Shiyi* 史繹 (*Unraveling of history*) 15 (1978).

Wu Zhenglong 吳正龍, "Nanjing zhi yi hou Zheng-Qing heyi zai jiantao (xia) 南京之役後鄭清和議在檢討 (下)" ("A reevaluation of the Zheng-Qing negotiations after the Nanjing campaign: part 2"), *Dalu zazhi* 大陸雜誌 (*Mainland journal*) 100.4 (2000).

Zheng Chenggong yu Qing zhengfu jian de tanpan 鄭成功與清政府間的談判 (*Negotiations between Zheng Chenggong and the Qing government*), Taipei: Wenjin, 2000.

Yang Yanjie 杨彦杰, *Heju shidai Taiwan shi* 荷據時代臺灣史 (*History of Taiwan under the Dutch occupation*), Taipei: Linking, 2000.

"1650 zhi 1662 nian Zheng Chenggong haiwai maoyi de maoyi'e he lirun'e gusuan 1650至1662年郑成功海外贸易的贸易额和利润额估算" ("Rough estimation of the revenues and profits from Zheng Chenggong's overseas trade from 1650 to 1662"), in Academic Division of the Zheng Chenggong Scholarly Discussion Group (ed.), *Zheng Chenggong yanjiu lunwen xuan xuji* 郑成功研究论文选续集 (*Selection of research papers on Zheng Chenggong, second part*), Fuzhou: Fujian People's Publishing House, 1984.

"Zheng Chenggong bujiang Gampea kao 郑成功部将GAMPEA 考" ("A study of Gampea, Zheng Chenggong's subordinate commander"), in Fang Youyi 方友义 (ed.), *Zheng Chenggong yanjiu* 郑成功研究 (*Research on Zheng Chenggong*), Xiamen: Xiamen University Press, 1994.

Yang Yihong 楊逸宏, "Zheng Chenggong di jiu dai sun Taiwan shengen 鄭成功第九代孫台灣生根" ("The ninth-generation descendant of Zheng Chenggong has formed roots in Taiwan"), *China Times Weekly Magazine* 1534 (July 17, 2007).

Yang Yongzhi 楊永智, *Ming Qing shiqi Tainan chuban shi* 明清時期台南出版史 (*History of the Tainan publishing industry during the Ming and Qing*). Taipei: Taiwan Student Bookstore, 2007.

Yuan Bingling 袁冰凌 and Bao Leshi 包乐史 (Leonard Blussé) (trans.), "Guanyu Zheng Zhilong gei Helan Badaweiya cheng zongdu Sibeikesi de liang feng xin 关于郑芝龙给荷兰巴达维亚城总督斯贝克斯的两封信" ("Regarding two letters written by Zheng Zhilong to governor-general Specx of Dutch Batavia"), *Fujian shizhi* 福建史志 (*Fujian historical journal*) (July 1994).

Zheng Guangnan and Shanghai China Maritime Museum, *Xinbian Zhongguo haidao shi* 新编中国海盗史 (*Newly annotated history of Chinese pirates*), Beijing: Encyclopedia of China Press, 2014.

Zhang Kaiyuan 章开沅, Rao Huaimin 饶怀民, and Yan Changhong 严昌洪 (eds), *Qing tongjian* 清通鉴 (*Comprehensive mirror of the Qing*), 4 vols., Changsha, Hunan: Yuelu shushe, 2000.

Zheng Ruiming 鄭瑞明, "Taiwan Ming-Zheng yu Dongnanya zhi maoyi guanxi chutan: Fazhan Dongnanya maoyi zhi dongji, shiwu ji waishang zhi qianlai 臺

灣明鄭與東南亞之貿易關係初探: 發展東南亞貿易之動機、實務及外商之前來" ("Preliminary investigation of the trading relationship between the Ming-Zheng regime and Southeast Asia: the motivation and actual circumstances of the development of trade with Southeast Asia and arrivals of foreign merchants"), *Guoli Taiwan shifan daxue lishixue bao* 國立臺灣師範大學歷史學報 (*National Taiwan Normal University journal of the study of history*) 14 (1986).

Zheng Weizhong (Cheng Wei-chung) 鄭維中, *Helan shidai de Taiwan shehui: Ziranfa de nanti yu wenminghua de licheng* 荷蘭時代的臺灣社會: 自然法的難題與文明化的歷程 (*Taiwanese society under Dutch rule: the conundrum of natural law and the civilizing process*), Taipei: Qianwei, 2004.

"Shi Lang 'Taiwan guihuan Helan' miyi 施琅'臺灣歸還荷蘭'密議" ("Admiral Shi Lang's secret proposal to return Taiwan to the Dutch"), *Taiwan wenxian* 臺灣文獻 (*Taiwan historica*) 61.3 (2010).

Zhu Delan 朱德蘭, "Qing chu Qianjieling shi Zhongguo hanghai shang maoyi zhi yanjiu 清初遷界令時中國航海上貿易之研究" ("Research on Chinese maritime trade under the coastal evacuation order in the early Qing"), in *Zhongguo haiyang fazhan shi lunwenji* 中國海洋發展史論文集 (*Essays in Chinese maritime history*), 10 vols., vol. II, Taipei: Three People's Principles Research Institute, 1986.

Zhu Shuangyi 朱双一, "'Zheng Jing shi Taidu fenzi' shuo zhiyi: yi *Dongbilou ji* wei zuo zheng '郑经是台独分子'说质疑: 以《东壁楼集》为佐证" ("Critiquing the saying 'Zheng Jing is a Taiwanese independence activist': using the *Collections from the Eastern Wall Pavilion* as evidence"), *Xiamen daxue xuebao: zhexue shehui kexueban* 厦门大学学报: 哲学社会科学版 (*Xiamen University journal: philosophy and social sciences edition*) 167.1 (2005).

Zhuang Jinde 莊金德, "Zheng-Qing heyi shimo 鄭清和議始末" ("An account of the Zheng-Qing negotiations from beginning to end"), *Taiwan wenxian* 臺灣文獻 (*Taiwan historica*) 12.4 (1961).

"Zheng shi junliang wenti de yantao 鄭氏軍糧問題的研討" ("A discussion of the problem of Zheng military provisions"), *Taiwan wenxian* 臺灣文獻 (*Taiwan historica*) 12.1 (1961).

Western languages

Abu-Lughod, Janet L., *Before European hegemony: the world-system, AD 1250–1350*, Oxford, UK: Oxford University Press, 1991.

Adams, Julia. "Principals and agents, colonialists and company men: the decay of colonial control in the Dutch East Indies," *American Sociological Review* 61.1 (1996).

"Trading states, trading places: the role of patrimonialism in early modern Dutch development," *Comparative Studies in Society and History* 36.2 (1994).

Anderson, Benedict, *Imagined communities: reflections on the origin and spread of nationalism*, London: Verso Press, 1983.

Anderson, John L., "Piracy and world history: an economic perspective on maritime predation," in C. R. Pennell, *Bandits at sea: a pirates reader*, New York: New York University Press, 2001.

Andrade, Tonio. "Chinese under European Rule: the case of Sino-Dutch mediator He Bin," *Late Imperial China* 28.1 (2007).

"The company's Chinese pirates: how the Dutch East India Company tried to lead a coalition of pirates to war against China, 1621–1662," *Journal of World History* 15.4 (2004).

How Taiwan became Chinese: Dutch, Spanish, and Han colonization in the seventeenth century, Gutenberg E-book www.gutenberg-e.org/andrade, 2008.

Lost colony: the untold story of China's first great victory over the west, Princeton, NJ: Princeton University Press, 2011.

Antony, Robert J., *Like froth floating on the sea: the world of pirates and seafarers in late imperial China*, Berkeley, CA: University of California Institute for East Asian Studies, 2003.

"'Righteous Yang': pirate, rebel, and hero on the Sino-Vietnamese water frontier, 1644–1684," *Cross-Currents: East Asian History and Culture Review* 11 (2014).

Arrighi, Giovanni, Hui Po-keung, Hung Ho-fung, and Mark Selden, "Historical capitalism, east and west," in Arrighi, Hamashita, and Selden (eds.), *The resurgence of East Asia: 500, 150, and 50 year perspectives*, London: Routledge, 2003.

Arrighi, Giovanni, Hamashita Takeshi, and Mark Selden, "Introduction," in Arrighi, Hamashita, and Selden (eds.), *The resurgence of East Asia: 500, 150, and 50 year perspectives*, London: Routledge, 2003.

Atwell, William S., "Ming China and the emerging world economy, c. 1470–1650," in Denis Twitchett and Frederick W. Mote (eds.), *The Cambridge history of China*, vol. VIII.2: the Ming dynasty, 1368–1644, Cambridge, UK: Cambridge University Press, 1998.

"A seventeenth-century 'general crisis' in East Asia?" *Modern Asian Studies* 24.4 (1990).

Bajpaee, Chietigj, "Hong Kong, Taiwan wilt in the dragon's glare," *Asia Times* (August 16, 2007).

Batchelor, Robert K, *London: the Selden Map and the making of a global city, 1549–1689*, Chicago: University of Chicago Press, 2014.

Beasley, W. G., *The Japanese experience: a short history of Japan*, Berkeley, CA: University of California Press, 2000.

Bellah, Robert, *Tokugawa religion: the cultural roots of modern Japan*, New York: Free Press, 1985.

Blussé, Leonard, "Junks to Java: Chinese shipping to the Nanyang in the second half of the eighteenth century," in Eric Tagliacozzo and Chang Wen-chin (eds.), *Chinese circulations: capital, commodities, and networks in Southeast Asia*, Durham, NC: Duke University Press, 2011.

"Minnan-jen or cosmopolitan? The rise of Cheng Chih-lung alias Nicolas Iquan," in E. B. Vermeer (ed.), *Development and decline of Fukien province in the 17th and 18th centuries*, Leiden: E. J. Brill, 1990.

"No boats to China: the Dutch East India Company and the changing pattern of the China Sea trade, 1635–1690," *Modern Asian studies* 30.1 (1996).

"The VOC as sorcerer's apprentice: stereotypes and social engineering on the China coast," in W. L. Idema (ed.), *Leyden studies in Sinology: papers presented* at the conference held in celebration of the fiftieth anniversary of the Sinological Institute of Leyden University, December 8–12, 1980, Leiden: Brill, 1980.

Visible cities: Canton, Nagasaki, and Batavia and the coming of the Americans, Cambridge, MA: Harvard University Press, 2008.

Borao-Mateo, José Eugenio, The Spanish experience in Taiwan, 1626–1642: the Baroque ending of a Renaissance endeavour, Hong Kong: Hong Kong University Press, 2009.

Boxer, Charles Ralph, The Christian century in Japan: 1549–1650, Berkeley, CA: University of California Press, 1951.

Dutch merchants and mariners in Asia, 1602–1795, London: Variorum Reprints, 1988.

"The rise and fall of Nicholas Iquan (Cheng Chih-lung)," T'ien Hsia monthly 11.5 (1941).

Brook, Timothy. The confusions of pleasure: commerce and culture in Ming China, Berkeley, CA: University of California Press, 1999.

Vermeer's hat: the seventeenth century and the dawn of the global world, New York: Bloomsbury Press, 2008.

Buch, W. J. M., "La Compagnie des Indes néerlandaises et l'Indochine" ("The Netherlands East India Company and Indochina"), Bulletin de l'Ecole française d'Extrême-Orient (Bulletin of the French School of the Far East) 37 (1937).

Bulbeck, David, Anthony Reid, Cheng Tan Lay, and Wu Yiqi (eds.), Southeast Asian exports since the fourteenth century: cloves, pepper, coffee, and sugar, Singapore: Institute of Southeast Asian Studies, 1998.

Busquets i Alemany, Anna, "Dreams in the Chinese periphery: Victorio Riccio and Zheng Chenggong's regime," in Tonio Andrade and Xing Hang (eds.), Sea rovers, silver, and samurai: maritime East Asia in global history, 1550–1700, Honolulu: University of Hawaii Press, forthcoming.

Carioti, Patrizia, "The Zheng regime and the Tokugawa bakufu: asking for intervention," in Tonio Andrade and Xing Hang (eds.), Sea rovers, silver, and samurai: maritime East Asia in global history, 1550–1700, Honolulu: University of Hawaii Press, forthcoming.

"The Zhengs' maritime power in the context of the 17th century far eastern seas: the rise of a 'centralised piratical organisation' and its gradual development into an informal 'state,'" Ming-Qing yanjiu (Ming-Qing studies) 5 (1996).

Chang Pin-ts'un, "Chinese maritime trade: the case of sixteenth-century Fu-ch'ien," unpublished PhD dissertation, Princeton University, 1993.

"Maritime trade and local economy in late Ming Fukien," in E. B. Vermeer (ed.), Development and decline of Fukien province in the 17th and 18th centuries, Leiden: E. J. Brill, 1990.

Chaunu, Pierre, Les Philippines et le Pacifique des Ibériques (XVIe, XVIIe, XVIIIe siècles): introduction méthodologique et indices d'activité (The Philippines and the Iberian Pacific, 16th, 17th, 18th centuries: methodological introduction and indices of activity), Paris: S.E.V.P.E.N., 1960.

Chen, Janet, Cheng Pei-kai, Michael Lestz, and Jonathan Spence (eds.), The search for modern China: a documentary collection, third edition, New York: W. W. Norton, 2014.

320   Bibliography

Cheng Wei-chung (Zheng Weizhong 鄭維中), *War, trade and piracy in the China Seas, 1622–1683*, Leiden: Brill, 2013.
Chun Hae-jong, "Sino-Korean tributary relations in the Ch'ing period," in John King Fairbank (ed.), *The Chinese world order: traditional China's foreign relations*, Cambridge, MA: Harvard University Press, 1968.
Clulow, Adam, *The company and the shogun: the Dutch encounter with Tokugawa Japan*, New York: Columbia University Press, 2014.
"Unjust, cruel and barbarous proceedings: Japanese mercenaries and the Amboyna incident of 1623," *Itinerario* 31.1 (2007).
Clunas, Craig, *Superfluous things: material culture and social status in early modern China*, Honolulu: University of Hawaii Press, 2004.
Cranmer-Byng, John L. and John E. Wills, Jr., "Trade and diplomacy with maritime Europe, 1644–c. 1800," in Wills (ed.), *China and maritime Europe, 1500–1800: trade, settlement, diplomacy, and missions*, Cambridge, UK: Cambridge University Press, 2011.
Croizier, Ralph C., *Koxinga and Chinese nationalism: myth, history, and the hero*, Cambridge, MA: East Asian Research Center, Harvard University, 1977.
Crossley, Pamela Kyle, *The Manchus*, Oxford, UK: Blackwell, 2002.
de Korte, J. P., *De jaarlijkse financiële verantwoording in de VOC, Verenigde Oostindische Compagnie* (*The annual financial accounting in the VOC, the Dutch East India Company*), Leiden: Martinus Nijhoff, 1984.
de Vries, Jan, "Connecting Europe and Asia: a quantitative analysis of the Cape route trade, 1497–1795," in Dennis Flynn, Arturo Giráldez, and Richard von Glahn (eds.), *Global connections and monetary history, 1470–1800*, London: Ashgate, 2003.
Deng Gang, *Maritime sector, institutions, and sea power of premodern China*, Westport, CT: Greenwood Press, 1999.
Duara, Prasenjit, *Rescuing history from the nation*, Chicago: University of Chicago Press, 1995.
Elisonas, Jurgis, "The inseparable trinity: Japan's relations with China and Korea," in John Whitney Hall (ed.), *The Cambridge history of Japan*, Cambridge, UK: Cambridge University Press, 1991, vol. IV: early modern Japan.
Fairbank, John King, "Maritime and continental in China's history," in Fairbank and Denis Crispin Twitchett (eds.), *The Cambridge history of China*, vol. XII.1: Republican China, 1912–1949, Cambridge, UK: Cambridge University Press, 1983.
Trade and diplomacy on the China coast: the opening of the treaty ports, 1842–1854, Stanford, CA: Stanford University Press, 1964.
Flynn, Dennis O. and Arturo Giráldez, "Arbitrage, China, and world trade in the early modern period," *Journal of the Economic and Social History of the Orient* 38.4 (1995).
"Born with a 'silver spoon': the origin of world trade in 1571," *Journal of World History* 6.2 (1995).
Frank, André Gunder, *ReOrient: global economy in the Asian age*, Berkeley, CA: University of California Press, 1998.
Giersch, C. Patterson, *Asian borderlands: the transformation of Qing China's Yunnan frontier*, Cambridge, MA: Harvard University Press, 2006.

"Cotton, copper, and caravans: trade and the transformation of southwest China," in Eric Tagliacozzo and Chang Wen-chin (eds.), *Chinese circulations: capital, commodities, and networks in Southeast Asia*, Durham, NC: Duke University Press, 2011.

Gipouloux, François and Jonathan Hall and Dianna Martin (trans.), *The Asian Mediterranean: port cities and trading networks in China, Japan and Southeast Asia, 13th–21st century*, Cheltenham, UK: Edward Elgar, 2011.

Hamashita Takeshi 浜下武志, "The *Lidai baoan* and the Ryukyu maritime tributary trade network with China and Southeast Asia, the fourteenth to seventeenth centuries," in Eric Tagliacozzo and Chang Wen-chin (eds.), *Chinese circulations: capital, commodities, and networks in Southeast Asia*, Durham, NC: Duke University Press, 2011.

Hang Xing, "The contradictions of legacy: reimagining the Zheng family in the People's Republic of China," *Late Imperial China* 34.2 (2013).

Ho, Dahpon David, *"Sealords live in vain: Fujian and the making of a maritime frontier in seventeenth-century China,"* unpublished PhD dissertation, University of California-San Diego, 2011.

Ho Pingti, *Ladder of success in imperial China*, New York: Columbia University Press, 1962.

Hoàng Anh Tuấn, *Silk for silver: Dutch-Vietnamese relations, 1637–1700*, Leiden: Brill, 2007.

Hsu, Jennifer Y. J. and Reza Hasmath, *The Chinese corporatist state: adaptation, survival, and resistance*, London: Routledge, 2012.

Huang, Philip, *The peasant family and rural development in the Yangzi delta, 1350–1988*, Stanford, CA: Stanford University Press, 1990.

Huang, Ray, *1587: a year of no significance, the Ming dynasty in decline*, New Haven, CT: Yale University Press, 1981.

Huber, Johannes, "Chinese settlers against the Dutch East India Company: the rebellion led by Kuo Huai-i on Taiwan in 1652," in E. B. Vermeer (ed.), *Development and decline of Fukien province in the 17th and 18th centuries*, Leiden: E. J. Brill, 1990.

Hung Chien-Chao, *"Taiwan under the Cheng family 1662–1683: sinicization after Dutch rule,"* unpublished PhD dissertation, Georgetown University, 1981.

Igawa Kenji, "At the crossroads: Limahon and *wakō* in sixteenth-century Philippines," in Robert J. Antony (ed.), *Elusive pirates, pervasive smugglers: violence and clandestine trade in the greater China Seas*, Hong Kong: Hong Kong University Press, 2010.

Israel, Jonathan I., *Dutch primacy in world trade, 1585–1740*, Oxford, UK: Oxford University Press, 1989.

Jones, Eric, *The European miracle: environments, economies, and geopolitics in the history of Europe and Asia*, third edition, Cambridge, UK: Cambridge University Press, 2003.

Kang, David C., *East Asia before the West: five centuries of trade and tribute*, New York: Columbia University Press, 2011.

Kang, Peter, "Koxinga and his maritime regime in the popular historical writings of post-Cold War Taiwan and China," in Tonio Andrade and Xing Hang (eds.), *Sea rovers, silver, and samurai: maritime East Asia in global history, 1550–1700*, Honolulu: University of Hawaii Press, forthcoming.

Kuhn, Philip, *Chinese among others: emigration in modern times*, Lanham, MD: Rowman and Littlefield, 2008.

Laver, Michael S., *The sakoku edicts and the politics of Tokugawa hegemony*, Amherst, NY: Cambria Press, 2011.

Levathes, Louise, *When China ruled the seas: the treasure fleet of the dragon throne, 1405–1433*, New York: Oxford University Press, 1996.

Li Tana, *Nguyễn Cochinchina: southern Vietnam in the seventeenth and eighteenth centuries*, Ithaca, NY: Southeast Asia Program Publications, 1998.

Lieberman, Victor, *Strange parallels: Southeast Asia in global context, c. 800–1830*, 2 vols., Cambridge, UK: Cambridge University Press, 2003.

Lintner, Bertil, "China's third wave," *Asia Times* (April 17, 2007).

Massarella, Derek, "Chinese, Tartars and 'thea' or a tale of two companies: the English East India Company and Taiwan in the late seventeenth century," *Journal of the Royal Asiatic Society*, 3rd series, 3.3 (1993).

Masselman, George, "Dutch colonial policy in the seventeenth century," *Journal of economic history* 21.4 (1961).

Matsuda, Matt, *Pacific worlds: a history of seas, peoples, and cultures*, New York: Cambridge University Press, 2012.

Myers, Ramon H. and Wang Yeh-chien, "Economic developments, 1644–1800," in Willard J. Peterson (ed.), *The Cambridge history of China*, vol. IX.1: the Ch'ing empire to 1800, Cambridge, UK: Cambridge University Press, 2002.

Naohiro Asao and Bernard Susser (trans.), "The sixteenth-century Unification," in Johon Whitney Hall (ed.), *The Cambridge history of Japan*, vol. IV: early modern Japan, Cambridge, UK: Cambridge University Press, 1991,.

Nara Shuichi, "Zeelandia, the factory in the Far Eastern trading network of the VOC," in Leonard Blussé (ed.), *Around and about Formosa: essays in honor of Professor Ts'ao Yung-ho*, Taipei: Ts'ao Yung-ho Foundation for Culture and Education, 2003.

Ng Chin-keong, *Trade and society: the Amoy network on the China coast, 1683–1735*, Singapore: Singapore University Press, 1983.

Pan, Lynn, *Sons of the Yellow Emperor: a history of the Chinese diaspora*, New York: Kodansha International, 1994.

Parker, Geoffrey and Lesley M. Smith, "Introduction," in Parker and Smith (eds.), *The general crisis of the seventeenth century*, second edition, London: Routledge, 1997.

Perdue, Peter, *China marches west: the Qing conquest of central Eurasia*, Cambridge, MA: Harvard University Press, 2005.

Phoeun, Mak and Po Dharma, "La deuxième intervention militaire vietnamienne au Cambodge (1673–1679)" ("The second Vietnamese military intervention in Cambodia: 1673–1679"), *Bulletin de l'Ecole française d'Extrême-Orient* (Bulletin of the French School of the Far East) 77 (1988).

Pomeranz, Kenneth, *The great divergence: China, Europe, and the making of the modern world economy*, Princeton, NJ: Princeton University Press, 2001.

Prakash, Om, *The Dutch East India Company and the economy of Bengal*, Princeton, NJ: Princeton University Press, 1985.

Ptak, Roderich, "Sino-Japanese maritime trade, circa 1550: merchants, ports and networks," in Ptak (ed.), *China and the Asian seas: trade, travel, and visions of the other (1400–1750)*, Brookfield, VT: Ashgate Variorum, 1998.

Rawski, Evelyn Sakakida, *Agricultural change and the peasant economy of south China*, Cambridge, MA: Harvard University Press, 1972.

Reid, Anthony, "Chinese on the mining frontier of Southeast Asia," in Eric Tagliacozzo and Chang Wen-chin (eds.), *Chinese circulations: capital, commodities, and networks in Southeast Asia*, Durham, NC: Duke University Press, 2011.

Southeast Asia in the age of commerce: 1450–1680, 2 vols., New Haven, CT: Yale University Press, 1988–1993.

Robinson, Kenneth R., "Centering the king of Chosŏn: aspects of Korean maritime diplomacy, 1392–1592," *Journal of Asian Studies* 59.1 (2000).

Rosenthal, Jean-Laurent and R. Bin Wong, *Before and beyond divergence: the politics of economic change in China and Europe*, Cambridge, MA: Harvard University Press, 2011.

Schottenhammer, Angela, "Characteristics of Qing China's maritime trade policies, *Shunzhi* through *Qianlong* reigns," in Schottenhammer (ed.), *Trading networks in early modern East Asia*, Wiesbaden, Germany: Otto Harrassowitz, 2010.

(ed.), *The East Asian Mediterranean: crossroads of knowledge, commerce, and human migration*, Wiesbaden, Germany: Otto Harrassowitz, 2008.

Shepherd, John Robert, *Statecraft and political economy on the Taiwan frontier*, Stanford, CA: Stanford University Press, 1993.

Skinner, G. William. "Regional urbanization in nineteenth-century China," in Skinner (ed.), *The city in late imperial China*, Stanford, CA: Stanford University Press, 1977.

Struve, Lynn, *The Ming-Qing conflict, 1619–1683: a historiography and source guide*, Ann Arbor, MI: Association for Asian Studies, 1998.

Southern Ming: 1644–1662, New Haven CT: Yale University Press, 1984.

Suzuki Yasuko, *Japan-Netherlands trade, 1600–1800: the Dutch East India Company and beyond*, Kyoto: Kyoto University Press, 2012.

Swope, Kenneth, *A dragon's head and a serpent's tail: Ming China and the first Great East Asian War, 1592–1598*, Norman, OK: University of Oklahoma Press, 2009.

Szonyi, Michael, *Practicing kinship: lineage and descent in late imperial China*, Stanford, CA: Stanford University Press, 2002.

Teng, Emma Jinhua, *Taiwan's imagined geography: Chinese colonial travel writing and pictures, 1683–1895*, Cambridge, MA: Harvard University Asia Center, 2004.

Tilly, Charles, *Coercion, capital, and European states: AD 990–1992*, London: Wiley, 1992.

Toby, Ronald, *State and diplomacy in early modern Japan: Asia in the development of the Tokugawa Bakufu*, Stanford, CA: Stanford University Press, 1991.

Totman, Conrad, *Early modern Japan*, Berkeley, CA: University of California Press, 1993.

Trocki, Carl A., "Boundaries and transgressions: Chinese enterprise in eighteenth- and nineteenth-century Southeast Asia," in Ong Aihwa and

Donald M. Nonini (eds.), *Ungrounded empires: the cultural politics of modern Chinese transnationalism*, London: Routledge, 1997.

Ts'ao Yung-ho (Cao Yonghe 曹永和), "Taiwan as an entrepôt in East Asia in the seventeenth century," in John E. Wills, Jr. (ed.), *Eclipsed entrepôts of the Western Pacific: Taiwan and central Vietnam, 1500–1800*, Burlington, VT: Ashgate, 2002.

Viraphol, Sarasin, *Tribute and profit: Sino-Siamese trade, 1652–1853*, Cambridge, MA: Council on East Asian Studies, Harvard University, 1977.

von Glahn, Richard, *Fountain of fortune: money and monetary policy in China, 1000–1700*, Berkeley, CA: University of California Press, 1996.

Wakeman, Frederic, *The great enterprise: the Manchu reconstruction of imperial order in seventeenth-century China*, 2 vols., Berkeley, CA: University of California Press, 1985.

Wang Gungwu, "Foreword," in Eric Tagliacozzo and Chang Wen-chin (eds.), *Chinese circulations: capital, commodities, and networks in Southeast Asia*, Durham, NC: Duke University Press, 2011.

"Merchants without empire: the Hokkien sojourning communities," in James D. Tracy (ed.), *The rise of merchant empires: long-distance trade in the early modern world, 1350–1750*, Cambridge, UK: Cambridge University Press, 1990.

Wilbur, Marguerite Eyer, *The East India Company: and the British empire in the Far East*, Stanford, CA: Stanford University Press, 1945.

Wills, John E., Jr., "Contingent connections: Fujian, the empire, and the early modern world," in Lynn Ann Struve (ed.), *The Qing formation in world-historical time*, Cambridge, MA: Harvard University Asia Center, 2004.

"The Dutch reoccupation of Chi-lung, 1664–1668," in Leonard Blussé (ed.), *Around and about Formosa: essays in honor of Professor Ts'ao Yung-ho*, Taipei: Ts'ao Yung-ho Foundation for Culture and Education, 2003.

Embassies and illusions: Dutch and Portuguese envoys to K'ang-hsi, 1666–1687, Cambridge, MA: Council on East Asian Studies, Harvard University, 1984.

"The hazardous missions of a Dominican: Victorio Riccio, O. P., in Amoy, Taiwan, and Manila," in *Actes du IIe colloque international de sinologie: les rapports entre la Chine et l'Europe au temps des lumières* (*Acts of the Second International Colloquium of Sinology: the relationship between China and Europe during the Age of Enlightenment*), Paris: Les belles lettres, 1980, vol. IV.

"Introduction," in Wills (ed.), *China and maritime Europe, 1500–1800: trade, settlement, diplomacy, and missions*, Cambridge, UK: Cambridge University Press, 2011.

"Maritime China from Wang Chih to Shih Lang: themes in peripheral history," in Jonathan D. Spence and Wills (eds.), *From Ming to Ch'ing: conquest, region, and continuity in seventeenth-century China*, New Haven, CT: Yale University Press, 1979.

"Maritime Europe and the Ming," in Wills (ed.), *China and maritime Europe, 1500–1800: trade, settlement, diplomacy, and missions*, Cambridge, UK: Cambridge University Press, 2011.

Mountain of fame: portraits in Chinese history, Princeton, NJ: Princeton University Press, 1994.

Pepper, guns, and parleys: the Dutch East India Company and China, 1662–1681, Cambridge, MA: Harvard University Press, 1974.

"Relations with maritime Europeans, 1514–1662," in Denis Twitchett and Frederick W. Mote (eds.), *The Cambridge history of China,* vol. VIII.2: the Ming dynasty, 1368–1644, Cambridge, UK: Cambridge University Press, 1998.

"The South China Sea is not a Mediterranean," in Tang Xiyong 湯熙勇 (ed.), *Zhongguo haiyang fazhan shi lunwenji* 中國海洋發展史論文集 (*Essays in Chinese maritime history*), vol. X, Taipei: Research Center for Humanities and Social Sciences, Academia Sinica, 2008.

"Yiguan's origins: clues from Chinese, Japanese, Dutch, Spanish, Portuguese, and Latin sources," in Tonio Andrade and Xing Hang (eds.), *Sea rovers, silver, and samurai: maritime East Asia in global history, 1550–1700,* Honolulu: University of Hawaii Press, forthcoming.

Wong, R. Bin, *China transformed: historical change and the limits of European experience,* Ithaca, NY: Cornell University Press, 1997.

Wong Young-tsu, "Security and warfare on the China coast: the Taiwan question in the seventeenth century," *Monumenta Serica: Journal of Oriental Studies* 35 (1981–1983).

Wray, William D, "The seventeenth-century Japanese diaspora: questions of boundary and policy," in Ina Baghdiantz McCabe, Gelina Harlaftis, and Ioanna Pepelasis Minoglou (eds.), *Diaspora entrepreneurial networks: four centuries of history,* New York: Berg, 2005.

Yamawaki Teijirō, "The great trading merchants, Cocksinja and his son," *Acta Asiatica: Bulletin of the Institute of Eastern Culture* 30 (1976).

Yao Keisuke, "Two rivals on an island of sugar: the sugar trade of the VOC and overseas Chinese in Formosa in the seventeenth century," in Leonard Blussé (ed.), *Around and about Formosa: essays in honor of Professor Ts'ao Yung-ho,* Taipei: Ts'ao Yung-ho Foundation for Culture and Education, 2003.

Yeh Wen-hsin, *Provincial passages: culture, space, and the origins of Chinese communism,* Berkeley, CA: University of California Press, 1996.

Yuan Bingling 袁冰凌, *Chinese democracies: a study of the kongsis of west Borneo (1776–1884),* Leiden: Leiden University Press, 1999.

Yumio Sakurai, "Eighteenth-century Chinese pioneers on the water frontiers of Indochina," in Nola Cooke and Li Tana (eds.), *Water frontiers: commerce and the Chinese in the lower Mekong region, 1735–1880,* Lanham, MD: Roman and Littlefield, 2004.

Zhao Gang, *The Qing opening to the ocean: Chinese maritime policies, 1684–1757,* Honolulu: University of Hawai`i Press, 2013.

Index

CPSIA information can be obtained
at www.ICGtesting.com
Printed in the USA
LVHW020210081221
705586LV00008B/425

9 781107 558458